Retracing Our Steps

Studies in Documents From the American Past, Vol. 1

Retracing Our Steps

Studies in Documents From the American Past, Vol. 1

MYRON A. MARTY

H. THEODORE FINKELSTON

Florissant Valley Community College
St. Louis, Missouri

Canfield Press

San Francisco
A Department of Harper & Row, Publishers, Inc.
New York • Evanston • London

About the Cover

"A Chorographical Map of the Country Round Philadelphia" by Bernard Romans. The map was advertised as "Just published at New Haven" in the *Connecticut Courant* of June 2, 1778.

By courtesy of John Carter Brown Library of Brown University, Providence, Rhode Island.

Cover and Interior Book Design by Gracia A. Alkema

E
173
.M315
1972
V.1

RETRACING OUR STEPS: STUDIES IN DOCUMENTS FROM THE AMERICAN PAST, Vol. 1

Copyright © 1972 by Myron A. Marty and H. Theodore Finkelston

Standard Book Number: 06–385435–X

Library of Congress Catalog Card Number: 76–170130

Contents

17. Jim-Crowism in the Making   381

Preface

How a nation looks at the future depends to a great extent on how it looks at the past. In 1801 President Thomas Jefferson could regard the nation's brief history with satisfaction, and his inaugural address reflected his confidence in the future of the young republic. Today, however, as the country approaches its 200th birthday in the 1970s, national confidence is threatened by uncertainty and apprehension. Now is the time, perhaps more than ever, for a new look at the past.

Jefferson himself invited a retracing of the past in uncertain times. In his inaugural address, after outlining what he believed to be essential principles of government, he asserted:

> These principles form the bright constellation which has gone before us and guided our steps through an age of revolution and reformation. The wisdom of our sages and blood of our heroes have been devoted to their attainment. They should be the creed of our political faith, the text of civic instruction, the touchstone by which to try the services of those we trust; and should we wander from them in moments of error or of alarm, let us hasten to retrace our steps and to regain the road which alone leads to peace, liberty, and safety.

Our aim in this book is to assist students in retracing some of the important steps of the American past. If they conclude that the nation has wandered from the principles Jefferson held so dear, they may be encouraged to help the country "regain the road," or perhaps motivated to redefine the principles in light of historical developments and present circumstances.

The text is edited on the premise that retracing the past is done best through an in-depth study of selected topics. The real value, as well as the real excitement, in studying history comes from digging in here and there to discover what is below the surface. This is most rewarding when documents from primary sources provide the focus of study.

This volume is comprised of seventeen self-contained chapters, each built around a single topic or theme. They are purposely narrow in scope. Our goal has been to select specific issues and ideas from the story of America's development and to retrace them through appropriate documents. Since the documents we have chosen represent only a small portion of those available, students and instructors should exercise caution in drawing conclusions or making judgments on the basis of material included in this text.

Each chapter is organized around a core document. The chapter introduction provides information concerning the document's author, its context, its purpose or function, and perhaps an appropriate comment about its subject and organization. It has not been our practice to recount factual information generally presented in basic history textbooks or lectures. To help students analyze the source materials, specific points to note are suggested in the document introductions. Difficult or confusing matters have explanatory footnotes. Following the core documents are several questions designed to promote a better understanding of the documents and to provide starters for class discussion. We have tried to phrase the questions so that there is no one answer; in other words, they are open-ended questions. Also included in each chapter is a cluster of related, shorter documents. The brief introductions to these readings include a question or two that help to illustrate the relationship. We have tried to keep each chapter to a manageable length so that supplementary books, especially paperbacks, may also be used. Each chapter concludes with a suggested list of such books.

The nature of this volume's organization permits a selective use of topics. Neither continuity nor understanding of the textual material will be sacrificed if the instructor decides to skip certain chapters, and selection within chapters is also possible. For example, cluster documents may be assigned to the entire class or used for individual assignments. They may be omitted if time does not allow an examination of all of the material during a given semester or quarter.

Reading might have been made easier had we modernized spelling and punctuation in the documents. We did this in early drafts and concluded that appreciably more was lost in historical flavor than was gained in reading ease. Consequently, we have chosen to rely on authoritative scholarly editions or on the original sources themselves and to present them unchanged, except for occasional paragraphing. In editing the documents it has been necessary at times to delete sentences or even entire paragraphs. Standard use of ellipses indicates minor omissions, and line spaces within a document indicate the deletion of complete paragraphs.

In presenting this work we express our appreciation to our students and colleagues for the stimulation they have provided us and to Gracia Alkema of Canfield Press for her invaluable editorial guidance. We are also indebted to the library staffs at Florissant Valley Community College (Sidney Reedy was particularly helpful), Washington University, and St. Louis University. The encouragement and assistance we received from our wives, Shirley Marty and Karen Finkelston, is immeasurable. They join us in the hope that teachers and students will find this volume to be an effective, flexible teaching instrument—a worthy supplement to their ingenuity.

Myron A. Marty

H. Theodore Finkelston

1. The Rebel
and the Establishment

What does it take to make a rebellion? The ingredients are easily identified: grievances, an establishment judged to be unresponsive, and a popular leader to exploit the grievances and attack the establishment.

The colony of Virginia was primed for rebellion in 1676. The grievances of the frontiersmen were severe, the establishment—the colonial government —was regarded as unresponsive, and a popular leader was ready to emerge from the ranks.

The grievances of Virginia's frontiersmen grew out of a set of frustrated desires. The source of frustration, as the frontiersmen saw it, was the government dominated by Governor William Berkeley, who at the age of 70 had served two long terms spanning 35 years. The rebel leader, Berkeley's antagonist, was Nathaniel Bacon, 29 years old and a resident in the colony for less than two years.

Most of the other English colonies in North America were experiencing discontent similar to that in Virginia, and before 1692 Massachusetts, New York, and Maryland also witnessed rebellions. But Bacon's Rebellion was the most significant because it most clearly pitted East against West, aristocrat against frontiersman, entrenched establishment against popular rebel, and because it occurred almost independently of political developments in England.

Although in 1676 the Virginia frontier extended only about as far west as the present location of Richmond, the farmers on this frontier shared a distinct set of interests. They wanted land, good prices for their products (principally tobacco), and low taxes. Those who were also aspiring traders sought fair trading policies, and all of them wanted not only protection against the Indians, but an aggressive policy to drive them back and open up new lands.

Governor Berkeley, the frontiersmen judged, was not heeding their call for help. His method and manner seemed to be arbitrary and tyrannical, and his economic policies seemed to serve only his own interests, not theirs. Furthermore, they interpreted his efforts to distinguish between friendly and unfriendly Indians and to pursue a defensive policy against Indian attacks as an abandonment of their interests. Finally, the differences over Indian policy precipitated the rebellion. As the established authority, the governor was concerned with the very practical problem of maintaining peace with the Indians; he perhaps even hoped to treat them with a measure of justice. The rebelling frontiersmen demanded more. They wanted to take the offensive, regardless of the consequences.

In March 1676, in response to frontier pressures, the Virginia House of Burgesses declared war on the Indians, but the restraints imposed in the declaration were unacceptable to the dissatisfied frontiersmen. Their feeling of unrest was intensified by the knowledge that the war would have to be supported by higher taxes, even though the entire colony was already suffering economic distress. Disgusted with this action, Bacon decided to take matters into his own hands and called for volunteers to move against the Indians. His call was heeded, and the rebellion was out in the open.

Events moved rapidly in the subsequent months. In May Bacon was proclaimed a rebel by the governor and expelled from his seat in the colony's council, but his followers promptly elected him to a seat in the newly convened House of Burgesses. (Bacon had been appointed to the council by Berkeley shortly after his arrival, an indication that Bacon was not of the lower classes in Virginia.) While continuing his sorties against the Indians, Bacon persistently demanded an official commission as leader of the war. June and July were tense months, filled with frequent confrontations between the governor and the rebel. By the end of July, Bacon's power and popularity were sufficient to force Governor Berkeley to flee to Accomac County on Virginia's eastern shore.

In September Berkeley managed to return for a final showdown with Bacon. Some weeks of virtual stalemate followed until the rebellion collapsed suddenly with Bacon's death, probably of malaria, on October 26, 1676. His followers carried on for a time, but the driving force was gone. Nevertheless, Berkeley was not able to savor his success, limited though it was, for he was soon recalled to England and died shortly thereafter, apparently in disfavor with the King.

Core Documents

A History of Our Miseries: A Letter to Henry Coventry

WILLIAM BERKELEY

The personalities of the two principal foes in Bacon's Rebellion contrast sharply. Historians generally agree that the irascibility of the aging Berkeley was a good match for the impetuosity of the youthful Bacon, but beyond this interpretations vary. Some assert that Berkeley had become willful, vindictive, despotic, vengeful, and cruel. They point particularly to the hangings of twenty-three Baconites as stark evidence. To these historians Bacon was the people's champion, the foe of aristocracy, the reformer of government, "the torchbearer of the revolution."

Other historians regard Bacon as having been an opportunistic, demagogic hell-raiser, who used unsuspecting people and noble words for his own ends, whatever they were. To these historians Berkeley, despite his excesses, was the real defender of liberty.

Which interpretation is more accurate cannot be explored here, for the question is too complex and would require the use of numerous sources, many not even in print. Some understanding of the two men can be reached, however, by considering their view of themselves and each other and how they were judged by their contemporaries. This part of the chapter includes two documents that offer rich insights into the viewpoints of both Bacon and Berkeley. The first is an account of the rebellion written by Governor Berkeley several months before he departed for England early in 1677. It was addressed to Henry Coventry, an English secretary of state. In studying the document, note how Governor Berkeley:

- *revealed a degree of personal disorganization and confusion.*
- *attempted both openly and subtly to justify his actions.*
- *tried to balance pride in his record with expressions of humility and subservience to God and the King.*
- *interpreted actions of the Baconites in their conflicts with Indians.*
- *accounted for Bacon's popularity and strength.*
- *described the course of events leading to the suppression of the rebellion.*

Right Honorable

After my rendering thankes to God who hath raysed me in this my greate necessity and perhaps unparaled misery so Noble a frend to be my Protector I shal then tel you that this will not be a letter but a History of our miseries

Wilcomb E. Washburn, ed., "A History of Our Miseries: Sir William Berkeley to Henry Coventry," *William and Mary Quarterly*, Third Series, XIV (1957), 405–13. Paragraphing has been added by the editors.

but before I enter into it I must cleere one just accusation which you have against me til you heare my justification and that is this that I wrote not to you the state and condition of this afflicted country.

Sir if a miserable man can find so much Charity as to be beleev'd then I must humbly besseech you to heare this truth that I wrote to you at large Entending my letters should goe by Captain Eveling but he was so justly frighted by Mr. Bland and one Captain Carver who were comming to Cease [seize] him with a ship Bacon had taken . . . that he was forced to make al the hast he could to Sea without calling for my letters or giving Bills of lading to Divers Gentlemen that had put goods and Tobaccoes aboard him. Right honorable this is al truth and I have your letters stil by me at my house but being now aboard Sir John Berries shipp who has been in the country three dayes cannot send them now But by the next shipp that goes for England wil doe it and then I hope your Goodnesse and mercy wil absolve me from my supposed Crime and neglect of my Duty.

And now most Honord Sir I will give you a relation of the original grouth of al our miseries only premising this that I thinke I should unpardonably offend that God who has shewed such miraculous mercyes to me in my deliverance (I say miraculous mercyes) if now after the feeling of them I should in the presence of God my deliverer write any thing in my owne favor or in the Exagerating the Crimes of the Rebels.

And thus I shal begin when seaven moneths since I was Exalted with pride that I had governed this Country fower and twenty Yeares in peace and plenty and was most certaine that no pretence of a fault could be alleaged against me. Then did God to humble me and take away the pride of my hart and thoughts rayse this ungrounded (for any real Grevance) and unexpected rebellion against his most sacred Majestie the country and me and thus it was

When those that were resolved to stirr up the people to sedition had divulged amongst the Rabble what feare there was of a sodaine [sudden] invasion from the Indians Then did Bacon by his servants and other Emissaries send into al parts of the Country that his father had five and twenty hundred pounds per annum in England and that he would spend al that Estate to free the Country from the Charge of the Warr on condition they would make him their General. Sir it is hardly to be beleeved how this promise and undertaking tooke with the country who did or made others beleeve that al was truth he promisd them so that like a trayne of powder as it were in a moment it enfected not only Virginia but Maryland who by the Experience of our miseries were forced to keepe a Gaurd to prevent the rising of the seditious there.

But Sir his first greate Act (and this to try what followers and abetters he was likely to procure) was to goe to a nation one hundred miles from any English plantation called the Ocannoeches[1] who were ever frends to the English and seated in an Island Very wel fortified by nature. But to this place he

---

[1]The Occaneechi (or Occaneechee) Indians lived on an island at the juncture of the Dan and the Roanoke rivers near the present town of Clarksville, Virginia. The island has been flooded in recent years by the construction of a dam a few miles down the river.

comes Hollowes[2] to the Indians to bring him and his men over into the Island which they civilly and courteously did in their Canoes and Bacon himselfe confesd to me and my Councel that he could not have forced his way by day if they had had intelligence of their intentions. But Sir being frendly entertained in the Island the Cheife of the Indians asked the English what businesse or desinge [design] brought them thither. The English replied they came to seeke the Sesquasahannochs and destroy as many of them as they could find for they were their Ennimies. The Indians very civilly replied that they were no frends of theirs that the English were tired with a long march that there was a nation of these sesquasahannoch aboute twenty miles of[f] that they would destroy them for the English sakes and bring in what prisoners they could to be disposed of by the English which they performed Exactly and brought in Divers prisoners most of which the Indians Knockt in the head in sight and instance of the Inglish.

But now Sir begins the quarrel with thes Innocent and courteous Indians. With the prisoners they brought in a consiserable [*sic*] quantity of beavor and a considerable quantity of Beads the only Indian Coyne. This . . . the English pretended to be theirs. To this the Indians modestly replied that they had brought them the prisoners to manifest their desires of Amitie with the Inglish But for the Beavor and the other wealth they had got it with the hazard of their lives and that they knew not how any one besidese themselves could pretend any title to it: But this satisfied not the avarice and as they then thought the Power of the English to compel the Indians to what they pleased, and with this confidence they fel roundly to worke with the Indians. But the Indians retiring to their fort quicly made the Inglish know how much they were deceavd and in fower howers time forced them to wade out of the Iland to the maine land and on my faith according to the best intelligence I could ever get, Bacon was the first man that leapt his horse into the River and so escaped to the maine land and was followed by al that were not Killed on the Iland. But it is not be imagined how cowardly treacherous and ungratefui soever this Act was what opinion it got him with the base rabble who were resolved to approve of al he did and Bacon heightned with the concurrane [*sic*] of this Rabble sends out his Emissaries againe to make them Vote him their General and cry out for a new Assembly which by the feares and sollicitations of the Councel I granted for I had alwaise this fault predominant in me not to resist the opinions and sollicitations of my Councel thoughe I knew almost demonstrably I was in the right and they in the wrong. . . .

But Sir to returne to Bacon when he knew the Assembly was thus Packt to his likeing he came downe to James Towne with about threescore men thinking to surprise me and the Councel. . . . But I prevented him and with the helpe of thes . . . Gentlemen and after some resistance tooke him and al his sloopes as he fled and Brought him backe to James Towne. And now Sir I know it wil be deservedly objected against me why I did not put him to death when I had him in my power. Truly Sir I must have beene Judge Jury and

---

[2]Hollowes: halloos or shouts.

Executioner my selfe to have donne it for the Assembly as I sayde were al packt
for him, the Councel frighted with hearing two thousand men were armed to
deliver him (which was a greate truth) so that al we could doe was to make
him confesse his fault which he willingly did not from any repentance but that
he might sooner head his Party.

Now Sir behold the misery I was envolved in. I did almost with teares
beg of the Assembly to have one hundred Voluntier Gentlemen to be my gaurd
for the Rabble I durst not trust which was scornefully and peremptorily denied
me though five or six dayes after they payde and allowed Bacon one thousand
men for his Gaurd (Sir Pardon my many Excursions which I am forced for
want of time and preperation to make). When Bacon was assured of the
inclination of the people to him he came downe to James-Towne with six
hundred of the meanest of the People, Came into the court and Assembly with
their Guns ready to fire, Clamourd for a commission for their General and
though it is known thes terrors moved not me yet at last I submitted to the
feares of the Councel and Assembly who told me as I have it stil under al their
several hands that unlesse I would yeald to invincible necessity they and their
wives and children were al undone. This with the consideration I could doe
the King little service by dying for him and might doe him service by living
inclined me to sute my Judgement to theirs and Grant him a commission
which was no soner signed but al his Rabble veryly beleevd I had resigned al
my power to their New General and Bacon himselfe made them beleeve he
thought so too and accordingly fel to worke confiscating and Plundering divers
good mens houses. For one moneth he came not to mine so that I had
opertunity to save al my plate and secure it in Captain Evelings shipp. And
hearing that Bacon entended to make me and Sir Harry Chicheley prisoners,
and perhaps deale more sevearly with us for hee had proclaimed us both
Traytors at the heade of his rebellious Army, I went to Sir Harry Chicheleys
house perswading him to retire with me to Accomach which place I understood continued Loyal (and indeed halfe of it was so). . . .

But now Sir begins Gods Visible mercyes to shine uppon me for thoughe
I went to Accomach but with fower Gentlemen yet I had in three dayes at least
fowrty Gentlemen of the best qualitie in Virginia that came over to me many
of them with their wives and children and left their estates to the mercy that
is Rapine of Bacons Barbarous Soldiers. And within a weeke after Bacon sent
a shipp with two hundred men under the Command of one Bland and Captain
Carver with joynt commission to take me and al my frends and Bring us to
him deade or alive which Bland swore a thousand God damme him he would
doe.

But now Sir observe the mercy of God. This Carver was an able stoute
seamen and soldier who under pretence of treating with me came from his
shipp with one hundred and threescore men. But it pleasd God he could not
goe backe with the Pinnace he brought his men in which I beleeve he was glad
of for I had charged him to begon in Eight howers and this contrary wind gave
him a pretence to stay longer for an opertunity to corrupt or cease [seize] my
Gaurd that wacthead [watched] his motions. Whilest this was acting on both

sides about twelve a clocke at night came a letter to me from the master of the shipp that Bacon had surprised and put Bland and thes soldiers aboard her that told me there were but fourty men that were left to gaurd the shipp that if I would send thirty or fourty Gentlemen he would so employ and secure the soldiers that we should easily enter and retake the shipp al which was undertaken and performed in six howers. And Carver seeing wherries goe to the shipp and suspecting the Cause made after them in a smal boate and was within musket shot of the shipp side when our men were possest of her who let him come on til [he] was within Pistol shot and then commanded him on Board which he ascended like a Chased Bore and would have stabd his lieu-Tenant if he had not been prevented by our men. This great and miraculous mercy put al the soldiers into our hands. . . . However this action gave the Loyal party a great reputation in the country and now the feare of me made many declare for the King who never after durst goe backe to Bacon.

And now Sir this miraculous mercy of God, for we were no more contrivers of it then the Axe is in the Carpenters hand, [was such] that we thought the whole country was owr owne but we afterward found we were not Ripe for Gods ful mercy: However, elevated with this sucesse we resolvd with al speed to make for James-Towne and sodainely raysing two hundred men we shipt them in the shipp we had taken and six or seaven Sloopes more which we got together and as soone as we came to the Westerne Shoar were met by one hundred men more. With thes we sayled for James Towne where we found five hundred of Bacons men but our numbers being trebled in the opinion of the Ennimie and I issuing out a Proclamation pardoning al the Common soldiers that would lay down their Armes and al the officers but three Bacon Drumer [Drummond] and and [*sic*] lawrance, thoughe they would not lay downe their Armes Yet the same night we arrived at James-Towne, they al fled to Bacon. . . .But the newes of James Towne being delivered and our smal numbers when landed being certainely Knowne he swore a Thousand of his usual execrable oaths he would put us al to the sword and with this resolution Joyning his forces with the others that fled from James Towne beseeged us. And the first thing he did was to Issue out a Proclamation that he would neither take nor give Quarter to which he bound al his soldiers with a most Horrid Oath.

But Sir twice Bacons forces had not beene able to hurt us if our officers and soldiers had had Courage or loyalty but there was a want of both in both for the common soldiers mutinied and the officers did not doe their whole Duty to surpresse them but some of them as I afterwards found did al they could to foment the mutiny.

One night having rode from Gaurd to gaurd and from quarter to quarter al day long to encourage the soldiers I went to bed about six or seaven at night. I was no sooner layne Downe but there came three or fower of the cheefe officers to me and told me I must presently rise and to goe to the shipp for the soldiers were al mutinying and running away. I told them I left them al ful of courage and as I thought fidelity. They replied they seemed so to me but I was no sooner gone but they fel afresh to mutiny and that two or three hundred men were landed at the backe of us. This made me cal for my clothes and horse and with fourty men that I could confide in I went to the place where thes men were reported to [be] landed but found not one man landed. When I obbrayded this to the officers they told me twas confidently so reported to them and in the condition I was then in was forced to take this for answere. The next day came more officers to me and represented to me againe the necessity of my quitting the towne. I represented to them the reputation we should loose and not only that but many hundreds that were now declaring for us which we found afterwards to be true desiring them with al passionate Earnestnesse to keepe the Towne but three dayes, that Bacons men sufferd more than we did and were as like to mutiny as ours.

When thes reasons would not prevaile I told them I could neither answere this to the King nor to any man that ever was a soldier unlesse they gave under their hands the necessity of my dishonorable quitting the place. This they swallowed too and presently drew up a declaration to that purpose and signed it with theire several hands which I have stil with me.

I no sooner quitted the Towne but Bacon enterd it burned five houses of mine and twenty of other Gentlemen and they say a very commodious Church he set fire too with his owne sacriligious handes. But within three weekes after the Justice and Judgement of God overtooke him. His usual oath was which he swore at least a Thousand times a day was God damme my Blood and God so infected his blood that it bred Lice in an incredible number so that for twenty dayes he never washt his shirts but burned them. To this God added the Bloody flux and an honest Minister wrote this Epitaph on him

> *Bacon is Dead I am sorry at my hart*
> *that Lice and flux should take the hangmans part.*

And now Right honorable that God has brought this most Atheistical man to his deserved end I must Epitomise the rest and say that Bacon being deade the Rabble chose an other General which had beene Bland but he was out of their reach, continued the other officers who soone disagreed amongst themselves mistrusting one the other. In the meane time my soldiers Kild fower of their most obstinate officers, two are dead in Prison, and fourteen Executed. Their Lieutenant General first and after their General gave up al their men and Armes into my hands and are pardoned. More then one hundred I had in prison before this surrender. What my part has beene in this I would rather you should heare from any Pen then mine. I wil only say this I have ever been faithful Diligent and Loyal and have lost a Quarter as much as al the country besides. If the King wil give any thing to support my old Age I wil Blesse God and him for it. If not I wil never repine nor Dispute with my God nor my King. But I thinke I could doe him better service then any commissioner of the customes he has and sooner let him know the worth of al his customes especially those of Tobbacco of which If I be rightly enformed the King does not receave halfe his due. Right Honorable I humbly beg your pardon for thus long troubling you and doe most humbly beseech you to continue your favours to me though I shal never deserve them. Your most humble obleeged Dutiful and Devoted servant

WILL BERKELEY

From on Board Sir John Berries shipp February the 2d 1676/7. If his Majestie would write to the Assembly that in consideration of the Gracious favours his Majestie has donne the Country they wil provide that his Governors losses given in on Oath may be made good to him it would put him into a condition of living happyly the remainder of his old age and leaving something to his poore Vertuous and now distressed wife.

The Declaration of the People

NATHANIEL BACON

This second document was apparently written on the day after Berkeley fled to Accomac and just before a conference at Middle Plantation, where Bacon consolidated his support.

In this "Declaration," note how Bacon:
- *catalogued his grievances against Berkeley, emphasizing in particular the charge of favoritism.*
- *interpreted the position of Berkeley regarding the Indians.*
- *asserted his loyalty to the King.*
- *called for the surrender or capture of his foes and threatened those who might protect them.*
- *claimed to be working on behalf of the common people of Virginia.*

JULY 30, 1676

For having upon specious pretences of Publick works raised unjust Taxes upon the Commonalty for the advancement of private Favourits and other sinnister ends but noe visible effects in any measure adequate.

For not having dureing the long time of his Government in any measure advanced this hopefull Colony either by Fortification, Townes or Trade.

For having abused and rendered Contemptible the Majesty of Justice, of advancing to places of judicature scandalous and Ignorant favourits.

For having wronged his Majesties Prerogative and Interest by assuming the monopoley of the Beaver Trade.

By having in that unjust gaine Bartered and sould his Majesties Country and the lives of his Loyal Subjects to the Barbarous Heathen.

For haveing protected favoured and Imboldened the Indians against his Majesties most Loyall subjects never contriveing requireing or appointing any due or proper meanes of satisfaction for their many Invasions Murthers and Robberies Committed upon us.

For having when the Army of the English was Just upon the Track of the Indians, which now in all places Burne Spoyle and Murder, and when wee might with ease have destroyed them who then were in open Hostility for having expresly Countermanded and sent back our Army by passing his word for the peaceable demeanour of the said Indians, who imediately prosecuted their evill Intentions Committing horrid Murders and Robberies in all places being protected by the said Engagement and word pass'd of him the said S'r William Berkley having ruined and made desolate a great part of his Majesties Country, have now drawne themselves into such obscure and remote places and are by their successes soe imboldened and confirmed and by their Confederacy soe strengthened that the cryes of Bloud are in all places and the Terrour and consternation of the People soe great, that they are now become not only a difficult, but a very formidable Enemy who might with Ease have been destroyed &c. When upon the Loud Outcries of Blood the Assembly had with all care raised and framed an Army for the prevention of future Mischiefs and safeguard of his Majesties Colony.

For having with only the privacy of some few favourits without acquainting the People, only by the Alteration of a Figure forged a Commission by wee know not what hand, not only without but against the Consent of the People, for raising and effecting of Civill Warrs and distractions, which being happily and without Bloodshedd prevented.

For haveing the second tyme attempted the same thereby, calling downe our Forces from the defence of the Frontiers, and most weake Exposed Places, for the prevention of civill Mischief and Ruine amongst ourselves, whilst the barbarous Enemy in all places did Invade murder and spoyle us his Majesties most faithfull subjects.

Of these the aforesaid Articles wee accuse S'r William Berkely, as guilty of each and every one of the same, and as one, who hath Traiterously attempted, violated and Injured his Majesties Interest here, by the losse of a great Part of his Colony, and many of his Faithfull and Loyall subjects by him betrayed, and in a barbarous and shamefull manner exposed to the Incursions and murthers of the Heathen.

And we further declare these the Ensueing Persons in this List, to have been his wicked, and pernitious Councellors, Aiders and Assisters against the Commonalty in these our Cruell Commotions

S'r Henry Chicherly, Knt.,	Jos. Bridger,
Col. Charles Wormley,	Wm. Clabourne,
Phil. Dalowell,	Thos. Hawkins, Juni'r,
Robert Beverly,	William Sherwood,
Robert Lee,	Jos. Page, Clerk,
Thos. Ballard,	Jo. Cliffe, "
William Cole,	Hubberd Farrell,
Richard Whitacre,	John West,
Nicholas Spencer,	Thos. Reade,

Mathew Kemp.

And wee doe further demand, That the said S'r William Berkley, with all the Persons in this List, be forthwith delivered upp, or surrender themselves, within foure dayes, after the notice hereof, or otherwise wee declare, as followeth, That in whatsoever house, place, or shipp, any of the said Persons shall reside, be hide, or protected, Wee doe declare, that the Owners, masters, or Inhabitants of the said places, to be Confederates, and Traitors to the People, and the Estates of them, as alsoe of all the aforesaid Persons to be Confiscated, This wee the Commons of Virginia doe declare desiring a prime Union among ourselves, that wee may Joyntly, and with one Accord defend ourselves against the Common Enemye. And Let not the Faults of the guilty, be the Reproach of the Innocent, or the Faults or Crimes of ye Oppressors divide and separate us, who have suffered by theire oppressions.

These are therefore in his Majesties name, to Command you forthwith to seize, the Persons above mentioned, as Traytors to ye King and Countrey, and them to bring to Middle Plantation, and there to secure them, till further Order, and in Case of opposition, if you want any other Assistance, you are forthwith to demand it in the Name of the People of all the Counties of Virginia

[signed] NATH BACON, Gen'l
By the Consent of ye People

Discussion Starters

1. Based on the information in these documents, what did Berkeley see in Bacon that Bacon did not see in himself? Similarly, what did Bacon see in Berkeley that Berkeley did not see in himself?

2. What difference, if any, would it make in one's judgment of Bacon to know that the "consent of the people" was only assumed by Bacon and that the declaration was never formally approved by the people?

3. From what middle ground, if any existed, might a conciliator have worked to achieve a peaceful resolution to the Berkeley-Bacon conflict? How might violent confrontation have been avoided? What was gained by violent confrontation?

4. What are the identifiable parallels (if any) between the governor's clash with the rebel in 1676 and conflicts in recent times between established authorities and rebellious protestors?

Related Documents

I. On Nathaniel Bacon: Narrative of the Commissioners

As continuing reports on the rebellion in Virginia reached England in the latter part of 1676, it became apparent that the English government would have to intervene. Three actions were agreed upon: replacing Governor Berkeley, sending a special commission to conciliate the dispute, and dispatching a contingent of English troops to Virginia.

The rebellion had been quelled by the time Governor Berkeley finally agreed to leave the colony, and the troops arrived too late to be of use in the conflict. The commissioners found that their efforts at conciliation were limited to moderating the consequences of the rebellion and relieving some of the sources of the discontent that had caused it. They nevertheless carried on rather extensive investigations and reported their findings to the King. Their final report included "A True Narrative of the Late Rebellion in Virginia," in which they tried to give an impartial account of the events that had torn the colony apart.

After describing the nature of the conflict with the Indians, they gave an account of Nathaniel Bacon's assumption of leadership. The excerpt below contains this account, along with some insights into Bacon's character. Considering that their relations with Governor Berkeley had become increasingly strained, one might suspect that the commissioners would look charitably on Bacon. On what points is their appraisal consistent with Bacon's self-image? Where does it agree with Berkeley's perception of Bacon? Judging from this report, which qualities of Bacon appear to have made him a successful rebel leader?

The Rout being got together now wanted nor waited for nothing but one to head and lead them out on their design. It soe happen'd that one Nathaniel Bacon Junr, a person whose lost and desperate fortunes had thrown him into that remote part of the world about 14 months before, and fram'd him fitt for such a purpose, as by the Sequel will appear, which may make a short character of him no impertinent Digression.

Hee was a person whose erratique fortune had carryed and shewne him many Forraigne Parts, and of no obscure Family. Upon his first comming into Virginia hee was made one of the Councill, the reason of that advancement (all on a suddain) being best known to the Governour, which honor made him the more considerable in the eye of the Vulgar, and gave some advantage to his pernicious designes. Hee was said to be about four or five and thirty yeares of age, indifferent tall but slender, blackhair'd and of an ominous, pensive,

Charles M. Andrews, ed., *Narratives of the Insurrections* (New York: Barnes and Noble, 1915; reprinted, 1959), pp. 109–11.

melancholly Aspect, of a pestilent and prevalent Logical discourse tending to atheisme in most companyes, not given to much talke, or to make suddain replyes, of a most imperious and dangerous hidden Pride of heart, despising the wisest of his neighbours for their Ignorance, and very ambitious and arrogant. But all these things lay hidd in him till after hee was a councillor, and untill he became powerfull and popular.

Now this man being in Company with one Crews, Isham and Bird, who growing to a highth of Drinking and making the Sadnesse of the times their discourse, and the Fear they all lived in, because of the Susquahanocks who had settled a little above the Falls of James River, and comitted many murders upon them, among whom Bacon's overseer happen'd to be one, Crews and the rest persuaded Mr. Bacon to goe over and see the Soldiers on the other Side James river and to take a quantity of Rum with them to give the men to drinke, which they did, and (as Crews etc. had before laid the Plot with the Soldiers) they all at once in field shouted and cry'd out, a Bacon! a Bacon! a Bacon! w'ch taking Fire with his ambition and Spirit of Faction and Popularity, easily prevail'd on him to Resolve to head them, His Friends endeavouring to fix him the Faster to his Resolves by telling him that they would also goe along with him to take Revenge upon the Indians, and drink Damnation to their Soules to be true to him, and if hee could not obtain a Comission they would assist him as well and as much as if he had one; to which Bacon agreed.

This Forwardnesse of Bacons greatly cheer'd and animated the People, who looked upon him as the onely Patron of the Country and preserver of their Lives and Fortunes.

For he pretended and bosted what great Service hee would doe for the country, in destroying the Comon Enemy, securing their Lives and Estates, Libertyes, and such like fair frauds hee subtily and Secretly insinuated by his owne Instruments over all the country, which he seduced the Vulgar and most ignorant People to believe (two thirds of each county being of that Sort) Soe that theire whole hearts and hopes were set now upon Bacon. Next he charges the Governour as negligent and wicked, treacherous and incapable, the Lawes and Taxes as unjust and oppressive and cryes up absolute necessity of redress.

Thus Bacon encouraged the Tumult and as the unquiet crowd follow and adhere to him, he listeth them as they come in upon a large paper, writing their name circular wise, that their Ring-Leaders might not be found out.

Having conjur'd them into this circle, given them Brandy to wind up the charme, and enjoyn'd them by an oth to stick fast together and to him, and the othe being administered, he went and infected New Kent County ripe for Rebellion.

Bacon having gott about 300 men together in armes prepared to goe out against the Indians, the Governour and his Friends endeavour to divert his designes, but cannot.

II. Charles City County Grievances

Among the reports brought together by the commissioners were statements of grievances in each of Virginia's counties. The nature of the grievances varied widely; generally, the closer the counties were to the conflicts with the Indians, the more hostile they were to the governor. Charles City County, upriver from the seat of government in Jamestown, offered the most comprehensive criticism of Governor Berkeley and his administration. This excerpt from its list of grievances is preceded by expressions of apology and loyalty and a simple statement on how the residents of the county understood they were to be governed.

To what extent does this assessment of the situation coincide with Bacon's? These grievances were compiled when Berkeley's departure was in sight, after the rebellion was quelled; what difference does this fact make in evaluating the grievances?

Nevertheless (as wee were informed and seduced to believe) the said Sir Wm. Berkley mindeing and aspiring to a sole and absolute power and command over us his majesties subjects, greatly neglecting the assistance of his majesties said councell in most weighty affairs (as in the nominating and appointing other fitt persons in the roome or place of those of the councell soe nominated by his majesty . . . which are dead or absent) did take upon him the sole nameing and appointing of other persons in theire room and place such as himselfe best liked and thought fittest for his purposes, and without the approval of his majesty or the Lords of his majesties councell for plantacons, as by his majesties commicon (which he the said Sir Wm. Berkeley religiously swore to observe) he is enjoyned and commanded.

And not herewith contented hath very often (as wee were informed and seduced to believe) discountenanced and placed his frowns on such of them as he observed in the least to thrust or cross his humour, soe that if by chance he had at any time choice of a person of honor or conscience, that durst like a noble Patriot speake his minde freely for the good of his majesty and of us his majesties poore distressed subjects, such person by some means or other was soone made weary of comeing to councell, and others overawed from the like boldness.

And that the said Sir Wm. Berkeley haveing for the end and purpose aforesaid for divers yeares last thus layde aside his majesties councell here, and in the stead thereof formed a councell of his owne, the better to support this his single power, hath likewise assumed to himself the sole nominating, appointing and commissionating of all commicon officers both civil and military amongst us (which power as we're seduced to believe is only granted to his majesties councell by his majesties commicon aforesaid) and alsoe other offices of profitt, which said several offices being by him the said Sir. Wm. Berkeley (the better to increase the number of his party) multiplyed to a great number,

Virginia Magazine of History and Biography, III (1896), 134–37. Paragraphing has been added by the editors.

some of them as his councell, commissioners of the peace in the several counties and to twice the number they ought to be by law, all which offices he bestowed on such persons (how unfitt or unskillfull soever) as he conceived would be most for his designs.

And that the more firmely to binde and oblige them thereunto and to allure others to his party, he the said Sir Wm. Berkeley permitted or connived at the persons soe commissionated by him (for the end and purpose aforesaid) unwarrantly and contrary to his majesties the very fundamental lawes, to lay and impose what levies and imposicons upon us they should or did please, which they would often extort from us by force and violence, and which for the most part they converted to their owne private lucre and gaine.

And that Sir Wm. Berkeley haveing by these wayes and meanes, and by takeing uppon him contrary to law the granting collectors places, sherifs, and other offices of profitt to whome he best pleased, he soe gained uppon and obliged all or the greatest number of the men of parts and estates in the whole country (out of which it was necessary our representatives and Burgesses should be elected) hath thereby soe fortifyed his power, over us, as of himselfe without respect to our laws, to doe what soever he best pleased and from time to time (besides the vast sums of Tobacco and money raised for building of the towne and forte, neither of which were ever finished or made usefull for habitation or security, and for Tanworks, Weavers &c.) to gaine and procure greate quantities of Tobacco and mony from us to his proper use over and besides the Thousand pounds yearly Sallary appointed him by the King's majesty and over and besides the fees, profitts and per quisetts to the place of Governor belonging to the great impovishment of this his majesties country.

All which besides the great quantities of armes and ammunicon his majesty hath been gratiously pleased to bestow upon us, and hath been raised amongst us for magazines and stores, have (as wee have been seduced to believe) been embezzled and consumed betwixt him and his officers, and very few or noe good acts done for us or this his majesties country, but on the contrary the same made rather worse, more open to all invaders, worse provided with armes and ammunicon, much poorer and more unable to purchase them.

Whereby we have been forced to submit to the Invasions of our Enimies, as in the two late Dutch warrs, and in the present warr against the Indians wee have wofully experienced. Nor hath there bin dureing the long Government of the said Sir Wm. Berkeley any competent security provided to defend the Merchants shipps tradeing into this country, though many vast sums have been raised on the people under the pretence of fortifications, and money's actually payd by all shipps in the name of Castle Duties, but on the contrary the gunns sent in by his majesty for that end lye buried in the sand and rust to the great incouragement of any Invador, and the apparent hazzard of this his majesties Country.

All which grievances and pressures and many others we still should continue to have patiently suffered under (had the same been really true as we were seduced to believe as aforesaid and it is possible on your Honors enquiry may be found to prove true) rather then in the least manner mannifest any contempt or disobedience to his majesties gracious Government, had he the said Sir Wm. Berkeley after all this been zealous or active in our defence or preservacon against our said Barbarous enimy the Indian, but when instead thereof we heard and found he not onely slighted and rejected the grate and lamentable cries of blood, rapine, devatacon, and distraction that came to his ears, from most parts of this his majesties distressed country, and tooke noe suffitient course to prevent or revenge the same allthough, (as himselfe confesseth), he had notice of a very formidable body of Indians comeing downe upon James river within fifty or sixty miles of the English Plantacons that did lye hovering over us and could not guess where the storme would fall, but on the contrary threatened those of this County of Charles City that with humble peticon came voluntary to offer their service at their own charge, and the hazard of their lives and fortunes to defend themselves and us, and to finde out and destroy the enimy (onely desireing his leave or commicon, and to be ledd by any commander or commanders he should please to appoint) whom with threatening language and much scorne he rejected, and instead of granting their request, by proclamacon under great pennalty prohibited the like petitioning for the future, giving us thereby . . . just cause to suspect that for the lucre of Gaine made by him and his friends by trading with them, and furnishing them with armes and ammunicon whilst wee ourselves wanted it he rather sought to protect them than us.

And this wee were rather induced to believe for that after he had (to satisfye the cryes of the people who dayly sawe the traders issue forth quantities of arms and ammunicon to ye Indian) by his publeque proclamacon prohibited all trading with the said Indians, he privately gave commicon to trade to some of his friends, who accordingly did sell store of powder and shott &c. to ye Indians then in arms against us.

These things being apparent and many more insinuated into our beliefe, togeather with violent and deadly fears of danger wee apprehended from the Indian, many of ye people haveing left their plantacons and stocks and drawne togeather inwards to secure their wives and children, whose daylye cryes made our lives uncomfortable. To confesse the truth to your Honors, we doe acknowledge wee were soe unadvised then and not till then as to believe it our duty incumbent on us both by the laws of God and nature, and our duty to his sacred majesties notwithstanding his the said Sir Wm. Berkeley's prohibition and comands to ye contrary to take up armes, many of us for the just defence of ourselves, wives and children and this his majesties Country against ye Indians.

III. A Conversation Between Nathaniel Bacon and John Goode

Some historians believe that Bacon may have hurt his cause by pursuing too radical a policy. An account of a conversation between Bacon and John Goode, one of his frontiersman followers, provides some insights into Bacon's attitudes. This conversation, which took place in early September 1676, was later reported to Governor Berkeley by Goode, who, as the conversation indicates, was compelled to part company with Bacon.

Do Bacon's comments suggest rebellious recklessness or courage? Why would an attitude like Bacon's prompt Governor Berkeley to pursue a harsh policy of repression?

JANUARY 30, 1677

Hon'd Sr.—In obedient submission to your honours command directed to me by Capt. Wm. Bird I have written the full substance of a discourse Nath: Bacon, deceased, propos'd to me on or about the 2d day of September last, both in order and words as followeth:—

BACON.—There is a report Sir Wm. Berkeley hath sent to the king for 2,000 Red Coates, and I doe believe it may be true, tell me your opinion, may not 500 Virginians beat them, wee having the same advantages against them the Indians have against us.

GOODE.—I rather conceive 500 Red Coats may either Subject or ruine Virginia.

B.—You talk strangely, are not wee acquainted with the Country, can lay Ambussadoes, and take Trees and putt them by, the use of their discipline, and are doubtlesse as good or better shott than they.

G.—But they can accomplish what I have sayd without hazard or coming into such disadvantages, by taking Opportunities of landing where there shall bee noe opposition, firing out [our?] houses and Fences, destroying our Stocks and preventing all Trade and supplyes to the Country.

B.—There may bee such prevention that they shall not bee able to make any great Progresse in Mischiefes, and the Country or Clime not agreeing with their Constitutions, great mortality will happen amongst them, in their Seasoning which will weare and weary them out.

G.—You see Sir that in a manner all the principall Men in the Countrey dislike your manner of proceedings, they, you may bee sure will joine with the Red Coates.

B.—But there shall none of them bee [permitted?].

G.—Sir, you speake as though you design'd a totall defection from Majestie, and our native Country.

B.—Why (smiling) have not many Princes lost their Dominions soe.

John Fiske, *Old Virginia* (Boston: Houghton Mifflin, 1897), II, pp. 83–86.

G.—They have been such people as have been able to subsist without their Prince. The poverty of Virginia is such, that the Major part of the Inhabitants can scarce supply their wants from hand to mouth, and many there are besides can hardly shift, without Supply one yeare, and you may bee sure that this people which soe fondly follow you, when they come to feele the miserable wants of food and rayment, will bee in greater heate to leave you, then [than] they were to come after you, besides here are many people in Virginia that receive considerable benefitts, comforts, and advantages by Parents, Friends and Correspondents in England, and many which expect patrimonyes and Inheritances which they will by no meanes decline.

B.—For supply I know nothing: the Country will be able to provide it selfe withall, in a little time, save Amunition and Iron, and I believe the King of France or States of Holland would either of them entertaine a Trade with us.

G.—Sir, our King is a great Prince, and his Amity is infinitely more valuable to them, then [than] any advantage they can reape by Virginia, they will not therefore provoke his displeasure by supporting his Rebells here; besides I conceive that your followers do not think themselves ingaged against the King's Authority, but against the Indians.

B.—But I think otherwise, and am confident of it, that it is the mind of this country, and of Mary Land, and Caroline also, to cast off their Governor and the Governors of Carolina have taken no notice of the People, nor the People of them, a long time; and the people are resolv'd to own their Governour further; And if wee cannot prevaile by Armes to make our Conditions for Peace, or obtaine the Priviledge to elect our own Governour, we may retire to Roanoke.

And here hee fell into a discourse of seating a Plantation in a great Island in the River, as a fitt place to retire to for Refuge.

G.—Sir, the prosecuting what you have discoursed will unavoidably produce utter ruine and destruction to the people and Countrey, & I dread the thoughts of putting my hand to the promoting a designe of such miserable consequence, therefore hope you will not expect from me.

B.—I am glad I know your mind, but this proceeds from meer Cowardlynesse.

G.—And I desire you should know my mind, for I desire to harbour noe such thoughts, which I should fear to impart to any man.

B.—Then what should a Gentleman engaged as I am, doe, you doe as good as tell me, I must fly or hang for it.

G.—I conceive a seasonable Submission to the Authority you have your Commission from, acknowledging such Errors and Excesse, as are yett past, there may bee hope of remission.

I perceived his cogitations were much on this discourse, hee nominated, Carolina, for the watch word.

Three days after I asked his leave to goe home, hee sullenly Answered, you may goe, and since that time, I thank God, I never saw or heard from him.

IV. Thomas Mathews on Nathaniel Bacon

*A reluctant participant in Bacon's Rebellion was the Virginia planter, business-
man, and sometime legislator, Thomas Mathews. In 1705, working from mem-
ory and probably from notes, Mathews wrote "The Beginning, Progress, and
Conclusion of Bacon's Rebellion, 1675–1676." Mathews' account seems to be
fairly impartial, although for a time he was sympathetic with the rebellion and
acquainted with its leaders.*

*In his narrative Mathews stressed Bacon's role as leader, but in an appendix
he shed some light on other undercover activities. If his assertion that there was
outside agitation is valid, what does this say about the motives of the rebels?
What is there in Berkeley's letter that would confirm or refute Mathews' assertion?*

To avoid Incumbring the Body of the foregoing little discourse, I have not
therein mentioned the received Opinion in Virginia, which very much Attributed the promoting these Perturbacions to Mr. Laurance, and Mr. Bacon
with his other Adherents were esteemed, as but Wheels agitated by the Weight
of his former and present Resentments, after their Choler was raised up to a
very high Pitch, at having been (so long and often) trifled with on their humble
Supplications to the Governour for his immediate taking in hand the most
speedy meanes towards stopping the Continued Effusions of so much English
Bloud, from time to time by the Indians; Which Common Sentiments I have
the more reason to believe were not altogether groundlesse, because my self
have heard him (in his familiar discourse) Insinuate as if his fancy gave him
prospect of finding (at one time or other,) some expedient not only to repaire
his great Losse, but therewith to See those abuses rectified that the Countrey
was oppress'd with through (as he said) the frowardness avarice and french
Despotick Methods of the Governour and likewise I know him to be a thinking
Man, and tho' nicely honest, affable, and without Blemish, in his Conversation
and Dealings, yet did he manifest abundance of uneasiness in the Sense of his
hard Usages, which might prompt him to Improve[1] that Indian Quarrel to the
Service of his Animosities, and for this the more fair and frequent opportunities offered themselves to him by his dwelling at James Town, where was the
Concourse from all Parts to the Governour and besides that he had Married
a Wealthy Widow who kept a large house of publick Entertainment unto
which resorted those of the best quality, and such others as Businesse Called
to that Town, and his Parts with his even Temper made his Converse Coveted
by Persons of all Ranks; So that being Subtile, and having these advantages
he might with lesse Difficulty discover mens Inclinations, and Instill his No-

---

Charles M. Andrews, ed., *Narratives of the Insurrections* (New York: Barnes and Noble, 1915;
reprinted, 1959), pp. 40–41. The manuscript is signed "T. M.," but Andrews and other historians
attribute it to Thomas Mathews.

[1]Make use of.

tions where he found those woud be imbib'd with greatest Satisfaction.

As for Mr. Bacon fame did lay to his Charge the having run out his Patrimony in England Except what he brought to Virginia and of that the most Part to be Exhausted, which together made him Suspected of Casting an Eye to Search for Retrievment in the troubled Waters of popular Discontents, wanting Patience to wait the Death of his oppulent Cousin, old Collo. Bacon, Whose Estate he Expected to Inherit.

But he was too young, too much a Stranger there, and of a Disposition too precipitate, to Manage things to that length those were Carried, had not thoughtfull Mr. Laurence been at the Bottom.

For Further Reading

Sharply contrasting interpretations of Bacon's Rebellion are offered by Wilcomb E. Washburn in *The Governor and the Rebel: A History of Bacon's Rebellion in Virginia** (1957; new introduction, 1967), and by Thomas J. Wertenbaker in *Torchbearer of the Revolution: The Story of Bacon's Rebellion and its Leader* (1940). The latter volume is out of print, but the author restated his arguments in a short booklet, *Bacon's Rebellion** (1957). Both Washburn and Wertenbaker should be read before drawing conclusions.

Wesley Frank Craven presents a more balanced picture in *The Southern Colonies in the Seventeenth Century* (1949). *Narratives of the Insurrections, 1675–1690*, edited by Charles M. Andrews (1915; reprinted in 1959), contains accounts of rebellions in a number of colonies including Virginia; this chapter contains excerpts from several of these accounts.

Two problems books are *Bacon's Rebellion** (1964), edited by Robert Middlekauf, and *Bacon's Rebellion: Prologue to Revolution?** (1969), edited by John B. Frantz.

*Paperbound edition available.

2. Awakening America

"We must consider that we shall be as a city upon a hill," John Winthrop reminded his fellow emigrants as they sailed to Massachusetts Bay in 1630. "The eyes of all people are upon us."

The eyes that looked at Winthrop's "city on the hill" in the 1630s and 1640s were not disappointed if they looked charitably, for they saw Winthrop leading the Puritan company in a dedicated and single-minded effort to keep a covenant with God by establishing what they believed to be a true Bible commonwealth. Church membership alone opened the door to full participation in the new society. Town meeting places served both spiritual and civic purposes, manners and morals imposed by the church were endorsed and enforced by the government, and religious dissent and heresy brought expulsion from the colony. In sum, church and state were virtually one in the Puritan theocracy. Although Winthrop suffered disappointments and reversals, when death approached in 1649 he could look back with satisfaction at having lived up to his part of the covenant.

What was to be seen by looking at Massachusetts Bay, the "city on the hill," a century later? By the standards of its Puritan founders the view would not have been pleasing. Even though many of the outward forms of religious practice persisted, the original meaning and spirit of living under a covenant with God had disappeared.

Such a change in religious climate occurred in other colonies as well. No matter what the ideals or convictions of their founders were, by the early decades of the eighteenth century all the colonies showed a surprising uniformity in their religious aspects. Established churches seemed to have lost their appeal for common people, as large numbers were either unchurched or dissenters. And replacements for the religious stalwarts of earlier years did not appear. Instead, the clergy seemed to become too sophisticated, too worldly, too settled in its established position and orthodoxy to minister effectively to the religious needs of ordinary people. By the 1720s, the time was ripe for a religious revival.

Although the "great and general awakening" in America had parallels in Europe, what happened in the colonies was unique and significant in its own right. One distinct aspect of its impact is the principal focus of this chapter.

The first stirrings of America's "Great Awakening" came in New Jersey in the mid-1720s under the impetus of a "New Light" pastor in the Dutch Reformed Church. A revival among Presbyterians in Pennsylvania next attracted attention. The third wave of religious excitement centered in Northampton, Massachusetts, in the mid-1730s, under the driving force of Jonathan Edwards.

Signs of revival appeared elsewhere in the colonies in the 1730s, but it was not until the end of the decade that local events were tied together in a general, shared experience. This was in great part a consequence of the preaching tours of George Whitefield, who arrived from England in November 1739. This "Grand Itinerant," only 24 years old, had mastered the ability to use his superb voice and enunciation for the greatest dramatic effect. He stirred the emotions of his hearers wherever he spoke, and he preached to numerous large audiences, frequently outdoors. His methods provoked controversy in England and aroused considerable opposition among the established clergy in the colonies, but his popularity seemed to increase as his opposition intensified.

The Great Awakening spread into many areas of the colonies during the next several years, but by 1744 calm, even indifference, had returned. The movement was overcome by its own excesses, by the increasingly effective opposition it generated, and by its inability to maintain the high level of emotion necessary to its continuance.

The impact of the Awakening, however, was felt for many years. The most noticeable effects included the creation of a multiplicity of religious sects separated by unbridgeable gaps, the founding of several colleges (initially to perpetuate the sects), increased suspicion of ties between church and state, the loss of prestige by the established clergy, and the development of missionary zeal for Christianizing the continent.

Core Document

Thoughts Concerning the Revival of Religion

JONATHAN EDWARDS

The more subtle consequences of the Great Awakening were probably of greater significance than the obvious ones. They have attracted increased attention in recent years, and have prompted one historian of the Awakening, Perry Miller, to mark the 1740s as "a watershed in American development." Alan Heimert, another historian writing on this period, sees it as "America's final break with the Middle Ages and her entry into a new intellectual age in the church and society."

The Great Awakening was not a liberal movement, but its democratic implications, although only subtly evident, cannot be overlooked. According to recent interpretations, the Awakening had a leveling effect in education and politics, elevating the status of the common man. It broke the hold of establishments and encouraged a spirit of individualism and independence. And because it was intercolonial and, at first, intersectarian, it helped to create a spirit of nationalism well before the onset of the Revolutionary period.

Ironically, the participant in the Great Awakening who seems to have best sensed its larger significance was a lonely minister in the Connecticut River Valley, Jonathan Edwards. A graduate of Yale and the leader of the Northampton revival in the 1730s, this quiet thinker and writer seems out of character as a revival preacher. He was more at ease while musing on the writing of John Locke and Isaac Newton than in ministering to his congregation. When preaching, even when delivering such well-known sermons as his "Sinners in the Hands of an Angry God," he either read from his manuscript or fixed his gaze on the bell rope.

Edwards, who now appears to have been the greatest theologian in American history, did much of his work during periods when he was engaged in disputes with his Northampton congregation over matters ranging from salary differences to disciplining of the town's youth and to doctrinal issues. Such disputes finally led to his removal from his congregation in 1750, but he continued his work as a missionary to Indians, a position allowing him more time for thinking and writing. In 1758, at the age of 54, he reluctantly became president of the College of New Jersey (now Princeton), but he died shortly after assuming office.

Much of Edwards' theological work was concerned with encouraging or defending the revival in which he participated. To this end he wrote three major treatises; included here are excerpts from the second one, Some Thoughts

Sereno E. Dwight, ed., *The Works of President Edwards with a Memoir of His Life in Ten Volumes* (New York: S. Converse, 1830), IV, pp. 82, 84–86, 90–91, 94–96, 98–99, 105–9, 128–33.

Concerning the Present Revival of Religion in New England *(1742). Of all his writings, this is probably the most easily understood by persons who are neither theologians nor philosophers.*

In reading this selection, identify the main points Edwards makes in:
- *challenging the critics of the Awakening.*
- *distinguishing the Awakening's good effects from its bad.*
- *pointing to the signs of real achievement of the Awakening.*
- *envisioning a new role and a bright future for America.*

I. Some make Philosophy, instead of the holy scriptures, their rule of judging of this work; particularly the philosophical notions they entertain of the nature of the soul, its faculties and affections. Some are ready to say, "There is but little sober solid religion in this work; it is little else but flash and noise. Religion now all runs out into transports and high flights of the passions and affections." In their philosophy, the affections of the soul are something diverse from the will, and not appertaining to the noblest part of the soul. They are ranked among the meanest principles that belong to men as partaking of animal nature, and what he has in common with the brute creation, rather than any thing whereby he is conformed to angels and pure spirits. And though they acknowledge that a good use may be made of the affections in religion, yet they suppose that the substantial part of religion does not consist in them, but that they are something adventitious and accidental in Christianity. . . .

If we take the scriptures for our rule, then the greater and higher our exercises of love to God, delight and complacency in him, desires and longings after him, delight in his children, love to mankind, brokenness of heart, abhorrence of sin, and self-abhorrence for it; the more we have of the peace of God which passeth all understanding, and joy in the Holy Ghost, unspeakable and full of glory: the higher our admiring thoughts of God, exulting and glorying in him; so much the higher is Christ's religion, or that virtue which he and his apostles taught, raised in the soul.

It is a stumbling to some, that religious affections should seem to be so powerful, or that they should be so violent (as they express it) in some persons. They are therefore ready to doubt whether it can be the Spirit of God; or whether this vehemence be not rather a sign of the operation of an evil spirit. But why should such a doubt arise? What is represented in scripture as more powerful in its effects than the Spirit of God? which is therefore called "the power of the Highest," . . . and its saving effect in the soul is called "the power of godliness." . . . So the Spirit is represented by a mighty wind, and by fire, things most powerful in their operation.

II. Many are guilty of not taking the holy scriptures as a sufficient and whole rule, whereby to judge of this work.—They judge by those things which the scripture does not give as any signs or marks whereby to judge one way or the other. viz. the effects that religious exercises and affections of mind have upon the body. Scripture rules respect the state of the mind, moral conduct, and voluntary behaviour; and not the physical state of the body. The design of the scripture is to teach us divinity, and not physic and anatomy. Ministers are made the watchmen of men's souls, and not their bodies; and therefore the great rule which God has committed into their hands, is to make them divines, and not physicians. . . . And therefore those ministers of Christ, and overseers of souls, who are full of concern about the involuntary motions of the fluids and solids of men's bodies, and who from thence are full of doubts and suspicions of the cause—when nothing appears but that the state and frame of their minds and their voluntary behaviour is good, and agreeable to God's word—go out of the place that Christ has set them in, and leave their proper business, as much as if they should undertake to tell who are under the influence of the Spirit by their looks or their gait. . . .

III. Another thing that some make their rule to judge of this work by, instead of the holy scriptures, is *history,* or former observation. Herein they err two ways:

First, If there be any thing extraordinary in the circumstances of this work, which was not observed in former times, theirs is a rule to reject this work which God has not given them, and they limit God, where he has not limited himself. And this is especially unreasonable in this case: For whosoever has well weighed the wonderful and mysterious methods of divine wisdom in carrying on the work of the new creation . . . may easily observe that it has all along been God's manner to open new scenes, and to bring forth to view things new and wonderful—such as eye had not seen, nor ear heard, nor entered into the heart of man or angels—to the astonishment of heaven and earth, not only in the revelations he makes of his mind and will, but also into the works of his hands. As the old creation was carried on through six days, and appeared all complete, settled in a state of rest on the seventh; so the new creation, which is immensely the greatest and most glorious work, is carried on in a gradual progress, from the fall of man to the consummation of all things. . . .

Secondly, Another way that some err in making history and former observation their rule instead of the holy scripture, is in comparing some external, accidental circumstances of this work, with what has appeared sometimes in enthusiasts. They find an agreement in some such things, and so they reject the whole work, or at least the substance of it, concluding it to be enthusiasm. Great use has been made to this purpose of many things that are found amongst the Quakers; however totally and essentially different in its nature this work is, and the principles upon which it is built, from the whole religion of the Quakers. . . .

IV. I wold propose it to be considered, whether or no some, instead of making the scriptures their only rule to judge of this work, do not make their own experience the rule, and reject such and such things as are now professed and experienced, because they themselves never felt them. Are there not many, who, chiefly on this ground, have entertained and vented suspicions, if not peremptory condemnations, of those extreme terrors, and those great, sudden, and extraordinary discoveries of the glorious perfections of God, and of the beauty and love of Christ? Have they not condemned such vehement affections, such high transports of love and joy, such pity and distress for the souls of others, and exercises of mind that have such great effects, merely, or chiefly, because they knew nothing about them by experience? Persons are very ready to be suspicious of what they have not felt themselves. It is to be feared that many good men have been guilty of this error: which however does not make it the less unreasonable. . . .

ANOTHER foundation error of those who reject this work, is, their not duly distinguishing the good from the bad, and very unjustly judging of the whole by a part; and so rejecting the work in general, or in the main substance of it, for the sake of some accidental evil in it. . . .

A great deal of noise and tumult, confusion and uproar, darkness mixed with light, and evil with good, is always to be expected in the beginning of something very glorious in the state of things in human society, or the church of God. After nature has long been shut up in a cold dead state, when the sun returns in the spring, there is, together with the increase of the light and heat of the sun, very tempestuous weather, before all is settled calm and serene, and all nature rejoices in its bloom and beauty. It is in the new creation as it was in the old: the Spirit of God first moved upon the face of the waters, which was an occasion of great uproar and tumult. Things were then gradually brought to a settled state, till at length all stood forth in that beautiful peaceful order, when the heavens and the earth were finished, and God saw every thing that he had made, and behold it was very good. When God is about to bring to pass something great and glorious in the world, nature is in a ferment and struggle, and the world as it were in travail. . . .

WHATEVER imprudences there have been, and whatever sinful irregularities; whatever vehemence of the passions, and heats of the imagination, transports and ecstacies; whatever error in judgment, and indiscreet zeal; and whatever outcries, faintings, and agitations of body; yet, it is manifest and notorious, that there has been of late a very uncommon influence upon the minds of a very great part of the inhabitants of New-England, attended with the best effects. . . . Multitudes in all parts of the land, of vain, thoughtless, regardless persons, are quite changed, and become serious and considerate. There is a vast increase of concern for the salvation of the precious soul, and of that inquiry, "What shall I do to be saved?" . . . They have also been awakened to a sense of the shortness and uncertainty of life, and the reality of another world and future judgment, and of the necessity of an interest in Christ. They are more afraid of sin, more careful and inquisitive that they may know what is contrary to the mind and will of God, that they may avoid it, and what he requires of them, that they may do it, more careful to guard against temptations, more watchful over their own hearts, earnestly desirous of knowing, and of being diligent in the use of the means that God has appointed in his word, in order to salvation. Many very stupid, senseless sinners, and persons of a vain mind, have been greatly awakened.

There is a strange alteration almost all over New-England amongst young people: by a powerful invisible influence on their minds, they have been

brought to forsake, in a general way, as it were at once, those things of which
they were extremely fond, and in which they seemed to place the happiness
of their lives, and which nothing before could induce them to forsake; as their
frolicking, vain company-keeping, night-walking, their mirth and jollity, their
impure language, and lewd songs. . . . It is astonishing to see the alteration
there is in some towns, where before there was but little appearance of religion,
or any thing but vice and vanity. And now they are transformed into another
sort of people; their former vain, worldly, and vicious conversation and dispositions seem to be forsaken, and they are, as it were, gone over to a new world.
Their thoughts, their talk, and their concern, affections and inquiries, are now
about the favour of God, an interest in Christ, a renewed sanctified heart, and
a spiritual blessedness, acceptance, and happiness in a future world.

Now, through the greater part of New-England, the holy Bible is in much
greater esteem and use than before. . . . The Lord's day is more religiously and
strictly observed. And much has been lately done at making up differences,
confessing faults one to another, and making restitution: probably more within
two years, than was done in thirty years before. It has been undoubtedly so
in many places. And surprising has been the power of this spirit in many
instances, to destroy old grudges, to make up long continued breaches, and to
bring those who seemed to be in a confirmed irreconcilable alienation, to
embrace each other in a sincere and entire amity. . . .

Multitudes in New-England have lately been brought to a new and great
conviction of the truth and certainty of the things of the gospel; to a firm
persuasion that Christ Jesus is the son of God, and the great and only Saviour
of the world, and that the great doctrines of the gospel touching reconciliation
by his blood, and acceptance in his righteousness, and eternal life and salvation
through him, are matters of undoubted truth. . . .

And, under the influences of this work, there have been many of the
remains of those wretched people and dregs of mankind, the poor Indians, that
seemed to be next to a state of brutality, and with whom, till now, it seemed
to be to little more purpose to use endeavours for their instruction and awakening, than with the beasts. Their minds have now been strangely opened to
receive instruction, and been deeply affected with the concerns of their precious souls; they have reformed their lives, and forsaken their former stupid,
barbarous and brutish way of living; and particularly that sin to which they
have been so exceedingly addicted, their drunkenness. Many of them to appearance brought truly and greatly to delight in the things of God, and to have
their souls very much engaged and entertained with the great things of the
gospel. And many of the poor Negroes also have been in like manner wrought
upon and changed. Very many little children have been remarkably enlightened, and their hearts wonderfully affected and enlarged, and their mouths
opened, expressing themselves in a manner far beyond their years, and to the
just astonishment of those who have heard them. Some of them for many
months, have been greatly and delightfully affected with the glory of divine
things, and the excellency and love of the Redeemer, with their hearts greatly

filled with love to, and joy in him; and they have continued to be serious and pious in their behaviour. . . .

IT is not unlikely that this work of God's Spirit, so extraordinary and wonderful, is the dawning, or at least a prelude of that glorious work of God, so often foretold in scripture, which, in the progress and issue of it, shall renew the world of mankind. If we consider how long since the things foretold as what should precede this great event, have been accomplished; and how long this event has been expected by the church of God, and thought to be nigh by the most eminent men of God, in the church; and withal consider what the state of things now is, and has for a considerable time been, in the church of God, and the world of mankind; we cannot reasonably think otherwise, than that the beginning of this great work of God must be near. And there are many things that make it probable that this work will begin in America.—It is signified that it shall begin in some very remote part of the world, with which other parts have no communication but by navigation, in Isa. lx. 9. "Surely the isles shall wait for me, and the ships of Tarshish first, to bring my sons from far." It is exceeding manifest that this chapter is a prophecy of the prosperity of the church, in its most glorious state on earth, in the latter days; and I cannot think that any thing else can be here intended but America by the isles that are far off, from whence the first-born sons of that glorious day shall be brought. Indeed, by *the isles,* in prophecies of gospel-times, is very often meant Europe. . . . But this prophecy cannot have respect to the conversion of Europe, in the time of that great work of God, in the primitive ages of the Christian church; for it was not fulfilled then. The isles and ships of Tarshish, thus understood, did not wait for God first; that glorious work did not begin in Europe, but in Jerusalem, and had for a considerable time been very wonderfully carried on in Asia, before it reached Europe. And as it is not *that* work of God which is chiefly intended in this chapter, but some more glorious work that should be in the latter ages of the Christian church; therefore, some other part of the world is here intended by the isles, that should be, as Europe then was, far separated from that part of the world where the church had before been, and with which it can have no communication but by the ships of Tarshish. And what is chiefly intended is not the British isles, nor any isles near the other continent; they are spoken of as at a great distance from that part of the world where the church had till then been. This prophecy therefore seems plainly to point out America, as the first-fruits of that glorious day.

God has made as it were two worlds here below, two great habitable continents, far separated one from the other: The latter is as it were now but newly created; it has been, till of late, wholly the possession of Satan, the church of God having never been in it, as it has been in the other continent, from the beginning of the world. This new world is probably now discovered, that the new and most glorious state of God's church on earth might commence there; that God might in it begin a new world in a spiritual respect, when he creates the *new heavens* and *new earth.*

God has already put that honour upon the other continent, that Christ was born there literally, and there made the "purchase of redemption." So, as Providence observes a kind of equal distribution of things, it is not unlikely that the great spiritual birth of Christ, and the most glorious "application of redemption," is to begin in this. . . .

The other continent hath slain Christ, and has from age to age shed the blood of the saints and martyrs of Jesus, and has often been as it were, deluged with the church's blood.—God has, therefore, probably reserved the honour of building the glorious temple to the daughter that has not shed so much blood, when those times of the peace, prosperity and glory of the church, typified by the reign of Solomon, shall commence. . . .

The old continent has been the source and original of mankind in several respects. The first parents of mankind dwelt there; and there dwelt Noah and his sons; there the second Adam was born, and crucified, and raised again: And it is probable that, in some measure to balance these things, the most glorious renovation of the world shall originate from the new continent, and the church of God in that respect be from hence. And so it is probable that will come to pass in spirituals, which has taken place in temporals, with respect to America: that whereas, till of late, the world was supplied with its silver, and gold, and earthly treasures from the old continent, now it is supplied chiefly from the new; so the course of things in spiritual respects will be in like manner turned. —And it is worthy to be noted, that America was discovered about the time of the reformation, or but little before: Which reformation was the first thing that God did towards the glorious renovation of the world, after it had sunk into the depths of darkness and ruin, under the great anti-christian apostacy. So that, as soon as this new world stands forth in view, God presently goes about doing some great thing in order to make way for the introduction of the church's latter-day glory—which is to have its first seat in, and is to take its rise from that new world.

It is agreeable to God's manner, when he accomplishes any glorious work in the world, in order to introduce a new and more excellent state of his church, to begin where no foundation had been already laid, that the power of God might be the more conspicuous; that the work might appear to be entirely God's, and be more manifestly a creation out of nothing. . . . When God is about to turn the earth into a paradise, he does not begin his work where there is some good growth already, but in the wilderness, where nothing grows, and nothing is to be seen but dry sand and barren rocks; that the light may shine out of darkness, the world be replenished from emptiness, and the earth watered by springs from a droughty desert: agreeable to many prophecies of scripture. . . . Now as when God is about to do some great work for his church, his manner is to begin at the lower end; so, when he is about to renew the whole habitable earth, it is probable that he will begin in this utmost, meanest, youngest and weakest part of it, where the church of God has been planted last of all: and so the first shall be last, and the last first: and that will be fulfilled in an eminent manner in Isa. xxiv. 19. "From the uttermost part of the earth have we heard songs, even glory to the righteous." . . .

. . . And if we may suppose that this glorious work of God shall begin in any part of America, I think, if we consider the circumstances of the settlement of New-England, it must needs appear the most likely, of all American colonies, to be the place whence this work shall principally take its rise. And, if these things be so, it gives us more abundant reason to hope that what is now seen in America, and especially in New-England, may prove the dawn of that glorious day; and the very uncommon and wonderful circumstances and events of this work, seem to me strongly to argue that God intends it as the beginning or forerunner of something vastly great.

I HAVE thus long insisted on this point, because, if these things are so, it greatly manifests how much it behoves us to encourage and promote this work, and how dangerous it will be to forbear so doing. It is very dangerous for God's professing people to lie still, and not to come to the help of the Lord, whenever he remarkably pours out his Spirit, to carry on the work of redemption in the application of it; but above all, when he comes forth to introduce that happy day of God's power and salvation, so often spoken of. . . .

Discussion Starters

1. It is difficult to define precisely what Edwards meant by "affections." Probably he meant deep and warm feelings leading to judgments and actions. If this definition is accurate, what judgments and actions might Edwards have expected to flow from the "affections" raised by religious revival? What, if anything, does all this have to do with the growth of a democratic spirit?

2. Which of the good effects of the Awakening, as judged by Edwards, would find approval in society today? By whom? To what extent could these good effects be achieved through a "patriotic awakening" apart from Christian teaching?

3. Evaluate the premises on which Edwards based his assertion that America was the land in which a new society would take shape. What would be the shape of this new society? What went wrong; i.e., why did the new society not come about?

4. How valid is the suggestion made by some historians that the seeds of a democratic spirit are apparent in this treatise?

Related Documents

I. Seasonable Thoughts on the State of Religion

CHARLES CHAUNCY

The most formidable antagonist Jonathan Edwards faced in the debate over the Great Awakening was Charles Chauncy, a Boston minister. Although they rarely mentioned names in their writings, there is no doubt that each had the other in mind when he wrote. The following selection is taken from Chauncy's Seasonable Thoughts on the State of Religion in New England *(1743), a vigorous attack on many features of the Great Awakening.*

In this excerpt, how effectively does he oppose Edwards' ideas on the future glories of America? What in this essay, if anything, can be considered as pessimistic, proestablishment, or antidemocratic?

'Tis true, we read of the coming on of a *glorious State* of Things in the LAST DAYS: Nor will the *Vision fail.*—We may rely upon it, the Prophesies, foretelling the Glory of the REDEEMER's *Kingdom,* will have their Accomplishment to the making this Earth of *Paradise,* in Compare with what it now is. But for the *particular Time* when this will be, it *is not for us to know it, the Father having put it in his own Power:* And whoever pretend to such Knowledge, they are wise above what is written; and tho' they may think they know much, they really know nothing as to this Matter.

It may be suggested,[1] that "the *Work of* GOD's SPIRIT that is so extraordinary and wonderful, is the *dawning,* or at lest, a *Prelude* of that glorious *Work of GOD,* so often foretold in Scripture, which, in the Progress and Issue of it, shall renew the whole World." But what are such Suggestions, but the Fruit of Imagination? Or at best, uncertain Conjecture? And can any good End be answered in endeavouring, upon Evidence absolutely precarious, to instill into the Minds of People a Notion of the *millenium* State, as what is NOW going to be introduced; yea, and of AMERICA,[2] as that Part of the World, which is

---

Alan Heimert and Perry Miller, eds., *The Great Awakening* (New York: Bobbs-Merrill, 1967), pp. 302–4.

[1]Mr. Edwards late book.

[2]While I was writing this Page, I received a Letter from a worthy Gentleman, in which, speaking of Mr. EDWARDS's late *Book,* he has these Words, "I am surpriz'd at his long Labour to prove the *Millennium* shall begin in AMERICA.—He has been so modest as to conceal the Reason of this; but it may easily be gathered from what he has *often said to private Persons,* viz. that he doubted not, the *Millennium* began when there was such an Awakening at NORTH-HAMPTON 8 Years past."—So that Salvation is gone forth from NORTH-HAMPTON, and NORTH-HAMPTON must have the Praise of being first brought into it.

To which let me add a few Words, from the late venerable Dr. INCREASE MATHER, which will shew, how widely good Men may differ from one another, in Matters of *meer Conjecture.* They are these, "I know there is a blessed Day to the visible Church not far off: But it is the Judgment

pointed out in the *Revelations* of GOD for the Place, where this glorious Scene of Things, "will, probably, first begin?" How often, at other Times, and in other Places, has the Conceit been propagated among People, as if the Prophecies touching the Kingdom of CHRIST, in the *latter Days*, were NOW to receive their Accomplishment? And what has been the Effect, but their running wild? So it was in GERMANY, in the Beginning of the Reformation. The *extraordinary* and *wonderful* Things in that Day, were look'd upon by the Men then thought to be most under the *SPIRIT's immediate* Direction, as "the Dawning of that glorious Work of GOD, which should renew the whole World;" and the Imagination of the Multitude being fired with this Notion, they were soon perswaded, that the Saints were now to reign on Earth, and the Dominion to be given into their Hands: And it was under the Influence of this vain Conceit, (in which they were strengthened by *Visions, Raptures* and *Revelations)* that they took up *Arms* against the lawful *Authority,* and were destroy'd, at one Time and another, to the Number of an HUNDRED THOUSAND. . . .

And 'tis well known, that this same Pretence of the near Approach of the MILLENIUM, the *promised Kingdom of the* MESSIAH, was the *Foundation-Error of* the *French Prophets,* and those in their Way, no longer ago than the Beginning of this Century: And so infatuated were they at last, as to publish it to the World, that the glorious Times they spake of, *would be manifest over the whole Earth, within the Term of* THREE YEARS. And what Set of Men have ever yet appear'd in the Christian World, whose Imaginations have been thorowly warmed, but they have, at length, wrought themselves up to a *full Assurance,* that NOW was the Time for the Accomplishment of the Scriptures, and the Creation of the *new Heavens,* and the *new Earth?* No one Thing have they more unitedly concurred in, to their own shameful Disappointment, and the doing unspeakable Damage to the Interest of Religion.—A sufficient Warning, one would think, to keep Men modest; and restrain them from Endeavours to lead People into a Belief of that, of which they have no sufficient *Evidence;* and in which, they may be deceived by their *vain Imaginations,* as Hundred and Thousands have been before them.

There are unquestionably many Prophecies concerning CHRIST, and the *Glory of his Kingdom,* still to be fulfilled; and it may be of good Service to labour to beget in People a Faith in these Things; or, if they have Faith, to quicken and strengthen it: But it can answer no good End to lead People into the Belief of any *particular* Time, as the Time *appointed* of GOD for the Accomplishment of these Purposes of his Mercy; because this is one of those Matters, his Wisdom has thought fit to keep conceal'd from the Knowledge of Man. Our own Faith therefore upon this Head can be founded only on *Conjecture;* and as 'tis only the like *blind Faith* we can convey to others, we should be cautious, lest their Conduct should be agreeable to their Faith. When they have imbib'd from us the Thought, as if the *glorious Things,* spoken of

---

of very learned Men, that, in the glorious Times promised to the Church on Earth, AMERICA will be HELL. And, although there is a Number of the Elect of GOD to be born here, I am verily afraid, that, in Process of Time, NEW-ENGLAND will be the wofullest Place in all AMERICA."

in Scripture, were to come forward in their Day, they will be apt (as has often been the Case) to be impatient, and from their *Officiousness* in tendring their Help where it is not needed, to disserve the Interest of the Redeemer.

II. Enthusiasm Described and Caution'd Against

CHARLES CHAUNCY

In another essay Chauncy stresses the importance of reason in religion as opposed to reliance on "enthusiasm." By "enthusiasm" antirevivalists generally referred to what they thought was mistaking some psychological or physical disturbance for the voice of God. The enthusiast acted, they believed, as though he was in direct communication with God.

This selection, taken from Enthusiasm Described and Caution'd Against *(1742), presents Chauncy's case for reason in religious experience. Which points in this essay most directly challenge the ideas of Edwards?*

3. Make use of the *Reason* and *Understanding* GOD has given you. This may be tho't an ill-advis'd direction, but 'tis as necessary as either of the former. Next to the *Scripture,* there is no greater enemy to *enthusiasm,* than *reason.* 'Tis indeed impossible a man shou'd be an *enthusiast,* who is in the just exercise of his understanding; and 'tis because men don't pay a due regard to the sober dictates of a well inform'd mind, that they are led aside by the delusions of a vain imagination. Be advised then to shew yourselves men, to make use of your reasonable powers; and not act as the *horse* or *mule,* as tho' you had no understanding.

'Tis true, you must not go about to set up your own *reason* in *opposition* to *revelation:* Nor may you entertain a tho't of making *reason* your *rule* instead of *scripture.* The bible, as I said before, is the *great rule* of religion, the grand test in matters of salvation: But then you must use your reason in order to understand the *bible:* Nor is there any other possible way, in which, as a reasonable creature, you shou'd come to an understanding of it.

You are, it must be acknowledged, in a corrupt state. The fall has introduc'd great weakness into your reasonable nature. You can't be too sensible of this; nor of the danger you are in of making a wrong judgment, thro' prejudice, carelessness, and the undue influence of sin and lust. And to prevent this, you can't be too solicitous to get your *nature sanctified:* Nor can you depend too strongly upon the divine grace to assist you in your search after truth: And 'tis in the way of due dependance on GOD, and the influences of his SPIRIT, that I advise you to the use of your reason: And in this way, you

Alan Heimert and Perry Miller, eds., *The Great Awakening* (New York: Bobbs-Merrill, 1967), pp. 246–49.

must make use of it. How else will you know what is a revelation from GOD? What shou'd hinder your entertaining the same tho't of a *pretended* revelation, as of a *real* one, but your reason discovering the falshood of the one, and the truth of the other? And when in the enjoyment of an undoubted revelation from GOD, as in the case of the *scripture,* How will you understand its meaning, if you throw by your reason? How will you determine, that this, and not that, is its true sense, in this and the other place? Nay, if no reasoning is to be made use of, are not all the senses that can be put on scripture equally proper? Yea, may not the most contrary senses be receiv'd at the same time, since reason only can point out the inconsistency between them? And what will be sufficient to guard you against the most monstrous extravagancies, in *principle* as well as *practice,* if you give up your understandings? What have you left, in this case, to be a check to the wantoness of your imaginations? What shou'd hinder your following every idle fancy, 'till you have lost yourselves in the wilds of falshood and inconsistency?

You may, it is true, misuse your reason: And this is a consideration that shou'd put you upon a due care, that you may use it well; but no argument why you shou'd not use it at all: And indeed, if you shou'd throw by your reason as a useless thing, you would at once put your selves in the way of all manner of delusion. . . .

4. You must not lay too great stress upon the *workings* of your *passions* and *affections.* These will be excited, in a less or greater degree, in the business of religion: And 'tis proper they shou'd. The passions, when suitably mov'd, tend mightily to awaken the *reasonable powers,* and put them upon a lively and vigorous exercise. And this is their proper use: And when address'd to, and excited to this purpose, they may be of good service: whereas we shall mistake the right use of the passions if we place our religion *only* or *chiefly,* in the heat and fervour of them. The *soul* is the *man:* And unless the *reasonable nature* is suitably wro't upon, the *understanding* enlightned, the *judgment* convinc'd, the *will* perswaded, and the *mind* intirely chang'd, it will avail but to little purpose; tho' the passions shou'd be set all in a blaze. This therefore you shou'd be most concern'd about. And if while you are sollicitous that you may be in transports of affection, you neglect your more noble part, your reason and judgment, you will be in great danger of being carried away by your imaginations. This indeed leads directly to *Enthusiasm:* And you will in vain, endeavour to preserve yourselves from the influence of it, if you a'nt duly careful to keep your passions in their proper place, under the government of a well inform'd understanding. While the passions are uppermost, and bear the chief sway over a man, he is in an unsafe state: None knows what he may be bro't to. You can't therefore be too careful to keep your passions under the regimen of a *sober judgment.* 'Tis indeed a matter of necessity, as you would not be led aside by delusion and fancy.

III. Spiritual Travels

NATHAN COLE

George Whitefield, the English revivalist, was regarded by establishment clergy-men as the chief and most dangerous of the emotion-arousing preachers they called "enthusiasts." An example of the excitement Whitefield aroused is apparent in the following account by one Nathan Cole, a farmer and carpenter who hurried to hear Whitefield at Middletown, Connecticut, in October 1740. Why would such a response to the "Grand Itinerant" shake or threaten the established church and clergy?

Now it pleased God to send Mr Whitefield into this land; and my hearing of his preaching at Philadelphia, like one of the Old apostles, and many thousands flocking to hear him preach the Gospel; and great numbers were converted to Christ; I felt the Spirit of God drawing me by conviction; I longed to see and hear him, and wished he would come this way. I heard he was come to New York and the Jerseys and great multitudes flocking after him under great concern for their Souls which brought on my Concern more and more hoping soon to see him but next I heard he was at long Island; then at Boston and next at Northampton; then on a Sudden, in the morning about 8 or 9 of the Clock there came a messenger and said Mr Whitfield preached at Hartford and Weathersfield yesterday and is to preach at Middletown this morning at ten of the Clock, I was in my field at Work, I dropt my tool that I had in my hand and ran home to my wife telling her to make ready quickly to go and hear Mr Whitfield preach at Middletown, then run to my pasture for my horse with all my might; fearing that I should be too late; having my horse I with my wife soon mounted the horse and went forward as fast as I thought the horse could bear, and when my horse got much out of breath I would get down and put my wife on the Saddle and bid her ride as fast as she could and not Stop or Slack for me except I bad her and so I would run untill I was much out of breath; and then mount my horse again, and so I did several times to favour my horse; we improved every moment to get along as if we were fleeing for our lives; all the while fearing we should be too late to hear the Sermon, for we had twelve miles to ride double in little more than an hour and we went round by the upper housen parish and when we came within about half a mile or a mile of the Road that comes down from Hartford weathersfield and Stepney to Middletown; on high land I saw before me a Cloud or fogg rising; I first thought it came from the great River, but as I came nearer the Road, I heard a noise something like a low rumbling thunder and presently found it was the noise of Horses feet coming down the Road and this Cloud was a Cloud of dust made by the Horses feet; it arose some Rods into the the [*sic*]

Leonard W. Labaree, ed., "George Whitefield Comes to Middletown," *William and Mary Quarterly,* Third Series, VII (1950), 590–91. This excerpt from "The Spiritual Travels of Nathan Cole" reprinted by permission of the Connecticut Historical Society.

air over the tops of Hills and trees and when I came within about 20 rods of the Road, I could see men and horses Sliping along in the Cloud like shadows and as I drew nearer it seemed like a steady Stream of horses and their riders, scarcely a horse more than his length behind another, all of a Lather and foam with sweat, their breath rolling out of their nostrils every Jump; every horse seemed to go with all his might to carry his rider to hear news from heaven for the saving of Souls, it made me tremble to see the Sight, how the world was in a Struggle; I found a Vacance between two horses to Slip in mine and my Wife said law our Cloaths will be all spoiled see how they look, for they were so Covered with dust, that they looked almost all of a Colour Coats, hats, Shirts, and horses: We went down in the Stream but heard no man speak a word all the way for 3 miles but every one pressing forward in great haste and when we got to Middletown old meeting house there was a great Multitude it was said to be 3 or 4000 of people Assembled together; we dismounted and shook of our Dust; and the ministers were then Coming to the meeting house; I turned and looked towards the Great River and saw the ferry boats Running swift backward and forward bringing Over loads of people and the Oars Rowed nimble and quick; every thing men horses and boats seemed to be Struggling for life; the land and banks over the river looked black with people and horses all along the 12 miles I saw no man at work in his field, but all seemed to be gone—When I saw Mr. Whitfield come upon the Scaffold he lookt almost Angelical; a young, Slim, slender youth before some thousands of people with a bold undaunted Countenance, and my hearing how God was with him every where as he came along it Solemnized my mind; and put me into a trembling fear before he began to preach; for he looked as if he was Cloathed with Authority from the Great God; and a sweet sollome solemnity sat upon his brow And my hearing him preach, gave me a heart wound; By Gods blessing: my old Foundation was broken up, and I saw that my righteousness would not save me.

IV. The Testimony of Harvard College Against George Whitefield

Although George Whitefield received a moderately warm acceptance in New England at first, the excesses of his methods and oratory soon aroused intense hostility. When he planned another tour of New England in 1744 his opponents took steps to resist him. Harvard College, stung by Whitefield's remark that the light of the universities had become darkness, drafted a lengthy testimony against him. Its main charges were applicable specifically to Whitefield, but generally to other Awakeners as well. To what extent, if any, does this testimony betray an antidemocratic spirit on the part of the establishment? What does the

Alan Heimert and Perry Miller, eds., *The Great Awakening* (New York: Bobbs-Merrill, 1967), pp. 342, 346, 349–53.

issuance of this testimony reveal about the concerns aroused by the Great Awakening?

First, as to the Man himself, whom we look upon as an Enthusiast, a censorious, uncharitable Person, and a Deluder of the People; which Things, if we can make out, all reasonable Men will doubtless excuse us, tho' some such, thro' a fascinating Curiosity, may still continue their Attachment to him.

First then, we charge him, with *Enthusiasm.* Now that we may speak clearly upon this Head, we mean by an *Enthusiast,* one that acts, either according to Dreams, or some sudden Impulses and Impressions upon his Mind, which he fondly imagines to be from the Spirit of God, perswading and inclining him thereby to such and such Actions, tho' he hath no Proof that such Perswasions or Impressions are from the holy Spirit: For the perceiving a strong Impression upon our Minds, or a violent Inclination to do any Action, is a very different Thing from perceiving such Impressions to be from the Spirit of God moving upon the Heart: For our strong Faith and Belief, that such a Motion on the Mind comes from God, can never be any Proof of it; and if such Impulses and Impressions be not agreeable to our Reason, or to the Revelation of the Mind of God to us, in his Word, nothing can be more dangerous than conducting ourselves according to them; for otherwise, if we judge not of them by these Rules, they may as well be the Suggestions of the evil Spirit: And in what Condition must that People be, who stand ready to be led by a Man that conducts himself according to his Dreams, or some ridiculous and unaccountable Impulses and Impressions on his Mind? . . .

In the next Place, we look upon Mr. *W.* as an uncharitable, censorious and slanderous Man; which indeed is but a natural Consequence of the heat of Enthusiasm, by which he was so evidently acted; for this Distemper of the Mind always puts a Man into a vain Conceit of his own Worth and Excellency, which all his Pretences to Humility will never hide, as long as he evidently shews, that he would have the World think he hath a greater Familiarity with God than other Men, and more frequent Communications from his Holy Spirit. Hence such a Man naturally assumes an Authority to dictate to others, and a Right to direct their Conduct and Opinions; and hence if any act not according to his Directions, and the Model of Things he had form'd in his own heated Brain, he is presently apt to run into slander, and stigmatize them as *Men of no Religion, unconverted,* and *Opposers of the Spirit of God:* And that such hath been the Behaviour of Mr. *W.* is also sufficiently evident. . . .

Again, We think it highly proper to bear our Testimony against Mr. *W.* as we look upon him a *Deluder of the People.* How he designs to manage in this Affair now, we know not: but we mean, that he hath much deluded them, and therefore suppose we have Reason in this respect to guard against him. And here we mean more especially as to the Collections of Money, which, when here before, by an extraordinary mendicant Faculty, he almost *extorted* from the People. As the Argument he then used was, *the Support and Education of his dear Lambs at the Orphan-House,* who (he told us, he hop'd) might in Time preach the Gospel to us or our Children; so it is not to be doubted, that the People were greatly encouraged to give him large'v of their Substance, supposing they were to be under the immediate Tuition and Instruction of himself, as he then made them to believe; and had not this been their Tho't, it is, to us, without all Peradventure, they would never have been perswaded to any considerable Contribution upon that Head; and this, notwithstanding, he hath scarce seen them for these four Years; and besides hath left the Care of them with a Person, whom these Contributors know nothing of, and we ourselves have Reason to believe is little better than a *Quaker;* so that in this Regard we think the People have been greatly deceiv'd. . . .

Secondly, We have as much Reason to dislike and bear Testimony against the *Manner* of his Preaching; and this in Two respects, both as an *Extempore* and as an *Itinerant* Preacher.

And first, as to his *extempore* Manner of preaching; this we think by no means proper, for that it is impossible that any Man should be able to manage any Argument with that Strength, or any Instruction with that Clearness in an *extempore* Manner, as he may with Study and Meditation. Besides, it is observable that your *extempore* Preachers give us almost always the same Things in the applicatory Part of their Sermons, so that it is often very little akin to their Text, which is just open'd in a cursory, and not seldom in a perverted Manner, and then comes the same kind of Harangue which they have often used before, as an *Application;* so that this is a most lazy Manner, and the Preacher offers that which cost him nothing, and is accordingly little Instructive to the Mind, and still less cogent to the reasonable Powers. . . .

But, *lastly,* We think it our Duty to bear our strongest Testimony against that *Itinerant* Way of preaching which this Gentleman was the first promoter of among us, and still delights to continue in: For if we had nothing against the *Man,* either as an *Enthusiast,* an *uncharitable* or *delusive* Person, yet we apprehend this Itinerant Manner of preaching to be of the worst and most pernicious Tendency.

Now by an *Itinerant* Preacher, we understand One that hath no particular Charge of his own, but goes about from Country to Country, or from Town to Town, in any Country, and stands ready to Preach to any Congregation that shall call him to it; and such an one is Mr. *W.* for it is but trifling for him to say (as we hear he hath) That he requires in order to his preaching any where, that the Minister also should invite him to it; for he knows the Populace have such an Itch after him, that when they generally desire it, the Minister (however diverse from their's, his own Sentiments may be) will always be in the utmost Danger of his People's quarrelling with, if not departing from him, shou'd he not consent to their impetuous Desires. Now as it is plain, no Man will find much Business as an *Itinerant* Preacher, who hath not something in his Manner, that is (however trifling, yea, and erroneous too, yet) very taking and agreeable to the People; so when this is the Case, as we have lately unhappily seen it, it is then in his Power to raise the People to any Degree of Warmth he pleases, whereby they stand ready to receive almost any Doctrine he is pleased to broach; as hath been the Case as to all the Itinerant Preachers who have followed Mr. *W's.* Example, and thrust themselves into Towns and

Parishes, to the Destruction of all Peace and Order, whereby they have to the great impoverishment of the Community, taken the People from their Work and Business, to attend their Lectures and Exhortations, always fraught with Enthusiasm, and other pernicious Errors: But, *which is worse, and it is the natural Effect of these Things,* the People have been thence ready to despise their own Ministers, and their usefulness among them, in too many Places, hath been almost destroy'd. . . .

And now, upon the whole, having, we think, made it evident to every one that is not prejedic'd on his Side (for such as are so, we have little hope to convince) that Mr. *W.* is chargeable with that *Enthusiasm, Censoriousness* and *delusive Management* that we have tax'd him with; and since also he seems resolv'd for that Itinerant Way of preaching, which we think so destructive to the Peace of the Churches of Christ; we cannot but bear our faithful Testimony against him, as a Person very unfit to preach about as he has done heretofore and as he has now begun to do.

And we wou'd earnestly, and with all due respect, recommend it to the Rev. Pastors of these Churches of Christ, to advise with each other in their several Associations, and consider whether it be not high Time to make a stand against the Mischiefs, which we have here suggested as coming upon the Churches.

Harvard College, Dec. 28. 1744.
EDWARD HOLYOKE, *President.* . . .

V. A Proposal for Promoting Useful Knowledge Among the British Plantations in America

BENJAMIN FRANKLIN

Jonathan Edwards' vision for America reveals a distinctly religious conviction. The great contemporary of Edwards, Benjamin Franklin, also had a vision for America, but his was in a secular, utilitarian vein. In 1743 he presented A Proposal for Promoting Useful Knowledge among the British Plantations in America. Compare his vision with that of Edwards. Why was Franklin's more realizable, or at least measurable? Which, from a contemporary point of view, was a more desirable vision? Which has had greater popularity in America?

MAY 14, 1743

The English are possess'd of a long Tract of Continent, from Nova Scotia to Georgia, extending North and South thro' different Climates, having different Soils, producing different Plants, Mines and Minerals, and capable of different Improvements, Manufactures, &c.

Leonard W. Labaree, ed., *The Papers of Benjamin Franklin* (New Haven: Yale University Press, 1960), II, pp. 380–83.

The first Drudgery of Settling new Colonies, which confines the Attention of People to mere Necessaries, is now pretty well over; and there are many in every Province in Circumstances that set them at Ease, and afford Leisure to cultivate the finer Arts, and improve the common Stock of Knowledge. To such of these who are Men of Speculation, many Hints must from time to time arise, many Observations occur, which if well-examined, pursued and improved, might produce Discoveries to the Advantage of some or all of the British Plantations, or to the Benefit of Mankind in general.

But as from the Extent of the Country such Persons are widely separated, and seldom can see and converse or be acquainted with each other, so that many useful Particulars remain uncommunicated, die with the Discoverers, and are lost to Mankind; it is, to remedy this Inconvenience for the future, proposed,

That One Society be formed of Virtuosi or ingenious Men residing in the several Colonies, to be called *The American Philosophical Society;* who are to maintain a constant Correspondence.

That Philadelphia being the City nearest the Centre of the Continent-Colonies, communicating with all of them northward and southward by Post, and with all the Islands by Sea, and having the Advantage of a good growing Library, be the Centre of the Society.

That at Philadelphia there be always at least seven Members, viz. a Physician, a Botanist, a Mathematician, a Chemist, a Mechanician, a Geographer, and a general Natural Philosopher, besides a President, Treasurer and Secretary.

That these Members meet once a Month, or oftner, at their own Expence, to communicate to each other their Observations, Experiments, &c. to receive, read and consider such Letters, Communications, or Queries as shall be sent from distant Members; to direct the Dispersing of Copies of such Communications as are valuable, to other distant Members, in order to procure their Sentiments thereupon, &c.

That the Subjects of the Correspondence be, All new-discovered Plants, Herbs, Trees, Roots, &c. their Virtues, Uses, &c. Methods of Propagating them, and making such as are useful, but particular to some Plantations, more general. Improvements of vegetable Juices, as Cyders, Wines, &c. New Methods of Curing or Preventing Diseases. All new-discovered Fossils in different Countries, as Mines, Minerals, Quarries, &c. New and useful Improvements in any Branch of Mathematicks. New Discoveries in Chemistry, such as Improvements in Distillation, Brewing, Assaying of Ores, &c. New Mechanical Inventions for saving Labour; as Mills, Carriages, &c. and for Raising and Conveying of Water, Draining of Meadows, &c. All new Arts, Trades, Manufactures, &c. that may be proposed or thought of. Surveys, Maps and Charts of particular Parts of the Sea-coasts, or Inland Countries; Course and Junction of Rivers and great Roads, Situation of Lakes and Mountains, Nature of the Soil and Productions, &c. New Methods of Improving the Breed of useful Animals, Introducing other Sorts from foreign Countries. New Improvements in Planting, Gardening, Clearing Land, &c. And all philosophical Experiments that let Light into the Nature of Things, tend to increase the Power of Man over Matter, and multiply the Conveniencies or Pleasures of Life.

That a Correspondence already begun by some intended Members, shall be kept up by this Society with the ROYAL SOCIETY of London, and with the DUBLIN SOCIETY.

That every Member shall have Abstracts sent him Quarterly, of every Thing valuable communicated to the Society's Secretary at Philadelphia; free of all Charge except the Yearly Payment hereafter mentioned.

That by Permission of the Postmaster-General, such Communications pass between the Secretary of the Society and the Members, Postage-free.

That for defraying the Expence of such Experiments as the Society shall judge proper to cause to be made, and other contingent Charges for the common Good, every Member send a Piece of Eight *per Annum* to the Treasurer, at Philadelphia, to form a Common Stock, to be disburs'd by Order of the President with the Consent of the Majority of the Members that can conveniently be consulted thereupon, to such Persons and Places where and by whom the Experiments are to be made, and otherwise as there shall be Occasion; of which Disbursements an exact Account shall be kept, and communicated yearly to every Member.

That at the first Meetings of the Members at Philadelphia, such Rules be formed for Regulating their Meetings and Transactions for the General Benefit, as shall be convenient and necessary; to be afterwards changed and improv'd as there shall be Occasion, wherein due Regard is to be had to the Advice of distant Members.

That at the End of every Year, Collections be made and printed, of such Experiments, Discoveries, Improvements, &c. as may be thought of publick Advantage: And that every Member have a Copy sent him.

That the Business and Duty of the Secretary be, To receive all Letters intended for the Society, and lay them before the President and Members at their Meetings; to abstract, correct and methodize such Papers, &c. as require it, and as he shall be directed to do by the President, after they have been considered, debated and digested in the Society; to enter Copies thereof in the Society's Books, and make out Copies for distant Members; to answer their Letters by Direction of the President, and keep Records of all material Transactions of the Society, &c.

Benjamin Franklin, the Writer of this Proposal, offers himself to serve the Society as their Secretary, 'till they shall be provided with one more capable.

For Further Reading

Jonathan Edwards has been the subject of numerous biographies. Perry Miller's (1959)* is a biography of Edwards' mind; A. O. Aldridge (1964) has emphasized the controversies in his life; Edward H. Davidson's (1966)* is an account of the development of his thought based on an analysis of his major writings and sermons; James Carse's (1967) is an easily understood interpretation of Edwards' philosophy and theology; the one by Ola Winslow (1940), giving a balanced story of his life, is out of print but available in many libraries.

The study of the Great Awakening most directly related to the thrust of this chapter is Alan Heimert's *Religion and the American Mind from the Great Awakening to the Revolution* (1966); it is a thorough, scholarly, and convincing but controversial reinterpretation of the movement. Another book relating the movement to the Revolution is Cedric Cowing's *The Great Awakening and the Revolution* (1971).

Besides the Heimert-Miller volume excerpted in this chapter, other available collections of primary sources include: Richard L. Bushman, ed., *The Great Awakening: Documents on the Revival of Religion, 1740–1745* * (1970); David Levin, ed., *Jonathan Edwards: A Profile* * (1969); David S. Lovejoy, ed., *Religious Enthusiasm and the Great Awakening* * (1969); and Clarence H. Faust and Thomas H. Johnson, eds., *Jonathan Edwards: Representative Selections* * (1935; extensive bibliography updated, 1962).

Problems books are: David Levin, ed., *The Puritan in the Enlightenment: Franklin and Edwards* * (1963); John Opie, ed., *Jonathan Edwards and the Enlightenment* * (1969); and Darrett B. Rutman, ed., *The Great Awakening in America: Event and Exegesis* * (1970).

Regional accounts are: Wesley M. Gewehr, *The Great Awakening in Virginia, 1740–1790* (1930; reprinted in 1965); Charles H. Maxson, *The Great Awakening in the Middle Colonies* (1920; reprinted in 1958); and Edwin S. Gaustad, *The Great Awakening in New England* * (1957).

---

*Paperbound edition available.

3. Mercantilism Measured

The English colonies in North America were founded and shaped haphazardly. Some began as the speculative projects of chartered companies, others as the adventures of privileged proprietors. In some colonies political ties with the English Crown were intimate, in others remote. Time, too, altered the closeness of ties. Religious motivation was a primary consideration in the plans and policies of some of the colonies, but in most it was nonexistent. In population growth, in social and political customs, in patterns of economic development, and in many other ways the colonies varied widely despite their common English heritage.

It was therefore no easy task for the mother country to manage this assortment of offspring. Yet a compelling desire that the colonies should prove economically profitable dictated the shaping of some type of management policy. It might be supposed that the policy was shaped primarily to ensure prosperity in the colonies, but this was not the case. Economic beliefs and attitudes in the seventeenth and eighteenth centuries required that the colonies first of all be profitable to the mother country. Toward this end, in keeping with the practice of other European powers, England developed a policy known as mercantilism.

Although mercantilism has sometimes been called a system, this is hardly accurate. No writer has ever worked out a theory supporting it. Instead it developed over a period of several centuries by patching together a series of practical expedients put forward by merchants and political leaders. Its development was a natural parallel to the emergence of nation-states and to the "Commercial Revolution," the name given to the general postmedieval expansion of trade and the practices associated with it, such as the uses of money and credit.

Nations attempting to implement the ideas of mercantilism hoped thereby to increase their national wealth. Acting on the assumption that the wealth of a nation, and therefore its economic well-being, depended on its possession of precious metals (thought to be fixed in quantity), mercantilists sought always to achieve a favorable balance of trade (that is, to ensure that the value of their exports exceeded the value of their imports). To be effective, mercantilism required extensive application and acceptance of legislative and administrative regulations and controls. In England, sentiment for such regulations and controls appeared as early as the sixteenth century, but the first important mercantilist law was not passed until 1651. Navigation Acts clarifying and expanding this law were passed in 1660, 1663, and 1673, and a comprehensive act, aimed at closing loopholes, was passed in 1696.

It was no accident that the passage of the Navigation Acts and the later Manufacturing Acts (1699, 1732, and 1750) took place as the North American colonies were assuming increasing significance in the English empire. If England could regulate the production and commerce of its colonies it could prevent rival states from using these colonies to their advantage. Features of the acts intended for this purpose provided, among other things, that goods and produce coming from or going to England could be carried only in English ships manned by English crews (colonials were counted as English), that colonial products going to Europe and purchases from Europe had to pass through English ports, and that certain "enumerated commodities" could be shipped only to England. The acts also stated that preferential treatment would be given to certain colonial products, and that the mother country would have a monopoly on manufactured goods in the colonies, with manufacturing there being restricted accordingly. The economies of the colonies, in sum, were to be complementary but subordinate to the economy of England.

Core Document

The Colonies and the Mercantile System

ADAM SMITH

Historical interpretation until the last several decades has asserted that the subordinate position of the colonies contributed to the accumulation of griev-ances that finally caused their separation from England. More recently histori-ans, notably Oliver Dickerson and Lawrence Harper, have demonstrated that although the mercantile system most certainly affected the course of the colonial economy, its effect was not generally felt to be adverse until after 1763, when the English government changed its application in relation to the colonies.

Here our concern is with issues suggested by the Scottish scholar Adam Smith, who probably deserves to be called the first economist. In his monumental work, An Inquiry into the Nature and Causes of the Wealth of Nations, *Smith not only gave mercantilism its name, but also laid it bare for analysis and helped to create sentiment for its abandonment. Historical circumstances joined with this sentiment to bring about such an abandonment by 1850.*

One of the many issues raised in The Wealth of Nations *concerns the relation between the interests of a state managing its economy and the interests of the individual within that state. Does the dominant interest of the state transcend the interests of the individual? What are the implications for, as the English expressed it, the "liberties of the subject" when the entire economy is managed by the state? These and other questions troubled Smith.*

There are two points that must be remembered when reading The Wealth of Nations. *First, the book is extremely comprehensive: it is economics, history, philosophy, and political theory all linked together to point to a practical pro-gram, a program written by a man who began his professional career as a moral philosopher. Any conclusions drawn out of a short excerpt must therefore be expressed tentatively.*

Second, because not all readers of Adam Smith have been cautious in drawing conclusions, his writings have been used to support economic ideas he most likely would have rejected. Smith should therefore be read without precon-ceptions as to what he stood for.

These excerpts are taken from Smith's accounting of the reasons for the prosperity of the colonies and his conclusions on mercantilism. In studying them, watch for his:

- *references to prosperity in the colonies and the liberality of England.*
- *judgments concerning the advantages and disadvantages experienced by*

Adam Smith, *The Wealth of Nations,* ed. Edwin Cannan (New York: Random House, Modern Library Edition, 1937), pp. 538–54, 625–26. Although Smith's first edition appeared in 1776, Cannan's volume is based on the fifth edition of 1789.

individuals and governments in the colonies by virtue of colonial management by England.

- *references to pursuit of English self-interest and, within this, of the self-interest of the merchants.*
- *explanations of the complexities involved in keeping a mercantilist state in balance and operating smoothly.*
- *interpretation of the slavery situation in the English colonies.*
- *conclusions on the adverse effect of mercantilist policy on the liberties of the subject.*

[There] are no colonies of which the progress has been more rapid than that of the English in North America.

Plenty of good land, and liberty to manage their own affairs their own way, seem to be the two great causes of the prosperity of all new colonies.

In the plenty of good land the English colonies of North America, though, no doubt, very abundantly provided, are, however, inferior to those of the Spaniards and Portugueze, and not superior to some of those possessed by the French before the late war. But the political institutions of the English colonies have been more favourable to the improvement and cultivation of this land, than those of any of the other three nations.

First, the engrossing of uncultivated land, though it has by no means been prevented altogether, has been more restrained in the English colonies than in any other. The colony law which imposes upon every proprietor the obligation of improving and cultivating, within a limited time, a certain proportion of his lands, and which, in case of failure, declares those neglected lands grantable to any other person; though it has not, perhaps, been very strictly executed, has, however, had some effect.

Secondly, in Pennsylvania there is no right of primogeniture,[1] and lands, like moveables, are divided equally among all the children of the family. In three of the provinces of New England the oldest has only a double share, as in the Mosaical law. Though in those provinces, therefore, too great a quantity of land should sometimes be engrossed by a particular individual, it is likely, in the course of a generation or two, to be sufficiently divided again. In the other English colonies, indeed, the right of primogeniture takes place, as in the law of England. But in all the English colonies the tenure of the lands . . . facilitates alienation, and the grantee of any extensive tract of land, generally finds it for his interest to alienate, as fast as he can, the greater part of it, reserving only a small quit-rent. . . .

Thirdly, the labour of the English colonists is not only likely to afford a greater and more valuable produce, but, in consequence of the moderation of their taxes, a greater proportion of this produce belongs to themselves, which they may store up and employ in putting into motion a still greater quantity of labour. The English colonists have never yet contributed any thing towards the defence of the mother country, or towards the support of its civil govern-

---

[1] *Editors' note:* Primogeniture laws provided for exclusive inheritance by the firstborn. "Alienation," later in the paragraph, refers to the conveying or transferring of property titles.

ment. They themselves, on the contrary, have hitherto been defended almost entirely at the expence of the mother country. But the expence of fleets and armies is out of all proportion greater than the necessary expence of civil government. The expence of their own civil government has always been very moderate. It has generally been confined to what was necessary for paying competent salaries to the governor, to the judges, and to some other offices of police, and for maintaining a few of the most useful public works. . . .

The ceremonial too of the civil government in the colonies, upon the reception of a new governor, upon the opening of a new assembly, &c. though sufficiently decent, is not accompanied with any expensive pomp or parade. Their ecclesiastical government is conducted upon a plan equally frugal. Tithes are unknown among them; and their clergy, who are far from being numerous, are maintained either by moderate stipends, or by the voluntary contributions of the people. . . .

Fourthly, in the disposal of their surplus produce, or of what is over and above their own consumption, the English colonies have been more favoured, and have been allowed a more extensive market, than those of any other European nation. Every European nation has endeavoured more or less to monopolize to itself the commerce of its colonies, and, upon that account, has prohibited the ships of foreign nations from trading to them, and has prohibited them from importing European goods from any foreign nation. But the manner in which this monopoly has been exercised in different nations has been very different. . . .

In the exportation of their own surplus produce . . . it is only with regard to certain commodities that the colonies of Great Britain are confined to the market of the mother country. These commodities having been enumerated in the act of navigation and in some other subsequent acts, have upon that account been called *enumerated commodities*. The rest are called *non-enumerated;* and may be exported directly to other countries, provided it is in British or Plantation ships, of which the owners and three-fourths of the mariners are British subjects.

Among the non-enumerated commodities are some of the most important productions of America and the West Indies; grain of all sorts, lumber, salt provisions, fish, sugar, and rum.

Grain is naturally the first and principal object of the culture of all new colonies. By allowing them a very extensive market for it, the law encourages them to extend this culture much beyond the consumption of a thinly inhabited country, and thus to provide beforehand an ample subsistence for a continually increasing population.

In a country quite covered with wood, where timber consequently is of little or no value, the expence of clearing the ground is the principal obstacle to improvement. By allowing the colonies a very extensive market for their lumber, the law endeavours to facilitate improvement by raising the price of a commodity which would otherwise be of little value, and thereby enabling them to make some profit of what would otherwise be mere expence.

In a country neither half-peopled nor half cultivated, cattle naturally multiply beyond the consumption of the inhabitants, and are often upon that account of little or no value. . . .

To increase the shipping and naval power of Great Britain, by the extension of the fisheries of our colonies, is an object which the legislature seems to have had almost constantly in view. Those fisheries, upon this account, have had all the encouragement which freedom can give them, and they have flourished accordingly. . . .

Sugar was originally an enumerated commodity which could be exported only to Great Britain. But in 1731, upon a representation of the sugar-planters, its exportation was permitted to all parts of the world. The restrictions, however, with which this liberty was granted, joined to the high price of sugar in Great Britain, have rendered it, in a great measure, ineffectual. . . .

Rum is a very important article in the trade which the Americans carry on to the coast of Africa, from which they bring back negroe slaves in return.

If the whole surplus produce of America in grain of all sorts, in salt provisions, and in fish, had been put into the enumeration, and thereby forced into the market of Great Britain, it would have interfered too much with the produce of the industry of our own people. It was probably not so much from any regard to the interest of America, as from a jealousy of this interference, that those important commodities have not only been kept out of the enumeration, but that the importation into Great Britain of all grain, except rice, and of salt provisions, has, in the ordinary state of the law, been prohibited.

The non-enumerated commodities could originally be exported to all parts of the world. Lumber and rice, having been once put into the enumeration, when they were afterwards taken out of it, were confined, as to the European market, to the countries that lie south of Cape Finisterre.[2] By the 6th of George III. c. 52.[3] all non-enumerated commodities were subjected to the like restriction. The parts of Europe which lie south of Cape Finisterre, are not manufacturing countries, and we were less jealous of the colony ships carrying home from them any manufactures which could interfere with our own.

The enumerated commodities are of two sorts: first, such as are either the peculiar produce of America, or as cannot be produced, or at least are not produced, in the mother country; . . . secondly, such as are not the peculiar produce of America, but which are and may be produced in the mother country, though not in such quantities as to supply the greater part of her demand, which is principally supplied from foreign countries. . . . The largest importation of commodities of the first kind could not discourage the growth or interfere with the sale of any part of the produce of the mother country. By confining them to the home market, our merchants, it was expected, would not only be enabled to buy them cheaper in the Plantations, and consequently

[2] *Editors' note:* Located at the northwesternmost point of Spain.
[3] *Editors' note:* This refers to chapter 52 of the laws passed in the sixth Parliamentary session during the reign of King George III.

to sell them with a better profit at home, but to establish between the Plantations and foreign countries an advantageous carrying trade, of which Great Britain was necessarily to be the center or emporium, as the European country into which those commodities were first to be imported. The importation of commodities of the second kind might be so managed too, it was supposed, as to interfere, not with the sale of those of the same kind which were produced at home, but with that of those which were imported from foreign countries; because, by means of proper duties, they might be rendered always somewhat dearer than the former, and yet a good deal cheaper than the latter. By confining such commodities to the home market, therefore, it was proposed to discourage the produce, not of Great Britain, but of some foreign countries with which the balance of trade was believed to be unfavourable to Great Britain. . . .

The tendency of some of these regulations to raise the value of timber in America, and thereby to facilitate the clearing of the land, was neither, perhaps, intended nor understood by the legislature. Though their beneficial effects, however, have been in this respect accidental, they have not upon that account been less real.

The most perfect freedom of trade is permitted between the British colonies of America and the West Indies, both in the enumerated and in the non-enumerated commodities. Those colonies are now become so populous and thriving, that each of them finds in some of the others a great and extensive market for every part of its produce. All of them taken together, they make a great internal market for the produce of one another.

The liberality of England, however, towards the trade of her colonies has been confined chiefly to what concerns the market for their produce, either in its rude state, or in what may be called the very first stage of manufacture. The more advanced or more refined manufactures even of the colony produce, the merchants and manufacturers of Great Britain chuse to reserve to themselves, and have prevailed upon the legislature to prevent their establishment in the colonies, sometimes by high duties, and sometimes by absolute prohibitions. . . .

While Great Britain encourages in America the manufactures of pig and bar iron, by exempting them from duties to which the like commodities are subject when imported from any other country, she imposes an absolute prohibition upon the erection of steel furnaces and slit-mills in any of her American plantations. She will not suffer her colonists to work in those more refined manufactures even for their own consumption; but insists upon their purchasing of her merchants and manufacturers all goods of this kind which they have occasion for.

She prohibits the exportation from one province to another by water, and even the carriage by land upon horseback or in a cart, of hats,[4] of wools and

[4]See page 60.

woollen goods, of the produce of America; a regulation which effectually prevents the establishment of any manufacture of such commodities for distant sale, and confines the industry of her colonists in this way to such coarse and household manufactures, as a private family commonly makes for its own use, or for that of some of its neighbours in the same province.

To prohibit a great people, however, from making all that they can of every part of their own produce, or from employing their stock and industry in the way that they judge most advantageous to themselves, is a manifest violation of the most sacred rights of mankind. Unjust, however, as such prohibitions may be, they have not hitherto been very hurtful to the colonies. Land is still so cheap, and, consequently, labour so dear among them, that they can import from the mother country, almost all the more refined or more advanced manufactures cheaper than they could make them for themselves. Though they had not, therefore, been prohibited from establishing such manufactures, yet in their present state of improvement, a regard to their own interest would, probably, have prevented them from doing so. In their present state of improvement, those prohibitions, perhaps, without cramping their industry, or restraining it from any employment to which it would have gone of its own accord, are only impertinent badges of slavery imposed upon them, without any sufficient reason, by the groundless jealousy of the merchants and manufacturers of the mother country. In a more advanced state they might be really oppressive and insupportable.

Great Britain too, as she confines to her own market some of the most important productions of the colonies, so in compensation she gives to some of them an advantage in that market; sometimes by imposing higher duties upon the like productions when imported from other countries, and sometimes by giving bounties upon their importation from the colonies. . . .

Of the greater part of the regulations concerning the colony trade, the merchants who carry it on, it must be observed, have been the principal advisers. We must not wonder, therefore, if, in the greater part of them, their interest has been more considered than either that of the colonies or that of the mother country. In their exclusive privilege of supplying the colonies with all the goods which they wanted from Europe, and of purchasing all such parts of their surplus produce as could not interfere with any of the trades which they themselves carried on at home, the interest of the colonies was sacrificed to the interest of those merchants. In allowing the same drawbacks upon the re-exportation of the greater part of European and East India goods to the colonies, as upon their re-exportation to any independent country, the interest of the mother country was sacrificed to it, even according to the mercantile ideas of that interest. It was for the interest of the merchants to pay as little as possible for the foreign goods which they sent to the colonies, and consequently, to get back as much as possible of the duties which they advanced upon their importation into Great Britain. They might thereby be enabled to sell in the colonies, either the same quantity of goods with a greater profit, or a greater quantity with the same profit, and, consequently, to gain something either in the one way or the other. It was, likewise, for the interest of the colonies to get all such goods as cheap and in as great abundance as possible. . . .

But though the policy of Great Britain with regard to the trade of her colonies has been dictated by the same mercantile spirit as that of other nations, it has, however, upon the whole, been less illiberal and oppressive than that of any of them.

In every thing, except their foreign trade, the liberty of the English colonists to manage their own affairs their own way is complete. It is in every respect equal to that of their fellow-citizens at home, and is secured in the same manner, by an assembly of the representatives of the people, who claim the sole right of imposing taxes for the support of the colony government. The authority of this assembly over-awes the executive power, and neither the meanest nor the most obnoxious colonist, as long as he obeys the law, has any thing to fear from the resentment, either of the governor or of any other civil or military officer in the province. The colony assemblies, though like the house of commons in England, they are not always a very equal representation of the people, yet they approach more nearly to that character; and as the executive power either has not the means to corrupt them, or, on account of the support which it receives from the mother country, is not under the necessity of doing so, they are perhaps in general more influenced by the inclinations of their constituents. The councils, which, in the colony legislatures, correspond to the house of lords in Great Britain, are not composed of an hereditary nobility. In some of the colonies, as in three of the governments of New England, those councils are not appointed by the king, but chosen by the representatives of the people. In none of the English colonies is there any hereditary nobility. In all of them, indeed, as in all other free countries, the descendant of an old colony family is more respected than an upstart of equal merit and fortune: but he is only more respected, and he has no privileges by which he can be troublesome to his neighbours. Before the commencement of the present disturbances, the colony assemblies had not only the legislative, but a part of the executive power. In Connecticut and Rhode Island, they elected the governor. In the other colonies they appointed the revenue officers who collected the taxes imposed by those respective assemblies, to whom those officers were immediately responsible. There is more equality, therefore, among the English colonists than among the inhabitants of the mother country. Their manners are more republican, and their governments, those of three of the provinces of New England in particular, have hitherto been more republican too. . .

[*In a digression from the main course of the chapter Smith commented on the lot of the slave in the English colonies.*]

In all European colonies the culture of the sugar-cane is carried on by negro slaves. The constitution of those who have been born in the temperate climate of Europe could not, it is supposed, support the labour of digging the ground under the burning sun of the West Indies; and the culture of the sugar-cane, as it is managed at present, is all hand labour, though, in the opinion of many, the drill plough might be introduced into it with great advantage. But, as the profit and success of the cultivation which is carried on by means of cattle, depend very much upon the good management of those cattle; so the profit and success of that which is carried on by slaves, must depend equally upon the good management of those slaves; and in the good management of their slaves the French planters, I think it is generally allowed, are superior to the English. The law, so far as it gives some weak protection to the slave against the violence of his master, is likely to be better executed in a colony where the government is in a great measure arbitrary, than in one where it is altogether free. In every country where the unfortunate law of slavery is established, the magistrate, when he protects the slave, intermeddles in some measure in the management of the private property of the master; and, in a free country, where the master is perhaps either a member of the colony assembly, or an elector of such a member, he dare not do this but with the greatest caution and circumspection. The respect which he is obliged to pay to the master, renders it more difficult for him to protect the slave. But in a country where the government is in a great measure arbitrary, where it is usual for the magistrate to intermeddle even in the management of the private property of individuals, and to send them, perhaps, a lettre de cachet if they do not manage it according to his liking, it is much easier for him to give some protection to the slave; and common humanity naturally disposes him to do so. The protection of the magistrate renders the slave less contemptible in the eyes of his master, who is thereby induced to consider him with more regard, and to treat him with more gentleness. Gentle usage renders the slave not only more faithful, but more intelligent, and therefore, upon a double account, more useful. He approaches more to the condition of a free servant, and may possess some degree of integrity and attachment to his master's interest, virtues which frequently belong to free servants, but which never can belong to a slave, who is treated as slaves commonly are in countries where the master is perfectly free and secure.

[*In the third edition (1784), Smith added some new sections to the book, including "Conclusions of the Mercantile System." The following excerpt consists of the closing paragraphs of this addition.*]

It is unnecessary, I imagine, to observe, how contrary such [trade and manufacturing] regulations are to the boasted liberty of the subject, of which we affect to be so very jealous; but which, in this case, is so plainly sacrificed to the futile interests of our merchants and manufacturers.

The laudable motive of all these regulations, is to extend our own manufactures, not by their own improvement, but by the depression of those of all our neighbours, and by putting an end, as much as possible, to the troublesome competition of such odious and disagreeable rivals. Our master manufacturers think it reasonable, that they themselves should have the monopoly of the ingenuity of all their countrymen. Though by restraining, in some trades, the number of apprentices which can be employed at one time, and by imposing the necessity of a long apprenticeship in all trades, they endeavour, all of them, to confine the knowledge of their respective employments to as small a number as possible; they are unwilling, however, that any part of this small number should go abroad to instruct foreigners.

Consumption is the sole end and purpose of all production; and the interest of the producer ought to be attended to, only so far as it may be necessary for promoting that of the consumer. The maxim is so perfectly self-evident that it would be absurd to attempt to prove it. But in the mercantile system, the interest of the consumer is almost constantly sacrified to that of the producer; and it seems to consider production, and not consumption, as the ultimate end and object of all industry and commerce.

In the restraints upon the importation of all foreign commodities which can come into competition with those of our own growth, or manufacture, the interest of the home-consumer is evidently sacrificed to that of the producer. It is altogether for the benefit of the latter, that the former is obliged to pay that enhancement of price which this monopoly almost always occasions.

It is altogether for the benefit of the producer that bounties are granted upon the exportation of some of his productions. The home-consumer is obliged to pay, first, the tax which is necessary for paying the bounty, and secondly, the still greater tax which necessarily arises from the enhancement of the price of the commodity in the home market.

By the famous treaty of commerce with Portugal, the consumer is prevented by high duties from purchasing of a neighbouring country, a commodity which our own climate does not produce, but is obliged to purchase it of a distant country, though it is acknowledged, that the commodity of the distant country is of a worse quality than that of the near one. The home-consumer is obliged to submit to this inconveniency, in order that the producer may import into the distant country some of his productions upon more advantageous terms than he would otherwise have been allowed to do. The consumer, too, is obliged to pay, whatever enhancement in the price of those very productions, this forced exportation may occasion in the home market.

But in the system of laws which has been established for the management of our American and West Indian colonies, the interest of the home-consumer has been sacrificed to that of the producer with a more extravagant profusion than in all our other commercial regulations. A great empire has been established for the sole purpose of raising up a nation of customers who should be obliged to buy from the shops of our different producers, all the goods with which these could supply them. For the sake of that little enhancement of price which this monopoly might afford our producers, the home-consumers have been burdened with the whole expence of maintaining and defending that empire. For this purpose, and for this purpose only, in the two last wars, more than two hundred millions have been spent, and a new debt of more than a hundred and seventy millions has been contracted over and above all that had been expended for the same purpose in former wars. The interest of this debt alone is not only greater than the whole extraordinary profit, which, it ever could be pretended, was made by the monopoly of the colony trade, but than the whole value of that trade, or than the whole value of the goods, which at an average have been annually exported to the colonies.

It cannot be very difficult to determine who have been the contrivers of this whole mercantile system; not the consumers, we may believe, whose interest has been entirely neglected; but the producers, whose interest has been so carefully attended to; and among this latter class our merchants and manufacturers have been by far the principal architects. In the mercantile regulations, which have been taken notice of in this chapter, the interest of our manufacturers has been most peculiarly attended to; and the interest, not so much of the consumers, as that of some other sets of producers, has been sacrificed to it.

Discussion Starters

1.   Assuming Smith's description of the colonial situation to be accurate, how satisfactorily were the liberties of the colonists protected against the potential oppression of mercantilist regulations and restrictions? What standards are used in measuring whether government-imposed restrictions infringe too heavily on personal freedom?

2.   If state-imposed regulations were necessary for a prospering economy, what might have been done to see that mercantile interests did not write them to their own advantage? Similarly, what might consumers today do to see that government-imposed restrictions are not written by and to the advantage of the business interests of the nation? How necessary are efforts directed toward this purpose?

3.   The general thrust of Smith's lengthy treatise was toward a free, unregulated, cosmopolitan economy. Smith recognized the problems that would be faced in working toward this end. What problems, both domestic and international, would be faced today if a similar goal were pursued? In what situations can government intervention successfully promote the general welfare?

4.   How does Smith's interpretation of the slavery situation contribute to our understanding of later racial problems in America?

Related Documents

I. Parliament Attacks Trade Abuses

Colonial trading practices frequently did not measure up to either the laws or the intentions of mercantilism, for evasion of the Navigation Acts became a regular part of trading. Most disconcerting to high English authorities was the suspicion that English customs officials and colonial governors were implicated in the evasion tactics. Although the rate of conformity with the laws was probably higher than the English supposed, reports of violations prompted Parliament to seek stricter law enforcement.

The following document records an effort by Parliament to compel the King to eliminate violations by seeking a greater degree of enforcement by the governors and proprietors. It should be noted that although the greatest concern expressed here was with the West Indies, where violations were most flagrant (or at least best reported), the message requested by Parliament was to go to all the colonies.

What reasons might account for Parliament's belief that it was necessary to particularly urge the King to see to the enforcement of the laws? What inferences might one draw about the actual liberties of the subjects in the colonies, particularly in economic matters?

MARCH 18, 1696

. . . The Earl of Rochester reported from the committee appointed to consider of the state of the trade of this kingdom, the address drawn by them, pursuant to the order yesterday.

Which was read, and agreed to, as follows;

We, the Lords Spiritual and Temporal in Parliament assembled, having taken into our consideration the state of the trade of this kingdom, with reference to the plantations in the West Indies, have found many great abuses of the several good laws that have been made for the government of the said plantations, and very illegal practices continually carried on, to the great detriment of this kingdom, and the lessening of your Majesty's customs here; and particularly, that the act passed in the eighth year of your Majesty's reign hath been greatly obstructed in the observing the rules therein appointed, by the non-compliance of some of the proprietors of several great tracts of land granted by your Majesty's predecessors where the governors are not immediately nominated by your Majesty, as also by the remissness or connivance of your Majesty's own governors:

Leo F. Stock, ed., *Proceedings and Debates of the British Parliament Respecting North America* (Washington, D.C.: Carnegie Institution, 1927), II, pp. 205–6. Courtesy of the Carnegie Institution.

Towards the remedying of which great abuses for the present, we humbly address to your Majesty, that, besides the instructions usually presented to your Majesty for your royal signature to be sent to the respective governors of the plantations, your Majesty may be pleased, as a further incitement to a stricter performance of their duty to your Majesty, at the close of all the rest of your instructions, that this following direction, or to this effect, may be signified as your Majesty's royal pleasure to every one of the said governors, and to the several proprietors and other governments where the governors are not immediately nominated by your Majesty:

And whereas, notwithstanding the many good laws made from time to time, for preventing of frauds in the plantation trade, which have been enumerated in these and former instructions, it is manifest that very great abuses have been, and continue still to be practised, to the prejudice of the same; which abuses must needs arise either from the insolvency of the persons who are accepted for security, or from the remissness or connivance of such as have been or are governors in the several plantations, who ought to take care that those persons who give bond should be duly prosecuted in case of non-performance: you are to take notice, that we take the good of our plantations, and the improvement of the trade thereof, by a strict and punctual observance of the several laws in force concerning the same, to be of so great importance to the benefit of England, and to the advancing of the duties of our customs here, that, if we shall be hereafter informed that at any time there shall be any failure in the due observance of these our present instructions, by any wilful fault or neglect on your part, we shall look upon it as a breach of the trust reposed in you by us, which we shall punish with the loss of your place in that government, and such further marks of our displeasure as we shall judge reasonable to be inflicted upon you for your offence against us, in a matter of this consequence, that we now so particularly charge you with.

And that your Majesty will be pleased further to direct, that the several proprietors of the plantations where your Majesty hath no governors of your own nomination may enter into security here, that their respective deputy governors shall, from, time to time, observe and obey all instructions that shall be sent to them from your Majesty, or any acting under your authority, pursuant to the several acts of trade relating to the plantations.

And whereas the colonies of Connecticut, of Roade Island, and Providence Plantation, have their governors and assistants chosen annually by the people there, are become a great receptacle for pirates, and carry on several illegal trades, contrary to the acts for the government of the plantations, which said colonies have no proprietors here in England; that your Majesty would be pleased to take care, that the governors in these several places be likewise obliged to give security to observe and obey all such instructions as shall be sent to them from your Majesty, or any acting under your authority.

II. The Commission of the Board of Trade

In the early years of mercantilism the matter of enforcement was in the hands of the Privy Council, a group of about 20 officials and advisers of the King who carried on the ordinary business of running the nation. Parliament's enactment of the Navigation Act in 1696, aimed at closing loopholes in the laws and in their enforcement, was accompanied by the King's commissioning a new agency, the Board of Trade (replacing the Lords of Trade), to look after the entire system. Economic, political, social, and religious questions were all within its sphere of responsibility. Much of its correspondence with colonial governors dealt with economic matters, and its reports were prepared for the Privy Council and the Parliament. Note the membership of the Board.

What concerns of the King are apparent in this commission? What in this commission would have been most objectionable to the ideological forerunners of Adam Smith (assuming there were some)?

MAY 15, 1696

William the third, by the grace of God, king of England, Scotland, France, and Ireland, Defender of the Faith, etc. To our Keeper of our Great Seal of England or Chancellor of England for the time being; our President of our Privy Council for the time being; our first commissioner of our Treasury and our Treasurer of England for the time being; our first commissioner of our Admiralty and our Admiral of England for the time being; and our Principal Secretaries of State for the time being, and our Chancellor of our Exchequer for the time being; to our right trusty and right well beloved cousin and councillor, John, earl of Bridgewater, and Ford, earl of Tankerville; to our trusty and well beloved Sir Philip Meadows, knight, William Blathwayt, John Pollexfen, John Locke, Abraham Hill, and John Methuen, esquires, Greeting:

Whereas we are extremely desirous that the trade of our kingdom of England, upon which the strength and riches thereof do in a great measure depend, should by all proper means be promoted and advanced; and whereas we are persuaded that nothing will more effectually contribute thereto than the appointing of knowing and fit persons to inspect and examine into the general trade of our said kingdom and the several parts thereof, and to inquire into the several matters and things hereinafter mentioned relating thereunto, with such powers and directions as are hereinafter specified and contained.

Know ye therefore that we, reposing especial trust and confidence in your discretions, abilities, and integrities, have nominated, authorized, and constituted, and do by these presents nominate, authorize, and appoint [you] . . . or any other three or more of you, to be our commissioners during our royal pleasure, for promoting the trade of our kingdom and for inspecting and

From *English Historical Documents, Vol. 9: American Colonial Documents to 1776*, edited by Merrill Jensen. Oxford University Press, New York, 1955. Also by permission of Eyre & Spottis-woode (Publishers) Ltd.

improving our plantations in America and elsewhere.

And to the end that our royal purpose and intention herein may the better take effect, our will and pleasure is, and we do hereby order, direct, and appoint that you do diligently and constantly as the nature of the service may require, meet together at some convenient place in our palace of Whitehall, which we shall assign for that purpose, or at any other place which we shall appoint for the execution of this our commission.

And we do by these presents authorize and empower you our said commissioners, or any three or more of you, to inquire, examine into and take an account of the state and condition of the general trade of England, and also of the several particular trades in all foreign parts, and how the same respectively are advanced or decayed, and the causes or occasions thereof; and to inquire into and examine what trades are or may prove hurtful, or are or may be made beneficial to our kingdom of England, and by what ways and means the profitable and advantageous trades may be more improved and extended, and such as are hurtful and prejudicial rectified or discouraged; and to inquire into the several obstructions of trade, and the means of removing the same. And also in what manner and by what proper methods the trade of our said kingdom may be most effectually protected and secured in all the parts thereof; and to consider by what means the several useful and profitable manufactures already settled in our said kingdom may be further improved, and how and in what manner new and profitable manufactures may be introduced.

And we do further by these presents authorize and require you, our said commissioners, or any three or more of you, to consider of some proper methods for setting on work and employing the poor of our said kingdom and making them useful to the public, and thereby easing our subjects of that burden; and by what ways and means such design may be made most effectual; and in general, by all such methods and ways as you in your discretions shall think best, to inform yourselves of all things relating to trade and the promoting and encouraging thereof; as also to consider of the best and most effectual means to regain, encourage, and establish the fishery of this kingdom.

And our further will and pleasure is that you, our said commissioners, or any five or more of you, do from time to time make representations touching the premises to us, or to our Privy Council, as the nature of the business shall require, which said representations are to be in writing, and to be signed by five or more of you.

And we do hereby further empower and require you, our said commissioners, to take into your care all records, grants, and papers remaining in the plantation office or thereunto belonging.

And likewise to inform yourselves of the present condition of our respective plantations, as well with regard to the administration of the government and justice in those places as in relation to the commerce thereof; and also to inquire into the limits of soil and product of our several plantations and how the same may be improved, and of the best means for easing and securing our colonies there, and how the same may be rendered most useful and beneficial to our said kingdom of England.

And we do hereby further empower and require you, our said commissioners, more particularly and in a principal manner to inform yourselves what naval stores may be furnished from our plantations and in what quantities and by what methods our royal purpose of having our kingdom supplied with naval stores from thence may be made practicable and promoted; and also to inquire into and inform yourselves of the best and most proper methods of settling and improving in our plantations such other staples and other manufactures as our subjects of England are now obliged to fetch and supply themselves withal from other princes and states; and also what staples and manufactures may be best encouraged there, and what trades are taken up and exercised there which are or may prove prejudicial to England, by furnishing themselves or other [of] our colonies with what has been usually supplied from England; and to find out proper means of diverting them from such trades, and whatsoever else may turn to the hurt of our kingdom of England.

And to examine and look into the usual instructions given to the governors of our plantations, and to see if anything may be added, omitted, or changed therein to advantage; to take an account yearly by way of journal of the administration of our governors there, and to draw out what is proper to be observed and represented unto us; and as often as occasion shall require to consider of proper persons to be governors or deputy governors, or to be of our council or of our council at law, or secretaries in our respective plantations in order to present their names to us in council.

And we do hereby further authorize and empower you, our said commissioners, to examine into and weigh such acts of the assemblies of the plantations respectively as shall from time to time be sent or transmitted hither for our approbation; and to set down and represent as aforesaid the usefulness or mischief thereof to our Crown and to our said kingdom of England, or to the plantations themselves, in case the same should be established for laws there; and also to consider what matters may be recommended as fit to be passed in the assemblies there; to hear complaints of oppressions and maladministrations in our plantations in order to represent as aforesaid what you in your discretions shall think proper; and also to require an account of all moneys given for public uses by the assemblies in our plantations, and how the same are and have been expended or laid out.

And we do by these presents authorize and empower you, our said commissioners, or any three of you, to send for persons and papers for your better information in the premises; and as occasion shall require to examine witnesses upon oath, which oath you are hereby empowered to administer in order to the matters aforesaid.

And we do declare our further will and pleasure to be, that you our said commissioners do from time to time report all your doings in relation to the premises in writing under the hands of any five of you as aforesaid, to us or to our Privy Council, as the nature of the thing shall require.

And we do hereby further authorize and empower you our said commissioners to execute and perform all other things necessary or proper for answering our royal intentions in the premises.

And we do further give power to you our said commissioners, or any three or more of you as aforesaid, from time to time, and as occasion shall require, to send for and desire the advice and assistance of our Attorney or Solicitor-General, or other our counsel at law.

And we do hereby further declare our royal will and pleasure to be that we do not hereby intend that our Chancellor of England or Keeper of our Great Seal for the time being, the President of our Privy Council for the time being, the Keeper of our Privy Seal for the time being, the Treasurer or first commissioner of our Treasury for the time being, our Admiral or first commissioner for executing the office of Admiral for the time being, our Principal Secretaries of State for the time being, or our Chancellor of the Exchequer for the time being, should be obliged to give constant attendance at the meeting of our said commissioners, but only so often and when the presence of them or any of them shall be necessary and requisite, and as their other public service will permit.

IN WITNESS whereof we have caused these our letters to be made patents, witness Thomas, archbishop of Canterbury, and the rest of the guardians and justices of the realm. At Westminister the fifteenth day of May in the eighth year of our reign.

III. The Hat Act

In addition to the acts regulating navigation, Parliament also passed a series of acts intended to ensure the subordinate status of colonial manufacturing. The Woolens Act of 1699, the Hat Act of 1732, and the Iron Act of 1750 all helped to define England's policy toward the colonies.

Excerpts from the Hat Act are included here to show the nature of the restrictions imposed on colonial manufacturing. Why would American colonists in 1732 be willing to accept such restrictions without protest? What changes occurred between 1732 and the 1770s (in both England and North America) to make the ideas of Adam Smith acceptable to some economic thinkers and practical politicians?

JUNE 1, 1732

Whereas the art and mystery of making hats in Great Britain hath arrived to great perfection, and considerable quantities of hats manufactured in this kingdom have heretofore been exported to his Majesty's plantations or colonies in America, who have been wholly supplied with hats from Great Britain; and whereas great quantities of hats have of late years been made, and the said manufacture is daily increasing in the British plantations in America, and is

From *English Historical Documents, Vol. 9: American Colonial Documents to 1776,* edited by Merrill Jensen. Oxford University Press, New York, 1955. Also by permission of Eyre & Spottiswoode (Publishers) Ltd.

from thence exported to foreign markets, which were heretofore supplied from Great Britain, and the hatmakers in the said plantations take many apprentices for very small terms, to the discouragement of the said trade, and debasing the said manufacture; wherefore for preventing the said ill practices for the future, and for promoting and encouraging the trade of making hats in Great Britain, be it enacted by the king's most excellent Majesty, by and with the advice and consent of the Lords Spiritual and Temporal, and Commons in this present Parliament assembled, and by the authority of the same, that from and after the twenty-ninth day of September in the year of our Lord one thousand seven hundred and thirty-two, no hats or felts whatsoever, dyed or undyed, finished or unfinished, shall be shipt, loaden, or put on board any ship or vessel in any place or parts within any of the British plantations, upon any pretence whatsoever, by any person or persons whatsoever, and also that no hats or felts, either dyed or undyed, finished or unfinished, shall be loaden upon any horse, cart, or other carriage, to the intent or purpose to be exported, transported, shipped off, carried, or conveyed out of any of the said British plantations to any other of the British plantations, or to any other place whatsoever, by any persons or persons whatsoever.

VII. And it is hereby further enacted by the authority aforesaid, that no person residing in any of his Majesty's plantations in America shall, from and after the said twenty-ninth day of September, one thousand seven hundred and thirty-two, make or cause to be made, any felt or hat of or with any wool or stuff whatsoever, unless he shall have first served as an apprentice in the trade or art of feltmaking during the space of seven years at the least; neither shall any feltmaker or hatmaker in any of the said plantations employ, retain, or set to work, in the said art or trade, any person as a journeyman or hired servant, other than such as shall have lawfully served an apprenticeship in the said trade for the space of seven years; nor shall any feltmaker or hatmaker in any of the said plantations have, take, or keep above the number of two apprentices at one time, or take any apprentice for any less term than seven years, upon pain to forfeit and pay the sum of five pounds for every month that he shall continue offending in the premises contrary to the true meaning of this act, of which one moiety shall go and be applied to the use of his Majesty, his heirs, and successors, and the other moiety thereof to such person or persons as will sue for the same by action of debt, bill, plaint, or information, to be commenced, brought, or prosecuted in any court in the said plantations, wherein no essoin, protection, or wager of law, or more than one imparlance shall be admitted or allowed for the defendant.

VIII. And be it further enacted by the authority aforesaid, that no person or persons inhabiting in the said plantations, from and after the said twenty-ninth day of September, one thousand seven hundred and thirty-two, shall retain or set on work, in the said art of hat or feltmaking, any black or Negro, upon pain to forfeit and pay the sum of five pounds for every month wherein such person or persons shall so offend, contrary to the meaning of this act; and to be recovered and applied in manner, and to the uses aforesaid.

IX. Provided always, that nothing in this act contained shall extend to charge any person or persons lawfully exercising the said art, with any penalty or forfeiture for setting or using his or their own son or sons to the making or working hats or felts in his or their own house or houses, so as every such son or sons be bound by indenture of apprenticeship, for the term of seven years at the least, which term shall not be to expire before he shall be of the full age of twenty-one years; anything herein contained to the contrary notwithstanding.

X. Provided also, and be it enacted by the authority aforesaid, that every feltmaker residing in the said plantations, who at the beginning of this present session of Parliament was a maker or worker of hats or felts, and being an householder, and likewise all such as were at the beginning of this present session apprentices, covenant servants, or journeymen in the same art or mystery of feltmaking so as such apprentices serve or make up their respective apprenticeships, shall and may continue and exercise the trade or art of making hats and felts in the said plantations, although the same persons were not bound apprentices to the same art for the term of seven years; anything in this act to the contrary notwithstanding.

XI. And be it further enacted by the authority aforesaid, that this present act shall be deemed, and is hereby declared to be a public act, of which all judges and justices are to take notice without special pleading the same.

IV. Considerations on the Causes of the State of Affairs in America

MALACHY POSTLETHWAYT

Malachy Postlethwayt was an economic journalist thoroughly dedicated to the principles and practices of mercantilism. In 1757 he prepared a lengthy report for the Duke of Rutland, a member of the Privy Council, on economic conditions in the British Empire. Because the Privy Council was the King's most direct advisory council, it might be assumed that the sentiment of this document reached some important ears.

As is apparent in the following selection, Postlethwayt favored a severe tightening of enforcement procedures and an increasing role for Parliament in the maintenance of mercantile policies. Had this treatise been circulated widely in the colonies, what would have been the likely response of the colonists? On what points would it have been most roundly attacked by Adam Smith?

Although there appears great wisdom in the framing the constitution of our colonies, especially, at the time when they were first settled; yet time and experience have shewn that there are still many things wanting to render the

Malachy Postlethwayt, *Britain's Commercial Interest Explained and Improved* (New York: Augustus M. Kelley, 1968; reprinted from the 1757 edition), I, pp. 465–70.

system complete: there seems a necessity, an indispensable necessity for the aid of the legislature in establishing the said constitutions by law, with penalties on such, who should presume to deviate therefrom. The best of laws are no more than a dead letter without they are duly executed. And what danger could arise from hence, either relative to the prerogative of the crown, or the safety of the subject?

The strengthening the hands of the crown, so as to guard against encroachments, cannot impede the due course of public business; the governors of our colonies being obliged to have all public concerns of the colonies registered in the journals of council, cannot obstruct the business of the crown. Those being timely transmitted to our council of trade at home, will occasion all things necessary to be laid occasionally before the parliament; and what is requisite to be done, will be duly and timely enforced by the authority of law. And will not this regular intercourse of business between the grand legislative power and the colonies give such strength and vigor to the latter, that they can never obtain without it? Has not a want of this proved one apparent, though gradual cause, of the present calamities under which our plantations labour?

The actions of the wisest men are formed agreeable to their informations. What may appear extremely wise and prudent, and in all respects well calculated to guard the crown from surprise, and the subject from injury, may yet have a different tendency, as it relates to our distant settlements; for without unity of design; without mutual relation between the systems observed abroad, and at home, and a uniform and inviolable course of proceedings, between both, it will be impossible to prevent the affairs of America from running into confusion, or free the crown, and the parliament from surprise. Nor can this, we humbly apprehend, be ever effectually prevented in any other manner than by the aid of parliament, in establishing an invariable rule of constant and timely intercourse, in relation to the transactions of the colony-councils abroad, and our board of trade at home.—It is impossible for the sovereign, or for those employed in the administration, to protect his Majesty's subjects abroad, otherwise than inviolably maintaining this uniform correspondence, in order to inflict penalties on such as shall act contrary to their duty, and regulate all colony-laws according to the eternal standard of a reciprocal interest between them and those of their parent kingdom.—Without such a steddy method of proceeding, the crown cannot protect and extend our trade and commerce, or in other respects exercise it's prerogatives.

For want of this, it may be useful to hint some of the methods which have been taken by several of our governors in our plantations to evade His Majesty's instructions, and to conceal acts of oppression.—Such governors do many acts of government without the advice or privity of their council, and, therefore, no records in the journals of their council appear thereof.—At other times, the acts of council, have, by a governor's influence, been imperfectly recorded, and in some cases wholly omitted.—When this precaution has not been used, and petitions of complaint have been preferred to his Majesty against them, they have, under frivolous pretences, kept back the records, and not duly transmitted them to England.

Such governors also have too often formed party and factious connections in assemblies, and past by-laws for the emission of paper-currency, and other laws, suited to their private interests, without suspending clauses to give the injured an opportunity to lay their grievances before the crown, previous to the carrying such detrimental laws into execution. Is it not notorious too, that such governors have dispossessed the crown-grantees of their lands, without legal trial or process? Have they not in more colonies than one issued blank patents or grants for lands, and afterwards affixed the seal of the colony thereto, and put them into private hands to be disposed of? Have not these detestable practises introduced the utmost confusion in some of the colonies? For when blank patents or grants are so issued, is it not in the power of such who hold them, by antedating the same, to claim the property of others? Will not this occasion such mixture of claims, and such confusion in property, as to put it out of the power of courts of law to determine the right of the subject? Must not these practices occasion every thing of this kind to be arbitrarily decided by acts of power and violence?

Acts of violence exercised in His Majesty's colonies, can scarce gain credit from those who enjoy the blessing of a regular government at home. Let those who have the power to redress pry into the complaints repeatedly made against his majesty's governors, and other officers employed in our colonies, and the proof sent home to support them, and they will find evidence enough of what has been only hinted; and they will find also that these grievances have been occasioned by want of a well-regulated system for the conduct of public affairs between Britain and her American colonies. Is it to be admired that these practises have sowed the seeds of confusion in our plantations, and given the enemies those advantages over us, which we at present experience? Have not these arbitrary and illegal proceedings been productive of these convulsions, which at different periods of time have happened in several of our colonies? Have not these things made the people uneasy in their situation, and caused them to think themselves unhappy under the best of governments and the best of kings? And have not such treatment often prompted them to act in opposition to His Majesty's measures, or to whatever else may have been wisely proposed for the benefit of the public?

England hath many difficulties to encounter in relation to the government of it's colonies, particularly, as we have observed, it's charter-governments; yet these, we humbly conceive, might easily be redressed by the aid of parliament. For it seems to be full time, at present, for the wisdom of the nation to determine upon such a union in government and constitution of every part of it's dominions as may tend to strengthen the whole British empire; for although she has hitherto maintained her power, with variety of dominions annexed, that have acted independently of her, as it were, though supported by her; yet this policy does not seem capable of much longer upholding her, against enemies, who govern every part of their dominions by one and the same steddy principle of union; by the same interesting laws, and regulations, the due execution of all which, is vigorously, and orderly enforced.

For Further Reading

A comprehensive and authoritative study of the Navigation Acts is provided by Lawrence A. Harper in *The English Navigation Laws: A Seventeenth Century Experiment in Social Engineering* (1939, 1964). Oliver M. Dickerson's *The Navigation Acts and the American Revolution** (1951) is the definitive study of the part the Navigation Acts played in precipitating the American Revolution.

Michael Kammen's *Empire and Interest: The American Colonies and the Politics of Mercantilism** (1970) is a thorough analysis of the title subject; it contains an extensive bibliography. Also worth noting is Philip W. Buck's *The Politics of Mercantilism* (1942). *Mercantilism* (1935, 1962), by Eli F. Hecksher, authorized translation by Mendel Shapiro, is a detailed study of the economic aspects of mercantilism as practiced internationally. *The Colonial Merchant** (1966), edited by Stuart W. Bruchey, is a good collection of primary sources.

*The Colonial Background of the American Revolution** (1924, 1958), by Charles M. Andrews, is a brief account of colonial conditions in the decades prior to the Revolution; considerable attention is given to trade relations.

Robert Heilbroner's *The Worldly Philosophers** (1961) has a good chapter on Adam Smith.

*Paperbound edition available.

4. Power and Protest

Whether the American Revolution was chiefly a struggle for home rule or a conflict over who should rule at home has been a point of debate among historians for several generations. Without taking sides, it is correct to observe that in the years immediately preceding the War for Independence ideological and constitutional questions provoked intense controversy on both sides of the Atlantic Ocean.

Prior to 1763 the British imperial system worked reasonably well, principally because the terms and management responsibilities of the system had not been clearly defined. Following the expulsion of the French from North America in 1763, the British government tried to bring a more rational order to the system and at the same time to generate revenue to support its administration. These efforts raised questions in the colonies concerning the proper disposition of power, for the colonists interpreted the new moves of the British as threats to their freedom. The Sugar and Currency Acts of 1764 put the colonists on the alert, but the Stamp Act in 1765 roused them to action. The repeal of the Stamp Act under colonial pressure the next year was only a partial palliative, accompanied as it was by the Declaratory Act, which asserted Parliament's right to make laws binding the colonies and people of America "in all cases whatsoever." The passage of the Townshend Acts in 1767 evoked a line of argument among the colonists that gradually led them to declare their independence from England.

Core Document

Letters From a Farmer in Pennsylvania

JOHN DICKINSON

Perhaps the most eloquent and most widely distributed representation of the colonists' viewpoint was offered in this document by John Dickinson, the well-known author of the Declaration of the Stamp Act Congress *and principal drafter of the* Declaration of the Causes and Necessity of Taking Up Arms *and the* Articles of Confederation. *He managed to maintain the respect of his compatriots even though he was not afraid to take unpopular positions. For reasons that appear to have been misunderstood, he refused to sign the Declaration of Independence, but he later served in the continental army.*

An independent but consistent thinker, Dickinson used his letters to express the colonial position that had been developing for several years. The letters were originally published in twelve installments in a weekly newspaper, beginning in November 1767. They were later printed in other newspapers and in pamphlet form in various editions, including some in foreign languages. The first three letters, which set the tone and direction of his argument, are included here.

In reading the letters, note:

- *attempts to show how acceptance of one British move would lead to another one still more perverse.*
- *distinctions made between powers of Parliament and of the crown.*
- *emphasis placed on united colonial action.*
- *efforts to define the extent and the limits of parliamentary power.*
- *the degree of willingness to accept a dependent position in the British mercantile system.*
- *concern over methods of protest and resistance.*

WINTER 1767

Letter I

My dear Countrymen,

I am a *Farmer,* settled, after a variety of fortunes, near the banks of the river *Delaware,* in the province of *Pennsylvania.* I received a liberal education, and have been engaged in the busy scenes of life; but am now convinced, that a man may be as happy without bustle, as with it. My farm is small; my servants are few, and good; I have a little money at interest; I wish for no more; my employment in my own affairs is easy; and with a contented grateful mind, (undisturbed by worldly hopes or fears, relating to myself,) I am completing the number of days allotted to me by divine goodness.

Paul L. Ford, ed., *The Life and Writings of John Dickinson* (Philadelphia: The Historical Society of Pennsylvania, 1895), I, pp. 307–28.

Being generally master of my time, I spend a good deal of it in a library, which I think the most valuable part of my small estate; and being acquainted with two or there gentlemen of abilities and learning who honour me with their friendship, I have acquired, I believe, a greater knowledge in history, and the laws and constitution of my country, than is generally attained by men of my class, many of them not being so fortunate as I have been in the opportunities of getting information.

From my infancy I was taught to love *humanity* and *liberty*. Enquiry and experience have since confirmed my reverence for the lessons then given me, by convincing me more fully of their truth and excellence. Benevolence to-wards mankind, excites wishes for their welfare, and such wishes endear the means of fulfilling them. *These* can be found in liberty only, and therefore her sacred cause ought to be espoused by every man, on every occasion, to the utmost of his power. As a charitable, but poor person does not withhold his *mite,* because he cannot relieve *all* the distresses of the miserable, so should not any honest man suppress his sentiments concerning freedom, however small their influence is likely to be. Perhaps he "may touch some wheel," that will have an effect greater than he could reasonably expect.

These being my sentiments, I am encouraged to offer to you, my country-men, my thoughts on some late transactions, that appear to me to be of the utmost importance to you. Conscious of my own defects, I have waited some time, in expectation of seeing the subject treated by persons much better qualified for the task; but being therein disappointed, and apprehensive that longer delays will be injurious, I venture at length to request the attention of the public, praying, that these lines may be *read* with the same zeal for the happiness of *British America,* with which they were *wrote.*

With a good deal of surprise I have observed, that little notice has been taken of an act of parliament, as injurious in its principle to the liberties of these colonies, as the *Stamp-Act* was: I mean the act for suspending the legislation of *New-York.*

The assembly of that government complied with a former act of parlia-ment, requiring certain provisions to be made for the troops in *America,* in every particular, I think, except the articles of salt, pepper and vinegar. In my opinion they acted imprudently, considering all circumstances, in not comply-ing so far as would have given satisfaction, as several colonies did: But my dislike of their conduct in that instance, has not blinded me so much, that I cannot plainly perceive, that they have been punished in a manner pernicious to *American* freedom, and justly alarming to all the colonies.

If the *British* parliament has a legal authority to issue an order, that we shall furnish a single article for the troops here, and to compel obedience to *that* order, they have the same right to issue an order for us to supply those troops with arms, cloths, and every necessary; and to compel obedience to *that* order also; in short, to lay *any burthens* they please upon us. What is this but *taxing* us at a *certain sum,* and leaving to us only the *manner* of raising it? How is this mode more tolerable than the *Stamp-Act?* Would that act have appeared more pleasing to *Americans,* if being ordered thereby to raise the sum total of the taxes, the mighty privilege had been left to them, of saying how much should be paid for an instrument of writing on paper, and how much for another on parchment?

An act of parliament, commanding us to do a certain thing, if it has any validity, is a *tax* upon us for the expence that accrues in complying with it; and for this reason, I believe, every colony on the continent, that chose to give a mark of their respect for *Great-Britain,* in complying with the act relating to the troops, cautiously avoided the mention of that act, lest their conduct should be attributed to its supposed obligation.

The matter being thus stated, the assembly of *New-York* either had, or had not, a right to refuse submission to that act. If they had, and I imagine no *American* will say they had not, then the parliament had *no right* to compel them to execute it. If they had not *that right,* they had *no right* to punish them for not executing it; and therefore *no right* to suspend their legislation, which is a punishment. In fact, if the people of *New-York* cannot be legally taxed but by their own representatives, they cannot be legally deprived of the privilege of legislation, only for insisting on that exclusive privilege of taxation. If they may be legally deprived in such a case, of the privilege of legislation, why may they not, with equal reason, be deprived of every other privilege? Or why may not every colony be treated in the same manner, when any of them shall dare to deny their assent to any impositions, that shall be directed? Or what signifies the repeal of the *Stamp-Act,* if these colonies are to lose their *other* privileges, by not tamely surrendering *that* of taxation?

There is one consideration arising from this suspension, which is not generally attended to, but shews its importance very clearly. It was not *necessary* that this suspension should be caused by an act of parliament. Ths crown might have restrained the governor of *New-York,* even from calling the assembly together, by its prerogative in the royal governments. This step, I suppose, would have been taken, if the conduct of the assembly of *New-York* had been regarded as an act of disobedience *to the crown alone;* but it is regarded as an act of "disobedience to the authority "of the BRITISH LEGISLATURE." This gives the suspension a consequence vastly more affecting. It is a parliamentary assertion of the *supreme authority* of the *British* legislature over these colonies, in *the point of taxation,* and is intended to COMPEL *New-York* into a submission to that authority. It seems therefore to me as much a violation of the liberty of the people of that province, and consequently of all these colonies, as if the parliament had sent a number of regiments to be quartered upon them till they should comply. For it is evident, that the suspension is meant as a *compulsion;* and the *method* of compelling is totally indifferent. It is indeed probable, that the sight of red coats, and the hearing of drums, would have been most alarming; because people are generally more influenced by their eyes and ears, than by their reason. But whoever seriously considers the matter, must perceive that a dreadful stroke is aimed at the liberty of these colonies. I say, of these colonies; for the cause of *one* is the cause of *all.* If the parliament may lawfully deprive *New-York* of any of *her* rights, it may deprive any, or all the other colonies of *their* rights; and nothing can possibly so much encourage such attempts, as a mutual inattention to the interests of each other. *To divide, and thus to destroy,* is the first political maxim in attacking those, who are powerful by their union. He certainly is not a wise man, who folds his arms, and reposes himself at home, viewing, with unconcern, the flames that have invaded his neighbour's house, without using any endeavours to extinguish them. When Mr. *Hampden's* ship money cause, for *Three Shillings* and *Fourpence,* was tried, all the people of *England,* with anxious expectations, interested themselves in the important decision;[1] and when the slightest point, touching the freedom of *one* colony, is agitated, I earnestly wish, that *all the rest* may, with equal ardour, support their sister. Very much may be said on this subject; but I hope, more at present is unnecessary.

With concern I have observed, that *two* assemblies of this province have sat and adjourned, without taking any notice of this act. It may perhaps be asked, what would have been proper for them to do? I am by no means fond of inflammatory measures; I detest them. I should be sorry that any thing should be done, which might justly displease our sovereign, or our mother country: But a firm, modest exertion of a free spirit, should never be wanting on public occasions. It appears to me, that it would have been sufficient for the assembly, to have ordered our agents to represent to the King's ministers, their sense of the suspending act, and to pray for its repeal. Thus we should have borne our testimony against it; and might therefore reasonably expect that, on a like occasion, we might receive the same assistance from the other colonies.

> *Concordia res parvae crescunt.*
> Small things grow great by concord.

A FARMER

Letter II

My dear Countrymen,

There is another late act of parliament, which appears to me to be unconstitutional, and as destructive to the liberty of these colonies, as that mentioned in my last letter; that is, the act for granting the duties on paper, glass, etc.

The parliament unquestionably possesses a legal authority to *regulate* the trade of *Great-Britain,* and all her colonies. Such an authority is essential to the relation between a mother country and her colonies; and necessary for the common good of all. He, who considers these provinces as states distinct from the *British Empire,* has very slender notions of *justice,* or of their *interests.* We are but parts of a *whole;* and therefore there must exist a power somewhere to preside, and preserve the connection in due order. This power is lodged in the parliament; and we are as much dependent on *Great-Britain,* as a perfectly free people can be on another.

---

[1] *Editors' note:* A case during the reign of Charles I in which John Hampden challenged attempts of the King to raise funds by royal order.

I have looked over *every statute* relating to these colonies, from their first settlement to this time; and I find every one of them founded on this principle, till the *Stamp-Act* administration. *All before,* are calculated to regulate trade, and preserve or promote a mutually beneficial intercourse between the several constituent parts of the empire; and though many of them imposed duties on trade, yet those duties were always imposed *with design* to restrain the commerce of one part, that was injurious to another, and thus to promote the general welfare. The raising a revenue thereby was never intended. Thus the King, by his judges in his courts of justice, imposes fines which all together amount to a very considerable sum, and contribute to the support of government: But this is merely a consequence arising from restrictions, that only meant to keep peace, and prevent confusion; and surely a man would argue very loosely, who should conclude from hence, that the King has a right to levy money in general upon his subjects. Never did the *British* parliament, till the period above mentioned, think of imposing duties in *America,* FOR THE PURPOSE OF RAISING A REVENUE. Mr. *Grenville* first introduced this language, in the preamble to the 4th of *Geo.* III., Chap. 15,[2] which has these words "And whereas it is just and necessary that A REVENUE BE RAISED IN YOUR MAJES-TY'S SAID DOMINIONS IN AMERICA, *for defraying the expences of defending, protecting, and securing the same:* We your Majesty's most dutiful and loyal subjects, THE COMMONS OF GREAT-BRITAIN, in parliament assembled, being desirous to make some provision in this present session of parliament, TO-WARDS RAISING THE SAID REVENUE IN AMERICA, have resolved to GIVE and GRANT unto your Majesty the several rates and duties herein after mentioned," &c.

A few months after came the *Stamp-Act,* which reciting this, proceeds in the same strange mode of expression, thus—"And whereas it is just and necessary, that provision be made FOR RAISING A FURTHER REVENUE WITHIN YOUR MAJESTY'S DOMINIONS IN AMERICA, *towards defraying the said expences,* we your Majesty's most dutiful and loyal subjects, the COMMONS OF GREAT-BRITAIN, &c. GIVE and GRANT, &c. as before.

The last act, granting duties upon paper, &c. carefully pursues these modern precedents. The preamble is, "Whereas it is expedient THAT A REVE-NUE SHOULD BE RAISED IN YOUR MAJESTY'S DOMINIONS IN AMERICA, *for making a more certain and adequate provision for defraying the charge of the administration of justice, and the support of civil government in such provinces, where it shall be found necessary; and towards the further defraying the expences of defending, protecting and securing the said dominions,* we your Majesty's most dutiful and loyal subjects, the COMMONS OF GREAT-BRITAIN, &c. GIVE and GRANT," &c. as before.

Here we may observe an authority *expressly* claimed and exerted to impose duties on these colonies; not for the regulation of trade; not for the

---

[2] *Editors' note:* A reference to chapter 15 of the laws passed in the fourth Parliamentary session during the reign of King George III; the specific act was the Revenue Act of 1764, commonly called the Sugar Act.

preservation or promotion of a mutually beneficial intercourse between the several constituent parts of the empire, heretofore the *sole objects* of parliamentary institutions; *but for the single purpose of levying money upon us.*

This I call an innovation; and a most dangerous innovation. It may perhaps be objected, that *Great-Britain* has a right to lay what duties she pleases upon her exports, and it makes no difference to us, whether they are paid here or there.

To this I answer. These colonies require many things for their use, which the laws of *Great-Britain* prohibit them from getting any where but from her. Such are paper and glass.

That we may legally be bound to pay any *general* duties on these commodities relative to the regulation of trade, is granted; but we being *obliged by the laws* to take from *Great-Britain,* any *special* duties imposed on their exportation *to us only, with intention to raise a revenue from us only,* are as much *taxes,* upon us, as those imposed by the *Stamp-Act.*

What is the difference in *substance* and *right* whether the same sum is raised upon us by the rates mentioned in the *Stamp-Act,* on the *use* of paper, or by these duties, on the *importation* of it. It is only the edition of a former book, shifting a sentence from the *end* to the *beginning.*

Suppose the duties were made payable in *Great-Britain.*

It signifies nothing to us, whether they are to be paid here or there. Had the *Stamp-Act* directed, that all the paper should be landed at *Florida,* and the duties paid there, before it was brought to the *British* colonies, would the act have raised less money upon us, or have been less destructive of our rights? By no means: For as we were under a necessity of using the paper, we should have been under the necessity of paying the duties. Thus, in the present case, a like *necessity* will subject us, if this act continues in force, to the payment of the duties now imposed.

Why was the *Stamp-Act* then so pernicious to freedom? It did not enact, that every man in the colonies *should* buy a certain quantity of paper—No: It only directed, that no instrument of writing should be valid in law, if not made on stamped paper, *&c.*

The makers of that act knew full well, that the confusions that would arise from the disuse of writings, would COMPEL the colonies to use the stamped paper, and therefore to pay the taxes imposed. For this reason the *Stamp-Act* was said to be a law THAT WOULD EXECUTE ITSELF. For the very same reason, the last act of parliament, if it is granted to have any force here, WILL EXECUTE ITSELF, and will be attended with the very same consequences to *American* liberty.

Some persons perhaps may say, that this act lays us under no necessity to pay the duties imposed, because we may ourselves manufacture the articles on which they are laid; whereas by the *Stamp-Act* no instrument of writing could be good, unless made on *British* paper, and that too stamped.

Such an objection amounts to no more than this, that the injury resulting to these colonies, from the total disuse of *British* paper and glass, will not be *so afflicting* as that which would have resulted from the total disuse of writing among them; for by that means even the *Stamp-Act* might have been eluded. Why then was it universally detested by them as slavery itself? Because it presented to these devoted provinces nothing but a choice of calamities,[3] imbittered by indignities, each of which it was unworthy of freemen to bear. But is no injury a violation of right but the *greatest* injury? If the eluding the payment of the taxes imposed by the *Stamp-Act,* would have subjected us to a more dreadful inconvenience, than the eluding the payment of those imposed by the late act; does it therefore follow, that the last is *no violation* of our rights, tho' it is calculated for the same purpose the other was, that is, *to raise money upon us,* WITHOUT OUR CONSENT.

This would be making *right* to consist, not in an exemption from *injury,* but from a certain *degree of injury.*

But the objectors may further say, that we shall suffer no injury at all by the disuse of *British* paper and glass. We might not, if we could make as much as we want. But can any man, acquainted with *America,* believe this possible? I am told there are but two or three *Glass-Houses* on this continent, and but very few *Paper-Mills;* and suppose more should be erected, a long course of years must elapse, before they can be brought to perfection. This continent is a country of planters, farmers, and fishermen; not of manufacturers. The difficulty of establishing particular manufactures in such a country, is almost insuperable. For one manufacture is connected with others in such a manner, that it may be said to be impossible to establish one or two, without establishing several others. The experience of many nations may convince us of this truth.

Inexpressible therefore must be our distresses in evading the late acts, by the disuse of *British* paper and glass. Nor will this be the extent of our misfortune, if we admit the legality of that act.

Great-Britain has prohibited the manufacturing [of] *iron* and *steel* in these colonies, without any objection being made to her *right* of doing it. The *like* right she must have to prohibit any other manufacture among us. Thus she is possessed of an undisputed *precedent* on that point. This authority, she will say, is founded on the *original intention* of settling these colonies; that is, that we should manufacture for them, and that they should supply her with materials. The *equity* of this policy, she will also say, has been universally acknowledged by the colonies, who never have made the least objections to statutes for that purpose; and will further appear by the *mutual benefits* flowing from this usage ever since the settlement of these colonies.

Our great advocate, Mr. *Pitt,* in his speeches on the debate concerning the repeal of the *Stamp-Act,* acknowledged, that *Great-Britain* could restrain our manufactures. His words are these—"This kingdom, as the supreme governing and legislative power, has ALWAYS bound the colonies by her regulations and RESTRICTIONS in trade, in navigation, in MANUFACTURES—in every thing, *except that of taking their money out of their pockets,* WITHOUT THEIR

---

[3] *Editors' note:* Either the disuse of writing or the payment of taxes without the consent of the colonists.

CONSENT." Again he says, "We may bind their trade, CONFINE THEIR MANU-
FACTURES, and exercise every power whatever, *except that of taking their
money out of their pockets,* WITHOUT THEIR CONSENT.

Here then, my dear countrymen, ROUSE yourselves, and behold the ruin
hanging over your heads. If you ONCE admit, that *Great-Britain* may lay
duties upon her exportations to us, *for the purpose of levying money on us only,*
she then will have nothing to do, but to lay those duties on the articles which
she prohibits us to manufacture—and the tragedy of *American* liberty is
finished. We have been prohibited from procuring manufactures, in all cases,
any where but from *Great-Britain* (excepting linens, which we are permitted
to import directly from *Ireland*). We have been prohibited, in some cases, from
manufacturing for ourselves; and may be prohibited in others. We are therefore
exactly in the situation of a city besieged, which is surrounded by the works
of the besiegers in every part *but one.* If *that* is closed up, no step can be taken,
but to surrender at discretion. If *Great-Britain* can order us to come to her for
necessaries we want, and can order us to pay what taxes she pleases before we
take them away, or when we land them here, we are as abject slaves as *France*
and *Poland* can shew in wooden shoes, and with uncombed hair. . . .

From what has been said, I think this uncontrovertible conclusion may
be deduced, that when a ruling state obliges a dependent state to take certain
commodities from her alone, it is implied in the nature of that obligation; is
essentially requisite to give it the least degree of justice; and is inseparably
united with it, in order to preserve any share of freedom to the dependent state;
that those commodities should never be loaded with duties, FOR THE SOLE
PURPOSE OF LEVYING MONEY ON THE DEPENDENT STATE.

Upon the whole, the single question is, whether the parliament can legally
impose duties to be paid *by the people of these colonies only,* FOR THE SOLE
PURPOSE OF RAISING A REVENUE, *on commodities which she obliges us to take
from her alone,* or, in other words, whether the parliament can legally take
money out of our pockets, without our consent. If they can, our boasted liberty
is but

> *Vox el praeterea nihil.*
> A sound and nothing else.

A FARMER

Letter III

My dear Countrymen, . . .

Sorry I am to learn, that there are some few persons, who shake their
heads with solemn motion, and pretend to wonder, what can be the meaning
of these letters. *"Great-Britain,"* they say, "is too powerful to contend with;
she is determined to oppress us; it is in vain to speak of right on one side, when
there is power on the other; when we are strong enough to resist, we shall
attempt it; but now we are not strong enough, and therefore we had better be

quiet; it signifies nothing to convince us that our rights are invaded, when we cannot defend them; and if we should get into riots and tumults about the late act, it will only draw down heavier displeasure upon us."

What can such men design? What do their grave observations amount to, but this—"that these colonies, totally regardless of their liberties, should commit them, with humble resignation, to *chance, time,* and the tender mercies of *ministers.*"

Are these men ignorant, that usurpations, which might have been successfully opposed at first, acquire strength by continuance, and thus become irresistable? Do they condemn the conduct of these colonies, concerning the *Stamp-Act?* Or have they forgot its successful issue? Ought the colonies at that time, instead of acting as they did, to have trusted for relief to the fortuitous events of futurity? If it is needless "to speak of rights" now, it was as needless then. If the behavior of the colonies was prudent and glorious then, and successful too; it will be equally prudent and glorious to act in the same manner now, if our rights are equally invaded, and may be as successful. Therefore it becomes necessary to enquire, whether "our rights *are* invaded." To talk of "defending" them, as if they could be no otherwise "defended" than by arms, is as much out of the way, as if a man having a choice of several roads to reach his journey's end, should prefer the worst, for no other reason, but because it *is* the worst.

As to "riots and tumults," the gentlemen who are so apprehensive of them, are much mistaken, if they think that grievances cannot be redressed without such assistance.

I will now tell the gentlemen, what is, "the meaning of these letters." The meaning of them is, to convince the people of these colonies, that they are at this moment exposed to the most imminent dangers; and to persuade them immediately, vigorously, and unanimously, to exert themselves, in the most firm, but most peaceable manner, for obtaining relief.

The cause of *liberty* is a cause of too much dignity to be sullied by turbulence and tumult. It ought to be maintained in a manner suitable to her nature. Those who engage in it, should breathe a sedate, yet fervent spirit, animating them to actions of prudence, justice, modesty, bravery, humanity and magnanimity.

To such a wonderful degree were the ancient *Spartans,* as brave and free a people as ever existed, inspired by this happy temperature of soul, that rejecting even in their battles the use of trumpets, and other instruments for exciting heat and rage, they marched up to scenes of havoc, and horror, with the sound of flutes, to the tunes of which their steps kept pace—"exhibiting," as *Plutarch* says, "at once a terrible and delightful sight, and proceeding with a deliberate valor, full of hope and good assurance, as if some divinity had sensibly assisted them."

I hope, my dear countrymen, that you will, in every colony, be upon your guard against those, who may at any time endeavour to stir you up, under pretences of patriotism, to any measures disrespectful to our Sovereign and our mother country. Hot, rash, disorderly proceedings, injure the reputation of a people, as to wisdom, valor and virtue, without procuring them the least benefit. I pray GOD, that he may be pleased to inspire you and your posterity, to the latest ages, with a spirit of which I have an idea, that I find a difficulty to express. To express it in the best manner I can, I mean a spirit, that shall so guide you, that it will be impossible to determine whether an *American's* character is most distinguishable, for his loyalty to his Sovereign, his duty to his mother country, his love of freedom, or his affection for his native soil.

Every government at some time or other falls into wrong measures. These may proceed from mistake or passion. But every such measure does not dissolve the obligation between the governors and the governed. The mistake may be corrected; the passion may subside. It is the duty of the governed to endeavour to rectify the mistake, and to appease the passion. They have not at first any other right, than to represent their grievances, and to pray for redress, unless an emergence is so pressing, as not to allow time for receiving an answer to their applications, which rarely happens. If their applications are disregarded, then that kind of *opposition* becomes justifiable, which can be made without breaking the laws, or disturbing the public peace.

This consists in the *prevention of the oppressors reaping advantage from their oppressions,* and not in their punishment. For experience may teach them, what reason did not; and harsh methods cannot be proper, till milder ones have failed.

If at length it become UNDOUBTED, that an inveterate resolution is formed to annihilate the liberties of the governed, the *English* history affords frequent examples of resistance by force. Whaat particular circumstances will in any future case justify such resistance, can never be ascertained, till they happen. Perhaps it may be allowable to say generally, that it never can be justifiable, until the people are FULLY CONVINCED, that any further submission will be destructive to their happiness.

When the appeal is made to the sword, highly probable is it, that the punishment will exceed the offence; and the calamities attending on war outweigh those preceding it. These considerations of justice and prudence, will always have great influence with good and wise men.

To these reflections on this subject, it remains to be added, and ought for ever to be remembered, that resistance, in the case of colonies against their mother country, is extremely different from the resistance of a people against their prince. A nation may change their king, or race of kings, and, retaining their antient form of government, be gainers by changing. Thus *Great-Britain,* under the illustrious house of *Brunswick,* a house that seems to flourish for the happiness of mankind, has found a felicity, unknown in the reigns of the *Stewarts.* But if once *we* are separated from our mother country, what new form of government shall we adopt, or where shall we find another *Britain,* to supply our loss? Torn from the body, to which we are united by religion, liberty, laws, affections, relation, language and commerce, we must bleed at every vein.

In truth—the prosperity of these provinces is founded in their dependence on *Great-Britain;* and when she returns to her "old good humour, and her old good nature," as Lord *Clarendon* expresses it, I hope they will always think it their duty and interest, as it most certainly will be, to promote her welfare by all the means in their power.

We cannot act with too much caution in our disputes. Anger produces anger; and differences, that might be accommodated by kind and respectful behavior, may, by imprudence, be enlarged to an incurable rage. In quarrels between countries, as well as in those between individuals, when they have risen to a certain height, the first cause of dissension is no longer remembered, the minds of the parties being wholly engaged in recollecting and resenting the mutual expressions of their dislike. When feuds have reached that fatal point, all considerations of reason and equity vanish; and a blind fury governs, or rather confounds all things. A people no longer regards their interest, but the gratification of their wrath. The sway of the *Cleons* and *Clodius's*,[4] the designing and detestable flatterers of the *prevailing passion,* becomes confirmed. Wise and good men in vain oppose the storm, and may think themselves fortunate, if, in attempting to preserve their ungrateful fellow citizens, they do not ruin themselves. Their *prudence* will be called *baseness;* their *moderation* will be called *guilt;* and if their virtue does not lead them to destruction, as that of many other great and excellent persons has done, they may survive to receive from their expiring country the mournful glory of her acknowledgment, that their counsels, if regarded, would have saved her.

The constitutional modes of obtaining relief, are those which I wish to see pursued on the present occasion; that is, by petitions of our assemblies, or where they are not permitted to meet, of the people, to the powers that can afford us relief.

We have an excellent prince, in whose good dispositions towards us we may confide. We have a generous, sensible and humane nation, to whom we may apply. They may be deceived. They may, by artful men, be provoked to anger against us. I cannot believe they will be cruel or unjust; or that their anger will be implacable. Let us behave like dutiful children, who have received unmerited blows from a beloved parent. Let us complain to our parent; but let our complaints speak at the same time the language of affliction and veneration.

If, however, it shall happen, by an unfortunate course of affairs, that our applications to his Majesty and the parliament for redress, prove ineffectual, let us THEN take *another step,* by withholding from *Great-Britain* all the advantages she has been used to receive from us. THEN let us try, if our ingenuity, industry, and frugality, will not give weight to our remonstrances. Let us all be united with one spirit, in one cause. Let us invent—let us work —let us save—let us, continually, keep up our claim, and incessantly repeat our complaints—But, above all, let us implore the protection of that infinitely good and gracious being, "by whom kings reign, and princes decree justice."

---

[4]Cleon was a popular firebrand of Athens, and Clodius of Rome; each of whom plunged his country into the deepest calamities.

Nil desperandum.
Nothing is to be despaired of.

A FARMER

Discussion Starters

1. If these letters were regarded as an attempt at conciliation with England, it would be possible to discover points in them where compromise was being suggested. Attempt to identify such points and then draw conclu- sions concerning Dickinson's purpose in writing them.

2. If it is true that the Anglo-American troubles started with England's efforts to define her relationship with the colonies more clearly, Dickinson might be blamed for aggravating the difficulties by proposing a different definition. What were the terms of his definition and how did they conflict with the English terms?

3. How might the points raised by Dickinson on the proper disposition of power be applied to the disposition of the power of the federal government in the United States today?

4. How does Dickinson's counsel on protest and resistance apply to those today who would protest and resist what they regard as the unjust use of power?

Related Documents

I. The Rights of Colonies Examined

STEPHEN HOPKINS

The arguments presented by John Dickinson were not original with him. Three years earlier, Governor Stephen Hopkins of Rhode Island, with the support of his legislature, published a pamphlet that sought both to resist British tax policies and to define the place of the colonies in the British Empire. Hopkins turned to history and to the colonial charters to determine the limits of British power.

In this brief excerpt, note how he attempted to restrict the power of Parlia- ment to tax the colonies. How do his arguments parallel Dickinson's? How feasible was his alternative plan for raising revenue?

DECEMBER 22, 1764

We are not insensible, that when liberty is in danger, the liberty of complaining is dangerous; yet, a man on a wreck was never denied the liberty of roaring as loud as he could, says Dean Swift. And we believe no good reason can be given, why the colonies should not modestly and soberly inquire, what right the parliament of Great Britain have to tax them. We know such inquiries, by a late letter writer, have been branded with the little epithet of *mushroom policy;* and he insinuates, that for the colonies to pretend to claim any privileges, will draw down the resentment of the parliament on them.—Is the defence of liberty become so contemptible, and pleading for just rights so dangerous? Can the guardians of liberty be thus ludicrous? Can the patrons of freedom be so jealous and so severe? If the British house of commons are rightfully possessed of a power to tax the colonies in America, this power must be vested in them by the British constitution, as they are one branch of the great legislative body of the nation; as they are the representatives of all the people in Britain, they have, beyond doubt, all the power such a representation can possibly give; yet, great as this power is, surely it cannot exceed that of their constituents. And can it possibly be shown that the people in Britain have a sovereign authority over their fellow subjects in America? Yet such is the authority that must be exercised in taking peoples' estates from them by taxes, or otherwise, without their consent. In all aids granted to the crown, by the parliament, it is said with the greatest propriety, "We freely give unto Your Majesty;" for they give their own money, and the money of those who have entrusted them with a proper power for that purpose. But can they, with the same propriety, give away the money of the Americans, who have never given any such power? Before a thing can be justly given away, the giver must certainly have acquired a property in it; and have the people in Britain justly acquired such a property in the goods and estates of the people in these colonies, that they may give them away at pleasure?

In an imperial state, which consists of many separate governments, each of which hath peculiar privileges, and of which kind it is evident the empire of Great Britain is; no single part, though greater than another part, is by that superiority entitled to make laws for, or to tax such lesser part; but all laws, and all taxations, which bind the whole, must be made by the whole. . . . Indeed, it must be absurd to suppose, that the common people of Great Britain have a sovereign and absolute authority over their fellow subjects in America, or even any sort of power whatsoever, over them; but it will be still more absurd to suppose they can give a power to their representatives, which they have not themselves. If the house of commons do not receive this authority from their constituents, it will be difficult to tell by what means they obtained it, except it be vested in them by mere superiority and power. . . .

If the colonies are not taxed by parliament, are they therefore exempted from bearing their proper share in the necessary burdens of government? This by no means follows. Do they not support a regular internal government in each colony, as expensive to the people here, as the internal government of Britain is to the people there? Have not the colonies here, at all times when called upon by the crown, raised money for the public service, done it as cheerfully as the parliament have done on like occasions? Is not this the most easy, the most natural, and most constitutional way of raising money in the colonies? What occasion then to distrust the colonies? What necessity to fall on an invidious and unconstitutional method, to compel them to do what they have ever done freely? Are not the people in the colonies as loyal and dutiful subjects as any age or nation ever produced? And are they not as useful to the kingdom, in this remote quarter of the world, as their fellow subjects are who dwell in Britain? The parliament, it is confessed, have power to regulate the trade of the whole empire; and hath it not full power, by this means, to draw all the money and all the wealth of the colonies into the mother country, at pleasure? What motive, after all this, can remain, to induce the parliament to abridge the privileges, and lessen the rights of the most loyal and dutiful subjects; subjects justly entitled to ample freedom, who have long enjoyed, and not abused or forfeited their liberties; who have used them to their own advantage, in dutiful subserviency to the orders and interests of Great Britain? Why should the gentle current of tranquillity, that has so long run with peace through all the British states, and flowed with joy and with happiness in all her countries, be at last obstructed, be turned out of its true course, into unusual and winding channels, by which many of those states must be ruined; but none of them can possibly be made more rich or more happy?

II. A Letter From a Gentleman at Halifax

MARTIN HOWARD, JR.

A prompt rebuttal to Stephen Hopkins was provided by Martin Howard, Jr., of Newport, Rhode Island (not Halifax, as the title suggests). He, too, looked to the colonial charters to support his position, but he reached different conclusions.

How successful does he appear to be in meeting Hopkins' arguments and in anticipating those offered later by Dickinson? Evaluate the feasibility of his definition of the colonies' place in the Empire.

FEBRUARY 13, 1765

I have endeavoured to investigate the true natural relation, if I may so speak, between colonies and their mother state, abstracted from compact or positive institution, but here I can find nothing satisfactory; till this relation is clearly defined upon a rational and natural principle, our reasoning upon the measure of the colonies obedience will be desultory and inconclusive. Every connection

From *Tracts of the American Revolution 1763–1776*, pp. 66–69, 77–78, ed. by Merrill Jensen. Copyright © 1967, by Bobbs-Merrill Company, Inc. Reprinted by permission of the publisher.

in life has its reciprocal duties; we know the relation between a parent and child, husband and wife, master and servant, and from thence are able to deduce their respective obligations; but we have no notices of any such precise natural relation between a mother state and its colonies, and therefore cannot reason with so much certainty upon the power of the one, or the duty of the others. The ancients have transmitted to us nothing that is applicable to the state of modern colonies, because the relation between these is formed by political compact; and the condition of each variant in their original, and from each other. The honourable author has not freed this subject from any of its embarrassments: Vague and diffuse talk of rights and privileges, and ringing the changes upon the words liberty and slavery, only serve to convince us, that words may affect without raising images, or affording any repose to a mind philosophically inquisitive. For my own part, I will shun the walk of metaphysicks in my enquiry, and be content to consider the colonies rights upon the footing of their charters, which are the only plain avenues, that lead to the truth of this matter.

The several New England charters ascertain, define and limit the respective rights and privileges of each colony, and I cannot conceive how it has come to pass that the colonies now claim any other or greater rights than are therein expresly granted to them. I fancy when we speak, or think of the rights of freeborn Englishmen, we confound those rights which are personal, with those which are political: There is a distinction between these, which ought always to be kept in view.

Our personal rights, comprehending those of life, liberty, and estate, are secured to us by the common law, which is every subject's birthright, whether born in Great Britain, on the ocean, or in the colonies; and it is in this sense we are said to enjoy all the rights and privileges of Englishmen. The political rights of the colonies, or the powers of government communicated to them, are more limited, and their nature, quality and extent depend altogether upon the patent or charter which first created and instituted them. As individuals, the colonists participate of every blessing the English constitution can give them: As corporations created by the crown, they are confined within the primitive views of their institution. Whether therefore their indulgence is scanty or liberal, can be no cause of complaint; for when they accepted of their charters, they tacitly submitted to the terms and conditions of them.

The colonies have no rights independant of their charters, they can claim no greater than those give them, by those the parliamentary jurisdiction over them is not taken away, neither could any grant of the king abridge that jurisdiction, because it is founded upon common law, as I shall presently shew, and was prior to any charter or grant to the colonies: Every Englishman, therefore, is subject to this jurisdiction, and it follows him wherever he goes. It is of the essence of government, that there should be a supreme head, and it would be a solecism in politicks to talk of members independant of it.

With regard to the jurisdiction of parliament, I shall endeavour to shew, that it is attached to every English subject, wherever he be: And I am led to do this from a clause in page nine of his honour's pamphlet, where he says,

"That the colonies do not hold their rights, as a privilege granted them, nor enjoy them as a grace and favour bestowed; but possess them, as an inherent, indefeasible right." This postulatum cannot be true with regard to political rights, for I have already shewn, that these are derived from your charters, and are held by force of the king's grant; therefore these inherent, indefeasible rights, as his honour calls them, must be personal ones, according to the distinction already made. Permit me to say, that inherent and indefeasible as these rights may be, the jurisdiction of parliament, over every English subject, is equally as inherent and indefeasible: That both have grown out of the same stock, and that if we avail ourselves of the one, we must submit to, and acknowlege the other.

It might here be properly enough asked, Are these personal rights self-existent? Have they no original source? I answer, They are derived from the constitution of England, which is the common law; and from the same fountain is also derived the jurisdiction of parliament over us.

But to bring this argument down to the most vulgar apprehension: The common law has established it as a rule or maxim, that the plantations are bound by British acts of parliament, if particularly named: And surely no Englishman, in his senses, will deny the force of a common law maxim. One cannot but smile at the inconsistency of these inherent, indefeasible men: If one of them has a suit at law, in any part of New England, upon a question of land property, or merchandize, he appeals to the common law, to support his claim, or defeat his adversary; and yet is so profoundly stupid as to say, that an act of parliament does not bind him; when, perhaps, the same page in a law book, which points him out a remedy for a libel, or a slap in the face, would inform him that it does.—In a word, The force of an act of parliament, over the colonies, is predicated upon the common law, the origin and basis of all those inherent rights and privileges which constitute the boast and felicity of a Briton.

Can we claim the common law as an inheritance, and at the same time be at liberty to adopt one part of it, and reject the other? Indeed we cannot: The common law, pure and indivisible in its nature and essence, cleaves to us during our lives, and follows us from Nova Zembla to Cape Horn: And therefore, as the jurisdiction of parliament arises out of, and is supported by it, we may as well renounce our allegiance, or change our nature, as to be exempt from the jurisdiction of parliament. Hence, it is plain to me, that in denying this jurisdiction, we at the same time, take leave of the common law, and thereby, with equal temerity and folly, strip ourselves of every blessing we enjoy as Englishmen: A flagrant proof this, that shallow draughts in politicks and legislation confound and distract us, and that an extravagant zeal often defeats its own purposes. . . .

You'l easily perceive, that what I have said is upon the general design of his honour's pamphlet; if he had divided his argument with any precision, I would have followed him with somewhat more of method; The dispute between Great Britain and the colonies consists of two parts; first, the jurisdiction of parliament,—and, secondly, the exercise of that jurisdiction. His honour hath blended these together, and no where marked the division between them: The first I have principally remarked upon: As to the second, it can only turn upon the expediency or utility of those schemes which may, from time to time, be adopted by parliament, relative to the colonies. Under this head, I readily grant, they are at full liberty to remonstrate, petition, write pamphlets and newspapers, without number, to prevent any improper or unreasonable imposition: Nay, I would have them do all this with that spirit of freedom which Englishmen always have, and I hope ever will, exert; but let us not use our liberty for a cloak of maliciousness. Indeed I am very sure the loyalty of the colonies has ever been irreproachable; but from the pride of some, and the ignorance of others, the cry against mother country has spread from colony to colony; and it is to be feared, that prejudices and resentments are kindled among them which it will be difficult ever, thoroughly, to sooth or extinguish. It may become necessary for the supreme legislature of the nation to frame some code, and therein adjust the rights of the colonies, with precision and certainty, otherwise Great Britain will always be teazed with new claims about liberty and privileges.

III. Lord Lyttelton on the Authority of Parliament

The controversy over colonial rights was naturally a matter of grave concern in Great Britain, particularly to members of Parliament. As the colonial response to the Stamp Act was being debated in Parliament, these remarks were offered by one member, Lord Lyttelton.

How valid is the case he makes? How do you suppose Dickinson would have answered him had he been present?

FEBRUARY 10, 1766

In treating this question, I must tire your lordships with repeating many self-evident truths, but when persons of eminent knowledge and abilities dispute this point, I even doubt of my own reason.

I shall therefore take the liberty of laying before your lordships a few general maxims, not of party, but such as no statesman, no lawyer, has ever denied.

The first foundation of civil government is, that a civil society was formed by men entering into society on what may properly be called an original compact, and entrusting government with a power over their persons, liberties, and estates, for the safety of the whole. In what form or manner this power is to be exercised depends on the laws and constitutions of different countries.

The Parliamentary History of England (London, 1813), XVI, pp. 166–68.

There cannot be two rights existing in government at the same time, which would destroy each other; a right in government to make laws, and a right in the people, or any part, to oppose or disobey such laws. Another great principle of policy is, that in all states, democratical, aristocratical, or monarchical, or in mixed states, as Great Britain, the government must rest somewhere, and that must be fixed, or otherwise there is an end of all government. "Imperium in imperio."

But these great maxims which imply a subjection to the supreme government or legislature, do not exclude the existence of inferior legislatures with restrained powers, subject to the superior legislature. That the colonies are of this kind the many statutes made here to bind them since their first settlement plainly evince.

They went out subjects of Great Britain, and unless they can shew a new compact made between them and the parliament of Great Britain (for the king alone could not make a new compact with them) they still are subjects to all intents and purposes whatsoever. If they are subjects, they are liable to the laws of the country. Indeed, they complain that the laying internal taxes on them takes away the right of laying such taxes: this I deny; they certainly may lay such internal taxes for local purposes, and the parliament here may lay such taxes on particular occasions.

The last great maxim of this and every other free government is, that "No subject is bound by any law to which he is not actually or virtually consenting." If the colonies are subjects of Great Britain, they are represented and consent to all statutes. . . .

The only question before your lordships is, whether the American colonies are a part of the dominions of the crown of Great Britain? If not, the parliament has no jurisdiction, if they are, as many statutes have declared them to be, they must be proper objects of our legislature: and by declaring them exempt from one statute or law, you declare them no longer subjects of Great Britain, and make them small independent communities not entitled to your protection.

If opinions of this weight are to be taken up, and argued upon through mistake or timidity, we shall have many legislators; we shall have Lycurguses, and Solons, in every coffee-house, tavern, and gin-shop in London.

The weight of taxes in England are heavy, and admit but this doctrine, many thousands who have no vote in electing representatives, will follow their brethren in America, in refusing submission to any taxes. The commons of this metropolis will with pleasure hear a doctrine propagated last week, of equality being the natural right of all.

We have a constitution which, with all its faults, is a good one, but the doctrine of equality may be carried to the destruction of this monarchy. Cromwell himself did not attempt to say that taxes were to be raised without the consent of the legislature.

IV. Lord Camden on the Authority of Parliament

A different point of view was presented by another member of Parliament, Lord Camden. He responded to Lord Lyttelton immediately in the parliamentary debate, and then, two weeks later, delivered the more formal speech from which these excerpts are taken.

What course of action might Parliament have followed had his view predominated? Why do you suppose it was not followed? How might governments be made to see their problems in larger historical perspectives?

FEBRUARY 24, 1766

My position is this—I repeat it—I will maintain it to my last hour,—taxation and representation are inseparable;—this position is founded on the laws of nature; it is more, it is itself an eternal law of nature; for whatever is a man's own, is absolutely his own; no man hath a right to take it from him without his consent, either expressed by himself or representative; whoever attempts to do it, attempts an injury; whoever does it, commits a robbery; he throws down and destroys the distinction between liberty and slavery. Taxation and representation are coeval with and essential to this constitution. I wish the maxim of Machiavel was followed, that of examining a constitution, at certain periods, according to its first principles; this would correct abuses and supply defects. I wish the times would bear it, and that men's minds were cool enough to enter upon such a task, and that the representative authority of this kingdom was more equally settled. I am sure some histories, of late published, have done great mischief; to endeavour to fix the æra when the House of Commons began in this kingdom, is a most pernicious and destructive attempt; to fix it in an Edward's or Henry's reign, is owing to the idle dreams of some whimsical, ill-judging antiquarians: but, my lords, this is a point too important to be left to such wrong-headed people. When did the House of Commons first begin? when, my lords? it began with the constitution, it grew up with the constitution; there is not a blade of grass growing in the most obscure corner of this kingdom, which is not, which was not ever, represented since the constitution began; there is not a blade of grass, which when taxed, was not taxed by the consent of the proprietor. . . . My lords, I challenge any one to point out the time when any tax was laid upon any person by parliament, that person being unrepresented in parliament. My lords, the parliament laid a tax upon the palatinate of Chester, and ordered commissioners to collect it there: as commissioners were ordered to collect it in other counties; but the palatinate refused to comply; they addressed the king by petition, setting forth, that the English parliament had no right to tax them, that they had a parliament of their own, that they had always taxed themselves, and therefore desired the king to order his commissioners not to proceed. My lords, the king received the petition; he did not declare them either seditious or rebellious, but allowed their plea, and they taxed themselves. Your lordships may see both the petition and the king's answer in the records in the Tower. The clergy taxed themselves; when the parliament attempted to tax them, they stoutly refused; said they were not represented there; that they had a parliament of their own, which represented the clergy; that they would tax themselves; they did so. Much stress has been laid upon Wales, before it was united as it now is, as if the King, standing in the place of their former princes of that country, raised money by his own authority; but the real fact is otherwise; for I find that, long before Wales was subdued, the northern counties of that principality had representatives, and a parliament or assembly. As to Ireland, my lords, before that kingdom had a parliament as it now has, if your lordships will examine the old records, you will find, that when a tax was to be laid on that country, the Irish sent over here representatives; and the same records will inform your lordships, what wages those representatives received from their constituents. In short, my lords, from the whole of our history, from the earliest period, you will find that taxation and representation were always united; so true are the words of that consummate reasoner and politician Mr. Locke. I before alluded to his book; I have again consulted him; and finding what he writes so applicable to the subject in hand, and so much in favour of my sentiments, I beg your lordships' leave to read a little of this book.

"The supreme power cannot take from any man, any part of his property, without his own consent." Such are the words of this great man, and which are well worth your serious attention. His principles are drawn from the heart of our constitution, which he thoroughly understood, and will last as long as that shall last; and, to his immortal honour, I know not to what, under providence, the Revolution and all its happy effects, are more owing, than to the principles of government laid down by Mr. Locke. For these reasons, my lords, I can never give my assent to any bill for taxing the American colonies, while they remain unrepresented; for as to the distinction of virtual representation, it is so absurd as not to deserve an answer; I therefore pass it over with contempt. The forefathers of the Americans did not leave their native country, and subject themselves to every danger and distress, to be reduced to a state of slavery: they did not give up their rights; they looked for protection, and not for chains, from their mother country; by her they expected to be defended in the possession of their property, and not to be deprived of it: for, should the present power continue, there is nothing which they can call their own; or, to use the words of Mr. Locke, "What property have they in that, which another may, by right, take, when he pleases, to himself?"

For Further Reading

Books on the American Revolution abound. Among the best narratives treating all or part of the Revolutionary period are: Lawrence H. Gipson, *The*

Coming of the Revolution, 1763–1775* (1954); Merrill Jensen, *The Founding of a Nation: A History of the American Revolution, 1763–1776* (1968); Bernhard Knollenberg, *Origin of the American Revolution, 1759–1766** (1961); John C. Miller, *Origins of the American Revolution** (1948); Edmund S. Morgan, *The Birth of the Republic, 1763–1789** (1956); and Esmond Wright, *The Fabric of Freedom, 1763–1800** (1961). A detailed study of the Stamp Act is found in *The Stamp Act Crisis** (1953), by Edmund S. and Helen M. Morgan.

A brief summary of revolutionary political thought is found in *The Political Thought of the American Revolution** (1963), by Clinton Rossiter. Bernard Bailyn's *Pamphlets of the American Revolution, Vol. I, 1750–1765* (1965) contains an excellent introductory essay and important prewar pamphlets; the essay is published separately in *The Ideological Origins of the American Revolution* (1967). The thought of John Dickinson is the subject of D. L. Jacobson's *John Dickinson and the Revolution in Pennsylvania* (1965).

Of the numerous collections of interpretive essays, the most comprehensive are *The Reinterpretation of the American Revolution** (1968), edited by Jack P. Greene; and *Essays on the American Revolution** (1970), edited by David L. Jacobsen. Another book edited by Greene is *The Ambiguity of the American Revolution** (1968).

Problems books include: Robert F. Berkhofer, Jr., ed., *The American Revolution: The Critical Issues** (1971); Richard J. Hooker, ed., *The American Revolution: The Search for Meaning** (1970); John R. Howe, Jr., ed., *The Role of Ideology in the American Revolution** (1970); Edmund S. Morgan, ed., *The American Revolution: Two Centuries of Interpretation** (1965); Charles R. Ritcheson, ed., *The American Revolution: The Anglo-American Relation, 1763–1794** (1969); and John C. Wahlke, ed., *The Causes of the American Revolution** (1962).

Tracts of the American Revolution* (1967), edited by Merrill Jensen, is an excellent collection of primary sources; several excerpts were used in this chapter. *The Debate on the American Revolution** (1965), edited by Max Beloff, is another good collection. *Empire and Nation** (1962), Forrest McDonald, ed., contains the complete Dickinson letters.

A number of the volumes suggested at the end of the next chapter are also appropriate here.

*Paperbound edition available.

5. Revolution or Reconciliation?

During the winter of 1775–76 the Second Continental Congress pondered the alternatives it could follow in the growing crisis between the American colonies and Great Britain. First, if it chose to do so, the Continental Congress could try to forget or overlook everything that had happened since 1763, thereby accepting the English government's view of the relationship between herself and the colonies. Second, the colonies could remain in the Empire but resist by arguments and by force of arms until Great Britain recognized the colonial position. Third, the colonies could declare their independence and fight to be separated from Great Britain so they could practice on their own what they believed to be their "natural" rights. In the summer of 1776, the faction in Congress favoring the third alternative was able to persuade a majority of the delegates to vote for independence.

In their quest for independence the Americans faced one of the greatest military powers in the Western world, and every advantage appeared to be on the side of the forces of King George III. Because of this factor, many Americans hoped that even though independence had been declared, some type of accommodation could be reached. Both sides gave lip service to this hope for reconciliation, but only the British made serious attempts to start negotiations aimed at keeping the colonies within the Empire. The colonies, represented by the Continental Congress, had committed themselves to independence, and as the rebellion progressed they became more and more convinced of the justice of their cause. Just or not, however, the attempts at reconciliation did worry those who advocated independence. These attempts, then, were bitterly attacked as mere shams by the patriot pamphleteers who thought the British were attempting to win by promises what they could never do by force of arms.

Core Document

Crisis: II

THOMAS PAINE

When Thomas Paine arrived in America in 1774, the crisis between the colonies and Great Britain was approaching the breaking point. Almost immediately Paine began a long career of political agitation. On January 10, 1776, he published anonymously the influential pamphlet Common Sense, *which by his count sold 120,000 copies in three months. After the Second Continental Congress declared America's independence in July 1776, Paine wrote the first in a series of pamphlets entitled* The American Crisis, *which appeared from 1776 to 1783. These pamphlets were intended to help strengthen the resolve of the patriots, for Paine well knew, as he declared in* Crisis: I, *that these were "the times that try men's souls."*

In Crisis: II *(1777) he lectured Lord Howe, the British military commander in America, on the British presence in America. This pamphlet was prompted by Howe's issuance of several proclamations in 1776 promising clemency to the American rebels if they would end their resistance. Paine tried to overcome the danger of these promises being accepted by pointing out to Howe, and especially to the Americans, the injustices Howe had committed and why the British could never win the war. If Howe were a reasonable man, Paine believed, he would recognize the failure of his mission and the failure of Britain in America, for the patriots were committed to a policy of independence and would never retreat from the path they had taken.*

In studying Crisis: II, *note what Paine believed to be:*
- *his purpose in writing this pamphlet.*
- *the meaning of reconciliation on George III's terms.*
- *the relationship between the Congress and the people.*
- *Howe's injustices toward the people of America.*
- *the prospects of an American victory.*
- *the necessity of the British making peace at once.*

Universal empire is the prerogative of a writer. His concerns are with all mankind, and though he cannot command their obedience, he can assign them

Daniel Edwin Wheeler, ed., *The Life and Writings of Thomas Paine* (New York: Vincent Parke, 1908), III, pp. 17–47.

their duty. The Republic of Letters is more ancient than monarchy, and of far higher character in the world than the vassal Court of Britain; he that rebels against reason is a real rebel, but he that in defense of reason, rebels against tyranny, has a better title to *"Defender of the Faith,"* than George III.

As a military man, Your Lordship may hold out the sword of war, and call it the *"ultima ratio regum:"* the last reason of Kings; we in return can show you the sword of justice, and call it, "the best scourge of tyrants." The first of these two may threaten, or even frighten for a while, and cast a sickly languor over an insulted people, but reason will soon recover the debauch, and restore them again to tranquil fortitude.

Your Lordship, I find, has now commenced [to be an] author, and published a *Proclamation:* I have published a *Crisis;* as they stand, they are the antipodes of each other; both cannot rise at once, and one of them must descend; and so quick is the revolution of things, that Your Lordship's performance, I see, has already fallen many degrees from its first place, and is now just visible on the edge of the political horizon.

It is surprising to what a pitch of infatuation, blind folly and obstinacy will carry mankind, and Your Lordship's drowsy proclamation is a proof that it does not even quit them in their sleep. Perhaps you thought America too was taking a nap, and therefore chose, like Satan to Eve, to whisper the delusion softly, lest you should awaken her. This continent, Sir, is too extensive to sleep all at once, and too watchful, even in its slumbers, not to startle at the unhallowed foot of an invader. You may issue your proclamations, and welcome, for we have learned to "reverence ourselves," and scorn the insulting ruffian that employs, you.

. . . But your master has commanded, and you have not enough of nature left to refuse. Surely! there must be something strangely degenerating in the love of monarchy, that can so strangely wear a man down to an ingrate, and make him proud to lick the dust that kings have trod upon.

A few more years, should you survive them, will bestow on you the title of "an old man": and in some hour of future reflection you may probably find the fitness of Wolsey's despairing penitence—"had I served my God as faithfully as I have served my king, he would not thus have forsaken me in my old age." . . .

. . . [Y]ou sunk yourself below the character of a private gentleman. That I may not seem to accuse you unjustly, I shall state the circumstance: by a verbal invitation of yours, communicated to Congress by General Sullivan, then a prisoner on his parole, you signified your desire of conferring with some members of that body as private gentlemen. It was beneath the dignity of the American Congress to pay any regard to a message that at best was but a genteel affront, and had too much of the ministerial complexion of tampering with private persons; and which might probably have been the case, had the gentlemen who were deputed on the business, possessed that kind of easy virtue which an English courtier is so truly distinguished by. Your request, however, was complied with, for honest men are naturally more tender of their civil than their political fame.

The interview ended as every sensible man thought it would; for Your Lordship knows, as well as the writer of the "Crisis" that it is impossible for the King of England to promise the repeal, or even the revisal of any acts of Parliament; wherefore, on your part, you had nothing to say, more than to request, in the room of demanding, the entire surrender of the continent; and then, if that was complied with, to promise that the inhabitants should escape with their lives. This was the upshot of the conference. You informed the conferees that you were two months in soliciting these powers. We ask, what powers? for as commissioner you have none. If you mean the power of pardoning, it is an oblique proof that your master was determined to sacrifice all before him; and that you were two months in dissuading him from his purpose. Another evidence of his savage obstinacy!

From your own account of the matter we may justly draw these two conclusions: first, that you serve a monster; and second, that never was a messenger sent on a more foolish errand than yourself. This plain language may perhaps sound uncouthly to an ear vitiated by courtly refinements; but words were made for use, and the fault lies in deserving them, or the abuse in applying them unfairly.

Soon after your return to New York, you published a very illiberal and unmanly handbill against the Congress; for it was certainly stepping out of the line of common civility, first to screen your national pride by soliciting an interview with them as private gentlemen. and in the conclusion to endeavor to deceive the multitude by making a handbill attack on the whole body of the Congress; you got them together under one name, and abused them under another. But the king you serve, and the cause you support, afford you so few instances of acting the gentleman, that out of pity to your situation the Congress pardoned the insult by taking no notice of it.

You say in that handbill, "that they, (the Congress,) disavowed every purpose for reconciliation not consonant with their extravagant and inadmissible claim of independence." Why, God bless me! what have you to do with our independence? We ask no leave of yours to set it up; we ask no money of yours to support it; we can do better without your fleets and armies than with them; you may soon have enough to do to protect yourselves without being burdened with us. We are very willing to be at peace with you, to buy of you and sell to you, and, like young beginners in the world, to work for our living; therefore, why do you put yourselves out of cash, when we know you cannot spare it, and we do not desire you to run into debt?

I am willing, Sir, you should see your folly in every point of view I can place it in, and for that reason descend sometimes to tell you in jest what I wish you to see in earnest. But to be more serious with you, why do you say, "their independence"? To set you right, Sir, we tell you, that the independency is ours, not theirs. The Congress were authorized by every state on the continent to publish it to all the world, and in so doing are not to be considered as the inventors, but only as the heralds that proclaimed it, or the office from which the sense of the people received a legal form; and it was as much as any or all their heads were worth, to have treated with you on the subject of submission under any name whatever. But we know the men in whom we have trusted; can England say the same of her Parliament? . . .

I am not for declaring war with every man that appears not so warm as myself: difference of constitution, temper, habit of speaking, and many other things, will go a great way in fixing the outward character of a man, yet simple honesty may remain at bottom. Some men have naturally a military turn, and can brave hardships and the risk of life with a cheerful face; others have not; no slavery appears to them so great as the fatigue of arms, and no terror so powerful as that of personal danger.

What can we say? We cannot alter nature, neither ought we to punish the son because the father begot him in a cowardly mood. However, I believe most men have more courage than they know of, and that a little at first is enough to begin with. I knew the time when I thought that the whistling of a cannon ball would have frightened me almost to death: but I have since tried it, and find that I can stand it with as little discomposure, and, I believe, with a much easier conscience than Your Lordship.

The same dread would return to me again were I in your situation, for my solemn belief of your cause is, that it is hellish and damnable, and, under that conviction, every thinking man's heart *must* fail him. . . .

Your avowed purpose here, is to kill, conquer, plunder, pardon, and enslave: and the ravages of your army through the Jerseys have been marked with as much barbarism as if you had openly professed yourself the prince of ruffians; not even the appearance of humanity has been preserved, either on the march or the retreat of your troops; no general order, that I could ever learn, has ever been issued to prevent or even forbid your troops from robbery, whereever they came; and the only instance of justice, if it can be called such, which has distinguished you for impartiality, is, that you treated and plundered all alike: what could not be carried away has been destroyed, and mahogany furniture has been deliberately laid on fire for fuel, rather than the men should be fatigued with cutting wood.

There was a time when the Whigs confided much in your supposed candor, and the Tories rested themselves in your favor; the experiments have now been made, and failed; in every town, nay, every cottage in the Jerseys, where your arms have been, is a testimony against you. How you may rest under this sacrifice of character I know not; but this I know, that you sleep and rise with the daily curses of thousands upon you: perhaps the misery which the Tories have suffered by your proffered mercy, may give them some claim to their country's pity, and be in the end the best favor you could show them.

In a folio general-order book belonging to Colonel Rhal's battalion, taken at Trenton, and now in the possession of the Council of Safety for the state, the following barbarous order is frequently repeated: "His Excellency the *commander-in-chief* orders, that all inhabitants who shall be found with arms, not having an officer with them, shall be immediately taken and hung up."

How many you may thus have privately sacrificed, we know not, and the account can only be settled in another world. Your treatment of prisoners, in order to distress them to enlist into your infernal service, is not to be equaled by any instance in Europe. Yet this is the humane Lord Howe and his brother, whom the Tories and their three-quarter kindred, the Quakers, or some of them at least, have been holding up for patterns of justice and mercy!

A bad cause will ever be supported by bad means and bad men; and whoever will be at the pains of examining strictly into things, will find that one and the same spirit of oppression and impiety, more or less, governs through your whole party in both countries. Not many days ago, I accidentally fell in company with a person of this city noted for espousing your cause, and on my remarking to him, "that it appeared clear to me, by the late providential turn of affairs, that God Almighty was visible on our side," he replied, "We care nothing for that, you may have Him, and welcome; if we have but enough of the devil on our side, we shall do." However carelessly this might be spoken, matters not, 'tis still the insensible principle that directs all your conduct, and will at last most assuredly deceive and ruin you.

If ever a nation was mad and foolish, blind to its own interest and bent on its own destruction, it is Britain. There are such things as national sins, and though the punishment of individuals may be reserved to *another* world, national punishment can only be inflicted in *this* world.

Britain, as a nation, is, in my inmost belief, the greatest and most ungrateful offender against God on the face of the whole earth: blessed with all the commerce she could wish for, and furnished, by a vast extension of dominion, with the means of civilizing both the eastern and western world, she has made no other use of both than proudly to idolize her own "thunder," and rip up the bowels of whole countries for what she could get. Like Alexander, she has made war her sport, and inflicted misery for prodigality's sake. The blood of India is not yet repaid, nor the wretchedness of Africa yet requited. Of late she has enlarged her list of national cruelties, by her butcherly destruction of the Caribs of St. Vincent's, and returning an answer by the sword to the meek prayer for *"Peace, liberty and safety."*

These are serious things, and whatever a foolish tyrant, a debauched court, a trafficking legislature, or a blinded people may think, the national account with heaven must some day or other be settled: all countries have sooner or later been called to their reckoning; the proudest empires have sunk when the balance was struck; and Britain, like an individual penitent, must undergo her day of sorrow, and the sooner it happens to her the better: as I wish it over, I wish it to come, but withal wish that it may be as light as possible.

Perhaps Your Lordship has no taste for serious things; by your connections in England I should suppose not: therefore I shall drop this part of the subject, and take it up in a line in which you will better understand me.

By what means, may I ask, do you expect to conquer America? If you could not effect it in the summer, when our army was less than yours, nor in the winter, when we had none, how are you to do it? In point of generalship you have been outwitted, and in point of fortitude outdone: your advantages turn out to your loss, and show us that it is in our power to ruin you by gifts: like a game of drafts, we can move out of *one* square to let you come in, in order that we may afterwards take two or three for one; and as we can always keep a double corner for ourselves, we can always prevent a total defeat.

You cannot be so insensible, as not to see that we have two to one the advantage of you, because we conquer by a drawn game, and you lose by it. Burgoyne might have taught Your Lordship this knowledge; he has been long a student in the doctrine of chances.

I have no other idea of conquering countries than by subduing the armies which defend them: have you done this, or can you do it? If you have not, it would be civil in you to let your proclamations alone for the present; otherwise, you will ruin more Tories by your grace and favor, than you will Whigs by your arms.

Were you to obtain possession of this city, you would not know what to do with it more than to plunder it. To hold it in the manner you hold New York, would be an additional dead weight upon your hands; and if a general conquest is your object, you had better be without the city than with it. When you have defeated all our armies, the cities will fall into your hands of themselves; but to creep into them in the manner you got into Princeton, Trenton, etc., is like robbing an orchard in the night before the fruit be ripe, and running away in the morning.

Your experiment in the Jerseys is sufficient to teach you that you have something more to do than barely to get into other people's houses; and your new converts, to whom you promised all manner of protection, and seduced into new guilt by pardoning them from their former virtues, must begin to have a very contemptible opinion both of your power and your policy. Your authority in the Jerseys is now reduced to the small circle which your army occupies, and your proclamation is nowhere else seen unless it be to be laughed at.

The mighty subduers of the continent have retreated into a nut shell, and the proud forgivers of our sins are fled from those they came to pardon; and all this at a time when they were dispatching vessel after vessel to England with the great news of every day. In short, you have managed your Jersey expedition so very dexterously, that the dead, only, are conquerors, because none will dispute the ground with them.

In all the wars which you have formerly been concerned in, you had only armies to contend with; in this case you have both an army and a country to combat with. In former wars, the countries followed the fate of their capitals; Canada fell with Quebec, and Minorca with Port Mahon or St. Philip's; by subduing those, the conquerors opened a way into, and became masters of the country: here it is otherwise; if you get possession of a city here, you are obliged to shut yourselves up in it, and can make no other use of it than to spend your country's money in. This is all the advantage you have drawn from New York; and you would draw less from Philadelphia, because it requires more force to keep it, and is much further from the sea. A pretty figure you and the Tories would cut in this city, with a river full of ice, and a town full of fire; for the immediate consequence of your getting here would be, that you would be cannonaded out again, and the Tories be obliged to make good the damage; and this, sooner or later, will be the fate of New York.

I wish to see the city saved, not so much from military as from natural motives. 'Tis the hiding place of women and children, and Lord Howe's proper business is with our armies. When I put all the circumstances together which ought to be taken, I laugh at your notion of conquering America. Because you live in a little country, where an army might run over the whole in a few days, and where a single company of soldiers might put a multitude to the rout, you expected to find it the same here.

It is plain that you brought over with you all the narrow notions you were bred up with, and imagined that a proclamation in the King's name was to do great things; but Englishmen always travel for knowledge, and Your Lordship, I hope, will return, if you return at all, much wiser than you came.

We may be surprised by events we did not expect, and in that interval of recollection you may gain some temporary advantage. Such was the case a few weeks ago, but we soon ripen again into reason, collect our strength, and while you are preparing for a triumph, we come upon you with a defeat. Such it has been, and such it would be were you to try it a hundred times over.

Were you to garrison the places you might march over, in order to secure their subjection (for remember you can do it by no other means), your army would be like a stream of water running to nothing. By the time you reached from New York to Virginia, you would be reduced to a string of drops not capable of hanging together; while we, by retreating from state to state, like a river turning back upon itself, would acquire strength in the same proportion as you lost it, and in the end be capable of overwhelming you. The country, in the meantime, would suffer, but it is a day of suffering, and we ought to expect it.

What we contend for is worthy the affliction we may go through. If we get but bread to eat, and any kind of raiment to put on, we ought not only to be contented, but thankful. More than *that* we ought not to look for, and less than *that* heaven has not yet suffered us to want. He that would sell his birthright for a little *salt,* is as worthless as he that sold it for *porridge* without salt. And he that would part with it for a gay coat, or a *plain* coat, ought forever to be a slave in buff.

What are salt, sugar and finery, to the inestimable blessings of "liberty and safety"! Or what are the inconveniences of a few months to the tributary bondages of ages? The meanest peasant in America, blest with these sentiments, is a happy man compared with a New York Tory; he can eat his morsel without repining, and when he has done, can sweeten it with a repast of wholesome air; he can take his child by the hand and bless it, without feeling the conscious shame of neglecting a parent's duty.

In making these remarks I have several objects in view.

On your part, they are to expose the folly of your pretended authority as a commissioner; the wickedness of your cause in general; and the impossibility of your conquering us at any rate. On the part of the public, my intention is, to show them their true and solid interest: to encourage them to their own good, to remove the fears and falsities which bad men have spread, and weak men have encouraged; and to excite in all men a love for union, and a cheerfulness for duty. I shall submit one more case to you respecting your conquest of this country, and then proceed to new observations.

Suppose our armies in every part of this continent were immediately to disperse, every man to his home, or where else he might be safe, and engage to re-assemble again on a certain future day; it is clear that you would then have no army to contend with, yet you would be as much at a loss in that case as you are now; you would be afraid to send your troops in parties over the continent, either to disarm, or prevent us from assembling, lest they should not return; and while you kept them together, having no army of ours to dispute with, you could not call it a conquest; you might furnish out a pompous page in the *London Gazette* or a New York paper, but when we returned, at the appointed time, you would have the same work to do that you had at first.

It has been the folly of Britain to suppose herself more powerful than she really is, and by that means she has arrogated to herself a rank in the world she is not entitled to: for more than this century past she has not been able to carry on a war without foreign assistance. In Marlborough's campaigns, and from that day to this, the number of German troops and officers assisting her have been about equal with her own; ten thousand Hessians were sent to England last war to protect her from a French invasion; and she would have cut but a poor figure in her Canadian and West Indian expeditions, had not America been lavish both of her money and men to help her along. The only instance in which she was engaged singly, that I can recollect, was against the rebellion in Scotland, in the years 1745 and 1746, and in that, out of three battles, she was twice beaten, till by thus reducing their numbers (as we shall yours), and taking a supply ship that was coming to Scotland with clothes, arms and money (as we have often done), she was at last enabled to defeat them.

England was never famous by land; her officers have generally been suspected of cowardice, have more of the air of a dancing-master than a soldier, and by the samples which we have taken prisoners, we give the preference to ourselves. Her strength, of late, has lain in her extravagance; but as her finances and credit are now low, her sinews in that line begin to fail fast.

As a nation she is the poorest in Europe; for were the whole kingdom, and all that is in it, to be put up for sale like the estate of a bankrupt, it would not fetch as much as she owes; yet this thoughtless wretch must go to war, and with the avowed design, too, of making us beasts of burden, to support her in riot and debauchery, and to assist her afterward in distressing those nations who are now our best friends. This ingratitude may suit a Tory, or the unchristian peevishness of a fallen Quaker, but none else.

'Tis the unhappy temper of the English to be pleased with any war, right or wrong, be it but successful; but they soon grow discontented with ill fortune, and it is an even chance that they are as clamorous for peace next summer, as the King and his ministers were for war last winter. In this natural view of things, Your Lordship stands in a very critical situation: your whole character is now staked upon your laurels; if they wither, you wither with them; if they flourish, you cannot live long to look at them; and at any rate, the black account hereafter is not far off.

What lately appeared to us misfortunes, were only blessings in disguise; and the seeming advantages on your side have turned out to our profit. Even our loss of this city, as far as we can see, might be a principal gain to us: the more surface you spread over, the thinner you will be, and the easier wiped away; and our consolation under that apparent disaster would be, that the estates of the Tories would become securities for the repairs. In short, there is no old ground we can fail upon, but some new foundation rises again to support us. "We have put, Sir, our hands to the plow, and cursed be he that looketh back."

Your King, in his speech to Parliament last spring, declared, "That he had no doubt but the great force they had enabled him to send to America, would effectually reduce the rebellious colonies." It has not, neither can it; but it has done just enough to lay the foundation of its own next year's ruin. You are sensible that you left England in a divided, distracted state of politics, and, by the command you had here, you became a principal prop in the court party; their fortunes rest on yours; by a single expression you can fix their value with the public, and the degree to which their spirits shall rise or fall; they are in your hands as stock, and you have the secret of the *alley* with you.

Thus situated and connected, you became the unintentional mechanical instrument of your own and their overthrow. The King and his ministers put conquest out of doubt, and the credit of both depended on the proof. To support them in the interim, it was necessary that you should make the most of everything, and we can tell by Hugh Gaine's New York paper what the complexion of the *London Gazette* is.

With such a list of victories the nation cannot expect you will ask new supplies; and to confess your want of them, would give the lie to your triumphs, and impeach the King and his ministers of treasonable deception. If you make the necessary demand at home, your party sinks; if you make it not, you sink yourself; to ask it now is too late, and to ask it before was too soon, and unless it arrive quickly it will be of no use. In short, the part you have to act, cannot be acted; and I am fully persuaded that all you have to trust to is, to do the best you can with what force you have got, or little more.

Though we have greatly exceeded you in point of generalship and bravery of men, yet, as a people, we have not entered into the full soul of enterprise; for I, who know England and the disposition of the people well, am confident, that it is easier for us to effect a revolution there, than you a conquest here; a few thousand men landed in England with the declared design of deposing the present King, bringing his ministers to trial, and setting up the Duke of Gloucester in his stead, would assuredly carry their point, while you were grovelling here, ignorant of the matter. As I send all my papers to England, this, like "Common Sense," will find its way there; and though it may put one party on their guard, it will inform the other, and the nation in general, of our design to help them.

Thus far, Sir, I have endeavored to give you a picture of present affairs: you may draw from it what conclusions you please. I wish as well to the true prosperity of England as you can, but I consider INDEPENDENCE *as America's natural right and interest,* and never could see any real disservice it would be to Britain. If an English merchant receives an order, and is paid for it, it signifies nothing to him who governs the country. This is my creed of politics. If I have anywhere expressed myself over-warmly, 'tis from a fixed, immovable hatred I have, and ever had, to cruel men and cruel measures. I have likewise an aversion to monarchy, as being too debasing to the dignity of man; but I never troubled others with my notions till very lately, nor ever published a syllable in England in my life.

What I write is pure nature, and my pen and my soul have ever gone together. My writings I have always given away, reserving only the expense of printing and paper, and sometimes not even that. I never courted either fame or interest, and my manner of life, to those who know it, will justify what I say. My study is to be useful, and if Your Lordship loves mankind as well as I do, you would, seeing you cannot conquer us, cast about and lend your hand toward accomplishing a peace.

Our independence, with God's blessing, we will maintain against all the world; but as we wish to avoid evil ourselves, we wish not to inflict it on others. I am never over-inquisitive into the secrets of the Cabinet, but I have some notion, that if you neglect the present opportunity, that it will not be in our power to make a separate peace with you afterwards; for whatever treaties or alliances we form, we shall most faithfully abide by; wherefore you may be deceived if you think you can make it with us at any time. A lasting independent peace is my wish, end and aim; and to accomplish that, *"I pray God the Americans may never be defeated, and I trust while they have good officers, and are well commanded,"* and willing to be commanded, *"that they* NEVER WILL."

COMMON SENSE
Philadelphia, Jan. 13, 1777

Discussion Starters

1. What issues of the American Revolution did this pamphlet bring to the reader?

2. Identify and evaluate the wartime conditions on which Paine based his boast that "we conquer by a drawn game"?

3. Speculate on Lord Howe's likely response to *Crisis: II.* Similarly, speculate on how "public opinion" in England might have reacted.

4. In what respects are the points on winning wars raised by Paine applicable to other wars? What is the difference, for example, between the Germans

fighting on their own soil in World War II and the Vietnamese fighting
at home against France and the United States in the 1950s and 1960s?

Related Documents

I. Letter to the President of the Congress

GEORGE WASHINGTON

*On August 27, 1776, the American army under George Washington was badly
defeated on Long Island. The defeat forced the Americans to retreat from New
York City, leaving it open to occupation by the British forces of Sir William
Howe. The retreat caused the Americans to pull back to their fortified positions
at Harlem, where they watched to see what the British would do next. It was
during this waiting period that Washington wrote to the President of the Congress about the condition of his army.*

*How could Washington be so pessimistic about the very military prospects
Paine viewed so optimistically? What measures did Washington believe the army
had to take before it could become an effective force?*

SEPTEMBER 24, 1776

Sir: From the hours allotted to sleep, I will borrow a few moments to convey
my thoughts on sundry important matters to Congress. I shall offer them, with
that sincerity which ought to characterize a man of candour; and with the
freedom which may be used in giving useful information without incurring the
imputation of presumption.

We are now as it were, upon the eve of another dissolution of our Army.
The remembrance of the difficulties which happened upon that occasion last
year, the consequences which might have followed the change, if proper advantages had been taken by the Enemy; added to a knowledge of the present
temper and situation of the troops, reflect but a very gloomy prospect upon
the appearance of things now and satisfy me beyond the possibility of doubt
that unless some speedy and effectual measures are adopted by Congress our
cause will be lost.

It is in vain to expect that any (or more than a trifling) part of this Army
will again engage in the service on the encouragement offered by Congress.
When men find that their townsmen and companions are receiving 20, 30, and
more dollars for a few months service (which is truly the case) it cannot be
expected; without using compulsion; and to force them into the service would

John C. Fitzpatrick, ed., *The Writings of George Washington* (Washington, D.C.: United States
Printing Office, 1932), VI, pp. 106–16.

answer no valuable purpose. When men are irritated and the Passions inflamed they fly hastily and cheerfully to arms. But after the first emotions are over, to expect, among such people as compose the bulk of an army, that they are influenced by any other principles than those of interest, is to look for what never did, and I fear never will happen; the Congress will deceive themselves therefore if they expect it.

A soldier reasoned with upon the goodness of the cause he is engaged in and the inestimable rights he is contending for hears you with patience, and acknowledges the truth of your observations, but adds, that it is of no more importance to him than others—The officer makes you the same reply, with this further remark, that his pay will not support him, and he cannot ruin himself and family to serve his Country when every member of the community is equally interested and benefited by his labours. The few therefore, who act upon principles of disinterestedness are, comparatively speaking, no more than a drop in the Ocean. It becomes evidently clear then that as this contest is not likely to be the work of a day. The War must be carried on systematically, and to do it you must have good officers. There are, in my judgment, no other possible means to obtain them but by establishing your army upon a permanent footing and giving your officers good pay. This will induce gentlemen, and men of character to engage; and till the bulk of your officers are composed of such persons as are actuated by principles of honour and a spirit of enterprise, you have little to expect from them. They ought to have such allowances as will enable them to live like, and support the characters of gentlemen. Not be driven by a scanty pittance to the low and dirty arts which many of them practice to filch the Public of more than the difference of pay would amount to upon an ample allowance. Besides, something is due to the man who puts his life in his hands, hazards his health, and forsakes the sweets of domestic enjoyments. . . .

With respect to the men, nothing but a good bounty can obtain them upon a permanent establishment; and for no shorter time than the continuance of the war ought they to be engaged. As facts incontestibly prove that the difficulty and cost of enlistments increase with time. When the Army was first raised at Cambridge, I am persuaded the men might have been got without a bounty from the War. After this they began to see that the contest was not likely to end so speedily as was imagined and to feel their consequence, by remarking, that to get the militia in, in the course of last year, many towns were induced to give them a bounty. . . . I shall therefore take the freedom of giving it as my opinion, that a good Bounty be immediately offered, aided by the proffer of at least 100, or 150 acres of land and a suit of clothes and blanket, to each non-commissioned officer and soldier. As I have good authority for saying that however high the men's pay may appear it is barely sufficient in the present scarcity and dearness of all kinds of goods to keep them in clothes much less afford support to their families. If this encouragement then is given to the men and such pay allowed the officers as will induce gentlemen of character and liberal sentiments to engage, and proper care and precaution are used in the nomination (having more regard to the characters of persons than the number of men they can enlist) we should in a little time have an army able to cope with any that can be opposed to it as there are excellent materials to form one out of. But while the only merit an officer possesses is his ability to raise men while those men consider and treat him as an equal, and (in the character of an officer) regard him no more than a broomstick being mixed together as one common herd. No order, nor no discipline can prevail. Nor will the officer ever meet with that respect which is essentially necessary to due subordination.

To place any dependence upon militia is assuredly resting upon a broken staff. Men just dragged from the tender scenes of domestic life, unaccustomed to the din of arms, totally unacquainted with every kind of military skill which being followed by a want of confidence in themselves when opposed to troops regularly trained, disciplined, and appointed, superior in knowledge, and superior in arms makes them timid and ready to fly from their own shadows. Besides, the sudden change in their manner of living, (particularly in the lodging) brings on sickness in many, impatience in all, and such an unconquerable desire of returning to their respective homes that it not only produces shameful and scandalous desertions among themselves, but infuses the like spirit in others. Again, men accustomed to unbounded freedom and no control cannot brook the restraint which is indispensably necessary to the good order and government of an army; without which licentiousness and every kind of disorder triumphantly reign. To bring men to a proper degree of subordination is not the work of a day, a month or even a year. Unhappily for us and the cause we are engaged in the little discipline I have been labouring to establish in the army under my immediate command is in a manner done away by having such a mixture of troops as have been called together within these few months.

Relaxed and unfit as our Rules and Regulations of War are for the Government of an army the Militia (those properly so called, for of these we have two sorts, the Six Months Men and those sent in as a temporary aid) do not think themselves subject to them and therefore take liberties which the soldier is punished for. This creates jealousy; jealousy begets dissatisfaction, and these by degrees ripen into mutiny keeping the whole army in a confused and disordered state; rendering the time of those who wish to see regularity and good order prevail more unhappy than words can describe. Besides this, such repeated changes take place that all arrangement is set at nought and the constant fluctuation of things deranges every plan as fast as adopted.

These Sir, Congress may be assured are but a small part of the inconveniences which might be enumerated and attributed to Militia, but there is one that merits particular attention and that is the expense. Certain I am that it would be cheaper to have 50 or 100,000 men in constant pay then to depend upon half the number and supply the other half occasionally by militia. The time the latter is in pay before and after they are in camp, assembling and marching, the waste of ammunition, the consumption of stores which in spite of every resolution and requisition of Congress they must be furnished with or sent home. Added to other incidental expenses consequent upon their coming and conduct in camp surpasses all idea and destroys every kind of regularity and economy which you could establish among fixed and settled troops; and will, in my opinion prove (if the scheme is adhered to) the ruin of our cause.

The jealousies of a standing army and the evils to be apprehended from one are remote, and in my judgment, situated and circumstanced as we are, not at all to be dreaded. But the consequence of wanting one, according to my ideas, formed from the present view of things is certain and inevitable ruin. For if I was called upon to declare upon oath whether the Militia have been most serviceable or hurtful upon the whole I should subscribe to the latter. I do not mean by this however to arraign the conduct of Congress. In so doing I should equally condemn my own measures, (if I did not my judgment), but experience which is the best criterion to work by, so fully, so clearly, and decisively reprobates the practice of trusting to Militia that no man who regards order, regularity, and economy, or who has any regard for his own honor, character, or peace of mind, will risk them upon this issue. . . .

In a word the difficulties which have forever surrounded me since I have been in the service, and kept my mind constantly upon the stretch . . . added to consciousness of my inability to govern an army composed of such discordant parts and under such a variety of intricate and perplexing circumstances, induces not only a belief, but a thorough conviction in my mind that it will be impossible unless there is a thorough change in our military systems for me to conduct matters in such a manner as to give satisfaction to the public which is all the recompence I aim at, or ever wished for.

Before I conclude I must apologize for the liberties taken in this letter and for the blots and scratchings therein, not having time to give it more correctly. With truth I can add that with every sentiment of respect and esteem. I am, etc.

II. The Carlisle Commission of 1778

On February 6, 1778, the representatives of the United States and France signed a military alliance in Paris. The American commissioners, led by Benjamin Franklin, had played a waiting game based on the hope of an American military victory. This hope had been realized with the victories at Saratoga in September and October 1777. Once the French were convinced that the Americans had a good chance of success, as demonstrated by Saratoga, they were willing to enter openly into the conflict. Earlier, when the threat of a Franco-American alliance had reached England, the ministry of Lord North began to investigate the possibility of reconciliation with the rebels. This concern became formally translated in the winter of 1777–78 into a Peace Commission consisting of the Earl

Samuel E. Morison, ed., *Sources and Documents Illustrating the American Revolution* (Oxford, England: Clarendon Press, 1929), pp. 187–90, 192–93, 202–3.

of Carlisle, William Eden, George Johnstone, Lord Howe, and Sir William Howe. The following royal instructions to the commission made it quite clear that reconciliation was to be considered a serious policy of the British government.

What concessions were the British government ready to make to bring the colonies back into the Empire? In what sense do these concessions represent an admission of weakness and an acknowledgement that Paine's assertions were correct?

With these our instructions you will receive our commission under the great seal of Great Britain, constituting you, or any three of you our Commissioners with certain powers to treat, consult, and agree upon the means of quieting the disorders now subsisting in certain of our colonies, plantations, and provinces in North America. You are therefore to repair with all convenient speed to New York, or such other place in North America as you shall judge most proper; and when you shall have arrived in any of them you are to proceed to the execution of the trust we have reposed in you. For that purpose you, or any three of you are to communicate your arrival to the Commander-in-Chief of the American forces, or to any body of men, by whatever name known or distinguished, who may be supposed to represent the different provinces, colonies, and plantations in America.

And you are hereby directed to address them by any style or title which may describe them, and to lay before them a copy of the Act of Parliament by virtue of which we are enabled to appoint commissioners, together with a copy of our commission. We do direct you, or any three of you, to express your desire and readiness to receive or meet them or any of them authorized for that purpose at New York or any place which shall be mutually agreed upon; and that upon notice of the intention of all or any such persons constituting such body as aforesaid to confer with you, or any three of you, upon the subject of this our commission and these our instructions you do immediately dispatch safe conduct for them to the place at which it may be agreed to consult and confer.

You may likewise assure them that as soon as peace is established they shall thenceforth be protected in the antient course of their trade and commerce by the power of Great Britain; and we authorize you to admit of any claim or title to independency in any description of men during the time of treaty and for the purpose of treaty.

If, under pretence of diffidence and distrust, they should decline treating upon the ground that you are not authorized finally to conclude any treaty or agreement, inasmuch as any resolution must be reserved for the future approbation or disapprobation of us and our two Houses of Parliament, after observing that the Legislature might reasonably imagine that the matters to be discussed were of too great concernment to be delegated to individuals. Especially as you could not expect to meet with equal and corresponding powers in those persons who might act for and on the behalf of the thirteen revolted colonies, who may remind them that as a proof of the good faith and sincerity of the intentions of Great Britain, to promote a full and permanent reconciliation between Great Britain and the said colonies, the Legislature have spontaneously passed 'An Act for removing all doubt and apprehensions concerning taxation by the Parliament of Great Britain in any of the colonies, provinces, and plantations in North America and the West Indies; and for repealing so much of an Act made in the 7th year of our reign as imposes a duty upon tea imported from Great Britain into any colony or plantation in America, or relates thereto.' And they have also passed 'An Act for repealing an Act . . . entitled, An Act for the better regulating the Government of the Province of Massachusetts Bay in New England;' and also the Act enabling us to vest you, or any three of you, with the powers and authorities with which we have entrusted you and do intrust you, of suspending all Acts passed since 1763, and for other purposes therein mentioned.

And as a further proof of such sincerity, you, or any three of you, are authorized to consent as you are hereby authorized to consent to make any propositons that they can offer, and that you shall think reasonable and fit to be entertained, the subject of an immediate reference to us and our two Houses of Parliament separate from the other points of the treaty in which the disposition of us and our two said Houses of Parliament to promote, by every proper concession, the restoration of peace and union can with no probability be doubted. You may particularly agree to a proposal that if in the ensuing treaty any mode can be settled of providing by provincial forces for the sufficient security and protection of our subjects, no standing army shall be raised or kept within the said Colonies in time of Peace without their consent. And also that none of the antient governments or constitutions in the said colonies shall be changed or varied without the consent or request of such of our respective colonies, signified by their general assemblies.

If this should likewise fail to produce the desired effect of entering into a treaty, it may be proper that such propositions and offers should, in such manner as you shall see fit, be made public and known as generally as possible. . . . You are however, to avoid giving umbrage or jealousy to the powers with which you are publicly treating, and you are not to make any public appeal to the inhabitants of America at large until you shall be satisfied that such public body of men and the Commander-in-Chief of the American forces shall refuse to enter into or proceed in such treaty.

But such caution is not to prevent you, or any three of you, from entering into any correspondence or treaty with particular colonies, bodies of men, or individual persons to answer the purposes of the commission wherewith we have entrusted you if your attempt to enter into a treaty, or come to any conclusion with such representative body of men as we have before described should fail or miscarry.

And if you should at length despair of bringing such body or bodies of men to a treaty, or effectually to proceed in such treaty, you are, if you find it proper, finally to set forth a declaration, for the information of our well disposed subjects at large, in which, after reciting the Act and the commission with which we have thought fit to empower you, or any three of you, you shall, if you think proper, publish a proclamation, containing a declaration of the earnest wishes of us and our Parliament for composing any differences that have unhappily subsisted between Great Britain and our said colonies, and for the re-establishment of peace and union upon firm and lasting foundations, and the means which have been used to obtain such salutary and happy purposes.

The propriety, nature, and extent of a suspension of arms will be best determined upon the spot in conjunction with the commanders-in-chief of our Army and Navy. But in the present apparent situation of things it does not seem to us to be necessary or advantageous that the first overture should come from you. Nevertheless you, or any three of you, are to determine on this point as you shall deem most expedient on due deliberation. . . .

It being to be understood that the design expressed by our subjects in America to return to their condition in 1763 is the principle of the present negotiation. That proposition in general terms must be agreed to at once. But the explanation of it will lead into some discussion, and it is very essential not only to evince the good faith of Great Britain, but for the successful result of the treaty, to proceed by ascertaining in the first place the demands of our subjects in America, and the extent to which we mean to acquiesce in those demands reserving the terms to be proposed to them as a subsequent consideration.

If they should require any security that the benefits held out to them . . . should not be at any future time annulled or revoked, the demand is not to be rejected. But it would be proper to place it in the class of those demands which have been made to us and our two Houses of Parliament for the alteration and improvement of their Constitution, which Great Britain is desirous to consider with the utmost attention; and it will be reasonable to put them upon proposing the security they may require.

As to contribution, it is just and reasonable that you should remind those with whom you treat that you are led to hope they will now make good, in the name and on the part of our subjects in America, their own repeated declarations of their readiness to contribute to the public charge, in common with all our other subjects, seeing they are to enjoy the common privileges of all our other subjects; and they are the rather called upon to exercise this act of justice, as such contribution would now be a mere act of free will. . . .

If obstacles should arise . . . in which the point of the contribution . . . have been stated, there is still another mode in which the proposition may be put.

There are duties payable in the colonies under Acts of the Legislature passed long before 1763 to which they never made any objection: the port duties, postage, the escheats, the forfeited grants of lands, and the quit-rents. These, though not considerable in the state of collection which will ever prevail while they are to be accounted for here would form a very considerable article of revenue if collected under a vigilant authority upon the spot. In lieu of all these, and upon a cession of them to the respective colonies, let their assemblies grant a certain sum for the service of the public and for a certain term.

If all these points should fail, you must then propose to let the question rest in oblivion and to secure them in fact by concessions upon the repeal of such Acts as you have power to suspend, and such others as they may represent as fit to be repealed. . . .

As to the Declaration of Independence dated the 4th of July 1776, and all votes, resolutions, and orders passed since the rupture began, it is not necessary to insist on a formal revocation of them as such declaration, votes, orders and resolutions, not being legal acts, will be in effect rescinded by the conclusion of the treaty. . . .

As it is impossible to foresee and enumerate all the matters which may arise during such an inquiry, you are not to consider these instructions as precluding you from entering into the examination and decision of any matters not contained herein, nor of any additional circumstances relative to such things as are the subject matter of these instructions. But you are at liberty to proceed upon every matter within the compass of your commission and to give all possible satisfaction to the minds of our subjects in America consistent with that degree of connection which is essentially necessary for preserving the relation between us and our subjects there.

Lastly. If there should be a reasonable prospect of bringing the treaty to a happy conclusion, you are not to lose so desirable an end by breaking off the negotiation on the adverse party absolutely insisting on some point which you are hereby directed, or which, from your own judgment and discretion you should be disposed not to give up or yield to provided the same be short of open and avowed Independence (except such independence as relates only to the purpose of treaty).

But in such case you will suspend coming to any final resolution till you shall have received our further orders thereupon. . . .

III. The Continental Congress Responds to the Carlisle Commission

The defeat of the British forces of General Burgoyne at Saratoga and the Franco-American alliance made the question of reconciliation a moot point to many in the Continental Congress. Even so, the Congress agreed to receive dispatches from the Carlisle Commission when it arrived at Philadelphia in the spring of 1778. The response of Congress to the commission was first one of caution, then one of anger, leading to a rejection of their proposals.

Why did Congress reject the overtures of the Carlisle Commission?

Journals of the Continental Congress (Washington, D.C.: Government Printing Office, 1908), XI, 605–11, 613–16.

SATURDAY, JUNE 13, 1778: Congress resumed the consideration of the report of the committee on the letter, of the 9th, from General Washington with the papers enclosed:

During the debate an express arrived with a letter of the 11th from General Washington which was read and a packet in which was enclosed together with other papers a letter signed "Carlisle, William Eden, George Johnstone," dated at Philadelphia, 9 June, 1778, and directed "to his excellence Henry Laurens, the president, and others, the members of Congress." Which letter was read to the words "insidious interposition of a power which has, from the first settlement of these colonies, been actuated with enmity to us both; and, notwithstanding the pretended date or present form of the French offers. . . ." Whereupon the reading was interrupted and a motion was made not to proceed farther because of the offensive language against His Most Christian Majesty: debates arising thereon.

Ordered, that the further consideration of the motion be postponed.

Adjourned to 10 o'clock on Monday.

MONDAY, JUNE 15, 1778: Congress resumed the consideration of the motion respecting the letter from the commissioners of the King of Great Britain. After debate:

Adjourned to 10 o'clock tomorrow.

TUESDAY, JUNE 16, 1778: Congress resumed the consideration of the motion respecting the letter from the commissioners of the King of Great Britain, which was amended, and is as follows: "That this Congress cannot hear any language reflecting upon the honor of His Most Christian Majesty, the good and faithful ally of these states." On motion, that the consideration thereof be postponed . . . so it was resolved in the affirmative.

A motion was then made, that the letter from the commissioners of the King of Great Britain lie on the table: passed in the negative.

On motion, *Resolved,* that the letter and papers accompanying it be read. Whereupon, the letter of the 9th and one dated June, 1778, both signed Carlisle . . . were read and also three acts of the parliament of Great Britain.

Ordered, that they be referred to a committee of five. . . .

The committee to whom were referred the letters and papers from the Earl of Carlisle, &c. commissioners from the King of Great Britain, reported the draught of a letter, which was read, and after debate:

Resolved, that the further consideration thereof be postponed until tomorrow.

WEDNESDAY, JUNE 17, 1778: Congress resumed the consideration of the draught of a letter in answer to the letter and papers received from the Earl of Carlisle, &c. commissioners from the King of Great Britain.

On motion to agree to the letter . . . it was unanimously agreed to, and is as follows:

I have received the letter from your excellencies of the 9th instant, with the enclosures, and laid them before Congress. Nothing but an earnest desire to spare the further effusion of human blood could have induced them to read a paper containing expressions so disrespectful to His Most Christian Majesty, the good and great ally of these states, or to consider propositions so derogatory to the honor of an independent nation.

The acts of the British Parliament, the commission from your sovereign, and your letter, suppose the people of these states to be subjects of the crown of Great Britain, and are founded on the idea of dependence, which is utterly inadmissable.

I am further directed to inform your excellencies, that Congress are inclined to peace, notwithstanding the unjust claims from which this war originated, and the savage manner in which it has been conducted.

They will, therefore, be ready to enter upon the consideration of a treaty of peace and commerce not inconsistent with treaties already subsisting, when the king of Great Britain shall demonstrate a sincere disposition for that purpose. The only solid proof of this disposition will be, an explicit acknowledgment of the independence of these states, or the withdrawing his fleets and armies.

I have the honor to be,
Your excellencies most obedient and humble servant.
. . .

The committee appointed to report upon the means of preventing a correspondence with the enemy brought in a report, Whereupon, Congress came to the following resolution:

Whereas, many letters addressed to individuals of these United States have been lately received from England, through the conveyance of the enemy, and some of them which have been under the inspection of members of Congress are found to contain ideas insidiously calculated to divide and delude the good people of these states:

Resolved, that it be, and it is hereby earnestly recommended to the legislative and executive authorities of the several states, to exercise the utmost care and vigilance, and take the most effectual measures to put a stop to so dangerous and criminal a correspondence.

Resolved, that the Commander in Chief and the commanders in each and every military department be, and he and they are hereby directed to carry the measures recommended in the above resolution into the most effectual execution.

Ordered, that the foregoing resolutions be forthwith published and it is recommended to the several printers in the United States to re-publish the same.

Adjourned to 10 o'clock tomorrow.

IV. Yorktown: A Letter From Cornwallis

The British invasion of the southern colonies (1779) had met with success at Charleston (1780) and defeat at King's Mountain (1780) and Cowpens (1781). In the summer of 1781 the British forces, under the leadership of Earl Cornwallis, invaded Virginia. They met little opposition and in August encamped on the seacoast at Yorktown to establish better communications with the Royal Navy. In October a Franco-American land and sea force isolated them, forcing the surrender of Cornwallis and his army on October 19, 1781. The following letter, dated after the surrender, was from Cornwallis to Sir Henry Clinton, explaining the British position at Yorktown.

According to Cornwallis, what was the primary cause of the British disaster? How does this letter affirm Paine's earlier observations?

OCTOBER 20, 1781

Sir,

    I have the mortification to inform your Excellency that I have been forced to give up the posts of York and Gloucester, and to surrender the troops under my command, by capitulation on the 19th inst. as prisoners of war to the combined forces of America and France.

    I never saw this post in a very favorable light, but when I found I was to be attacked in it in so unprepared a state, by so powerful an army and artillery, nothing but the hopes of relief would have induced me to attempt its defence; for I would either have endeavored to escape to New York, by rapid marches from the Gloucester side, immediately on the arrival of General Washington's troops at Williamsburgh, or I would notwithstanding the disparity of numbers have attacked them in the open field, where it might have been just possible that fortune would have favored the gallantry of the handful of troops under my command: but being assured by your Excellency's letters, that every possible means would be tried by the navy and army to relieve us, I could not think myself at liberty to venture upon either of those desperate attempts; therefore . . . I withdrew within the works on the night of the 29th of September, hoping by the labor and firmness of the soldiers, to protract the defence until you could arrive. Everything was to be expected from the spirit of the troops, but every disadvantage attended their labor, as the works were to be continued under the enemy's fire, and our stock of intrenching tools, which did not much exceed four hundred, when we began to work in the latter end of August, was now much diminished.

    The enemy broke ground on the night of the 30th, and constructed on that night, and the two following days and nights, two redoubts, which, with some works that had belonged to our outward position, occupied a gorge between two creeks or ravines, which come from the river on each side of the town.

Jack P. Greene, ed., *Colonies to Nation: 1763–1789* (New York: McGraw-Hill, 1967), pp. 415–18.

On the night of the 6th of October they made their first parallel, extending from its right on the river to a deep ravine on the left, nearly opposite to the center of this place, and embracing our whole left at the distance of six hundred yards. Having perfected this parallel, their batteries opened on the evening of the 9th . . . The fire continued incessant from heavy cannon and from mortars and howitzers, throwing shells from eight to sixteen inches, until all our guns on the left were silenced, our work much damaged, and our loss of men considerable . . . On the evening of the 14th, they assaulted and carried two redoubts that had been advanced about three hundred yards for the purpose of delaying their approaches . . . on the morning of the 16th, I ordered a sortie of about three hundred and fifty men under the direction of Lieutenant-colonel Abercrombie to attack two batteries, which appeared to be in the greatest forwardness, and to spike the guns. A detachment of guards with the eightieth company of Grenadiers . . . and one of Light Infantry . . . both succeeded by forcing the redoubts that covered them, spiking eleven guns, and killing or wounding about one hundred of the French troops, who had the guard of that part of the trenches, and with little loss on our side. This action, though extremely honorable to the officers and soldiers who executed it, proved of little public advantage, for the cannon having been spiked in a hurry, were soon rendered fit for service again, and before dark the whole parallel and batteries appeared to be nearly complete. At this time we knew that there was no part of the whole front attacked, on which we could show a single gun, and our shells were nearly expended; I therefore had only to choose between preparing to surrender next day, or endeavoring to get off with the greatest part of the troops, and I determined to attempt the latter, reflecting that though it should prove unsuccessful in its immediate object, it might at least delay the enemy in the prosecution of further enterprizes: sixteen large boats were prepared . . . but at this critical moment, the weather from being moderate and calm, changed to a most violent storm of wind and rain, and drove all the boats, some of which had troops on board, down the river . . . at day break . . . the boats having now returned, they were ordered to bring back the troops that had passed during the night, and they joined us in the forenoon without much loss. Our works in the mean time were going to ruin . . . my opinion entirely coincided with that of the engineer and principal officers of the army, that they were in many places assailable in the forenoon, and that by the continuence of the same fire for a few hours longer, they would be in such a state as to render it desperate with our numbers to attempt to maintain them. We at that time could not fire a single gun . . . Our numbers had been diminished by the enemy's fire, but particularly by sickness, and the strength and spirits of those in the works were much exhausted by the fatigue of constant watching and unremitting duty. Under all these circumstances, I thought it would have been wanton and inhuman to the last degree to sacrifice the lives of this small body of gallant soldiers, who had ever behaved with so much fidelity and courage, by exposing them to an assault, which from the numbers and precautions of the enemy could not fail to succeed. I therefore proposed to capitulate

... I sincerely lament that better could not be obtained, but I have neglected nothing in my power to alleviate the misfortune and distress of both officers and soldiers. The men are well cloathed and provided with necessaries, and I trust will be regularly supplied by the means of the officers that are permitted to remain with them. The treatment, in general, that we have received from the enemy since our surrender, has been perfectly good and proper. . . .

Although the event has been so unfortunate, the patience of the soldiers in bearing the greatest fatigues, and their firmness and intrepidity under a persevering fire of shot and shells, that I believe has not often been exceeded, deserved the highest admiration and praise. A successful defence, however, in our situation was perhaps impossible, for the place could only be reckoned an entrenched camp, subject in most places to enfilade, and the ground in general so disadvantageous, that nothing but the necessity of fortifying it as a post to protect the navy, could have induced any person to erect works upon it. Our force diminished daily by sickness and other losses, and was reduced when we offered to capitulate on this side to little more than three thousand two hundred rank and file fit for duty, including officers, servants and artificers; and at Gloucester about six hundred, including cavalry. The enemy's army consisted of upwards of eight thousand French, nearly as many continentals, and five thousand militia. They brought an immense train of heavy artillery, most amply furnished with ammunition, and perfectly well manned.

The constant and universal cheerfulness and spirit of the officers in all hardships and danger, deserve my warmest acknowledgments. . . .

CORNWALLIS

For Further Reading

The military history of the American Revolution can be followed through two short histories of the war: Howard Peckham, *The War for Independence** (1958), and Willard M. Wallace, *Appeal to Arms* (1951). For a more detailed account of the war, John R. Alden's *A History of the American Revolution* (1969) and John C. Miller's *Triumph of Freedom* (1948) should be consulted.

Two outstanding biographies of military men are: Douglas S. Freeman, *George Washington* (1948–1957), and Samuel Eliot Morison, *John Paul Jones* (1959). Elisha P. Douglass' *Rebels and Democrats** (1955) deals with the question of who would rule at home once the British were gone. *Man of Reason: The Life of Thomas Paine* (1959), by Alfred Owen Aldridge, is an interesting biography of the author of *Common Sense* and *The Crisis.*

Philip Davidson's *Propaganda and the American Revolution* (1941) offers a good account of the uses of propaganda by the patriots during the war. John C. Miller's *Sam Adams: Pioneer in Propaganda* (1936) is concerned with how

---

*Paperbound edition available.

one man reacted to the crisis between the colonies and the mother country. A problems book that covers the period of the war and its consequences is *The American Revolution: How Revolutionary Was It?** (1965), edited by George Athan Billias; also note the suggestions at the end of Chapter Five.

---

*Paperback edition available.

6. Debating the Dangers of Despotism: The Ratification Contest

The odds seemed to be against the newly drafted Constitution of the United States even before its 39 signers affixed their names to it. Four months of arduous debate behind closed doors had yielded a document that none of its signers could endorse without some misgivings. Fourteen delegates, either out of indifference or opposition, left Philadelphia before the convention adjourned on September 17, 1787, and three who remained refused to sign it. Instead, these three—Elbridge Gerry of Massachusetts and George Mason and Edmund Randolph of Virginia—prepared to return to their home states to organize opposition to its ratification.

In other states, too, opponents of the proposed Constitution mobilized their forces. Within days after adjournment the contest for men's minds and votes began to occupy the young nation's attention. The approval of nine states was needed for ratification, but everyone knew that the nation would not be a true nation without the inclusion of the four big states, Massachusetts, New York, Pennsylvania, and Virginia. In these states, therefore, heated battles were waged between those favoring and those opposing ratification.

It is a credit to the persuasiveness, shrewdness, and even deviousness of the Constitution's supporters that the contest for ratification proved a success. Styling themselves as "Federalists" when they were in fact nationalists, they hung the label "Antifederalists" on those who opposed the Constitution. The well-organized Federalists, arguing on a take-it-or-leave-it basis for an affirmative vote, eventually proved to be too formidable for the loose coalition of opposition the Antifederalists put together.

History is not generous to losers, and the case of the Antifederalists is no exception. Because their opposition reflected many points of view, the arguments of the Antifederalists have seemed incomplete and inconsistent. Their doctrinaire ideologies and attitudes have been judged too inflexible to make effective government possible in a world of uncertainties. Their dire predictions of despotism have not come true, and their fears of centralized power have generally been regarded as exaggerated. No leader of national reputation came forward to espouse their cause, and they could not counter the influence of the endorsement given to the Constitution by George Washington, Benjamin Franklin, and Thomas Jefferson. Finally, no single collection of essays was produced to match the brilliant defense of the Constitution in *The Federalist,* a series of papers by Alexander Hamilton, James Madison, and John Jay.

Yet there was substantial agreement among the Antifederalists in both their general criticisms and their specific objections. To them, the new Constitution seemed to be a rejection of the ideals they had fought for in the Revolution. They were virtually unanimous in calling for a bill of rights and in expressing fear of "consolidated" government and the powers given to it. The powers they feared most concerned taxation, the maintenance of a standing army, regulation of interstate commerce, and control of elections in the states, no matter how indirect.

Their fears intensified as they pondered what Patrick Henry referred to as the "sweeping clause" (Article I, Section 8, clause 16), the federal supremacy clause (Article VI), the powers of the presidency, and the wide jurisdiction given to the federal courts. They were distressed by the system of representation in the new frame of government. Considering the geographic size and the heterogeneity of the population, they were convinced that the ratio of representatives to constituents (1:30,000) was too small, that the two-year terms in the House of Representatives were too long, and that rotation in office should be assured.

Wrapping all their objections into one issue, what stands out is their conviction that the new Constitution did not adequately guard against the dangers of despotism by an elite few.

Core Document

Centinel Letter No. 1

The Federalists, united by a single cause, pushed for prompt ratification, and they worked effectively in the smaller states. They hoped early conventions would give ratification a momentum that the reluctant states would find irresistible. The uncertainties and the ambiguous interpretations the Constitution allowed, they believed, could be worked out through moderation and compromise in practical situations.

The Antifederalists, on the other hand, wanted more precise limitations on the possible ramifications of the new Constitution. They therefore wanted to slow down the ratification process to permit time for debate and clarification. Some called for conditional ratification, pending adoption of specific amendments. Others saw the need for a second convention to consider detailed objections and new ideas. A few pleaded for outright rejection.

Where the Antifederalists were strong there was protracted debate over ratification. Moreover, the debate was carried on not only in meeting halls but also in newspapers and through pamphlets. Woven prominently and persistently through the Antifederalist arguments were several specific themes. Perhaps most noteworthy were the assertions that the proposed Constitution placed governmental power in the hands of an aristocratic few, that "the people" would be at the mercy of this aristocracy, and that the Constitution could be made acceptable only by taking specific steps to guard against aristocratic despotism.

The following document was the first in a series of 24 letters signed "Centinel" and published between October 5, 1787, and November 24, 1788, in the Independent Gazetteer *of Philadelphia. Although the author was probably Samuel Bryan, the letters no doubt reflect the views of his father, George Bryan, a judge of the Supreme Court of Pennsylvania and a prominent and vociferous Antifederalist.*

In reading this letter, note:

- *the contrasts drawn between the Constitution of Pennsylvania and the proposed federal Constitution.*
- *attempts to minimize or discredit the endorsement of the proposed Constitution by prominent persons.*
- *judgments concerning the ability of "the people" to make sound decisions.*
- *judgments concerning the "wealthy and ambitious."*
- *the catalogue of objections raised against the new Constitution.*

John B. McMaster and Frederick C. Stone, eds., *Pennsylvania and the Federal Constitution* (Lancaster: The Historical Society of Pennsylvania, 1888), pp. 565–76.

OCTOBER 5, 1787

To the FREEMEN of PENNSYLVANIA. *Friends, Countrymen and Fellow Citizens.*

Permit one of yourselves to put you in mind of certain *liberties* and *privileges* secured to you by the constitution of this commonwealth, and to beg your serious attention to his uninterested opinion upon the plan of federal government submitted to your consideration, before you surrender these great and valuable privileges up forever. Your present frame of government secures to you a right to hold yourselves, houses, papers and possessions free from search and seizure, and therefore warrants granted without oaths or affirmations first made, affording sufficient foundations for them, whereby any officer or messenger may be commanded or required to search your houses or seize your persons or property not particularly described in such warrant, shall not be granted. Your constitution further provides "that in controversies respecting property, and in suits between man and man, the parties have a right *to trial by jury, which ought to be held sacred.*" It also provides and declares, "*that the people have a right of* FREEDOM OF SPEECH, *and of* WRITING *and* PUBLISHING *their sentiments,* therefore THE FREEDOM OF THE PRESS OUGHT NOT TO BE RESTRAINED." The constitution of Pennsylvania is *yet* in existence, *as yet* you have the right to *freedom of speech,* and of *publishing your sentiments.* How long those rights will appertain to you, you yourselves are called upon to say; whether your *houses* shall continue to be your *castles,* whether your *papers,* your *persons* and your *property,* are to be held sacred and free from *general warrants,* you are now to determine. Whether the *trial by jury* is to continue as your birth-right, the freemen of Pennsylvania, nay, of all America, are now called upon to declare.

Without presuming upon my own judgment, I cannot think it an unwarrantable presumption to offer my private opinion, and call upon others for theirs; and if I use my pen with the boldness of a freeman, it is because I know that *the liberty of the press yet remains unviolated and juries yet are judges.*

The late Convention have submitted to your consideration a plan of a new federal government. The subject is highly interesting to your future welfare. Whether it be calculated to promote the great ends of civil society, viz., the happiness and prosperity of the community, it behoves you well to consider, uninfluenced by the authority of names. Instead of that frenzy of enthusiasm, that has actuated the citizens of Philadelphia, in their approbation of the proposed plan, before it was possible that it could be the result of a rational investigation into its principles, it ought to be dispassionately and deliberately examined on its own intrinsic merit, the only criterion of your patronage. If ever free and unbiased discussion was proper or necessary, it is on such an occasion. All the blessings of liberty and the dearest privileges of freemen are now at stake and dependent on your present conduct. Those who are compe-

John B. McMaster and Frederick C. Stone, eds., *Pennsylvania and the Federal Constitution* (Lancaster: The Historical Society of Pennsylvania, 1888), pp. 565–76.

tent to the task of developing the principles of government, ought to be encouraged to come forward, and thereby the better enable the people to make a proper judgment; for the science of government is so abstruse, that few are able to judge for themselves. Without such assistance the people are too apt to yield an implicit assent to the opinions of those characters whose abilities are held in the highest esteem, and to those in whose integrity and patriotism they can confide; not considering that the love of domination is generally in proportion to talents, abilities and superior requirements, and that the men of the greatest purity of intention may be made instruments of despotism in the hands of the *artful and designing*. If it were not for the stability and attachment which time and habit gives to forms of government, it would be in the power of the enlightened and aspiring few, if they should combine, at any time to destroy the best establishments, and even make the people the instruments of their own subjugation.

The late revolution having effaced in a great measure all former habits, and the present institutions are so recent, that there exists not that great reluctance to innovation, so remarkable in old communities, and which accords with reason, for the most comprehensive mind cannot foresee the full operation of material changes on civil polity; it is the genius of the common law to resist innovation.

The wealthy and ambitious, who in every community think they have a right to lord it over their fellow creatures, have availed themselves very successfully of this favorable disposition; for the people thus unsettled in their sentiments, have been prepared to accede to any extreme of government. All the distresses and difficulties they experience, proceeding from various causes, have been ascribed to the impotency of of the present confederation, and thence they have been led to expect full relief from the adoption of the proposed system of government; and in the other event, immediately ruin and annihilation as a nation. These characters flatter themselves that they have lulled all distrust and jealousy of their new plan, by gaining the concurrence of the two men in whom America has the highest confidence, and now triumphantly exult in the completion of their long meditated schemes of power and aggrandizement.[1] I would be very far from insinuating that the two illustrious personages alluded to, have not the welfare of their country at heart; but that the unsuspecting goodness and zeal of the one has been imposed on, in a subject of which he must be necessarily inexperienced, from his other arduous engagements; and that the weakness and indecision attendant on old age, has been practiced on in the other.

I am fearful that the principles of government inculcated in Mr. Adams' treatise,[2] and enforced in the numerous essays and paragraphs in the newspapers, have misled some well designing members of the late Convention. But it will appear in the sequel, that the construction of the proposed plan of government is infinitely more extravagant.

[1] *Editors' note:* George Washington and Benjamin Franklin.
[2] *Editors' note: Defense of the Constitution of the American States.*

I have been anxiously expecting that some enlightened patriot would, ere this, have taken up the pen to expose the futility, and counteract the baneful tendency of such principles. Mr. Adams' *sine qua non* of a good government is three balancing powers; whose repelling qualities are to produce an equilibrium of interests, and thereby promote the happiness of the whole community. He asserts that the administrators of every government, will ever be actuated by views of private interest and ambition, to the prejudice of the public good; that therefore the only effectual method to secure the rights of the people and promote their welfare, is to create an opposition of interests between the members of two distinct bodies, in the exercise of the powers of government, and balanced by those of a third. This hypothesis supposes human wisdom competent to the task of instituting three co-equal orders in government, and a corresponding weight in the community to enable them respectively to exercise their several parts, and whose views and interests should be so distinct as to prevent a coalition of any two of them for the destruction of the third. Mr. Adams, although he has traced the constitution of every form of government that ever existed, as far as history affords materials, has not been able to adduce a single instance of such a government; he indeed says that the British constitution is such in theory, but this is rather a confirmation that his principles are chimerical and not to be reduced to practice. If such an organization of power were practicable, how long would it continue? Not a day—for there is so great a disparity in the talents, wisdom and industry of mankind, that the scale would presently preponderate to one or the other body, and with every accession of power the means of further increase would be greatly extended. The state of society in England is much more favorable to such a scheme of government than that of America. There they have a powerful hereditary nobility, and real distinctions of rank and interests; but even there, for want of that perfect equality of power and distinction of interests in the three orders of government, they exist but in name; the only operative and efficient check upon the conduct of administration, is the sense of the people at large.

Suppose a government could be formed and supported on such principles, would it answer the great purposes of civil society? If the administrators of every government are actuated by views of private interest and ambition, how is the welfare and happiness of the community to be the result of such jarring adverse interests?

Therefore, as different orders in government will not produce the good of the whole, we must recur to other principles. I believe it will be found that the form of government, which holds those entrusted with power in the greatest responsibility to their constituents, the best calculated for freemen. A republican, or free government, can only exist where the body of the people are virtuous, and where property is pretty equally divided. In such a government the people are the sovereign and their sense or opinion is the criterion of every public measure; for when this ceases to be the case, the nature of the government is changed, and an aristocracy, monarchy or despotism will rise on its ruin. The highest responsibility is to be attained in a simple structure of government, for the great body of the people never steadily attend to the operations of government, and for want of due information are liable to be imposed on. If you complicate the plan by various orders, the people will be perplexed and divided in their sentiment about the source of abuses or misconduct; some will impute it to the senate, others to the house of representatives, and so on, that the interposition of the people may be rendered imperfect or perhaps wholly abortive. But, if imitating the constitution of Pennsylvania, you vest all the legislative power in one body of men (separating the executive and judicial) elected for a short period, and necessarily excluded by rotation from permanency, and guarded from precipitancy and surprise by delays imposed on its proceedings, you will create the most perfect responsibility; for then, whenever the people feel a grievance, they cannot mistake the authors, and will apply the remedy with certainty and effect, discarding them at the next election. This tie of responsibility will obviate all the dangers apprehended from a single legislature, and will the best secure the rights of the people.

Having premised this much, I shall now proceed to the examination of the proposed plan of government, and I trust, shall make it appear to the meanest capacity, that it has none of the essential requisites of a free government; that it is neither founded on those balancing restraining powers, recommended by Mr. Adams and attempted in the British constitution, or possessed of that responsibility to its constituents, which, in my opinion, is the only effectual security for the liberties and happiness of the people; but on the contrary, that it is a most daring attempt to establish a despotic aristocracy among freemen, that the world has ever witnessed.

I shall previously consider the extent of the powers intended to be vested in Congress, before I examine the construction of the general government.

It will not be controverted that the legislative is the highest delegated power in government, and that all others are subordinate to it. The celebrated *Montesquieu*[3] establishes it as a maxim, that legislation necessarily follows the power of taxation. By sect. 8, of the first article of the proposed plan of government, "the Congress are to have power to lay and collect taxes, duties, imposts, and excises, to pay the debts and provide for the common defense and *general welfare* of the United States; but all duties, imposts and excises, shall be uniform throughout the United States." Now what can be more comprehensive than these words? Not content by other sections of this plan, to grant all the great executive powers of a confederation, and a STANDING ARMY IN TIME OF PEACE, that grand engine of oppression, and moreover the absolute control over the commerce of the United States and all external objects of revenue, such as unlimited imposts upon imports, etc., they are to be vested with every species of *internal* taxation; whatever taxes, duties and excises that they may deem requisite for the *general welfare,* may be imposed on the citizens of these states, levied by the officers of Congress, distributed through every district in America; and the collection would be enforced by the standing army, however

---

[3]*Editors' note:* A French philosopher (1689–1755) whose ideas on republicanism were frequently cited by the Antifederalists.

grievous or improper they may be. The Congress may construe every purpose for which the State legislatures now lay taxes, to be for the *general welfare,* and thereby seize upon every object of revenue.

The judicial power by Article 3d sect. 1st shall extend to all cases, in law and equity, arising under this constitution, the laws of the United States, and treaties made or which shall be made under their authority; to all cases affecting ambassadors, other public ministers and consuls; to all cases of admiralty and maritime jurisdiction, to controversies to which the United States shall be a party, to controversies between two or more States, between a State and citizens of another State, between citizens of different States, between citizens of the same State claiming lands under grants of different States, and between a State, or the citizens thereof, and foreign States, citizens or subjects.

The judicial power to be vested in one Supreme Court, and in such inferior Courts as the Congress may from time to time ordain and establish.

The objects of jurisdiction recited above are so numerous, and the shades of distinction between civil causes are oftentimes so slight, that it is more than probable that the State judicatories would be wholly superseded; for in contests about jurisdiction, the federal court, as the most powerful, would ever prevail. Every person acquainted with the history of the courts in England, knows by what ingenious sophisms they have, at different periods, extended the sphere of their jurisdiction over objects out of the line of their institution, and contrary to their very nature; courts of a criminal jurisdiction obtaining cognizance in civil causes.

To put the omnipotency of Congress over the State government and judicatories out of all doubt, the 6th article ordains that "this constitution and the laws of the United States which shall be made in pursuance thereof, and all treaties made, or which shall be made under the authority of the United States, shall be the *supreme law of the land,* and the judges in every State shall be bound thereby, anything in the constitution or laws of any State to the contrary notwithstanding."

By these sections the all-prevailing power of taxation, and such extensive legislative and judicial powers are vested in the general government, as must in their operation necessarily absorb the States legislatures and judicatories; and that such was in the contemplation of the framers of it, will appear from the provision made for such event, in another part of it (but that, fearful of alarming the people by so great an innovation, they have suffered the forms of the separate governments to remain, as a blind). By Article 1st sect. 4th, "the times, places and manner of holding elections for senators and representatives, shall be prescribed in each State by the legislature thereof; *but the Congress may at any time, by law, make or alter such regulations, except as to the place of choosing senators.*" The plain construction of which is, that when the State legislatures drop out of sight, from the necessary operation of this government, then Congress are to provide for the election and appointment of representatives and senators.

If the foregoing be a just comment, if the United States are to be melted down into one empire, it becomes you to consider whether such a government, however constructed, would be eligible in so extended a territory; and whether it would be practicable, consistent with freedom? It is the opinion of the greatest writers, that a very extensive country cannot be governed on democratical principles, on any other plan than a confederation of a number of small republics, possessing all the powers of internal government, but united in the management of their foreign and general concerns.

It would not be difficult to prove, that anything short of despotism could not bind so great a country under one government; and that whatever plan you might, at the first setting out, establish, it would issue in a depotism.

If one general government could be instituted and maintained on principles of freedom, it would not be so competent to attend to the various local concerns and wants, of every particular district, as well as the peculiar governments, who are nearer the scene, and possessed of superior means of information; besides, if the business of the *whole* union is to be managed by one government, there would not be time. Do we not already see, that the inhabitants in a number of larger States, who are remote from the seat of government, are loudly complaining of the inconveniences and disadvantages they are subjected to on this account, and that, to enjoy the comforts of local government, they are separating into smaller divisions?

Having taken a review of the powers, I shall now examine the construction of the proposed general government.

Article 1st, sect. 1st. "All legislative powers herein granted shall be vested in a Congress of the United States, which consist of a senate and house of representatives." By another section, the President (the principal executive officer) has a conditional control over their proceedings.

Sect. 2d. "The house of representatives shall be composed of members chosen every second year, by the people of the several States. The number of representatives shall not exceed one for every 30,000 inhabitants."

The senate, the other constituent branch of the legislature, is formed by the legislature of each State appointing two senators, for the term of six years.

The executive power by Article 2d, sect 1st, is to be vested in a President of the United States of America, elected for four years: Sec. 2 gives him "power, by and with the consent of the senate to make treaties, provided two-thirds of the senators present concur; and he shall nominate, and by and with the advice and consent of the senate, shall appoint ambassadors, other public ministers and consuls, judges of the Supreme Court, and all other officers of the United States, whose appointments are not herein otherwise provided for, and which shall be established by law, etc. And by another section he has the absolute power of granting reprieves and pardons for treason and all other high crimes and misdemeanors, except in case of impeachment.

The foregoing are the outlines of the plan.

Thus we see, the house of representatives are on the part of the people to balance the senate, who I suppose will be composed of the *better sort,* the *well born,* etc. The number of the representatives (being only one for every 30,000 inhabitants) appears to be too few, either to communicate the requisite information of the wants, local circumstances and sentiments of so extensive an empire, or to prevent corruption and undue influence, in the exercise of such great powers; the term for which they are to be chosen, too long to preserve a due dependence and accountability to their constituents; and the mode and places of their election not sufficiently ascertained, for as Congress have the control over both, they may govern the choice, by ordering the *representatives* of a *whole* State, to be *elected* in *one* place, and that too may be the most *inconvenient.*

The senate, the great efficient body in this plan of government, is constituted on the most unequal principles. The smallest State in the Union has equal weight with the great States of Virginia, Massachusetts or Pennsylvania. The senate, besides its legislative functions, has a very considerable share in the executive; none of the principal appointments to office can be made without its advice and consent. The term and mode of its appointment will lead to permanency; the members are chosen for six years, the mode is under the control of Congress, and as there is no exclusion by rotation, they may be continued for life, which, from their extensive means of influence, would follow of course. The President, who would be a mere pageant of State, unless he coincides with the views of the senate, would either become the head of the aristocratic junto in that body, or its minion; besides, their influence being the most predominant, could the best secure his re-election to office. And from his power of granting pardons, he might screen from punishment the most treasonable attempts on the liberties of the people, when instigated by the senate.

From this investigation into the organization of this government, it appears that it is devoid of all responsibility or accountability to the great body of the people, and that so far from being a regular balanced government, it would be in practice a *permanent* ARISTOCRACY.

The framers of it, actuated by the true spirit of such a government, which ever abominates and suppresses all free inquiry and discussion, have made no provision for the *liberty of the press,* that grand *palladium of freedom,* and *scourge of tyrants;* but observed a total silence on that head. It is the opinion of some great writers, that if the liberty of the press, by an institution of religion or otherwise, could be rendered *sacred,* even in *Turkey,* that despotism would fly before it. And it is worthy of remark that there is no declaration of personal rights, premised in most free constitutions; and that trial by *jury* in *civil* cases is taken away; for what other construction can be put on the following, viz: Article 3d, sect. 2d, "In all cases affecting ambassadors, other public ministers and consuls, and those in which a State shall be party, the Supreme Court shall have *original* jurisdiction. In all the other cases above mentioned, the Supreme Court shall have *appellate* jurisdiction, both as to *law and fact!*" It would be a novelty in jurisprudence, as well as evidently improper, to allow an appeal from the verdict of a jury, on the matter of fact; therefore it implies and allows of a dismission of the jury in civil cases, and especially when it is considered, that jury trial in criminal cases is expressly stipulated for, but not in civil cases.

But our situation is represented to be so *critically* dreadful, that, however reprehensible and exceptionable the proposed plan of government may be, there is no alternative between the adoption of it and absolute ruin. My fellow citizens, things are not at that crisis; it is the argument of tyrants; the present distracted state of Europe secures us from injury on that quarter, and as to domestic dissensions, we have not so much to fear from them, as to precipitate us into this form of government, without it is a safe and a proper one. For remember, of all *possible* evils, that of *despotism* is the *worst* and the most to be dreaded.

Besides, it cannot be supposed that the first essay on so difficult a subject, is so well digested as it ought to be; if the proposed plan, after a mature deliberation, should meet the approbation of the respective States, the matter will end; but if it should be found to be fraught with dangers and inconveniences, a future general Convention, being in possession of the objections, will be the better enabled to plan a suitable government.

> *"Who's here so base, that would a bondman be?*
> *If any, speak; for him have I offended.*
> *Who's here so vile, that will not love his country?*
> *If any, speak; for him have I offended."*

CENTINEL

Discussion Starters

1. How would one measure the validity of Centinel's assertions concerning the aspirations and inclinations of the wealthy?

2. Who were "the people" to whom Centinel referred and how would one measure the validity of his judgments concerning their capabilities?

3. What advantages and disadvantages would we obtain today if our national legislature were organized as Centinel would have preferred it? What standard should be used in determining advantages and disadvantages?

4. As judged by Centinel, the Constitution threatened to become an instrument of oppression, the tool of a permanent aristocracy. To what extent have his predictions come true?

5. What suggestions of Centinel might be incorporated into a proposal that would truly place more political power in the hands of the common people to be used for their protection and benefit? How might this be done?

Related Documents

I. Opposition in New York: A Speech by Melancton Smith

In February 1787, when the Continental Congress reluctantly called for a convention to meet in Philadelphia the following May, its charge to the convention was specific. It was called "for the sole and express purpose of revising the Articles of Confederation and reporting to Congress and the several legislatures such alterations and provisions therein as shall when agreed to in Congress and confirmed by the states render the federal constitution adequate to the exigencies of government and the preservation of the Union."

The final act of the convention thus called together was the passing of a resolution presenting the entirely new Constitution to the Congress and expressing the opinion that it should be submitted to conventions of delegates in each state for assent and ratification. To this was added the opinion that when the Constitution was ratified by nine states, proceedings for establishing the new government under the new Constitution should commence.

The Continental Congress reluctantly yielded to this opinion, thus setting the stage for vigorous contests in the state conventions. Matching wits and words in the New York convention were Melancton Smith and Alexander Hamilton, among others. In the following selection, Smith, a merchant, lawyer, and politician, attacked the Constitution's representation formula, charging that the formation of a permanent aristocracy seemed likely.

Compare his arguments with those of Centinel. From the point of view of one who favors fair distribution of political power, how convincing are Smith's arguments? Who, in his opinion, were "the people"?

JUNE 21, 1788

To determine whether the number of representatives proposed by this Constitution is sufficient, it is proper to examine the qualifications which this house ought to possess, in order to exercise their power discreetly for the happiness of the people. The idea that naturally suggests itself to our minds, when we speak of representatives, is, that they resemble those they represent. They should be a true picture of the people, possess a knowledge of their circumstances and their wants, sympathize in all their distresses, and be disposed to seek their true interests. The knowledge necessary for the representative of a free people not only comprehends extensive political and commercial information, such as is acquired by men of refined education, who have leisure to attain to high degrees of improvement, but it should also comprehend that kind of

Jonathan Elliott, ed., *The Debates in the Several State Conventions on the Adoption of the Federal Constitution* (Philadelphia: Lippincott, 1836), II, pp. 245–48.

acquaintance with the common concerns and occupations of the people, which men of the middling class of life are, in general, more competent to than those of a superior class. To understand the true commercial interests of a country, not only requires just ideas of the general commerce of the world, but also, and principally, a knowledge of the productions of your own country, and their value, what your soil is capable of producing, the nature of your manufactures, and the capacity of the country to increase both. To exercise the power of laying taxes, duties, and excises, with discretion, requires something more than an acquaintance with the abstruse parts of the system of finance. It calls for a knowledge of the circumstances and ability of the people in general—a discernment how the burdens imposed will bear upon the different classes.

From these observations results this conclusion—that the number of representatives should be so large, as that, while it embraces the men of the first class, it should admit those of the middling class of life. I am convinced that this government is so constituted that the representatives will generally be composed of the first class in the community, which I shall distinguish by the name of the *natural aristocracy* of the country. I do not mean to give offence by using this term. I am sensible this idea is treated by many gentlemen as chimerical. I shall be asked what is meant by the *natural aristocracy*, and told that no such distinction of classes of men exists among us. It is true, it is our singular felicity that we have no legal or hereditary distinctions of this kind; but still there are real differences. Every society naturally divides itself into classes. The Author of nature has bestowed on some greater capacities than others; birth, education, talents, and wealth, create distinctions among men as visible, and of as much influence, as titles, stars, and garters. In every society, men of this class will command a superior degree of respect; and if the government is so constituted as to admit but few to exercise the powers of it, it will, according to the natural course of things, be in their hands. Men in the middling class, who are qualified as representatives, will not be so anxious to be chosen as those of the first. When the number is so small, the office will be highly elevated and distinguished; the style in which the members live will probably be high; circumstances of this kind will render the place of a representative not a desirable one to sensible, substantial men, who have been used to walk in the plain and frugal paths of life.

Besides, the influence of the great will generally enable them to succeed in elections. It will be difficult to combine a district of country containing thirty or forty thousand inhabitants,—frame your election laws as you please,—in any other character, unless it be in one of conspicuous military, popular, civil, or legal talents. The great easily form associations; the poor and middling class form them with difficulty. If the elections be by plurality,—as probably will be the case in this state—it is almost certain none but the great will be chosen, for they easily unite their interests: the common people will divide, and their divisions will be promoted by the others. There will be scarcely a chance of their uniting in any other but some great man, unless in some popular demagogue, who will probably be destitute of principle. A substantial yeoman, of sense and discernment, will hardly ever be chosen. From these remarks, it appears that the government will fall into the hands of the few and the great. This will be a government of oppression. I do not mean to declaim against the great, and charge them indiscriminately with want of principle and honesty. The same passions and prejudices govern all men. The circumstances in which men are placed in a great measure give a cast to the human character. Those in middling circumstances have less temptation; they are inclined by habit, and the company with whom they associate, to set bounds to their passions and appetites. If this is not sufficient, the want of means to gratify them will be a restraint: they are obliged to employ their time in their respective callings; hence the substantial yeomanry of the country are more temperate, of better morals, and less ambition, than the great. The latter do not feel for the poor and middling class; the reasons are obvious—they are not obliged to use the same pains and labor to procure property as the other. They feel not the inconveniences arising from the payment of small sums. The great consider themselves above the common people, entitled to more respect, do not associate with them; they fancy themselves to have a right of preëminence in every thing. In short, they possess the same feelings, and are under the influence of the same motives, as an hereditary nobility. I know the idea that such a distinction exists in this country is ridiculed by some; but I am not the less apprehensive of danger from their influence on this account. Such distinctions exist all the world over, have been taken notice of by all writers on free government, and are founded in the nature of things. It has been the principal care of free governments to guard against the encroachments of the great. Common observation and experience prove the existence of such distinctions. Will any one say that there does not exist in this country the pride of family, of wealth, of talents, and that they do not command influence and respect among the common people? . . . We ought to guard against the government being placed in the hands of this class. They cannot have that sympathy with their constituents which is necessary to connect them closely to their interests. Being in the habit of profuse living, they will be profuse in the public expenses. They find no difficulty in paying their taxes, and therefore do not feel public burdens. Besides, if they govern, they will enjoy the emoluments of the government. The middling class, from their frugal habits, and feeling themselves the public burdens, will be careful how they increase them.

But I may be asked, Would you exclude the first class in the community from any share in legislation? I answer, By no means. They would be factious, discontented, and constantly disturbing the government. It would also be unjust. They have their liberties to protect, as well as others, and the largest share of property. But my idea is, that the Constitution should be so framed as to admit this class, together with a sufficient number of the middling class to control them. You will then combine the abilities and honesty of the community, a proper degree of information, and a disposition to pursue the public good. A representative body, composed principally of respectable yeomanry, is the best possible security to liberty. When the interest of this part of the community is pursued, the public good is pursued, because the body of every nation consists of this class, and because the interest of both the rich and the poor are involved in that of the middling class. No burden can be laid on the poor but what will sensibly affect the middling class. Any law rendering property insecure would be injurious to them. When, therefore, this class in society pursue their own interst, they promote that of the public, for it is involved in it.

II. Alexander Hamilton Speaks for the Constitution

A reply to Melancton Smith came from Alexander Hamilton, a rising young political figure. Following a disappointing performance in the Constitutional Convention, Hamilton made a powerful contribution to the Federalist cause as one of the contributors to The Federalist *and as a defender of the Constitution in the New York convention.*

Evaluate the aptness of Hamilton's replies to Smith's assertions. Based on this selection, what was the extent of Hamilton's interest in the broad distribution of political power? Speculate on the sort of attack Centinel might have made on Hamilton's arguments.

JUNE 21, 1788

Sir, we hear constantly a greal deal which is rather calculated to awake our passions, and create prejudices, than to conduct us to the truth, and teach us our real interests. I do not suppose this to be the design of the gentlemen. Why, then, are we told so often of an aristocracy? For my part, I hardly know the meaning of this word, as it is applied. If all we hear be true, this government is really a very bad one. But who are the aristocracy among us? Where do we find men elevated to a perpetual rank above their fellow-citizens, and possessing powers entirely independent of them? The arguments of the gentlemen only go to prove that there are men who are rich, men who are poor, some who are wise, and others who are not; that, indeed, every distinguished man is an aristocrat. This reminds me of a description of the aristocrats I have seen in a late publication styled the Federal Farmer.[1] The author reckons in the aristocracy all governors of states, members of Congress, chief magistrates, and all officers of the militia. This description, I presume to say, is ridiculous. The image is a phantom. Does the new government render a rich man more elegible than a poor one? No. It requires no such qualification. It is bottomed on the broad and equal principle of your state constitution.

Sir, if the people have it in their option to elect their most meritorious men, is this to be considered as an objection? Shall the Constitution oppose

[1] *Editors' note:* A reference to the letters of Richard Henry Lee of Virginia.

Jonathan Elliot, ed., *The Debates in the Several State Conventions on the Adoption of the Federal Constitution* (Philadelphia: Lippincott, 1836), II, pp. 256–58.

their wishes, and abridge their most invaluable privilege? While property continues to be pretty equally divided, and a considerable share of information pervades the community, the tendency of the people's suffrages will be to elevate merit even from obscurity. As riches increase and accumulate in few hands, as luxury prevails in society, virtue will be in a greater degree considered as only a graceful appendage of wealth, and the tendency of things will be to depart from the republican standard. This is the real disposition of human nature: it is what neither the honorable member nor myself can correct; it is a common misfortune, that awaits our state constitution as well as all others.

There is an advantage incident to large districts of election, which perhaps the gentlemen, amidst all their apprehensions of influence and bribery, have not averted to. In large districts, the corruption of the electors is much more difficult; combinations for the purposes of intrigue are less easily formed; factions and cabals are little known. In a small district, wealth will have a more complete influence, because the people in the vicinity of a great man are more immediately his dependents, and because this influence has fewer objects to act upon. It has been remarked, that it would be disagreeable to the middle class of men to go to the seat of the new government. If this be so, the difficulty will be enhanced by the gentleman's proposal. If his argument be true, it proves that the larger the representation is, the less will be your chance of having it filled. But it appears to me frivolous to bring forward such arguments as these. It has answered no other purpose than to induce me, by way of reply, to enter into discussion, which I consider as useless, and not applicable to our subject.

It is a harsh doctrine that men grow wicked in proportion as they improve and enlighten their minds. Experience has by no means justified us in the supposition that there is more virtue in one class of men than in another. Look through the rich and the poor of the community, the learned and the ignorant. Where does virtue predominate? The difference indeed consists, not in the quantity, but kind, of vices which are incident to various classes; and here the advantage of character belongs to the wealthy. Their vices are probably more favorable to the prosperity of the state than those of the indigent, and partake less of moral depravity.

After all, sir, we must submit to this idea, that the true principle of a republic is, that the people should choose whom they please to govern them. Representation is imperfect in proportion as the current of popular favor is checked. This great source of free government, popular election, should be perfectly pure, and the most unbounded liberty allowed. Where this principle is adhered to; where, in the organization of the government, the legislative, executive, and judicial branches are rendered distinct; where, again, the legislature is divided into separate houses, and the operations of each are controlled by various checks and balances, and, above all, by the vigilance and weight of the state governments,—to talk of tyranny, and the subversion of our liberties, is to speak the language of enthusiasm. This balance between the national and state governments ought to be dwelt on with peculiar attention, as it is of the utmost importance. It forms a double security to the people. If one encroaches on their rights, they will find a powerful protection in the other. Indeed, they will both be prevented from overpassing their constitutional limits, by a certain rivalship, which will ever subsist between them. I am persuaded that a firm union is as necessary to perpetuate our liberties as it is to make us respectable; and experience will probably prove that the national government will be as natural a guardian of our freedom as the state legislature themselves.

III. The Popular Basis of the House of Representatives—Federalist Number 57

JAMES MADISON

An analytical reply to the charge of the Antifederalists—that the scheme of representation in the new Constitution worked to the disadvantage of the common people—came in the 57th Federalist *paper, written by James Madison.*

Evaluate from the point of view of a farmer or a city worker each of the points Madison makes. How might Centinel have responded to Madison's arguments?

To the People of the State of New York:

The *Third* charge against the House of Representatives is, that it will be taken from that class of citizens which will have least sympathy with the mass of the people, and be most likely to aim at an ambitious sacrifice of the many to the aggrandizement of the few.

Of all the objections which have been framed against the federal Constitution, this is perhaps the most extraordinary. Whilst the objection itself is levelled against a pretended oligarchy, the principle of it strikes at the very root of republican government.

The aim of every political constitution is, or ought to be, first to obtain for rulers men who possess most wisdom to discern, and most virtue to pursue, the common good of the society; and in the next place, to take the most effectual precautions for keeping them virtuous whilst they continue to hold their public trust. The elective mode of obtaining rulers is the characteristic policy of republican government. The means relied on in this form of government for preventing their degeneracy are numerous and various. The most effectual one, is such a limitation of the term of appointments as will maintain a proper responsibility to the people.

Let me now ask what circumstance there is in the constitution of the House of Representatives that violates the principles of republican government, or favors the elevation of the few on the ruins of the many? Let me ask whether every circumstance is not, on the contrary, strictly comfortable to

Reprinted by permission of the publishers from Benjamin F. Wright, ed., *The Federalist,* pp. 383–85. Cambridge, Mass.: The Belknap Press of Harvard University Press. Copyright 1961 by the President and Fellows of Harvard College.

these principles, and scrupulously impartial to the rights and pretentions of every class and description of citizens?

Who are to be the electors of the federal representatives? Not the rich, more than the poor; not the learned, more than the ignorant; not the haughty heirs of distinguished names, more than the humble sons of obscurity and unpropitious fortune. The electors are to be the great body of the people of the United States. They are to be the same who exercise the right in every State of electing the corresponding branch of the legislature of the State.

Who are to be the objects of popular choice? Every citizen whose merit may recommend him to the esteem and confidence of his country. No qualification of wealth, of birth, of religious faith, or of civil profession is permitted to fetter the judgment or disappoint the inclination of the people.

If we consider the situation of the men on whom the free suffrages of their fellow-citizens may confer the representative trust, we shall find it involving every security which can be devised or desired for their fidelity to their constituents.

In the first place, as they will have been distinguished by the preference of their fellow-citizens, we are to presume that in general they will be somewhat distinguished also by those qualities which entitle them to it, and which promise a sincere and scrupulous regard to the nature of their engagements.

In the second place, they will enter into the public service under circumstances which cannot fail to produce a temporary affection at least to their constituents. There is in every breast a sensibility to marks of honor, of favor, of esteem, and of confidence, which, apart from all considerations of interest, is some pledge for grateful and benevolent returns. Ingratitude is a common topic of declamation against human nature; and it must be confessed that instances of it are but too frequent and flagrant, both in public and in private life. But the universal and extreme indignation which it inspires is itself a proof of the energy and prevalence of the contrary sentiment.

In the third place, those ties which bind the representative to his constituents are strengthened by motives of a more selfish nature. His pride and vanity attach him to a form of government which favors his pretensions and gives him a share in its honors and distinctions. Whatever hopes or projects might be entertained by a few aspiring characters, it must generally happen that a great proportion of the men deriving their advancement from their influence with the people, would have more to hope from a preservation of the favor, than from innovations in the government subversive of the authority of the people.

All these securities, however, would be found very insufficient without the restraint of frequent elections. Hence, in the fourth place, the House of Representatives is so constituted as to support in the members an habitual recollection of their dependence on the people. Before the sentiments impressed on their minds by the mode of their elevation can be effaced by the exercise of power, they will be compelled to anticipate the moment when their power is to cease, when their exercise of it is to be reviewed, and when they must descend to the level from which they were raised; there forever to remain unless a faithful discharge of their trust shall have established their title to a renewal of it.

I will add, as a fifth circumstance in the situation of the House of Representatives, restraining them from oppressive measures, that they can make no law which will not have its full operation on themselves and their friends, as well as on the great mass of the society. This has always been deemed one of the strongest bonds by which human policy can connect the rulers and the people together. It creates between them that communion of interests and sympathy of sentiments, of which few governments have furnished examples; but without which every government degenerates into tyranny. If it be asked, what is to restrain the House of Representatives from making discriminations in favor of themselves and a particular class of the society? I answer: the genius of the whole system; the nature of just and constitutional laws; and above all, the vigilant and manly spirit which actuates the people of America—a spirit which nourishes freedom, and in return is nourished by it.

If this spirit shall ever be so far debased as to tolerate a law not obligatory on the legislature, as well as on the people, the people will be prepared to tolerate any thing but liberty.

IV. Cursory Remarks

HUGH HENRY BRACKENRIDGE

The polemics of the Antifederalists were ordinarily met by reasoned arguments. Occasionally, however, the Federalists resorted to satire to discredit their opponents' arguments. Hugh Henry Brackenridge, a jurist, author, and the foremost champion of the Constitution in Western Pennsylvania, wrote what was perhaps the cleverest satirical piece of the entire contest over ratification.

Identify the clues that betray this essay as satire. Which specific Antifederalist objections raised in Centinel's letter are satirized by Brackenridge?

It is not my intention to enter largely into a consideration of this plan of government, but to suggest some ideas in addition to, and of the same nature with, those already made, showing the imperfections and the danger of it.

The first thing that strikes a diligent observer, is the want of precaution with regard to the *sex* of the president. Is it provided that he shall be of the male gender? The Salii, a tribe of the Burgundians, in the 11th century, excluded females from the sovereignty. Without a similar exclusion, what shall we think, if, in progress of time, we should come to have an *old woman* at the head of our affairs? But what security have we that he shall be a *white man?* What would be the national disgrace if he should be elected from one of the southern states, and a *vile negro* should come to rule over us? Treaties would

Paul L. Ford, ed., *Essays on the Constitution of the United States* (Brooklyn: Historical Printing Club, 1892), pp. 319–21.

then be formed with the tribes of Congo and Loango, instead of the civilized nations of Europe. But is there any security that he shall be a *freeman?* Who knows but the electors at a future period, in days of corruption, may pick up a man-servant, a convict perhaps, and give him the dominion? Is any care taken that he shall be of *perfect parts?* Shall we, in affairs of a civil nature, leave a door open to lame men, bastards, eunuchs, and the devil knows what?

A senate is the next great constituent part of the government; and yet there is not a word said with regard to the ancestry of any of them; whether they should be altogether Irish, or only Scots Irish. If any of them have been in the war of the White Boys, the Heart of Oak, or the like, they may overturn all authority, and make Shilelah the supreme law of the land.

The house of representatives is to be so large, that it can never be built. They may begin it, but it can never be finished. Ten miles square! Babylon itself, unless the suburbs are taken into view, was not of greater extent.

But what avails it to dwell on these things? The want of a *bill of rights* is the great evil. There was no occasion for a bill of *wrongs;* for there will be wrongs enough. But oh! a *bill of rights!* What is the nature of a bill of rights? "It is a schedule of inventory of those powers which Congress do not possess." But if it is clearly ascertained what powers they have, what need of a catalogue of those powers they have not? Ah! there is the mistake. A minister preaching, undertook, first, to show what was in his text; second, what was not in it. When it is specified what powers are given, why not also what powers are not given? A bill of rights is wanting, and all those things which are usually secured under it—

1. The *rights of conscience* are swept away. The Confession of Faith, the Prayer-Book, the Manual and Pilgrim's Progress are to go. The psalms of Watts, I am told, are the only thing of the kind that is to have any quarter at all.

2. The *liberty of the press*—that is gone at the first stroke. Not so much as an advertisement for a stray horse, or a runaway negro, can be put in any of the gazettes.

3. The *trial by jury*—that is knocked in the head, and all that worthy class of men, the lawyers, who live by haranguing and bending the juries, are demolished.

I would submit it to any candid man, if in this constitution there is the least provision for the privilege of shaving the beard? or is there any mode laid down to take the measure of a pair of breeches? Whence is it then, that men of learning seem so much to approve, while the ignorant are against it? The cause is perfectly apparent, viz., that reason is an erring guide, while instinct, which is the governing principle of the untaught, is certain. Put a pig in a poke, carry it half a day's journey through woods and by-ways, let it out, and it will run home without deviation. Could Dr. Franklin do this? What reason have we then to suppose that his judgment, or that of Washington, could be equal to that of Mr. Smilie in state affairs?

Were it not on this principle that we are able to account for it, it might be thought strange that old Livingston, of the Jersies, could be so hoodwinked as to give his sanction to such a diabolical scheme of tyranny amongst men —a constitution which may well be called hell-born. For if all the devils in Pandemonium had been employed about it, they could not have made a worse.

Neil MacLaughlin, a neighbor of mine, who has been talking with Mr. Findley, says that under this constitution all weavers are to be put to death. What have these innocent manufacturers done that they should be proscribed?

Let other states think what they will of it, there is one reason why every Pennsylvanian should execrate this imposition upon mankind. It will make his state most probably the seat of government, and bring all the officers, and cause a great part of the revenue to be expended here. This must make the people rich, enable them to pay their debts, and corrupt their morals. Any citizen, therefore, on the Delaware and Susquehannah waters, ought to be hanged and quartered, that would give it countenance.

I shall content myself at present with these strictures, but shall continue them from time to time as occasion may require.

V. Ploughjogger Smith Favors the Constitution

The Massachusetts convention provided the scene for a series of dramatic confrontations. At one point in the debate, Amos Singletary, an outspoken Antifederalist, gave this reason for his fear of the new Constitution: "These lawyers, and men of learning, and moneyed men, that talk so finely, and gloss over matters so smoothly, to make us, poor illiterate people, swallow down the pill, expect to get into Congress themselves; they expect to be the managers of this Constitution, and get all the power and all the money into their own hands, and then they will swallow up all us little folks."

The response to Mr. Singletary came from Jonathan Smith of Berkshire County, the westernmost county in Massachusetts. Why might this speech be regarded by some (perhaps Centinel) as selling out the interests of the common people, including "ploughjoggers"? How should it be regarded?

JANUARY 25, 1788

. . . Mr. President, I am a plain man, and get my living by the plough. I am not used to speak in public, but I beg your leave to say a few words to my brother ploughjoggers in this house. I have lived in a part of the country where I have known the worth of good government by the want of it. There was a black cloud that rose in the east last winter, and spread over the west.[1] [Here Mr. Widgery interrupted. Mr. President, I wish to know what the gentleman means by the east.] I mean, sir, the county of Bristol; the cloud rose there, and burst upon us, and produced a dreadful effect. It brought on a state of anarchy,

---

[1] *Editors' note:* An apparent reference to Shays' Rebellion.

Jonathan Elliot, ed., *The Debates in the Several State Conventions on the Adoption of the Federal Constitution* (Philadelphia: Lippincott, 1836), II, pp. 102–4.

and that led to tyranny. I say, it brought anarchy. People that used to live peaceably, and were before good neighbors, got distracted, and took up arms against government. [Here Mr. Kingsley called to order, and asked, what had the history of last winter to do with the Constitution. Several gentlemen, and among the rest the Hon. Mr. Adams, said the gentleman was in order—let him go on in his own way.] I am going, Mr. President, to show you, my brother farmers, what were the effects of anarchy, that you may see the reasons why I wish for good government. People I say took up arms; and then, if you went to speak to them, you had the musket of death presented to your breast. They would rob you of your property; threaten to burn your houses; oblige you to be on your guard night and day; alarms spread from town to town; families were broken up; the tender mother would cry, "O, my son is among them! What shall I do for my child!" Some were taken captive, children taken out of their schools, and carried away. Then we should hear of an action, and the poor prisoners were set in the front, to be killed by their own friends. How dreadful, how distressing was this! Our distress was so great that we should have been glad to snatch at any thing that looked like a government. Had any person, that was able to protect us, come and set up his standard, we should all have flocked to it, even if it had been a monarch; and that monarch might have proved a tyrant;—so that you see that anarchy leads to tyranny, and better have one tyrant than so many at once.

Now, Mr. President, when I saw this Constitution, I found that it was a cure for these disorders. It was just such a thing as we wanted. I got a copy of it, and read it over and over. I had been a member of the Convention to form our own state constitution, and had learnt something of the checks and balances of power, and I found them all here. I did not go to any lawyer, to ask his opinion; we have no lawyer in our town, and we do well enough without. I formed my own opinion, and was pleased with this Constitution. My honorable old daddy there [pointing to Mr. Singletary] won't think that I expect to be a Congress-man, and swallow up the liberties of the people. I never had any post, nor do I want one. But I don't think the worse of the Constitution because lawyers, and men of learning and moneyed men, are fond of it. I don't suspect that they want to get into Congress and abuse their power. I am not of such a jealous make. They that are honest men themselves are not apt to suspect other people. I don't know why our constituents have not a good right to be as jealous of us as we seem to be of the Congress; and I think those gentlemen, who are so very suspicious that as soon as a man gets into power he turns rogue, had better look at home.

We are, by this Constitution, allowed to send ten members to Congress. Have we not more than that number fit to go? I dare say, if we pick out ten, we shall have another ten left, and I hope ten times ten; and will not these be a check upon those that go? Will they go to Congress, and abuse their power, and do mischief, when they know they must return and look the other ten in the face, and be called to account for their conduct? Some gentlemen think that our liberty and property are not safe in the hands of moneyed men, and men of learning? I am not of that mind.

Brother farmers, let us suppose a case, now: Suppose you had a farm of 50 acres, and your title was disputed, and there was a farm of 5000 acres joined to you, that belonged to a man of learning, and his title was involved in the same difficulty; would you not be glad to have him for your friend, rather than to stand alone in the dispute? Well, the case is the same. These lawyers, these moneyed men, these men of learning, are all embarked in the same cause with us, and we must all swim or sink together; and shall we throw the Constitution overboard because it does not please us alike? Suppose two or three of you had been at the pains to break up a piece of rough land, and sow it with wheat; would you let it lie waste because you could not agree what sort of a fence to make? Would it not be better to put up a fence that did not please every one's fancy, rather than not fence it at all, or keep disputing about it until the wild beasts came in and devoured it? Some gentlemen say, Don't be in a hurry; take time to consider, and don't take a leap in the dark. I say, Take things in time; gather fruit when it is ripe. There is a time to sow and a time to reap; we sowed our seed when we sent men to the federal Convention; now is the harvest, now is the time to reap the fruit of our labor; and if we won't do it now, I am afraid we never shall have another opportunity.

For Further Reading

An interesting account of the contest for ratification is presented by Robert A. Rutland in *The Ordeal of the Constitution: The Antifederalists and the Ratification Struggle of 1787–1788* (1966). Clinton Rossiter, *1787: The Grand Convention** (1966), a detailed account of the convention, contains a chapter on ratification.

The economic motives and status of the founding fathers have been the subject of discussion since Charles A. Beard published *An Economic Interpretation of the Constitution of the United States** (1913, 1935). The Beard thesis has been attacked on different grounds by Robert F. Brown in *Charles Beard and the Constitution** (1956) and by Forrest McDonald in *We the People: The Economic Origins of the Constitution** (1958). *The Antifederalists: Critics of the Constitution, 1781–1788** (1961), by Jackson Turner Main, reaches conclusions compatible with Beard's.

Four books of documents, all containing informative introductions by their editors, are: Morton Borden, *The Antifederalist Papers* (1965); Cecelia Kenyon, *The Antifederalists** (1966); John D. Lewis, *Anti-Federalists vs. Federalists** (1967); Alpheus T. Mason, *The States Rights Debate: Antifederalism and the Constitution** (1964). The Mason volume also contains the "disunion amendments" proposed in the early 1960s.

*The Debate over the Constitution, 1787–1789** (1965), a brief problems book edited by Alfred Young, contains excerpts from significant documents.

*Paperbound edition available.

7. Politics and Parties

The political party system that has been the lifeblood of American politics originated in the conflicts over national policy during the last decade of the eighteenth century. Although a new government had been created with the ratification of the Constitution in 1788, it remained to be determined whether the "paper" government could be effectively organized and set in motion. The task of establishing it was placed under the leadership of a man of proven ability, President George Washington. The new president appointed as his chief advisers Alexander Hamilton (secretary of the treasury) and Thomas Jefferson (secretary of state). These two men, plus the secretary of war and the attorney general, constituted Washington's first cabinet. He hoped to use the cabinet as a primary instrument in the formation and implementation of federal policy, but to his dismay, it became the battleground of emerging party politics.

As secretary of the treasury, Hamilton was directly responsible for the financial integrity and stability of the new government. With this responsibility in mind, he formulated a series of policies designed to create a strong centralized nation. These policies were intended not only to guarantee sound fiscal policy, but also to promote the expansion of manufacturing in the United States. Hamilton's program, therefore, required the funding at par of the national debt and the assumption of the debts incurred by the states during the Revolution, the initiation of excise taxes for increased revenue, the creation of a national bank, and, finally, a protective tariff. Although the protective tariff was rejected, he was able to get Congress to enact the other provisions of his program.

But Hamilton's financial proposals were not consistent with Jefferson's beliefs. Jefferson preferred to have the United States remain an agrarian society as much as possible. Furthermore, he jealously guarded the rights of the states and was willing to relinquish power to the central government only when the need for such a transfer was satisfactorily demonstrated. His ideas closely paralleled those of James Madison, who became the anti-Hamilton leader in Congress. This group began to be identified, at least in its own mind, as the "Republicans" by the election of 1792.

Domestic policy was not the only point of controversy in the early National period. In foreign affairs Washington's determination to remain impartial in the French Revolution was interpreted by the pro-French Jefferson and his friends as being pro-British and prompted by Hamilton and his followers in the Congress. The President's tendency to heed Hamilton's advice not only on domestic affairs but also on foreign relations finally led Jefferson to resign as secretary of state in 1793. By this time the lines were being drawn, and the next three years saw the development of a well-organized opposition party in the United States. This chapter focuses on foreign policy as a partisan issue during Washington's tenure as president.

Core Document

The Partisans of Patience, Negotiation, and Peace

ALEXANDER HAMILTON

The wars of the French Revolution were watched with keen interest by many Americans, and some were prompted to take sides. Those who agreed with Jefferson generally saw it as a continuation of man's pursuit of liberty, while Hamilton and many in the business community saw it as a direct threat to the concept of property and its privileges. The Hamiltonians also felt that mobocracy could well be introduced into the American nation as a result of the turmoil in France.

The situation became critical when the English, at war with the French, began to seize neutral American shipping and to support the belligerent Indian tribes on the American frontier. The United States had the alternative of going

Henry Cabot Lodge, ed., *The Works of Alexander Hamilton* (New York; G.P. Putnam's Sons, 1903), V, pp. 97–102, 114–15.

to war against England or submitting to her overwhelming military superiority. *The Republicans were ready for war, but Washington, at the request of Hamilton, sent John Jay to London to negotiate the differences between the two nations. The agreement reached by these negotiations was called Jay's Treaty. Republicans regarded it as a sellout to English military power, using it as an issue to enhance their identity with the people and to form a solid front in Congress against Hamilton's party, which became known as the Federalist party.*

In reading the following letter from Hamilton to Washington, written before Jay's Treaty, note how Hamilton evaluated:
- *the emerging political parties in the United States.*
- *the question of whether to negotiate with England.*
- *the role of American military preparedness in negotiations.*
- *the need for American unity.*
- *the role of the president in the crisis.*
- *the selection of an envoy to be sent to England.*

APRIL 14, 1794

Sir:—The present is beyond question a great, a difficult, and a perilous crisis in the affairs of this country. . . . In such a crisis it is the duty of every man, according to situation, to contribute all in his power towards preventing evil and producing good. This consideration will, I trust, be a sufficient apology for the liberty I am about to take of submitting, without an official call, the ideas which occupy my mind concerning the actual posture of our public affairs. It cannot but be of great importance that the Chief Magistrate should be informed of the real state of things, and it is not easy for him to have this information but through those principal officers who have most frequent access to him. Hence an obligation on their part to communicate information on occasions like the present.

A course of accurate observation has impressed on my mind a full conviction, that there exists in our councils three considerable parties,—one, decided for preserving peace by every effort which shall any way consist with the ultimate maintenance of the national honor and rights, and disposed to cultivate with all nations a friendly understanding; another, decided for war, and resolved to bring it about by every expedient which shall not too directly violate the public opinion; a third, not absolutely desirous of war, but solicitous at all events to excite and keep alive irritation and ill-humor between the United States and Great Britain, and not unwilling in the pursuit of this object to expose the peace of the country to imminent hazards.

The views of the first party, in respect to the questions between Great Britain and us, favor the following course of conduct: to take effectual measures of military preparation, creating, in earnest, force and revenue; to vest the President with important powers respecting navigation and commerce for ulterior contingencies—to endeavor by another effort of negotiation, confided to hands able to manage it, and friendly to the object, to obtain reparation for the wrongs we suffer, and a demarkation of a line of conduct to govern in future; to avoid till the issue of that experiment all measures of a nature to occasion a conflict between the motives which might dispose the British Government to do us the justice to which we are entitled and the sense of its own dignity. If that experiment fails, then and not till then to resort to reprisals and war.

The views of the second party, in respect to the same questions, favor the following course of conduct: to say and to do every thing which can have a tendency to stir up the passions of the people and beget a disposition favorable to war; to make use of the inflammation which is excited in the community for the purpose of carrying through measures calculated to disgust Great Britain, and to render an accommodation impracticable without humiliation to her, which they do not believe will be submitted to; in fine, to provoke and bring on war by indirect means, without declaring it or even avowing the intention, because they know the public mind is not yet prepared for such an extremity, and they fear to encounter the direct responsibility of being the authors of a war.

The views of the third party lead them to favor the measures of the second —but without a perfect coincidence in the result. They weakly hope that they may hector and vapor with success—that the pride of Great Britain will yield to her interest, and that they may accomplish the object of perpetuating animosity between the two countries without involving war. There are some characters, not numerous, who do not belong to either of these classes, but who fluctuate between them as, in the conflict between Reason and Passion, the one or the other prevails.

It may seem difficult to admit, in the situation of this country, that there are parties of the description of the two last; men who can either systematically meditate war or can be willing to risk it otherwise than by the use of means which they deem necessary to insure reparation for the injuries we experience.

But a due attention to the course of the human passions, as recorded in history, and exemplified by daily occurrences, is sufficient to obviate all difficulty on this head.

Wars oftener proceed from angry and perverse passions, than from cool calculations of interest. This position is admitted without difficulty when we are judging of the hostile appearances in the measures of Great Britain toward this country. What reason can there be why it should not be as good a test of similar appearances on our part? As men it is equally applicable to us,—and the symptoms are strong of our being readily enough worked up into a degree of rage and frenzy, which goes very far toward silencing the voice of reason and interest.

Those who compose the parties whose measures have a war aspect, are under the influence of some of the strongest passions that can actuate human conduct. They unite from habitual feeling in an implacable hatred to Great Britain and a warm attachment to France. Their animosity against the former is inflamed by the most violent resentment for recent and unprovoked injuries —in many instances by personal loss and suffering of intimate friends and connections. Their sympathy with the latter is increased by the idea of her being engaged in defending the cause of liberty against a combination of despots, who meditate nothing less than the destruction of it throughout the world. In hostility with Britain, they seek the gratification of revenge upon a detested enemy with that of serving a favorite friend, and in this the cause of liberty. They anticipate, also, what is, in their estimation, a great political good, a more complete and permanent alienation from Great Britain, and a more close approximation to France. Those even of them who do not wish the extremity of war consider it as a less evil than a thorough and sincere accommodation with Great Britain, and are willing to risk the former rather than lose an opportunity so favorable as the present to extend and rivet the springs of ill-will against that nation.

However necessary it is to veil this policy in public, in private there are not much pains taken to disguise it. Some gentlemen do not scruple to say that pacification is and ought to be out of the question.

What has been heretofore said relates only to persons in public character. If we extend our view from these to the community at large, we shall there also find a considerable diversity of opinion—partisans of patience, negotiation, and peace, if possible, and partisans of war. There is no doubt much of irritation now afloat; many advocates for measures tending to produce war. But it would be a great mistake to infer from these appearances that the prevailing sentiment of the country is for war—or that there would be either a willing acquiescence or a zealous co-operation in it if the proceedings of the government should not be such as to render it manifest, beyond question, that war was inevitable, but by an absolute sacrifice of the rights and interests of the nation—that the race of prudence was completely run, and that nothing was done to invite hostility, or left undone to avoid it.

It is to my mind unequivocal that the great mass of opinion in the Eastern States and in the State of New York is against war, if it can be avoided without absolute dishonor or the ultimate sacrifice of essential rights and interests; and I verily believe that the same sentiment is the radical one throughout the United States, *some* of the towns, perhaps, excepted; where even it is much to be doubted whether there would not be a minority for the affirmative, if the naked question was presented of war, or of measures which should be acknowledged to have a tendency to promote or produce it.

The natural inference from such a state of the public mind is, that if measures are adopted with the disapprobation and dissent of a large and enlightened minority of Congress, which in the event should appear to have been obstacles to a peaceable adjustment of our differences with Great Britain, there would be, under the pressure of the evils produced by them, a deep and extensive dissatisfaction with the conduct of the government—a loss of confidence in it, and an impatience under the measures which war would render unavoidable.

Prosperous as is truly the situation of the country; great as would be the evils of war to it, it would hardly seem to admit of a doubt, that no chance for preserving peace ought to be lost or diminished, in compliance either with resentment, or the speculative ideas which are the arguments for a hostile course of conduct.

At no moment were the indications of a plan on the part of Great Britain to go to war with us sufficiently decisive to preclude the hope of averting it by a negotiation conducted with prudent energy, and seconded by such military preparations as should be demonstrative of a resolution eventually to vindicate our rights. The revocation of the instructions of the 6th of November, even with the relaxation of some pretensions which Great Britain has in former wars maintained against neutral powers, is full evidence that if the system was before for war, it was then changed. The events which have taken place in Europe are of a nature to render it probable that such a system will not be revived, and that by prudent management we may still escape a calamity which we have the strongest motives, internal, as well as external, to shun. . . .

To you, sir, it is unnecessary to urge the extreme precariousness of the events of war. The inference to be drawn is too manifest to escape your penetration. This country ought not to set itself afloat upon an ocean so fluctuating, so dangerous, and so uncertain, but in a case of absolute necessity.

That necessity is certainly not yet apparent. The circumstances which have been noticed with regard to the recent change of conduct on the part of Great Britain, authorize a strong hope that a negotiation, conducted with ability and moderation, and supported at home by demonstrations of vigor and seriousness, would obviate those causes of collision which are the most urgent —might even terminate others, which have so long fostered dissatisfaction and enmity. There is room to suppose that the moment is peculiarly favorable to such an attempt. On this point there are symptoms of a common sentiment between the advocates and the opposers of an unembarrassed attempt to negotiate: the former desiring it from the confidence they have in its probable success; the *latter, from the same cause, endeavoring either to prevent its going on under right auspices, or to clog it with impediments which will frustrate its effect.*

All ostensibly agree, that one more experiment of negotiation ought to precede actual war; but there is this serious difference in the practice. The sincere friends of peace and accommodation are for leaving things in a state which will enable Great Britain, without abandoning self-respect, to do us the justice we seek. The others are for placing things upon a footing which would involve the disgrace or disrepute of having receded through intimidation.

This last scheme indubitably ends in war. The folly is too great to be seriously entertained by the discerning part of those who affect to believe the position—that Great Britain, fortified by the alliances of the greatest part of Europe, will submit to our demands, urged with the face of coercion, and preceded by acts of reprisal. She cannot do it without renouncing her pride and her dignity, without losing her consequence and weight in the scale of nations; and, consequently, it is morally certain that she will not do it. A proper estimate of the operation of the human passions, must satisfy us that she would be less disposed to receive the law from us than from any other nation—a people recently become a nation, not long since one of her dependencies, and as yet, if a Hercules, a Hercules in the cradle.

When one nation inflicts injuries upon another, which are causes of war, if this other means to negotiate before it goes to war, the usual and received course is to prepare for war, and proceed to negotiation, avoiding reprisals till the issue of the negotiation. This course is recommended by all enlightened writers on the laws of nations, as the course of moderation, propriety, and wisdom; and it is that commonly pursued, except where there is a disposition to go to war, or a commanding superiority of power.

Preparation for war, in such cases, contains in it nothing offensive. It is a mere precaution for self-defence, under circumstances which endanger the breaking out of war. It gives rise to no point of honor which can be a bar to equitable and amicable negotiation. But acts of reprisal speak a contrary effect—they change negotiation into peremptory demand, and they brandish a rod over the party on whom the demand is made. He must be humble indeed, if he comply with the demand to avoid the stripe. . . .

The proposition for cutting off all intercourse with Great Britain has not yet sufficiently developed itself to enable us to pronounce what it truly is. It may be so extensive in its provisions as even to include in fact, though not in form, sequestration, by rendering remittances penal or impracticable. Indeed, it can scarcely avoid so far interfering with the payment of debts already contracted, as in a great degree to amount to a virtual sequestration. But, however this may be, being adopted for the express purpose of retaliating or punishing injuries, to continue until those injuries are redressed, it is in the spirit of a reprisal. Its principle is avowedly coercion—a principle directly opposite to that of negotiation, which supposes an appeal to the reason and justice of the party. Caustic and stimulant in the highest degree, it cannot fail to have a correspondent effect upon the minds of those against whom it is directed. It cannot fail to be viewed as originating in motives of the most hostile and overbearing kind; to stir up all the feelings of pride and resentment in the nation as well as in the Cabinet; and, consequently, to render negotiations abortive.

It will be wonderful if the immediate effect of either of these measures be not either war or the seizure of our vessels wherever they are found, on the ground of keeping them as hostages for the debts due to the British merchants, and on the additional ground of the measures themselves being either acts of hostility or evidence of a disposition to hostility.

The interpretation will naturally be that our views, originally pacific, have changed with the change in the affairs of France, and are now bent towards war.

The measures in question, besides the objection to them resulting from their tendency to produce war, are condemned by a comprehensive and enlightened view of their operation in other respects. They cannot but have a malignant influence upon our public and mercantile credit. They will be regarded abroad as violent and precipitate. It will be said, there is no reliance to be placed on the steadiness or solidity of concerns with this people. Every gust that arises on the political sky is the signal for measures tending to destroy their ability to pay or to obstruct the course of payment. Instead of a people pacific, forbearing, moderate, and of rigid probity, we see in them a people turbulent, hasty, intemperate, and loose, sporting with their individual obligations, and disturbing the general course of their affairs with levity and inconsiderateness.

Such will indubitably be the comment upon our conduct. The favorable impressions now entertained of the character of our government and nation will infallibly be reversed.

The cutting off of intercourse with Great Britain, to distress her seriously, must extend to the prohibition of all her commodities, indirectly as well as directly; else it will have no other operation than to transfer the trade between the two countries to the hands of foreigners, to our disadvantage more than to that of Great Britain.

If it extends to the total prohibition of her commodities, however brought, it deprives us of a supply, for which no substitute can be found elsewhere— a supply necessary to us in peace, and more necessary to us if we are to go to war. It gives a sudden and violent blow to our revenue, which cannot easily, if at all, be repaired from other resources. It will give so great an interruption to commerce as may very possibly interfere with the payment of the duties which have heretofore accrued, and bring the Treasury to an absolute stoppage of payment—an event which would cut up credit by the roots.

The consequences of so great and so sudden a disturbance of our trade, which must affect our exports as well as our imports, cannot be calculated. An excessive rise in the price of foreign commodities—a proportionable decrease of price and demand of our own commodities—the derangement of our revenue and credit,—these circumstances united may occasion the most dangerous dissatisfactions and disorders in the community, and may drive the government to a disgraceful retreat, independent of foreign causes. . . .

'T is as great an error for a nation to overrate us as to underrate itself. Presumption is as great a fault as timidity. 'T is our error to overrate ourselves and underrate Great Britain; we forget how little we can annoy, how much we may be annoyed.

'T is enough for us, situated as we are, to be resolved to vindicate our honor and rights in the last extremity. To precipitate a great conflict of any sort is utterly unsuited to our condition, to our strength, or to our resources. This is a truth to be well weighed by every wise and dispassionate man, as the rule of public action.

There are two ideas of immense consequence to us in the event of war: the disunion of our enemies; the perfect union of our own citizens. Justice and moderation, united with firmness, are the means to secure both these advantages; injustice or intemperance will lose both.

Unanimity among ourselves, which is the most important of the two ideas, can only be secured by its being manifest, if war ensues, that it was inevitable by another course of conduct. This cannot and will not be the case, if measures so intemperate as those which are meditated take place. The inference will be, that the war was brought on by the design of some and the rashness of others. This inference will be universal in the Northern States; and to you, sir, I need not urge the importance of those States in war.

Want of unanimity will naturally tend to render the operations of war feeble and heavy, to destroy both effort and perseverance. War, undertaken under such auspices, can scarcely end in any thing better than an inglorious and disadvantageous peace. What worse it may produce is beyond the reach of human foresight. . . .

The crisis is such a one as involves the highest responsibility on the part of every one who may have to act a part in it. It is one in which every man will be understood to be bound to act according to his judgment without concession to the ideas of others. The President, who has by the Constitution a right to object to laws which he deems contrary to the public interest, will be considered as under an indispensable obligation to exercise that right against any measure, relating to so vast a point as that of the peace of the country, which shall not accord with his opinion. The consideration of its having been adopted by both Houses of Congress, and of respect for their opinions, will have no weight in such a case as a reason for forbearing to exercise the right of objection. The consequence is, that the not objecting will be deemed conclusive evidence of approbation, and will implicate the President in all the consequences of the measure.

In such a position of things, it is therefore of the utmost importance to him, as well as to the community, that he should trace out in his own mind such a plan as he thinks it would be eligible to pursue, and should endeavor, by proper and constitutional means, to give the deliberations of Congress a direction towards that plan.

Else he runs the risk of being reduced to the dilemma either of assenting to measures which he may not approve, with a full responsibility for consequences, or of objecting to measures which have already received the sanction of the two Houses of Congress, with the responsibility of having resisted and probably prevented what they meditated. Neither of these alternatives is a desirable one.

It seems advisable, then, that the President should come to a conclusion whether the plan ought to be preparation for war, and negotiation unincumbered by measures which forbid the expectation of success, or immediate measures of a coercive tendency, to be accompanied with the ceremony of a demand of redress. For I believe there is no middle plan between those two courses.

If the former appears to him to be the true policy of the country, I submit it as my conviction, that it is *urgent* for him to demonstrate that opinion as a preventive of wrong measures and future embarrassment.

The mode of doing it which occurs is this: to nominate a person who will have the confidence of those who think peace still within our reach, and who may be thought qualified for the mission as Envoy Extraordinary to Great Britain; to announce this to the one as well as the other House of Congress, with an observation that it is done with an intention to make a solemn appeal to the justice and good sense of the British Government, to avoid if possible an ulterior rupture, and adjust the causes of misunderstanding between the two countries, and with *an earnest recommendation that vigorous and effectual measures may be adopted to be prepared for war, should it become inevitable, abstaining for the present from measures which may be contrary to the spirit of an attempt to adjust existing differences by negotiation.*

Knowing as I do, sir, that I am among the persons who have been in your contemplation to be employed in the capacity I have mentioned, I should not have taken the present step, had I not been resolved at the same time to advise you with decision to drop me from the consideration, and to fix upon another character. I am not unapprised of what has been the bias of your opinion on the subject. I am well aware of all the collateral obstacles which exist; and I assure you in the utmost sincerity that I shall be completely and entirely satisfied with the election of another.

I beg leave to add, that of the persons whom you would deem free from any constitutional objections, Mr. Jay is the only man in whose qualifications for success there would be thorough confidence, and him whom alone it would be advisable to send. I think the business would have the best chance possible in his hands, and I flatter myself that his mission would issue in a manner that would produce the most important good to the nation.

Let me add, sir, that those whom I call the sober-minded men of the country look up to you with solicitude upon the present occasion. If happily you should be the instrument of still rescuing the country from the dangers and calamities of war, there is no part of your life, sir, which will produce to you more real satisfaction or true glory than that which shall be distinguished by this very important service.

In any event, I cannot doubt, sir, that you will do justice to the motives which impel me, and that you will see in this proceeding another proof of my sincere wishes for your honor and happiness, and anxiety for the public weal.

With the truest respect and attachment,

I have the honor to be, etc.

Discussion Starters

1. Why did Hamilton believe that a peace-through-negotiation policy on the part of the American government would be beneficial to the future of the United States?

2. In what way could Hamilton's negotiation proposals be interpreted as pro-English?

3. How did Hamilton's description of the emergence of parties in the United States fit his later arguments as to the course the federal government must

follow in foreign affairs? How valid were his indictments of those who opposed his proposals?

4. As a member of Washington's cabinet, how far could Hamilton go in limiting dissent for the sake of national unity?

5. How does this letter demonstrate Hamilton's influence in Washington's administration?

6. Given Hamilton's arguments, how would Jefferson have answered his conclusions?

Related Documents

I. The Insidious Treaty: A Letter From James Madison

Jay's Treaty provided the springboard the Republicans needed to gain national prominence. Being anti-British (antimonarchy) and pro-French (prorepublican), they attacked the treaty as a renunciation of the hard-won freedoms of the American Revolution. In the following letter James Madison expressed his opinion on the treaty and thus on the relationship between Great Britain and the United States.

How do his views compare with those expressed by Hamilton in his letter to Washington? In what ways would Madison disagree with Hamilton's description of political parties in the United States?

AUGUST 23, 1795

Dear Sir

Your favor of the third instant did not come to hand till a few days ago, having been probably retarded by the difficulty the post met with in passing the water-courses which have been much swelled of late by excessive rains. It gives me much pleasure to learn that your health has been so much improved; as well as that you are taking advantage of it to co-operate in elucidating the great subject before the public. . . .

. . . The characteristics of the Treaty which I have wished to see more fully laid open to the public view are 1. its ruinous tendency with respect to the carrying trade. The increase of our shipping under the new Government has, in most legislative discussion, been chiefly ascribed to the advantage given to

Gaillard Hunt, ed., *The Writings of James Madison* (New York, G. P. Putnam's Sons, 1906), VI, pp. 239–44, 256–57.

American vessels by the difference of 10 Per Cent on the impost in their favor. This, in the valuable cargoes from G. B. has been sufficient to check the preference of British Merchants for British bottoms; and it has been not deemed safe hitherto by G. B. to force on a contest with us, in this particular, by any countervailing regulations. In consequence of the Treaty, she will no doubt establish such regulations; and thereby leave the British capital free to prefer British vessels. This will not fail to banish our tonnage from the trade with that Country. And there seems to have been no disposition in the Negociator to do better for our navigation in the W. India trade; especially if the exclusion of our vessels from the re-exportation of the enumerated articles Sugar Coffee &c be taken into the account. The nature of our exports & imports compared with that of the British, is a sufficient, but at the same time our only defence against the superiority of her capital. The advantage they give us in fostering our navigation ought never to have been abandoned. If this view of the subject be just and were presented to the public with mercantile skill, it could not fail to make a deep impression on England. In fact the whole Treaty appears to me to assassinate the interest of that part of the Union.— 2 the insidious hostility of the Treaty to France in general; but particularly the operation of the 15th article, which as far as I have seen has been but faintly touched on, tho it be in fact, pregnant with more mischief than any of them.

According to all our other Treaties as well as those of all other nations, the footing of the most favored nations is so qualified, that those entitled to it, must pay the price of any particular privilege that may be granted in a new Treaty. The Treaty of Jay makes every new privilege result to G. B., without her paying any price at all. Should France, Spain, Portugal or any other nation offer the most precious privileges in their trade, as the price of some particular favour in ours, no bargain could be made, unless they would agree, not only to let the same favor be extended to G. B., but extended gratuitously. They could not purchase for themselves, without at the same time purchasing for their rival. In this point of view, the 15th article may be considered as a direct bar to our Treating with other nations, and particularly with The French Republic. Much has been said of a suspected backwardness to improve our commerical arrangements with France; and a predilection for arrangements with G. B., who had less to give, as well as less inclination to give what she had. It was hardly imagined that we were so soon to grant every thing to G. B. for nothing in return; and to make it a part of this bad bargain with her, that we should not be able to make a good one with any other nation. 3. the spirit in which every point of the law of nations is regulated. It is the interest of the U. S. to enlarge the rights of Neutral nations. It is the general interest of humanity that this should be done. In all our other Treaties this policy has prevailed. The same policy has pervaded most of the modern Treaties of other nations. G. B. herself has been forced into it in several of her Treaties. In the Treaty of Jay, every principle of liberality, every consideration of interest has been sacrificed to the arbitrary maxims which govern the policy of G. B. Nay a new principle has been created, in the face of former complaints of our Executive. As well as against the fundamental rights of nations & duties of humanity, for the purpose of aiding the horrible scheme of starving a whole people out of their liberties. . . .

. . . A Treaty thus unequal in its conditions, thus derogatory to our national rights, thus insidious in some of its objects, and thus alarming in its operation to the dearest interests of the U. S. in their commerce and navigation, is in its present form unworthy the voluntary acceptance of an Independent people, and is not dictated in them by the circumstances in which providence has kindly placed them. It is sincerely believed, that such a Treaty would not have been listened to at any former period, when G. B. was most at her ease, and the U. S. without the respectability they now enjoy. To pretend that however injurious the Treaty may be it ought to be submitted to in order to avoid the hostile resentment of G. B. which would evidently be as impolitic as it would be unjust on her part, is an artifice too comtemptible to answer its purpose. It will not easily be supposed, that a refusal to part with our rights without an equivalent will be made the pretext of a war on us; much less that such a pretext will be founded on our refusal to mingle a sacrifice of our commerce & navigation with an adjustment of political differences. Nor is any evidence to be found, either in History or Human nature, that nations, are to be bribed out of a spirit of encroachment & aggressions by humiliations which nourish their pride, or by concessions which extend their resources & power.

To do justice to all nations; to seek it from them by peaceable means in preference to war; and to confide in this policy for avoiding that extremity; or securing the blessing of Heaven, when forced upon us, is the only course of which the United States can never have reason to repent.

II. A Crisis Full of Instruction

FISHER AMES

Fisher Ames of Massachusetts became the spokesman for the Federalist point of view in the House of Representatives during Washington's two terms in office. Ames, like many Federalists, was committed to the idea that the United States would prosper only if the government was based upon an aristocracy of demonstrated talent and honor. He felt the growth of democracy would only lead to disunion and the eventual collapse of the country. Ames believed in a strong central government that would perpetuate its power and prestige by a dynamic and tireless execution of federal policy.

In the following letter to his friend Thomas Dwight, what effect did he claim Jay's Treaty had upon the growing political parties in the nation? How does his opinion of parties compare with Hamilton's description in his letter to Washington?

Fisher Ames, *Works* (Boston: Little, Brown, 1854), II, p. 172.

AUGUST, 1795

My letter by Mr. Boylston expressed to you and Colonel W. a vehement suspicion the President would not ratify the treaty. This was grounded on confidential information that he had gone to Virginia, and had not done it. Since that time, I am happy to learn, through a channel that I believe pure, that he has ratified it. Now let the heathen rage. If the government dare act right, I still believe it can maintain it. The time will come when faction will make it afraid; nay, when it will become the instrument of faction, and be as little disposed as able, to uphold order. Is it not manifest that the violence of this storm springs from the anticipation of the election to the Presidency? . . . Jefferson's party seize the moment to discredit their most dreaded rival, Jay. Clinton's and Adams's parties in the two States, and State parties elsewhere, enlist under the banner of the Jefferson leaders. Does this augur an unbiased appointment, or a cordial support, of Washington's successor? An experienced sailor would say, these little whirlwinds of dry leaves and dirt portend a hurricane. How can a government be managed in adverse times; and when the chief magistrate asks support against the faction of his rival, but can give none, or almost none, to the laws—when we see that the splendid name of the present possessor, though stronger than a host, scarcely protects him, and the government is but just spared from destruction by the mobs of Philadelphia, Boston, &c., although their complaining mouths are actually stopped by the showers of manna? A ship that is sinking, or near sinking at her anchors in the port, will drown her crew if they venture to sea in her. We shall, at any rate, get along for some time; and if the country people see that the wounds attempted to be given by the mobs aforesaid will be mortal, they will become alarmed, and afford such a support to law and order, as possibly may enable government to stand its ground. It is a crisis full of instruction, perhaps of fate.

Yours, &c.

III. Federalist Number 10

JAMES MADISON

The maturation of political parties during the crisis over Jay's Treaty came as no surprise to many men in and out of government. The development of parties, and their danger and benefit to the Republic, had been argued during the debates over the ratification of the Constitution in 1787 and 1788. The advocates of the Constitution believed the new instrument of government would prevent the development of parties or factions and had enlisted the pen of James Madison to support their cause. Madison's essays, along with those of Alexander Hamilton and John Jay, became collectively known as The Federalist. *Whether these essays were decisive in the ratification of the Constitution, especially in the*

Benjamin F. Wright, ed., *The Federalist* (Cambridge, Mass.: Belknap Press, 1961), pp. 129–33.

strategic state of New York where they were given the widest possible press, is uncertain, but they are without doubt the most complete and cogent statement of the political theory of America's founding fathers.

How does Madison's description of factions written in 1787 compare with Hamilton's evaluation of the emerging political parties in 1794? Why would Madison condemn Jay's Treaty and promote opposition to Hamilton in 1795 (see page 149) when eight years earlier he had condemned such actions in "Federalist Number 10"?

1787

To the People of the State of New York:

Among the numerous advantages promised by a well-constructed Union, none deserves to be more accurately developed than its tendency to break and control the violence of faction. The friend of popular governments never finds himself so much alarmed for their character and fate, as when he contemplates their propensity to this dangerous vice. He will not fail, therefore, to set a due value on any plan which, without violating the principles to which he is attached, provides a proper cure for it. The instability, injustice, and confusion introduced into the public councils, have, in truth, been the mortal diseases under which popular governments have everywhere perished; as they continue to be the favorite and fruitful topics from which the adversaries to liberty derive their most specious declamations. The valuable improvements made by the American constitutions on the popular models, both ancient and modern, cannot certainly be too much admired; but it would be an unwarrantable partiality, to contend that they have as effectually obviated the danger on this side, as was wished and expected. Complaints are everywhere heard from our most considerate and virtuous citizens, equally the friends of public and private faith, and of public and personal liberty, that our governments are too unstable, that the public good is disregarded in the conflicts of rival parties, and that measures are too often decided, not according to the rules of justice and the rights of the minor party, but by the superior force of an interested and overbearing majority. However anxiously we may wish that these complaints had no foundation, the evidence of known facts will not permit us to deny that they are in some degree true. It will be found, indeed, on a candid review of our situation, that some of the distresses under which we labor have been erroneously charged on the operation of our governments; but it will be found, at the same time, that other causes will not alone account for many of our heaviest misfortunes; and, particularly, for that prevailing and increasing distrust of public engagements, and alarm for private rights, which are echoes from one end of the continent to the other. These must be chiefly, if not wholly, effects of the unsteadiness and injustice with which a factious spirit has tainted our public administrations.

By a faction, I understand a number of citizens, whether amounting to a majority or minority of the whole, who are united and actuated by some common impulse of passion, or of interest, adverse to the rights of other citizens, or to the permanent and aggregate interests of the community.

There are two methods of curing the mischiefs of faction: the one, by removing its causes; the other, by controlling its effects.

There are again two methods of removing the causes of faction: the one, by destroying the liberty which is essential to its existence; the other, by giving to every citizen the same opinions, the same passions, and the same interests.

It could never be more truly said than of the first remedy, that it was worse than the disease. Liberty is to faction what air is to fire, an aliment without which it instantly expires. But it could not be less folly to abolish liberty, which is essential to political life, because it nourishes faction, than it would be to wish the annihilation of air, which is essential to animal life, because it imparts to fire its destructive agency.

The second expedient is as impracticable as the first would be unwise. As long as the reason of man continues fallible, and he is at liberty to exercise it, different opinions will be formed. As long as the connection subsists between his reason and his self-love, his opinions and his passions will have a reciprocal influence on each other; and the former will be objects to which the latter will attach themselves. The diversity in the faculties of men, from which the rights of property originate, is not less an insuperable obstacle to a uniformity of interests. The protection of these faculties is the first object of government. From the protection of different and unequal faculties of acquiring property, the possession of different degrees and kinds of property immediately results; and from the influence of these on the sentiments and views of the respective proprietors, ensues a division of the society into different interests and parties.

The latent causes of faction are thus sown in the nature of man; and we see them everywhere brought into different degrees of activity, according to the different circumstances of civil society. A zeal for different opinions concerning religion, concerning government, and many other points, as well of speculation as of practice; an attachment to different leaders ambitiously contending for pre-eminence and power; or to persons of other descriptions whose fortunes have been interesting to the human passions, have, in turn, divided mankind into parties, inflamed them with mutual animosity, and rendered them much more disposed to vex and oppress each other than to co-operate for their common good. So strong is this propensity of mankind to fall into mutual animosities, that where no substantial occasion presents itself, the most frivolous and fanciful distinctions have been sufficient to kindle their unfriendly passions and excite their most violent conflicts. But the most common and durable source of factions has been the various and unequal distribution of property. Those who hold and those who are without property have ever formed distinct interests in society. Those who are creditors, and those who are debtors, fall under a like discrimination. A landed interest, a manufacturing interest, a mercantile interest, a moneyed interest, with many lesser interests, grow up of necessity in civilized nations, and divide them into different classes, actuated by different sentiments and views. The regulation of these various and interfering interests forms the principal task of modern legislation, and involves the spirit of party and faction in the necessary and ordinary operations of the government.

No man is allowed to be a judge in his own cause, because his interest would certainly bias his judgment, and, not improbably, corrupt his integrity. With equal, nay with greater reason, a body of men are unfit to be both judges and parties at the same time; yet what are many of the most important acts of legislation, but so many judicial determinations, not indeed concerning the rights of single persons, but concerning the rights of large bodies of citizens? And what are the different classes of legislators but advocates and parties to the causes which they determine? Is a law proposed concerning private debts? It is a question to which the creditors are parties on one side and the debtors on the other. Justice ought to hold the balance between them. Yet the parties are, and must be, themselves the judges; and the most numerous party, or, in other words, the most powerful faction must be expected to prevail. Shall domestic manufactures be encouraged, and in what degree, by restrictions on foreign manufactures? are questions which would be differently decided by the landed and the manufacturing classes, and probably by neither with a sole regard to justice and the public good. The apportionment of taxes on the various descriptions of property is an act which seems to require the most exact impartiality; yet there is, perhaps, no legislative act in which greater opportunity and temptation are given to a predominant party to trample on the rules of justice. Every shilling with which they overburden the inferior number, is a shilling saved to their own pockets.

It is in vain to say that enlightened statesmen will be able to adjust these clashing interests, and render them all subservient to the public good. Enlightened statesmen will not always be at the helm. Nor, in many cases, can such an adjustment be made at all without taking into view indirect and remote considerations, which will rarely prevail over the immediate interest which one party may find in disregarding the rights of another or the good of the whole.

The inference to which we are brought is, that the *causes* of faction cannot be removed, and that relief is only to be sought in the means of controlling its *effects*.

If a faction consists of less than a majority, relief is supplied by the republican principle, which enables the majority to defeat its sinister views by regular vote. It may clog the administration, it may convulse the society; but it will be unable to execute and mask its violence under the forms of the Constitution. When a majority is included in a faction, the form of popular government, on the other hand, enables it to sacrifice to its ruling passion or interest both the public good and the rights of other citizens. To secure the public good and private rights against the danger of such a faction, and at the same time to preserve the spirit and the form of popular government, is then the great object to which our inquiries are directed. Let me add that it is the great desideratum by which this form of government can be rescued from the opprobrium under which it has so long labored, and be recommended to the esteem and adoption of mankind.

By what means is this object attainable? Evidently by one of two only.

Either the existence of the same passion or interest in a majority at the same time must be prevented, or the majority, having such coexistent passion or interest, must be rendered, by their number and local situation, unable to concert and carry into effect schemes of oppression. If the impulse and the opportunity be suffered to coincide, we well know that neither moral nor religious motives can be relied on as an adequate control. They are not found to be such on the injustice and violence of individuals, and lose their efficacy in proportion to the number combined together, that is, in proportion as their efficacy becomes needful.

IV. Anti-Republicans and Republicans

THOMAS JEFFERSON

Thomas Jefferson became the standard-bearer of the Republicans in the presidential election of 1796. Although he subsequently lost the presidency, he did win enough electoral votes to gain the vice presidency. But Jefferson, along with Madison and Hamilton, had earlier in his career spoken out against political parties in the United States. He justified this change of heart in a letter to his friend William Branch Giles in 1795. He stated,

> *Were parties here divided merely by a greediness for office, as in England, to take a part with either would be unworthy of a reasonable or moral man, but where the principle of difference is as substantial and as strongly pronounced as between the republicans & the Monocrats of our country, I hold it as honorable to take a firm & decided part, and as immoral to pursue a middle line, as between the parties of Honest men, & Rogues, into which every country is divided.*

> *In the following extract Jefferson describes the formation of the political parties in the United States, and particularly the make-up of the two main parties. How does his viewpoint differ from that of Hamilton?*

The people of America, before the revolution-war, being attached to England, had taken up, without examination, the English ideas of the superiority of their constitution over every thing of the kind which ever had been or ever would be tried. The revolution forced them to consider the subject for themselves, and the result was an universal conversion to republicanism. Those who did not come over to this opinion, either left us, & were called Refugees, or staid with us under the name of tories; & some, preferring profit to principle took side with us and floated with the general tide. Our first federal constitution, or confederation as it was called, was framed in the first moments of our separation from England, in the highest point of our jealousies of independance as to her & as to each other. It formed therefore too weak a bond to produce an

Paul Leicester Ford, ed., *The Works of Thomas Jefferson* (New York: G.P. Putnam's Sons, 1904), VIII, pp. 206–10.

union of action as to foreign nations. This appeared at once on the establishment of peace, when the pressure of a common enemy which had hooped us together during the war, was taken away. Congress was found to be quite unable to point the action of the several states to a common object. A general desire therefore took place of amending the federal constitution. This was opposed by some of those who wished for monarchy to wit, the Refugees now returned, the old tories, & the timid whigs who prefer tranquility to freedom, hoping monarchy might be the remedy if a state of complete anarchy could be brought on. A Convention however being decided on, some of the monocrats got elected, with a hope of introducing an English constitution, when they found that the great body of the delegates were strongly for adhering to republicanism, & for giving due strength to their government under that form, they then directed their efforts to the assimilation of all the parts of the new government to the English constitution as nearly as was attainable. In this they were not altogether without success; insomuch that the monarchical features of the new constitution produced a violent opposition to it from the most zealous republicans in the several states. For this reason, & because they also thought it carried the principle of a consolidation of the states farther than was requisite for the purpose of producing an union of action as to foreign powers, it is still doubted by some whether a majority of the people of the U. S. were not against adopting it. However it was carried through all the assemblies of the states, tho' by very small majorities in the largest states. The inconveniences of an inefficient government, driving the people as is usual, into the opposite extreme, the elections to the first Congress run very much in favor of those who were known to favor a very strong government. Hence the anti-republicans appeared a considerable majority in both houses of Congress. They pressed forward the plan therefore of strengthening all the features of the government which gave it resemblance to an English constitution, of adopting the English forms & principles of administration, and of forming like them a monied interest, by means of a funding system, not calculated to pay the public debt, but to render it perpetual, and to make it an engine in the hands of the executive branch of the government which, added to the great patronage it possessed in the disposal of public offices, might enable it to assume by degrees a kingly authority. The biennial period of Congress being too short to betray to the people, spread over this great continent, this train of things during the first Congress, little change was made in the members to the second. But in the mean time two very distinct parties had formed in Congress; and before the third election, the people in general became apprised of the game which was playing for drawing over them a kind of government which they never had in contemplation. At the 3d. election therefore a decided majority of Republicans were sent to the lower house of Congress; and as information spread still farther among the people after the 4th. election the anti-republicans have become a weak minority. But the members of the Senate being changed but once in 6. years, the completion of that body will be much slower in it's assimilation to that of the people. This will account for the differences which may appear in the proceedings & spirit of the two houses. Still however it is inevitable that the Senate will at length be formed to the republican model of the people, & the two houses of the legislature, once brought to act on the true principles of the Constitution, backed by the people, will be able to defeat the plan of sliding us into monarchy, & to keep the Executive within Republican bounds, notwithstanding the immense patronage it possesses in the disposal of public offices, notwithstanding it has been able to draw into this vortex the judiciary branch of the government & by their expectancy of sharing the other offices in the Executive gift to make them auxiliary to the Executive in all it's views instead of forming a balance between that & the legislature as it was originally intended and notwithstanding the funding phalanx which a respect for public faith must protect, who it was engaged by false brethren. Two parties then do exist within the U. S. they embrace respectively the following descriptions of persons.

The Anti-republicans consist of

1. The old refugees & tories.

2. British merchants residing among us, & composing the main body of our merchants.

3. American merchants trading on British capital. Another great portion.

4. Speculators & Holders in the banks & public funds.

5. Officers of the federal government with some exceptions.

6. Office-hunters, willing to give up principles for places. A numerous & noisy tribe.

7. Nervous persons, whose languid fibres have more analogy with a passive than active state of things.

The Republican part of our Union comprehends

1. The entire body of landholders throughout the United States.

2. The body of labourers, not being landholders, whether in husbanding or the arts.

The latter is to the aggregate of the former party probably as 500 to one; but their wealth is not as disproportionate, tho' it is also greatly superior, and is in truth the foundation of that of their antagonists. Trifling as are the numbers of the Anti-republican party, there are circumstances which give them an appearance of strength & numbers. They all live in cities, together, & can act in a body readily & at all times; they give chief employment to the newspapers, & therefore have most of them under their command. The Agricultural interest is dispersed over a great extent of country, have little means of intercommunication with each other, and feeling their own strength & will, are conscious that a single exertion of these will at any time crush the machinations against their government. . . .

For Further Reading

The development of political parties has been examined by many historians over the years; some of the more recent studies are: Morton Borden, *Parties and Politics in the Early Republic, 1789–1815** (1967); William N. Chambers,

*Paperbound edition available.

Political Parties In a New Nation* (1963); Noble Cunningham, Jr., *The Jeffersonian Republicans** (1957); David Fischer, *The Revolution of American Conservatism** (1965); Joseph La Palombara and Myron Weiner, eds., *Political Parties and Political Development** (1966); and John C. Miller, *The Federalist Era, 1789–1801** (1960).

Since the formation of parties was influenced by the foreign policies of the new government, these books are important: Samuel F. Bemis, *Jay's Treaty** (1923; revised edition 1962); Joseph Charles, *The Origins of the American Party System** (1956); Jerald A. Combs, *The Jay Treaty* (1970); Felix Gilbert, *To the Farewell Address** (1961); and Paul Varg, *Foreign Policies of the Founding Fathers** (1963).

Biographies of some of the leading men of the period include: Irving Brant, *James Madison, Father of the Constitution* (1950); Dumas Malone, *Thomas Jefferson and the Ordeal of Liberty** (1962); John C. Miller, *Alexander Hamilton** (1959); and Page Smith, *John Adams* (1962).

An interesting collection of primary source material can be found in *The Making of the American Party System** (1965), edited by Noble Cunningham, Jr.; while problems books on the period are: George Athan Billias, ed., *The Federalists** (1970), and Paul Goodman, ed., *The Federalists vs. the Jeffersonian Republicans** (1967).

A book of interpretations by historians on the development of parties is *The Early American Party System** (1969), edited by Norman K. Risjord.

*Paperbound edition available.

8. Nationalism
American Style

American nationalism developed out of ideas made popular by the European Enlightenment. Two of those ideas—individual freedom and representative government—became the heart of the nationalistic spirit in the colonies and later in the nation. They helped the colonists to band together, sometimes reluctantly, to resist the British and to pursue independence. In the decades after the Revolution evidences of the spirit of nationalism ranged from Noah Webster's proposal to reform the language to George Washington's *Farewell Address*. But the recognition of true national identity, transcending the traditions of sectionalism, did not emerge until the end of the War of 1812.

Once the war was over and America entered the so-called "Era of Good Feelings," many newspaper editors, politicians, and clergymen hailed the late war as the Second War for Independence. They predicted a glorious future for the United States because the nation had finally established itself as a full-fledged member of the family of nations and was entering a promising period of national prosperity. To support their visions they pointed to the increasing importance of manufacturing in the Northeast, the rapidly developing cotton production in the South, and the expanding agriculture of the West. There were setbacks to their predictions, such as the Panic of 1819 and the controversy over the admission of Missouri as a state, but they were regarded as only temporary disturbances. To some men the sectional conflict leading to the Missouri Compromise may have been a fire bell in the night, but many either did not hear it or, if they did, tried to ignore its alarm. They believed America was no longer an experiment, but rather a thriving nation, destined to prove that it could and would survive.

Core Document

The Protection of Home Industry

HENRY CLAY

Henry Clay of Kentucky had been a spokesman for western interests and one of the leading "war hawks" in Congress prior to the War of 1812. After the war he became one of the chief advocates of a program for the economic development of the United States. Clay's plan, known as the American System, was based upon the concept of a protective tariff. He believed such protection would keep the United States politically independent of foreign machinations by making the nation economically self-sufficient.

In 1816 Clay and the other supporters of a protective system, including John C. Calhoun of South Carolina, passed a mildly protectionist tariff in Congress. But in 1820, when a new tariff providing for higher rates was introduced, the good will of 1816 had disappeared. The opponents of the Tariff of 1820 spoke of the disadvantages the tariff would work upon their particular section rather than on how it would affect the nation as a whole. Calhoun opposed the new tariff, for he believed it would cause a loss in southern buying power, which was dependent upon foreign markets for the sale of cotton. Daniel Webster of Massachusetts, who represented the commercial and shipping interests of the Northeast, had opposed the Tariff of 1816 and continued his opposition in 1820 because he believed the new tariff would artificially build up one segment of the economy to the detriment of all others.

But Clay, backed by many western farmers who wanted protection from cheap foreign foodstuffs and by many manufacturers in the Northeast and Middle states, defended the tariff as vital to the national development of the United States. The Tariff of 1820 passed the House, but lost in the Senate by one vote. Nationalism had emerged in the United States, but it did not yet dictate national policy.

In reading Clay's defense of his proposed American System, note his reasons for believing that:

- *the increasing population of the United States encouraged the growth of manufacturing.*

Henry Clay, *Life and Speeches,* ed. by Daniel Mallory (New York: Robert P. Bixby, 1843), I, pp. 405–16, 419, 423.

- *the future overseas marketability of tobacco, cotton, and foodstuffs was cause for protectionism.*
- *the independence of the United States was tied to food, clothing, and defense.*
- *America was politically free, but commercially a slave.*
- *the objectionable aspects of industrialization could be remedied.*
- *the frontier contributed to the growth of manufacturing.*
- *industry had certain virtues not found in agriculture.*
- *revenue for the federal treasury would be generated by industrialization.*
- *society was based upon mutual concession.*
- *domestic industry would promote peace.*

APRIL 26, 1820

In considering the subject, the first important inquiry that we should make is, whether it be desirable that such a portion of the capital and labor of the country should be employed in the business of manufacturing, as would furnish a supply of our necessary wants? Since the first colonization of America, the principal direction of the labor and capital of the inhabitants, has been to produce raw materials for the consumption or fabrication of foreign nations. We have always had, in great abundance, the means of subsistence, but we have derived chiefly from other countries our clothes, and the instruments of defence. Except during those interruptions of commerce arising from a state of war, or from measures adopted for vindicating our commercial rights, we have experienced no very great inconvenience heretofore from this mode of supply. The limited amount of our surplus produce, resulting from the smallness of our numbers, and the long and arduous convulsions of Europe, secured us good markets for that surplus in her ports, or those of her colonies. But those convulsions have now ceased, and our population has reached nearly ten millions. A new epoch has arisen; and it becomes us deliberately to contemplate our own actual condition, and the relations which are likely to exist between us and the other parts of the world. The actual state of our population, and the ratio of its progressive increase, when compared with the ratio of the increase of the population of the countries which have hitherto consumed our raw produce, seem, to me, alone to demonstrate the necessity of diverting some portion of our industry from its accustomed channel. We double our population in about the term of twenty-five years. If there be no change in the mode of exerting our industry, we shall double, during the same term, the amount of our exportable produce. Europe, including such of her colonies as we have free access to, taken altogether, does not duplicate her population in a shorter term, probably, than one hundred years. The ratio of the increase of her capacity of consumption, therefore, is, to that of our capacity of production, as one is to four. And it is manifest, from the simple exhibition of the powers of the consuming countries, compared with those of the supplying country, that the former are inadequate to the latter. It is certainly true, that a portion of the mass of our raw produce, which we transmit to her, reverts to us in a fabricated form, and that this return augments with our increasing population. This is, however, a very inconsiderable addition to her actual ability to afford a market for the produce of our industry.

I believe that we are already beginning to experience the want of capacity in Europe to consume our surplus produce. Take the articles of cotton, tobacco, and bread-stuffs. For the latter we have scarcely any foreign demand. And is there not reason to believe, that we have reached, if we have not passed, the maximum of the foreign demand for the other two articles? Considerations connected with the cheapness of cotton, as a raw material, and the facility with which it can be fabricated, will probably make it to be more and more used as a substitute for other materials. But, after you allow to the demand for it the utmost extension of which it is susceptible, it is yet quite *limited*—limited by the number of persons who use it, by their wants and their ability to supply them. If we have not reached, therefore, the maximum of the foreign demand, (as I believe we have,) we must soon fully satisfy it. With respect to tobacco, that article affording an enjoyment not necessary, as food and clothes are, to human existence, the foreign demand for it is still more precarious, and I apprehend that we have already passed its limits. It appears to me, then, that, if we consult our interest merely, we ought to encourage home manufactures. But there are other motives to recommend it, of not less importance.

The wants of man may be classed under three heads; food, raiment, and defence. They are felt alike in the state of barbarism and of civilization. He must be defended against the ferocious beasts of prey in the one condition, and against the ambition, violence, and injustice, incident to the other. If he seeks to obtain a supply of those wants without giving an equivalent, he is a beggar or a robber; if by promising an equivalent which he cannot give, he is fraudulent; and if by commerce, in which there is perfect freedom on his side, whilst he meets with nothing but restrictions on the other, he submits to an unjust and degrading inequality. What is true of individuals is equally so of nations. The country, then, which relies upon foreign nations for either of those great essentials, is not, in fact, independent. Nor is it any consolation for our dependence upon other nations, that they are also dependent upon us, even were it true. Every nation should anxiously endeavor to establish its absolute independence, and consequently be able to feed, and clothe, and defend itself. If it rely upon a foreign supply, that may be cut off by the caprice of the nation yielding it, by war with it, or even by war with other nations, it cannot be independent. But it is not true, that any other nations depend upon us in a degree any thing like equal to that of our dependence upon them for the great necessaries to which I have referred. Every other nation seeks to supply itself with them from its own resources; and, so strong is the desire which they feel to accomplish this purpose, that they exclude the cheaper foreign article, for the dearer home production. Witness the English policy in regard to corn. So selfish, in this respect, is the conduct of other powers, that, in some instances, they even prohibit the produce of the industry of their *own* colonies, when it comes into competition with the produce of the parent country. All other countries but our own, exclude by high duties, or absolute prohibitions, whatever they can respectively produce within themselves. The truth is, and it is in vain to disguise it, that we are a sort of independent colonies of England—politically free, commercially slaves. Gentlemen tell us of the advantages of a free exchange of the produce of the world. But they tell us of what has never existed, does not exist, and perhaps never will exist. . . .

But, say gentlemen, there are to the manufacturing system some inherent objections, which should induce us to avoid its introduction into this country; and we are warned by the example of England, by her pauperism, by the vices of her population, her wars, and so forth. It would be a strange order of Providence, if it were true, that he should create necessary and indispensable wants, and yet should render us unable to supply them without the degradation or contamination of our species.

Pauperism is, in general, the effect of an overflowing population. Manufactures may undoubtedly produce a redundant population; but so may commerce, and so may agriculture. In this respect they are alike; and from whatever cause the disproportion of a population to the subsisting faculty of a country may proceed, its effect of pauperism is the same. . . . France resembles this country more than England, in respect to the employments of her population; and we do not find that there is any thing in the condition of the manufacturing portion of it, which ought to dissuade us from the introduction of it into our own country. But even France has not that great security against the abuses of the manufacturing system, against the effects of too great a density of population, which we possess in our waste lands. While this resource exists, we have nothing to apprehend. Do capitalists give too low wages; are the laborers too crowded, and in danger of starving? the unsettled lands will draw off the redundancy, and leave the others better provided for. If an unsettled province, such as Texas, for example, could, by some convulsion of nature, be wafted alongside of, and attached to, the island of Great Britain, the instantaneous effect would be, to draw off the redundant portion of the population, and to render more comfortable both the emigrants and those whom they would leave behind. I am aware, that while the public domain is an acknowledged security against the abuses of the manufacturing, or any other system, it constitutes, at the same time, an impediment, in the opinion of some, to the success of manufacturing industry, by its tendency to prevent the reduction of the wages of labor. Those who urge this objection have their eyes too much fixed on the ancient system of manufacturing, when manual labor was the principal instrument which it employed. During the last half century, since the inventions of Arkwright, and the long train of improvements which followed, the labor of machinery is principally used. I have understood, from sources of information which I believe to be accurate, that the combined force of all the machinery employed by Great Britain, in manufacturing, is equal to the labor of one hundred millions of able-bodied men. If we suppose the aggregate of the labor of all the individuals which she employs in that branch of industry to be equal to the united labor of two millions of able-bodied men, (and I should think it does not exceed it,) machine labor will stand to manual labor, in the proportion of one hundred to two. There cannot be a doubt that we have skill and enterprise enough to command the requisite amount of machine power.

There are, too, some checks to emigration from the settled parts of our country to the waste lands of the west. Distance is one, and it is every day becoming greater and greater. There exists, also, a natural repugnance (felt less, it is true, in the United States than elsewhere, but felt even here,) to abandoning the place of our nativity. Women and children, who could not migrate, and who would be comparatively idle if manufactures did not exist, may be profitably employed in them. This is a very great benefit. I witnessed the advantage resulting from the employment of this description of our population, in a visit which I lately made to the Waltham manufactory, near Boston. There, some hundreds of girls and boys were occupied in separate apartments. The greatest order, neatness, and apparent comfort, reigned throughout the whole establishment. The daughters of respectable farmers, in one instance, I remember, the daughter of a senator in the state legislature, were usefully employed. They would come down to the manufactory, remain perhaps some months, and return, with their earnings, to their families, to assist them throughout the year. But one instance had occurred, I was informed by the intelligent manager, of doubtful conduct on the part of any of the females, and, after she was dismissed, there was reason to believe that injustice had been done her. Suppose that establishment to be destroyed, what would become of all the persons who are there engaged so beneficially to themselves, and so usefully to the state? Can it be doubted that, if the crowds of little mendicant boys and girls who infest this edifice, and assail us, every day, at its very thresholds, as we come in and go out, begging for a cent, were employed in some manufacturing establishment, it would be better for them and the city? Those who object to the manufacturing system should recollect, that constant occupation is the best security for innocence and virtue, and that idleness is the parent of vice and crime. They should contemplate the laboring poor with employment, and ask themselves what would be their condition without it. If there are instances of hard taskmasters among the manufacturers, so also are there in agriculture. The cause is to be sought for, not in the nature of this or that system, but in the nature of man. If there are particular species of unhealthy employment in manufactures, so there are in agriculture also. There has been an idle attempt to ridicule the manufacturing system, and we have heard the expression, 'spinning-jenny tenure.' It is one of the noblest inventions of human skill. It has diffused comforts among thousands who, without it, would never have enjoyed them; and millions yet unborn will bless the man by whom it was invented. Three important inventions have distinguished the last half century, each of which, if it had happened at long intervals of time from the other, would have been sufficient to constitute an epoch in the progress of the useful arts. The first was that of Arkwright; and our own country is entitled to the merit of the other two. The world is indebted to Whitney for the one, and to Fulton for the other. Nothing is secure against the shafts of ridicule. What would be thought of a man who should speak of a cotton-gin tenure, or a steamboat tenure?

In one respect there is a great difference in favor of manufactures, when compared with agriculture. It is the rapidity with which the whole manufacturing community avail themselves of an improvement. It is instantly communicated and put in operation. There is an avidity for improvement in the one system, an aversion to it in the other. . . . .

It is objected, that the effect of the encouragement of home manufactures, by the proposed tariff, will be, to diminish the revenue from the customs. The amount of the revenue from that source will depend upon the amount of importations, and the measure of these will be the value of the exports from this country. The quantity of the exportable produce will depend upon the foreign demand; and there can be no doubt that, under any distribution of the labor and capital of this country, from the greater allurements which agriculture presents than any other species of industry, there would be always a quantity of its produce sufficient to satisfy that demand. If there be a diminution in the ability of foreign nations to consume our raw produce, in the proportion of our diminished consumption of theirs, under the operation of this system, that will be compensated by the substitution of a home for a foreign market, in the same proportion. It is true, that we cannot remain in the relation of seller, only to foreign powers, for any length of time; but if, as I have no doubt, our agriculture will continue to supply, as far as it can profitably, to the extent of the limits of foreign demand, we shall receive not only in return many of the articles on which the tariff operates, for our own consumption, but they may also form the objects of trade with South America and other powers, and our comforts may be multiplied by the importation of other articles. Diminished consumption, in consequence of the augmentation of duties, does not necessarily imply diminished revenue. The increase of the duty may compensate the decrease in the consumption, and give you as large a revenue as you before possessed.

Can any one doubt the impolicy of government resting solely upon the precarious resource of such a revenue? It is constantly fluctuating. It tempts us, by its enormous amount, at one time, into extravagant expenditure; and we are then driven, by its sudden and unexpected depression, into the opposite extreme. We are seduced by its flattering promises into expenses which we might avoid; and we are afterwards constrained by its treachery, to avoid expenses which we ought to make. It is a system under which there is a sort of perpetual war, between the interest of the government and the interest of the people. Large importations fill the coffers of government, and empty the pockets of the people. Small importations imply prudence on the part of the people, and leave the treasury empty. In war, the revenue disappears; in peace it is unsteady. On such a system the government will not be able much longer exclusively to rely. We all anticipate that we shall have shortly to resort to some additional supply of revenue within ourselves. . . .

. . . By the encouragement of home industry, you will lay a basis of internal taxation, when it gets strong, that will be steady uniform, yielding alike in peace and in war. We do not derive our ability from abroad, to pay taxes. That depends upon our wealth and our industry; and it is the same, whatever may be the form of levying the public contributions.

But it is urged, that you tax other interests of the state to sustain manufacturers. The business of manufacturing, if encouraged, will be open to all. It is not for the sake of the particular individuals who may happen to be engaged in it, that we propose to foster it; but it is for the general interest. We think that it is necessary to the comfort and well-being of society, that fabrication, as well as the business of production and distribution, should be supported and taken care of. Now, if it be even true, that the price of the home fabric will be somewhat higher, in the first instance, than the rival foreign articles, that consideration ought not to prevent our extending reasonable protection to the home fabric. Present temporary inconvenience may be well submitted to for the sake of future permanent benefit. If the experience of all other countries be not utterly fallacious; if the promises of the manufacturing system be not absolutely illusory; by the competition which will be elicited in consequence of your parental care, prices will be ultimately brought down to a level with that of the foreign commodity. Now, in a scheme of policy which is devised for a nation, we should not limit our views to its operation during a single year, or for even a short term of years. We should look at its operation for a considerable time, and in war as well as in peace. Can there be a doubt, thus contemplating it, that we shall be compensated by the certainty and steadiness of the supply in all seasons, and the ultimate reduction of the price for any temporary sacrifices we make? Take the example of salt, which the ingenious gentleman from Virginia (Mr. Archer) has adduced. He says, during the war, the price of that article rose to ten dollars per bushel, and he asks if you would lay a duty, permanent in its duration, of three dollars per bushel, to secure a supply in war. I answer, no, I would not lay so high a duty. That which is now proposed, for the encouragement of the domestic production, is only five cents per bushel. In forty years the duty would amount only to two dollars. If the recurrence of war shall be only after intervals of forty years' peace, (and we may expect it probably oftener,) and if, when it does come, the same price should again be given, there will be a clear saving of eight dollars, by promoting the domestic fabrication. All society is an affair of mutual concession. If we expect to derive the benefits which are incident to it, we must sustain our reasonable share of burdens. The great interests which it is intended to guard and cherish, must be supported by their reciprocal action and reaction. The harmony of its parts is disturbed, the discipline which is necessary to its order is incomplete, when one of the three great and essential branches of its industry is abandoned and unprotected. If you want to find an example of order, of freedom from debt, of economy, of expenditure falling below rather than exceeding income, you will go to the well-regulated family of a farmer. You will go to the house of such a man as Isaac Shelby; you will not find him haunting taverns, engaged in broils, prosecuting angry lawsuits; you will behold every member of his family clad with the produce of their own hands, and usefully employed; the spinning-wheel and the loom in motion by daybreak. With what pleasure will his wife carry you into her neat dairy, lead you into her store-house, and point you to the table-cloths, the sheets, the counterpanes which lie on this shelf for one daughter, or on that for another, all prepared in advance by her provident care for the day of their respective marriages. If you want to see an opposite example, go to the house of a man who manufactures nothing at home, whose family resorts to the store for everything they consume. You will find him perhaps in the tavern, or at the shop at the cross-roads. He is engaged, with the rum-grog on the table, taking depositions to make out some case of usury or fraud. Or perhaps he is furnishing to his lawyer the materials to prepare a long bill of injunction in some intricate case. The sheriff is hovering about his farm to serve some new writ. On court-days—he never misses attending them—you will find him eagerly collecting his witnesses to defend himself against the merchant and doctor's claims. Go to his house, and, after the short and giddy period that his wife and daughters have flirted about the country in their calico and muslin frocks, what a scene of discomfort and distress is presented to you there! What the individual family of Isaac Shelby is, I wish to see the nation in the aggregate become. But I fear we shall shortly have to contemplate its resemblance in the opposite picture. If statesmen would carefully observe the conduct of private individuals in the management of their own affairs, they would have much surer guides in promoting the interests of the state, than the visionary speculations of theoretical writers. . . .

The manufacturing system is favorable to the maintenance of peace. Foreign commerce is the great source of foreign wars. The eagerness with which we contend for every branch of it, the temptations which it offers, operating alike upon us and our foreign competitors, produce constant collisions. No country on earth, by the extent of its superfices, the richness of its soil, the variety of its climate, contains within its own limits more abundant facilities for supplying all our rational wants than ours does. It is not necessary or desirable, however, to cut off all intercourse with foreign powers. But, after securing a supply within ourselves, of all the great essentials of life, there will be ample scope still left for preserving such an intercourse. If we had no intercourse with foreign states, if we adopted the policy of China, we should have no external wars. And in proportion as we diminish our dependence upon them, shall we lessen the danger of the recurrence of war. Our late war would not have existed if the counsels of the manufacturers in England had been listened to. They finally did prevail, in their steady and persevering effort to produce a repeal of the orders in council; but it was too late to prevent the war.

The tendency of reasonable encouragement to our home industry is favorable to the preservation and strength of our confederacy. Now our connection is merely political. For the sale of the surplus of the produce of our agricultural labor, all eyes are constantly turned upon the markets of Liverpool. There is scarcely any of that beneficial intercourse, the best basis of political connection, which consists of the exchange of the produce of our labor. On our maritime frontier there has been too much stimulus, an unnatural activity; in the great interior of the country, there exists a perfect paralysis. Encourage fabrication at home, and there will instantly arise animation and a healthful circulation throughout all the parts of the republic. The cheapness, fertility, and quantity of our waste lands, offer such powerful inducements to cultivation, that our countrymen are constantly engaging in it. I would not check this disposition, by hard terms in the sale of it. Let it be easily accessible to all who wish to acquire it. But I would countervail this predilection, by presenting to capital and labor motives for employment in other branches of industry. Nothing is more uncertain than the pursuit of agriculture, when we mainly rely upon foreign markets for the sale of its surplus produce. In the first place, it is impossible to determine, *a priori,* the amount of this surplus; and, in the second, it is equally impossible to anticipate the extent of the foreign demand. Both the one and the other depend upon the seasons. From the fluctuations incident to these, and from other causes, it may happen that the supplying country will, for a long series of years, have employed a larger share of its capital and labor than is wise, in production to supply the wants of the consuming countries, without becoming sensible of its defect of policy. The failure of a crop, or the failure of a market, does not discourage the cultivator. He renews his labors another year, and he renews his hopes. It is otherwise with manufacturing industry. The precise quantum of its produce, at least, can with some accuracy be previously estimated. And the wants of foreign countries can be with some probability anticipated. . . .

But, sir, friendly as I am to the existence of domestic manufactures, I would not give to them unreasonable encouragement, by protecting duties. Their growth ought to be gradual, but sure. I believe all the circumstances of the present period highly favorable to their success. But they are the youngest and the weakest interest of the state. Agriculture wants but little or no protection against the regulations of foreign powers. The advantages of our position, and the cheapness, and abundance, and fertility of our land, afford to that greatest interest of the state almost all the protection it wants. As it should be, it is strong and flourishing; or, if it be not, at this moment, prosperous, it is not because its produce is not ample, but because, depending, as we do altogether, upon a foreign market for the sale of the surplus of that produce, the foreign market is glutted. Our foreign trade, having almost exclusively engrossed the protecting care of government, wants no further legislative aid. . . .

Mr. Chairman, I frankly own that I feel great solicitude for the success of this bill. The entire independence of my country on all foreign states, as it respects a supply of our essential wants, has ever been with me a favorite object. The war of our revolution effected our political emancipation. The last war contributed greatly towards accomplishing our commercial freedom. But our complete independence will only be consummated after the policy of this bill shall be recognised and adopted. We have, indeed, great difficulties to contend with—old habits, colonial usages, the obduracy of the colonial spirit, the enormous profits of a foreign trade, prosecuted under favorable circumstances, which no longer continue. I will not despair; the cause, I verily believe, is the cause of the country. It may be postponed; it may be frustrated for the moment, but it must finally prevail. Let us endeavor to acquire for the present congress, the merit of having laid this solid foundation of the national prosperity. . . .

Discussion Starters

1. How valid were Clay's arguments that the growth of home industry in the United States could only be beneficial to the nation? Should not the possibility of industrial slums, industrial unemployment, and the exploitation and destruction of the environment also have been considered? If so, how? If not, why not?

2. Evaluate the argument that the imposition of a protective tariff would cause the consumer to pay inflated prices for American-produced articles when the same articles could be purchased from foreign states at a cheaper rate. In what ways does this same argument have, or not have, validity in the present tariff structure of the United States?

3. How might Clay have answered a charge that his system of economic nationalism was in reality economic isolationism? Consider whether this same charge would be applicable to the tariff policies of the United States at the present time.

Related Documents

I. The Reforming of Spelling

NOAH WEBSTER

Nationalism may have emerged as a popular impulse after the War of 1812, but even before the war men were concerned about building the United States into a strong, unified nation. One of the early nationalists was the lexicographer and educator Noah Webster.

In the following article Webster argued for the creation of an American language to replace the English that Americans had used during the Colonial period. How do the arguments in his proposal coincide with those in Clay's system of economic self-sufficiency?

Old South Leaflets (Boston: Directors of the Old South Work, n.d.) VIII, No. 196, pp. 385–90.

It has been observed by all writers on the English language, that the orthography or spelling of words is very irregular; the same letters often representing different sounds, and the same sounds often expressed by different letters. For this irregularity, two principal causes may be assigned:

1. The changes to which the pronunciation of a language is liable, from the progress of science and civilization.

2. The mixture of different languages, occasioned by revolutions in England, or by a predilection of the learned, for words of foreign growth and ancient origin.

To the first cause may be ascribed the difference between the spelling and pronunciation of Saxon words. The northern nations of Europe originally spoke much in gutturals. . . .

But as savages proceed in forming languages, they lose the guttural sounds, in some measure, and adopt the use of labials, and the more open vowels. . . .

In this progress, the English have lost the sounds of most of the guttural letters. The *k* before *n* in *know,* the *g* in *reign,* and in many other words, are become mute in practice; and the *gh* is softened into the sound of *f,* as in *laugh,* or is silent, as in *brought.*

To this practice of softening the sounds of letters, or wholly suppressing those which are harsh and disagreeable, may be added a popular tendency to abbreviate words of common use. Thus *Southwark,* by a habit of quick pronunciation, is become *Suthark; Worcester* and *Leicester* are become *Wooster* and *Lester; business, bizness; colonel, curnel; cannot, will not, cant, wont.* . . .

But such is the state of our language. The pronunciation of the words which are strictly *English,* has been gradually changing for ages, and since the revival of science in Europe, the language has received a vast accession of words from other languages, many of which retain an orthography very ill suited to exhibit the true pronunciation.

The question now occurs: ought the Americans to retain these faults which produce innumerable inconveniences in the acquisition and use of the language, or ought they at once to reform these abuses, and introduce order and regularity into the orthography of the AMERICAN TONGUE?

Let us consider this subject with some attention. . . .

The principal alterations necessary to render our orthography sufficiently regular and easy, are these:

1. The omission of all superfluous or silent letters; as *a* in *bread.* Thus *bread, head, give, breast, built, meant, realm, friend,* would be spelt *bred, hed, giv, brest, bilt, ment, relm, frend.* Would this alteration produce any inconvenience, any embarrassment or expense? By no means. On the other hand, it would lessen the trouble of writing, and much more, of learning the language; it would reduce the true pronunciation to a certainty; and while it would assist foreigners and our own children in acquiring the language, it would render the pronunciation uniform, in different parts of the country, and almost prevent the possibility of changes.

2. A substitution of a character that has a certain definite sound for one that is more vague and indeterminate. Thus by putting *ee* instead of *ea* or *ie*, the words *mean, near, speak, grieve, zeal,* would become *meen, neer, speek, greev, zeel.* This alteration would not occasion a moment's trouble; at the same time it would prevent a doubt respecting the pronunciation; whereas the *ea* and *ie* having different sounds, may give a learner much difficulty. Thus *greef* should be substituted for *grief; kee* for *key; beleev* for *believe; laf* for *laugh; dawter* for *daughter; plow* for *plough; tuf* for *tough; proov* for *prove; blud* for *blood;* and *draft* for *draught.* In this manner *ch* in Greek derivatives should be changed into *k;* for the English *ch* has a soft sound, as in *cherish;* but *k* always a hard sound. Therefore *character, chorus, cholic, architecture,* should be written *karacter, korus, kolic, arkitecture;* and were they thus written, no person could mistake their true pronunciation.

Thus *ch* in French derivatives should be changed into *sh; machine, chaise, chevalier,* should be written *masheen, shaze, shevaleer;* and *pique, tour, oblique,* should be written *peek, toor, obleek.* . . .

The advantages to be derived from these alterations are numerous, great and permanent.

1. The simplicity of the orthography would facilitate the learning of the language. It is now the work of years for children to learn to spell; and after all, the business is rarely accomplished. . . .

But with the proposed orthography, a child would learn to spell, without trouble, in a very short time, and the orthography being very regular, he would ever afterwards find it difficult to make a mistake. It would, in that case, be as difficult to spell *wrong* as it is now to spell *right.* . . .

2. A correct orthography would render the pronunciation of the language as uniform as the spelling in books. A general uniformity thro the United States would be the event of such a reformation as I am here recommending. All persons, of every rank, would speak with some degree of precision and uniformity. Such a uniformity in these states is very desirable; it would remove prejudice, and conciliate mutual affection and respect.

3. Such a reform would diminish the number of letters about one sixteenth or eighteenth. . . .

4. But a capital advantage of this reform in these states would be, that it would make a difference between the English orthography and the American. This will startle those who have not attended to the subject; but I am confident that such an event is an object of vast political consequence. . . .

The alteration, however small, would encourage the publication of books in our own country. It would render it, in some measure, necessary that all books should be printed in America. The English would never copy our orthography for their own use; and consequently the same impressions of books would not answer for both countries. The inhabitants of the present generation would read the English impressions; but posterity, being taught a different spelling, would prefer the American orthography.

Besides this, a *national language* is a bond of *national union.* Every engine should be employed to render the people of this country *national;* to call their attachments home to their own country; and to inspire them with the pride of national character. However they may boast of independence, and the freedom of their government, yet their *opinions* are not sufficiently independent; an astonishing respect for the arts and literature of their parent country, and a blind imitation of its manners are still prevalent among the Americans. Thus an habitual respect for another country, deserved indeed and once laudable, turns their attention from their own interests, and prevents their respecting themselves.

II. The Star-Spangled Banner

FRANCIS SCOTT KEY

The War of 1812 was, for the most part, a military debacle for the United States. But national tragedies such as the burning of Washington, D.C., and the failure to effectively break the British blockade were somewhat compensated for by the valiant defense of Baltimore and the success of Andrew Jackson at New Orleans. The defense of Baltimore and the attack on Fort McHenry did not produce a future president, as did the events at New Orleans, but it did produce a set of verses that became the national anthem of the United States.

Of what national significance did Francis Scott Key believe the flag to be that he saw "by the dawn's early light"? Why was patriotism like Key's basic to the success of Clay's plan for an American economy?

O! SAY can you see, by the dawn's early light,
    What so proudly we hail'd at the twilight's last gleaming,
Whose broad stripes and bright stars through the perilous fight,
    O'er the ramparts we watch'd were so gallantly streaming?
And the Rockets' red glare, the Bombs bursting in air,
Gave proof through the night that our Flag was still there;
    O! say, does that star-spangled Banner yet wave,
    O'er the Land of the free, and the home of the brave?

On that shore, dimly seen through the mists of the deep,
    Where the foe's haughty host in dread silence reposes,
What is that, which the breeze o'er the towering steep,
    As it fitfully blows, half conceals, half discloses?
Now it catches the gleam of the morning's first beam,
In full glory reflected now shines on the stream.
    'Tis the star-spangled banner. O! long may it wave,
    O'er the land of the free and the home of the brave.

National Intelligencer, September 27, 1814.

And where is that band who so vauntingly swore,
   That the havoc of war and the battle's confusion
A home and a country should leave us no more?
   Their blood has wash'd out their foul footsteps' pollution.
No refuge could save the hireling and slave,
From the terror of flight or the gloom of the grave;
      And the star-spangled banner in triumph doth wave,
      O'er the land of the free and the home of the brave.

O! thus be it ever when freemen shall stand,
   Between their lov'd home, and the war's desolation,
Blest with vict'ry and peace, may the Heav'n-rescued land,
   Praise the power that hath made and preserv'd us a nation!
Then conquer we must, when our cause it is just,
And this be our motto—"In God is our Trust!"
      And the star-spangled banner in triumph shall wave,
      O'er the land of the free and the home of the brave.

III. Mr. Wendover Moves for an Alteration of the National Flag

Every modern nation has its symbols of independence, from national seals to national mottoes to national flags. In 1818 the composition of the flag of the United States was not standardized, so one might see flags with thirteen stripes, nine stripes, or eighteen stripes, and in some cases the stripes ran perpendicular rather than horizontal. Such confusion in the appearance of the national banner seemed unnecessary to many of nationalists in and out of Congress. This led Congressman Robert H. Wendover of New York to introduce a bill for the standardization of the flag.

How does Wendover's defense of his bill illustrate the popular concepts of nationalism held in the United States during this period?

The House then resolved itself into a Committee of the Whole on the bill to alter the flag of the United States [providing that from and after the fourth day of July next, the flag of the United States be thirteen horizontal stripes, alternate red and white; that the Union be twenty stars, white in a blue field; and that, on the admission of every new State into the Union, one star be added to the Union of the flag, and that such addition shall take effect on the fourth day of July then next succeeding such admission].

Mr. Wendover . . . Sir, the importance attached to a national flag, both in its literal and figurative use, is so universal, and of such ancient origin, that we seldom inquire into the meaning of their various figures, as adopted by

Annals of the Congress of the United States, Fifteenth Congress, First Session, (Washington: Gales and Seaton, 1854), pp. 1458–63, 2524.

other nations, and are in some danger of forgetting the symbolical application of those composing that of our own.

Were we now about to devise suitable emblems for a national flag, I doubt not we should see much diversity of sentiment, and perhaps some efforts for local gratification; but I presume we should unite in some general and appropriate figures, referring not to sectional but national objects. But on this subject we need not differ. Suitable symbols were devised by those who laid the foundation of the Republic; and I hope their children will ever feel themselves in honor precluded from changing these, except so far as necessity may dictate, and with a direct view of expressing by them their original design. . . .

The flag of the United States was altered by law, from thirteen to fifteen stripes and stars, on the first of May, 1795, to apply to the admission of Vermont and Kentucky into the Union. . . .

Sir, it cannot be deemed proper to go on and increase the stripes in your flag. There are now twenty States; what number they will ultimately extend to none can conjecture. For my own part, I doubt not there will in time be accessions from the East, from the North, from the West, and from the South. Sir, I am willing every people should "manage their own affairs in their own way." But I can no more believe that any portion of the earth will remain in perpetual thraldom, and be forever tributary to a foreign Power, than I can subscribe to the doctrine of a ceaseless succession of legitimate kings.

Sir, it cannot be deemed desirable, under the existing state of things, in relation to the stripes and stars in the flag, to retain it in its present situation; it is not only inapplicable, but both parts refer to the same thing, and the one is a duplicate of the other; but the alteration proposed will direct the view to two striking facts in our national history, and teach the world an important reality, that republican government is not only practicable, but that it is also progressive. . . .

Mr. Chairman, I hope this bill will pass, and wish it to pass with much unanimity; not only because I believe it will meet the public approbation, and be best calculated to give sufficient permanency to the form of your flag, but because there yet remains a few, and, indeed, but few, who first nerved their arm to raise this banner of freedom, and nobly defended it, through carnage and blood, to victory and to peace. With hoary locks and tottering frame they have been preserved to see it acquire a renown which I trust will never fade; and have lived to witness in their sons that heroic spirit, which assures them that their privations and their arduous struggle in defence of liberty have not been in vain.

Sir, I believe it is now the time to legislate on this subject; your flag now stands pre-eminently high in the estimation of other nations, and it is justly the pride of your own. And although, for a moment, your flag was veiled at Detroit, and left to droop at Castine; and although (if I may so express it) it was made to weep at Washington, it has not lost its lustre—it remains unsullied. No disgrace has attached to your "star-spangled banner." It has been the signal of victory on the land, of successful valor on the lakes, and waved triumphantly on the ocean. And even on those who predicted that in "nine months the striped bunting would be swept from the ocean," it possessed the wonderful charm, that before the nine months had elapsed, "fir-built frigates" and "Yankee cock-boats" were magnified into "ships-of-the-line;" . . .

But, sir, whatever be the fate of this bill, I hope the time is not distant when you will give to your flag its deserved honor, as the guardian of your citizens; when your hardy seamen shall no longer be doomed to the degradation to ask for, nor you to give them, *paper protections;* but, when they shall point aloft to the flag of their country, and say, "This is the protection of freemen; under this we desire peacefully to traverse the ocean and sail to every clime. But perish the arm that shall attempt to seize upon our persons; and woe to the nation that shall dare to infringe our country's rights!" And whenever called to the contest by the voice of their country, may they rally round the "star-spangled banner," and emphatically exclaim—

> *"High-waving, unsullied, unstruck, proudly showeth,*
> *What each friend, and each foe, and each neutral well knoweth;*
> *That her path is etherial, high she aspires,*
> *Her stripes aloft streaming, like boreal fires."*
> *Joined with Stars, "They astonish, dismay, or delight,*
> *As the foe, or the friend, may encounter the sight."*

[*Representative Wendover's plea was not in vain for on April 4, 1818 the following act was approved.*]

An Act to Establish the Flag of the United States.

Be it *enacted,* &c.; That, from and after the fourth day of July next, the flag of the United States be thirteen horizontal stripes, alternate red and white: that the union be twenty stars, white in a blue field.

Sec. 2. *And be it further enacted,* That, on the admission of every new State into the Union, one star be added to the union of the flag; and that such addition shall take effect on the fourth day of July then next succeeding such admission.

IV. The Prospect Before Us

HEZEKIAH NILES

In 1815 Hezekiah Niles, editor of Niles' Weekly Register, *took it upon himself to look into the future for his readers to determine what might lie ahead for the United States. For Niles the future was bright enough, although he did see some signs of a growing sectionalism in the nation. But he believed that these signs*

Niles' Weekly Register, September 2, 1815.

served as a warning for all Americans to be vigilant against those that would jeopardize the nation. Such vigilance would, of course, be rewarded by the preservation of the American way of life.

In the following editorial how does Niles' concept of the national character supplement Clay's confidence in his American System?

The existing state of things, as well as the "prospect before us," is most happy for the American people. THE REPUBLIC, REPOSING ON THE LAURELS OF A GLORIOUS WAR, GATHERS THE RICH HARVEST OF AN HONORABLE PEACE. Every where the sound of the axe is heard opening the forest to the sun, and claiming for agriculture the range of the buffalo.—Our cities grow and towns rise up as by magic; commerce expands her proud sails in safety, and the "striped bunting" floats with majesty over every sea. The busy hum of ten thousand wheels fills our seaports, and the sound of the spindle and the loom succeeds the yell of the savage or screech of the night owl in the late wilderness of the interior. The *lord of the soil,* who recently deserted the plough to meet the enemies of his country on its threshold, and dispute the possession, has returned in quiet to his fields, exulting that the *republic lives,* and in honor! The hardy hunter, whose deadly rifle lately brought the foeman to the earth, has resumed his former life, and, in the trackless forest, employs the same weapon, with unerring aim, to stop the fleet deer in his course. Plenty crowns the works of peace with abundance, and scatters from her cornucopia all the good things of this life, with prodigal bounty. A high and honorable feeling generally prevails, and the people begin to assume, more and more, a NATIONAL CHARACTER: and to look at home for the only means, under Divine goodness, of preserving their religion and liberty—with all the blessings that flow from their unrestricted enjoyment. The 'bulwark' of these is in the sanctity of their principles, and the virtue and valor of those who profess to love them; and need no guarantee from the blood-stained and profligate princes and powers of *Europe.* Morality and good order ever prevails—canting hypocrisy has but few advocates, for the Great Architect of the universe worshipped on the altar of men's hearts, in the way that each believes most acceptable to HIM—undirected by the ministers of the "evil one," in the shape of *inquisitors* or *government* priests. The great body of the clergy of the United States are really "ambassadors of Christ," of moral lives and virtuous deportment; and the people, to whom *they* are amenable, liberally support them in these good dispositions. All sects unite, each in their own way, in love and unity, to seek the hidden treasure, and raise the grand anthem of "holiness to the Lord" when they find it in a conscience at ease. No man has a preference over another because he is supposed by the *law* to worship GOD more correctly than his neighbor. No man is compelled to contribute to the support of a sect that his own sense of reason does not approve. Every one is free to pursue what course he pleases in civil or religious matters, provided, only, he observes the rules laid down to preserve order and the moral law. . . .

Such are among the inestimable blessings that flow from a free constitution. May heaven, in mercy to mankind, preserve it as an example, and take our beloved country into its charge as the *permanent* asylum for the oppressed of all nations—as a city of refuge where the weary may find repose; acknowledging no throne but that of the CREATOR of all things; yielding to no law not built upon the public will.

V. A Proposal for a National Society of Literature

ROBERT LEE

The nationalistic impulse that emerged in the United States during the Era of Good Feelings had many facets, from economic nationalism to literary nationalism. Literary nationalism was based upon the untapped artistic resources of the American genius and was represented, in one instance, by the following letter written by Robert Lee of New Jersey.

How do Lee's arguments for the establishment of a national society for the promotion of literature, arts, and the sciences parallel Clay's arguments for a protective tariff and Webster's for a national language?

Among the various events which have tended most essentially to change the face of human affairs, may justly be ranked the discovery and colonization of America, the revolt of the colonies of North America from British dominion, and the establishment of a new empire in that portion of the new world which had disdained any longer being subjected to European domination.

Nor was the mere change of foreign rulers, for rulers chosen from among, and by ourselves, the only change which we experienced. New modes of thinking were adopted; new principles of government were established. Out of that chaos, darkness and night from which we emerged, has been brought order, light and the beauty of a glorious morn.

But, have we, the American people, done all that is required at our hands? —have we improved all the glorious opportunities offered us by our emancipation from European domination? do we appreciate the extent of the blessings which we enjoy? or have we considered the best means of securing these blessings to ourselves, of diffusing them among our cotemporaries, or of transmitting them to posterity?

And have we, in fact, considered how infinitely important is the present crisis of human affairs? that upon what has recently been done, and upon what is now transpiring, depends the destinies of all future generations of men; and, that next to the honor of having performed a part in the late glorious revolution, will be the honor of having contributed to the promotion of literature, the arts and sciences in the new world,—and from thence diffusing them, and with them the principles of our admirable system of government, to every distant land, and among all the scattered tribes of the earth. . . .

Have we considered the high destinies which await our country; the vast extent of territory and variety of soil which it embraces, the countless millions which are destined to inhabit it, the long vista of ages thro' which its course is, doubtless, to run, or the mighty influence which its systems of government, its modes of thinking and manner of acting, are to have over the destinies of other nations? If we have, we shall be irresistably compelled to believe that the American people are called upon to act a most distinguished part upon the great theatre of the universe.

In proposing the establishment of a society of the kind and for the objects here suggested, I have had equally in view to open wide the doors of the temple of fame to all, who, with a laudable ambition, desire to distinguish themselves by rendering essential service to their country; to induce a national manner of thinking and acting, on all important matters; and to transfer to other countries and to transmit to distant ages the influence of this manner of thinking and acting, so far as the same is connected with and may tend to perpetuate those rules and principles by which our country is now distinguished from the rest of the world, and from which it derives so many blessings.

I want to establish a society with ample means to reward every exertion of genius which may be displayed, and to call forth every latent genius which our country may possess, to give every possible encouragement to literature, the arts and sciences, and to give to them the stamp and character of *American;* to wipe away that reproach which foreigners have unjustly cast upon us, and to build up for our country a solid pyramid of fame.

I therefore propose;—that a national society be established for the encouragement of American literature, and for the promotion of arts and sciences.

VI. Cohens vs. Virginia

John Marshall served as Chief Justice of the United States Supreme Court from 1801 to 1835. During those years, he passed down many decisions that helped to create a strong central government for the nation. One of his decisions, Cohens vs. Virginia, *reaffirmed the power of the Supreme Court to review judgments of state courts that denied federal rights.*

In what ways does the following excerpt from Cohens vs. Virginia *complement Clay's concept of economic nationalism?*

FEBRUARY TERM, 1821

[The] objection to the jurisdiction of the court is that its appellate power cannot be exercised, in any case, over the judgment of a State court.

John Marshall, *Complete Constitutional Decisions,* ed. John M. Dillon (Chicago: Callaghan, 1903), pp. 402–4.

This objection is sustained chiefly by arguments drawn from the supposed total separation of the judiciary of a State from that of the Union, and their independence of each other. The argument considers the Federal judiciary as completely foreign to that of a State; and as being no more connected with it, in any respect whatever, than the court of a foreign State. If this hypothesis be just, the argument founded on it is equally so; but if the hypothesis be not supported by the Constitution, the argument fails with it.

This hypothesis is not founded on any words in the Constitution which might seem to countenance it, but on the unreasonableness of giving a contrary construction to words which seem to require it, and on the incompatibility of the application of the appellate jurisdiction to the judgments of State courts with that constitutional relation which subsists between the government of the Union and the governments of those States which compose it.

Let this unreasonableness, this total incompatibility, be examined.

That the United States form, for many and for most important purposes, a single nation has not yet been denied. In war we are one people. In making peace we are one people. In all commercial regulations we are one and the same people. In many other respects the American people are one. And the government which is alone capable of controlling and managing their interests in all these respects is the government of the Union. It is their government, and in that character they have no other. America has chosen to be, in many respects, and to many purposes, a nation; and for all these purposes her government is complete; to all these objects it is competent. The people have declared that in the exercise of all powers given for these objects it is supreme. It can, then, in effecting these objects, legitimately control all individuals or governments within the American territory. The Constitution and laws of a State, so far as they are repugnant to the Constitution and laws of the United States, are absolutely void. These States are constituent parts of the United States. They are members of one great empire,—for some purposes sovereign, for some purposes subordinate.

In a government so constituted is it unreasonable that the judicial power should be competent to give efficacy to the constitutional laws of the Legislature? That department can decide on the validity of the Constitution or law of a State, if it be repugnant to the Constitution or to a law of the United States. Is it unreasonable that it should also be empowered to decide on the judgment of a State tribunal enforcing such unconstitutional law? Is it so very unreasonable as to furnish a justification for controlling the words of the Constitution?

We think it is not. We think that, in a government acknowledgedly supreme with respect to objects of vital interest to the nation, there is nothing inconsistent with sound reason, nothing incompatible with the nature of government, in making all its departments supreme, so far as respects those objects, and so far as is necessary to their attainment. The exercise of the appellate power over those judgments of the State tribunals, which may contravene the Constitution or laws of the United States, is, we believe, essential to the attainment of those objects.

VII. The Monroe Doctrine

Nationalism in the United States was not confined to domestic issues. In a speech to Congress in 1823, President James Monroe upheld the American belief in the right of a people to determine their own government and extended this to the revolutions in South America. The resulting Monroe Doctrine became one of the basic policies of the United States, and continues, in some aspects, to the present day.

How did the Monroe Doctrine work to the advantage or disadvantage of Clay's economic plan?

DECEMBER 2, 1823

At the proposal of the Russian Imperial Government, made through the minister of the Emperor residing here, a full power and instructions have been transmitted to the minister of the United States at St. Petersburg to arrange by amicable negotiation the respective rights and interests of the two nations on the northwest coast of this continent. A similar proposal had been made by His Imperial Majesty to the Government of Great Britain, which has likewise been acceded to. The Government of the United States has been desirous by this friendly proceeding of manifesting the great value which they have invariably attached to the friendship of the Emperor and their solicitude to cultivate the best understanding with his Government. In the discussions to which this interest has given rise and in the arrangements by which they may terminate the occasion has been judged proper for asserting, as a principle in which the rights and interests of the United States are involved, that the American continents, by the free and independent condition which they have assumed and maintain, are henceforth not to be considered as subjects for future colonization by any European Powers. . . .

. . . In the wars of the European powers in matters relating to themselves we have never taken any part, nor does it comport with our policy so to do. It is only when our rights are invaded or seriously menaced that we resent injuries or make preparation for our defense. With the movements in this hemisphere we are of necessity more immediately connected, and by causes which must be obvious to all enlightened and impartial observers. The political system of the allied powers is essentially different in this respect from that of America. This difference proceeds from that which exists in their respective Governments; and to the defense of our own, which has been achieved by the loss of so much blood and treasure, and matured by the wisdom of their most enlightened citizens, and under which we have enjoyed unexampled felicity, this whole nation is devoted. We owe it, therefore, to candor and to the amicable relations existing between the United States and those powers to declare that we should consider any attempt on their part to extend their

James D. Richardson, ed., *A Compilation of the Messages and Papers of the Presidents* (Washington, D.C.: Government Printing Office, 1897), II, pp. 209, 218–19.

system to any portion of this hemisphere as dangerous to our peace and safety. With the existing colonies or dependencies of any European power we have not interfered and shall not interfere. But with the Governments who have declared their independence and maintained it, and whose independence we have, on great consideration and on just principles, acknowledged, we could not view any interposition for the purpose of oppressing them, or controlling in any other manner their destiny, by any European power in any other light than as the manifestation of an unfriendly disposition toward the United States. In the war between those new Governments and Spain we declared our neutrality at the time of their recognition, and to this we have adhered, and shall continue to adhere, provided no change shall occur which, in the judgment of the competent authorities of this Government, shall make a corresponding change on the part of the United States indispensable to their security.

. . . Our policy in regard to Europe, which was adopted at an early stage of the wars which have so long agitated that quarter of the globe, nevertheless remains the same, which is, not to interfere in the internal concerns of any of its powers; to consider the government *de facto* as the legitimate government for us; to cultivate friendly relations with it, and to preserve those relations by a frank, firm, and manly policy, meeting in all instances the just claims of every power, submitting to injuries from none. But in regard to those continents circumstances are eminently and conspicuously different. It is impossible that the allied powers should extend their political system to any portion of either continent without endangering our peace and happiness; nor can anyone believe that our southern brethren, if left to themselves, would adopt it of their own accord. It is equally impossible, therefore, that we should behold such interposition in any form with indifference. . . .

For Further Reading

The emergence of an American nationalism is analyzed in: Kendrick C. Babcock, *The Rise of American Nationality* (1906; reprinted in 1968); Marcus Cunliffe, *The Nation Takes Shape** (1959); Merle E. Curti, *The Roots of American Loyalty* (1946; reprinted in 1967); and George Dangerfield, *The Awakening of American Nationalism** (1965) and *The Era of Good Feelings** (1952).

The biographies of some of the leading men of the period also illustrate the development of nationalism and include: *John Quincy Adams and the Foundations of American Foreign Policy* (1949) and *John Quincy Adams and the Union* (1956), by Samuel F. Bemis; W. P. Cresson, *James Monroe* (1946); Clement Eaton, *Henry Clay and the Art of American Politics** (1957); J. H. Powell, *Richard Rush, Republican Diplomat* (1942); and Glyndon Van Deusen, *The Life of Henry Clay** (1937).

The economic development of the United States during this period is examined in: R. G. Albion, *The Rise of New York Port* (1939; reprinted in

*Paperbound edition available.

1970); Paul W. Gates, *The Farmer's Age** (1960); Bray Hammond, *Banks and Politics in America** (1957); Louis C. Hunter, *Steamboats on the Western Rivers* (1949; reprinted in 1970); P. D. Jordan, *The National Road* (1948); George R. Taylor, *The Transportation Revolution** (1951); Frederick Jackson Turner, *The Rise of the New West** (1907); and Richard C. Wade, *The Urban Frontier** (1959).

Nationalism in foreign affairs is examined in two studies: *The Monroe Doctrine* (1927; revised edition 1955), by Dexter Perkins, and *The United States and the Independence of Latin America, 1800–1830** (1941; reprinted in 1962), by Arthur P. Whitaker.

A problems book is *The Monroe Doctrine** (1966) edited by Armin Rappaport.

*Paperbound edition available.

9. Nullification: Challenge to the Union

In the winter of 1832–33 it seemed possible that a sectional war might break out in the United States. Immediately at issue were the protective tariffs of 1828 and 1832, but the underlying causes dated back to the plans for a protective system that had been proposed by Alexander Hamilton in the 1790s and the first protective tariff passed by Congress in 1816. Revenue tariffs had been enacted by Congress since 1789 to help pay the costs of government, but the 1816 tariff was the first passed with the primary intent of protecting the new industries of the country.

The 1816 tariff found general support in the different sections of the United States, including the South, where John C. Calhoun of South Carolina was among its principal advocates. The most notable resistance to protectionism came from Daniel Webster, who represented the shipping interests of New England. But the views held by these men and their constituencies changed during the 1820s: while manufacturing increased in importance in the North, it did not develop to any great extent in the South, thus prompting Southern resistance to protectionism. As producers of raw materials, they believed any protective tariff would increase the price of imported manufactured articles and decrease export markets. Protective tariffs were passed over Southern opposition in 1824 and 1828, the latter bill producing vigorous reactions among the adversely affected groups, who called it the "Tariff of Abominations."

This tariff, rigged by the Jacksonians to discredit President John Quincy

Adams, was designed to increase rates on manufactured goods and on some raw materials. When the protectionists passed the bill, many voting on principle rather than on how they would be affected, the Southerners and New England manufacturers became enraged. The New England interests were able to modify the aspects of the bill that had adversely affected them by the revised tariffs of 1830 and 1832, but these tariffs did little to reduce the rates on products imported into the South.

On November 24, 1832, a special convention in South Carolina passed a resolution declaring the federal tariffs of 1828 and 1832 "null, void, and no law, not binding upon this state, its officers or citizens." This action by the South Carolina Convention, based upon the principle of "nullification," ushered in a period of crisis that almost brought civil war between the federal government and the state of South Carolina.

Although the protective tariffs were the chief issue in the nullification crisis, the larger controversy was over the nature of the Union. By the late 1820s political leaders in the North generally held that the United States was a consolidated union with a central government that could pass legislation binding upon all of the states if it was for the general welfare. But Southern spokesmen asserted that the United States was a confederation of sovereign states that could either accept or reject federal legislation depending upon local conditions if they regarded it as unconstitutional.

Core Document

A Letter From John C. Calhoun

Vice President John C. Calhoun entered the tariff controversy anonymously in 1828 when he authored a report to a state committee of South Carolina that was concerned with federal tariff policies. The report, known as the "Exposition and Protest," became one of the first statements of the principle of nullification. From 1828 to 1833 (the year he resigned as vice president and was subsequently elected as senator from South Carolina), he played an expanding role in the developing crisis. The split between Jackson and Calhoun had become apparent to the public as early as 1830, in an exchange of toasts during a celebration of Jefferson's birthday. On that occasion Jackson toasted "The Federal Union— it must be preserved"; Calhoun quickly responded with "The Union—next to our liberty most dear."

By 1832 Calhoun had reached the conclusion that the tariff issue was only a symptom of a greater illness: the deterioration of the body politic of the United

Richard K. Cralle, ed., *Reports and Public Letters of John C. Calhoun* (New York: D. Appleton and Company, 1855), VI, pp. 144–45, 147–54, 158–63, 167–70, 174–75, 181–82, 185–93.

States by the destructive legislation passed for the benefit of the Northern commercial interests. To Calhoun these interests, even though they represented a majority in Congress, were passing legislation that was detrimental to the natural growth of the nation. He believed that the majority had acted in a tyrannical way and that the minority had to be guaranteed protection from this tyranny. The greatest guarantee, he thought, would be to give the minority the final say over all legislation passed by the federal government. The issue of the tariff, therefore, brought into focus the question of whether the United States was a consolidated union or a confederation of sovereign states. It pitted the rule of the majority against the rights of the minority.

　　Calhoun's most comprehensive statement of the principle of nullification is found in the following letter written to Governor James Hamilton, Jr., of South Carolina in August 1832. This letter was later published and became the doctrinal basis for future Southern arguments for nullification and states' rights.

　　In reading Calhoun's letter note what he says about:
- the relationship between the citizens of the States and the General government.
- the relationship between the States and the General government.
- the use of the amending process.
- where final sovereignty rests in the American system.
- the nature of the federal government.
- the principle of nullification.
- the difference between nullification and secession.
- reserved and delegated powers.
- the powers necessary for the existence and preservation of free states.
- majority rule.
- the diversity of the interests of individuals.

To General Hamilton on the Subject of State Interposition

Fort Hill, August 28th, 1832

My Dear Sir:

　　I have received your note of the 31st July, requesting me to give you a fuller development of my views than that contained in my address last summer, on the right of a State to defend her reserved powers against the encroachments of the General Government. . . .

　　Strange as the assertion may appear, it is nevertheless, true, that the great difficulty in determining whether a State has the right to defend her reserved powers against the General Government, or, in fact, any right at all beyond those of a mere corporation, is to bring the public mind to realize plain historical facts connected with the origin and formation of the Government. . . .

　　. . . From the beginning, and in all the changes of political existence through which we have passed, the people of the United States have been united as forming political communities, and not as individuals. Even in the first stage of existence, they formed distinct colonies, independent of each other, and politically united only through the British crown. In their first imperfect union, for the purpose of resisting the encroachments of the mother country, they united as distinct political communities; and passing from their colonial condition, in the act announcing their independence to the world, they declared themselves, by name and enumeration, free and independent States. In that character, they formed the old confederation; and, when it was proposed to supersede the articles of the confederation by the present Constitution, they met in convention as States, acted and voted as States; and the Constitution, when formed, was submitted for ratification to the people of the several States; it was ratified by them as States, each state for itself; each by its ratification binding its own citizens: the parts thus separately binding themselves, and not the whole the parts; to which, if it be added, that it is declared in the preamble of the Constitution to be ordained by the people of the *United States,* and in the article of ratification, when ratified, it is declared *"to be binding between the States so ratifying,"* the conclusion is inevitable, that the Constitution is the work of the people of the States, considered as separate and independent political communities; that they are its authors—their power created it, their voice clothed it with authority; that the government formed is, in reality, their agent; and that the Union, of which the Constitution is the bond, is a union of States, and not of individuals. . . .

I will next proceed to state some of the results which necessarily follow from the facts which have been established.

The first, and, in reference to the subject of this communication, the most important, is, that there is *no direct* and *immediate* connection between the individual citizens of a State and the General Government. The relation between them is through the State. The Union is a union of States as communities, and not a union of individuals. As members of a State, her citizens were originally subject to no control but that of the State, and could be subject to no other, except by the act of the State itself. The Constitution was, accordingly, submitted to the States for their separate ratification; and it was only by the ratification of the State that its citizens became subject to the control of the General Government. The ratification of any other, or all the other States, without its own, could create no connection between them and the General Government, nor impose on them the slightest obligation . . . it follows, as a necessary consequence, that the act of ratification bound the State as a community . . . and not the citizens of the State as individuals; the latter being bound through their State, and in consequence of the ratification of the former. Another, and a highly important consequence, as it regards the subject under investigation, follows with equal certainty; that, on a question whether a particular power exercised by the General Government be granted by the Constitution, it belongs to the State as a member of the Union, in her sovereign capacity in convention, to determine definitively, as far as her citizens are concerned, the extent of the obligation which she contracted; and if, in her opinion, the act exercising the power be unconstitutional, to declare it null and void, *which declaration would be obligatory on her citizens.* In coming to this conclusion, it may be proper to remark, to prevent misrepresentation, that I do not claim for a State the right to abrogate an act of the General Government. It is the Constitution that annuls an unconstitutional act. Such an act is of itself void and of no effect. What I claim is, the right of the State, *as far as its citizens are concerned, to declare the extent of the obligation, and that such declaration is binding on them*—a right, when limited to its citizens, flowing directly from the relation of the State to the General Government on the one side, and its citizens on the other, as already explained, and resting on the most plain and solid reasons. . . .

. . . It has been shown that the people of the States, acting as distinct and independent communities, are the authors of the Constitution, and that the General Government was organized and ordained by them to execute its powers. The Government, then, with all of its departments, is, in fact, the agent of the States, constituted to execute their joint will, as expressed in the Constitution.

In using the term agent, I do not intend to derogate in any degree from its character as a government. It is as truly and properly a government as are the State governments themselves. I have applied it simply because it strictly belongs to the relation between the General Government and the States, as, in fact, it does also to that between a State and its own government. Indeed, according to our theory, governments are in their nature but trusts, and those appointed to administer them, trustees or agents to execute the trust powers. The sovereignty resides elsewhere—in the people, not in the government; and with us, *the people* mean *the people of the several States* originally formed into thirteen distinct and independent communities, and now into twenty-four. Politically speaking, in reference to our own system, there are *no other people.* The General Government, as well as those of the States, is but the organ of their power: the latter, that of their respective States, through which are exercised separately that portion of power not delegated by the Constitution, and in the exercise of which each State has a local and peculiar interest; the former, the joint organ of all the States confederated into one general community, and through which they jointly and concurringly exercise the delegated powers, in which all have a common interest. Thus viewed, the Constitution of the United States, with the government it created, is truly and strictly the Constitution of each State,—as much so as its own particular Constitution and Government, ratified by the same authority,—in the same mode, and having, as far as its citizens are concerned, its powers and obligations from the same source,—differing only in the aspect under which I am considering the subject,—in the *plighted faith* of the State to its co-States, and of which as far as its citizens are considered, the State, in the last resort, is the exclusive judge.

Such, then, is the relation between the State and General Government, in whatever light . . . it may be viewed, I hold it as necessarily resulting, that, in the case of a power disputed between them, the Government, as the agent, has no right to enforce its construction against the construction of the State as one of the sovereign parties to the Constitution, any more than the State government would have against the people of the State in their sovereign capacity,—the relation being the same between them. . . . The General Government is a case of joint agency—the joint agent of the twenty-four sovereign States. It would be its duty, according to the principles established in such cases, instead of attempting to enforce its construction of its powers against that of the States, to bring the subject before the States themselves, in the only form which, according to the provision of the Constitution, it can be—by a proposition to amend, in the manner prescribed in the instrument, to be acted on by them in the only mode they can, by expressly granting or withholding the contested power. Against this conclusion there can be raised but one objection, that the States have surrendered or transferred the right in question. . . .

But, instead of showing any such grant, not a provision can be found in the Constitution *authorizing the General Government to exercise any control whatever over a State* by force, by veto, by judicial process, or in any other form —*a most important omission, designed, and not accidental,* and as will be shown in the course of these remarks,—omitted by the dictates of the profoundest wisdom.

The journal and proceedings of the Convention which formed the Constitution afford abundant proof that there was in the body a powerful party, distinguished for talents and influence, intent on obtaining for the General Government a grant of the very power in question, and that they attempted to effect this object in all possible ways, but, fortunately, without success. . . .

The opinion that the General Government has the right to enforce its construction of its powers against a State in any mode whatever, is, in truth, founded on a fundamental misconception of our system. At the bottom of this, and, in fact, almost every other misconception as to the relation between the States and the General Government, lurks the radical error, that the latter is a national, and not, as in reality it is, a confederated Government; and that it derives its powers from a higher source than the States. There are thousands influenced by these impressions without being conscious of it, and who, while they believe themselves to be opposed to consolidation, have infused into their conception of our Constitution almost all the ingredients which enter into that form of government. The striking difference between the present government and that under the old confederation (I speak of governments as distinct from constitutions) has mainly contributed to this dangerous impression. But however dissimilar their governments, the present *Constitution is as far removed from consolidation, and is as strictly and as purely a confederation, as the one which it superseded.* . . .

I have . . . shown that a State has a right, in her sovereign capacity, in convention, to declare an unconstitutional act of Congress to be null and void, and that such declarations would be obligatory on her citizens,—as highly so as the Constitution itself,—and conclusive against the General Government, which would have no right to enforce its construction of its powers against that of the State.

I next propose to consider the practical effect of the exercise of this high and important right—which, as the great conservative principle of our system, is known under the various names of nullification, interposition, and State veto —in reference to its operation viewed under different aspects: nullification,— as declaring null an unconstitutional act of the General Government, as far as the State is concerned; interposition,—as throwing the shield of protection between the citizens of a State and the encroachments of the Government; and veto,—as arresting or inhibiting its unauthorized acts within the limits of the State. . . .

From the adoption of the Constitution, we have had but one continued agitation of constitutional questions embracing some of the most important powers exercised by the Government; and yet, in spite of all the ability and force of argument displayed in the various discussions, backed by the high authority claimed for the Supreme Court to adjust such controversies, not a single constitutional question, of a political character, which has ever been agitated during this long period, has been settled in the public opinion. . . .

. . . The declaration of nullification would be obligatory on the citizens of the State;—as much so, in fact, as its declaration ratifying the Constitution, resting, as it does, on the same basis. It would *to them* be the highest possible evidence that the power contested was not granted, and, of course, that the act of the General Government was unconstitutional. They would be bound, in all the relations of life, private and political, to respect and obey it; and, when called upon as jurymen, to render their verdict accordingly,—or as judges, to pronounce judgment in conformity with it. . . .

Beaten, . . . the General Government would be compelled to abandon its unconstitutional pretensions, or resort to force; a resort, the difficulty (I was about to say, the impossibility) of which would very soon fully manifest itself, should folly or madness ever make the attempt.

In considering this aspect of the controversy, I pass over the fact that the General Government has no right to resort to force against a State—to coerce a sovereign member of the Union—which, I trust, I have established beyond all possible doubt. Let it, however, be determined to use force, and the difficulty would be insurmountable, unless, indeed, it be also determined to set aside the Constitution, and to subvert the system to its foundations. . . .

There is, indeed, one view, and one only, of the contest, in which force could be employed; but that view, as between the parties, would supersede the Constitution itself:—that nullification is secession,—and would, consequently, place the State, as to the others, in the relation of a foreign state. Such, clearly, would be the effect of secession; but it is equally clear that it would place the State beyond the pale of all her federal relations, and thereby, all control on the part of the other States over her. She would stand to them simply in the relation of a foreign state, divested of all federal connection, and having none other between them but those belonging to the laws of nations. Standing thus towards one another, force might, indeed, be employed against a State, but it must be a belligerent force, preceded by a declaration of war, and carried on with all its formalities. Such would be the certain effect of secession; and if nullification be secession—if it be but a different name for the same thing— such too, must be its effect; which presents the highly important question, Are they, in fact, the same . . . ?

First, they are wholly dissimilar in their nature. *One has reference to the parties themselves, and the other to their agents.* Secession is a *withdrawal from the Union;* a separation from *partners,* and, as far as depends on the member withdrawing, a *dissolution* of the partnership. It presupposes an association; a union of several States or individuals for a common object. Wherever these exist, secession may; and where they do not, it cannot. Nullification, on the contrary, *presupposes the relation of principal and agent:* the one granting a power to be executed,—the other, appointed by him with authority to execute it; *and is simply a declaration on the part of the principal, made in due form, that an act of the agent transcending his power is null and void.* It is a right belonging exclusively to the relation between principal and agent, to be found *wherever it exists, and in all its forms,* between several, or an association of principals, and their joint agents, as well as between a single principal and his agent.

The difference in their object is no less striking than in their nature. The object of secession is to *free* the withdrawing member from the *obligation* of the association or union, and is applicable to cases where the object of the association or union *has failed,* either by an abuse of power on the part of *its* members, or other causes. *Its direct and immediate object, as it concerns the withdrawing member, is the dissolution of the association or union,* as far as it is concerned. On the contrary, the object of nullification is to confine the agent within the limits of his powers, by arresting his acts transcending them, *not with the view of destroying the delegated or trust power, but to preserve it, by compelling the agent to fulfill the object for which the agency or trust was created; and is applicable only to cases where the trust or delegated powers are transcended on the part of the agent.* Without the power of secession, an association or union, formed for the common good *of all* the members, might prove ruinous to some, by the abuse of power on the part of the others; and without nullification the agent might, under color of construction, assume a power never intended to be delegated, or to convert those delegated to objects never intended to be comprehended in the trust, to the ruin of the principal, or, in case of a joint agency, to the ruin of some of the principals. Each has, thus, its appropriate object, but objects in their nature very dissimilar; so much so, that, in case of an association or union, where the powers are delegated to be executed by an agent, the abuse of power, on the part of the *agent,* to the injury of one or more of the members, would not justify secession on their part. The rightful remedy in that case would be nullification. There would be neither right nor pretext to secede: not right, because secession is applicable only to the acts of the members of the association or union, and not to the act of the agent; nor pretext, because there is another, and equally efficient remedy, short of the dissolution of the association or union, which can only be justified by necessity. Nullification may, indeed, be succeeded by secession. In the case stated, should the other members undertake to grant the power nullified, and should the nature of the power be such as to *defeat the object of the association or union,* at least as far as the member nullifying is concerned, it would then become an abuse of power on the part of the principals, and thus present a case where secession would apply; but in no other could it be justified, except it be for a failure of the association or union to effect the object for which it was created, independent of any abuse of power.

It now remains to show that their effect is as dissimilar as their nature or object.

Nullification leaves the members of the association or union in the condition it found them—subject to all its burdens, and entitled to all its advantages, comprehending the member nullifying as well as the others—its object being, not to destroy, but to preserve, as has been stated. It simply arrests the act of the agent, as far as the principal is concerned, leaving in every other respect the operation of the joint concern as before; secession, on the contrary, destroys, as far as the withdrawing member is concerned, the association or union, and restores him to the relation he occupied towards the other members before the existence of the association or union. He loses the benefit, but is released from the burden and control, and can no longer be dealt with, by his former associates, as one of its members.

Such are clearly the differences between them—differences so marked, that, instead of being identical, as supposed, they form a contrast in all the aspects in which they can be regarded. The application of these remarks to the political association or Union of these twenty-four States and the General Government, their joint agent, is too obvious, after what has been already said, to require any additional illustration. . . .

I propose next to consider this important modification of the sovereign powers of the States, in connection with the right of nullification.

It is acknowledged on all sides that the duration and stability of our system depend on maintaining *the equilibrium* between the States and the General Government—the reserved and delegated powers. . . .

On the side of the reserved powers, no check more effectual can be found or desired than nullification, or the right of arresting, within the limits of a State, the exercise, by the General Government, of any powers but the delegated—a right which, if the States be true to themselves and faithful to the Constitution, will ever prove, on the side of the reserved powers, an effectual protection to both.

Nor is the check on the side of the delegated less perfect. Though less strong, it is ample to guard against encroachments; and is as strong as the nature of the system would bear, as will appear in the sequel. It is to be found in the amending power. Without the modification which it contains of the rights of self-government on the part of the States, as already explained, the consent of each State would have been requisite to any additional grant of power, or other amendment of the Constitution. While, then, nullification would enable a State to arrest the exercise of a power not delegated, the right of self-government, if unmodified, would enable her to prevent the grant of a power not delegated; and thus her conception of what power ought to be granted would be as conclusive against the co-States, as her construction of the powers granted is against the General Government. In that case, the danger would be on the side of the States or reserved powers. The amending power, *in effect,* prevents this danger. In virtue of the provisions which it contains, the resistance of a State to a power cannot finally prevail, unless she be sustained by one fourth of the co-States; and in the same degree that her resistance is weakened, the power of the General Government, or the side of the delegated powers, is *strengthened.* It is true that the right of a State to arrest an unconstitutional act is of itself complete against the Government; but it is equally so that the controversy may, *in effect,* be terminated against her by a grant of the contested powers by three fourths of the States. It is thus by this simple, and apparently incidental contrivance, that the right of a State to nullify an unconstitutional act, so essential to the protection of the reserved rights, but which, unchecked, might too much debilitate the Government, is counterpoised. . . .

Of all the impediments opposed to a just conception of the nature of our political system, the impression that the right of a State to arrest an unconstitutional act of the General Government is inconsistent with the great and fundamental principle of all free states—that a majority has the right to govern—is the greatest. Thus regarded, nullification is, without farther reflection, denounced as the most dangerous and monstrous of all political heresies, as, in truth, it would be, were the objection as well-founded as, in fact, it is destitute of all foundation, as I shall now proceed to show.

Those who make the objection seem to suppose that the right of a majority to govern is a principle too simple to admit of any distinction; and yet, if I do not mistake, it is susceptible of the most important distinction—entering deeply into the construction of our system, and, I may add, into that of all free States in proportion to the perfection of their institutions—and is essential to the very existence of liberty.

When, then, it is said that a majority has the right to govern, there are two modes of estimating the majority, to either of which the expression is applicable. The one, in which the whole community is regarded in the aggregate, and the majority is estimated in reference to the entire mass. This may be called the majority of the whole, or the absolute majority. The other, in which it is regarded in reference to its different political interests, whether composed of different classes, of different communities, formed into one general confederated community, and in which the majority is estimated, not in reference to the whole, but to each class or community of which it is composed, —the assent of each taken separately,—and the concurrence of all constituting the majority. A majority thus estimated may be called the concurring majority.

When it is objected to nullification, that it is opposed to the principle that a majority ought to govern, he who makes the objection must mean the absolute, as distinguished from the concurring. It is only in the sense of the former the objection can be applied. In that of the concurring, it would be absurd, as the concurring assent of all the parts (with us, all the States) is of the very essence of such majority. Again, it is manifest, that in the sense in which it would be good against nullification, it would be equally so against the Constitution itself; for, in whatever light that instrument may be regarded, it is clearly not the work of the absolute, but of the concurring majority. It was formed and ratified by the concurring assent of all the States, and not by the majority of the whole taken in the aggregate, as has been already stated. Thus, the acknowledged right of each State, *in reference to the Constitution,* is unquestionably the same right which nullification attributes to each *in reference to the unconstitutional acts of the Government;* and, if the latter be opposed to the right of a majority to govern, the former is equally so. I go farther. The objection might, with equal truth, be applied to all free States that have ever existed: I mean States deserving the name,—excluding, of course, those which, after a factious and anarchical existence of a few years, have sunk under the yoke of tyranny or the dominion of some foreign power. There is not, with this exception, a single free State whose institutions were not based on the principle of the concurring majority: not one in which the community was not regarded in reference to its different political interests, and which did not, in some form or other, take the assent of each in the operation of the Government. . . .

Our first experiment in government was on the old form of a simple confederacy—unmodified, and extending the principle of the concurring majority alike to the Constitution (the articles of union) and to the Government which it constituted. It failed. . . .

The new Government was reared on the foundation of the old, strengthened, but not changed. It stands on the same solid basis of the concurring majority, perfected by the sanction of the people of the States directly given, and not indirectly through the State governments, as their representatives, as in the old confederation. With this difference, the authority which made the two Constitutions—which granted their powers, and ordained and organized their respective Governments to execute them—is the same. But, in passing from the Constitution to the Government (the law-making and the law-administering powers), the difference between the two becomes radical and essential. There, in the present, the concurring majority is dropped, and the absolute substituted. In determining, then, what powers ought to be granted, and how the Government appointed for their execution ought to be organized, the separate and concurring voice of the States was required—the union being regarded, for this purpose, in reference to its various and distinct interests; but in the execution of these powers (delegated only because all the States had a common interest in their exercise), the Union is no longer regarded in reference to its parts, but as forming, to the extent of its delegated powers, one great community—to be governed by a common will—just as the States are in reference to their separate interests, and by a Government organized on principles similar to theirs. By this simple but fortunate arrangement, we have ingrafted the absolute on the concurring majority, thereby giving to the administration of the powers of the Government, where they were required, all the energy and promptness belonging to the former—while we have retained in the power granting and organizing authority (if I may so express myself), the principle of the concurring majority, and with it that justice, moderation, and full and perfect representation of all the interests of the community which belong exclusively to it.

Such is the solidity and beauty of our admirable system—but which, it is perfectly obvious, can only be preserved by maintaining the ascendency of the CONSTITUTION–MAKING AUTHORITY OVER THE LAW–MAKING—THE CONCURRING OVER THE ABSOLUTE MAJORITY. Nor is it less clear that this can only be effected by the right of a State to annul the unconstitutional acts of the Government—a right confounded with the idea of a minority governing a majority, but which, so far from being the case, is indispensable to prevent the more energetic but imperfect majority which controls the movements of the Government from usurping the place of that more perfect and just majority which formed the Constitution and ordained Government to execute its powers.

Nor need we apprehend that this check, as powerful as it is, will prove excessive. . . .

The Constitution, while it grants powers to the Government, at the same time imposes restrictions on its action, with the intention of confining it within a limited range of powers, and of the means of executing them. The object of the powers is to protect the rights and promote the interests of all; and of the restrictions, to prevent the majority, or the dominant interests of the Government, from perverting powers intended for the common good into the means of oppressing the minor interests of the community. . . .

Two powers are necessary to the existence and preservation of free States: a power on the part of the ruled to prevent rulers from abusing their authority, by compelling them to be faithful to their constituents, and which is effected through the right of suffrage; and a power TO COMPEL THE PARTS OF SOCIETY TO BE JUST TO ONE ANOTHER, BY COMPELLING THEM TO CONSULT THE INTEREST OF EACH OTHER—which can only be effected, whatever may be the device for the purpose, by requiring the concurring assent of all the great and distinct interests of the community to the measures of the Government. This result is the sum-total of all the contrivances adopted by free States to preserve their liberty, by preventing the conflicts between the several classes or parts of the community. Both powers are indispensable. The one as much so as the other. The rulers are not more disposed to encroach on the ruled than the different interests of the community on one another; nor would they more certainly convert their power from the just and legitimate objects for which governments are instituted into an instrument of aggrandizement, at the expense of the ruled,—unless made responsible to their constituents,—than would the stronger interests theirs, at the expense of the weaker, unless compelled to consult them in the measures of the Government by taking their separate and concurring assent. The same cause operates in both cases. The constitution of our nature, which would impel the rulers to oppress the ruled, unless prevented, would in like manner, and with equal force, impel the stronger to oppress the weaker interest. To vest the right of government in the absolute majority, would be, in fact—BUT TO EMBODY THE WILL OF THE STRONGER INTEREST IN THE OPERATIONS OF THE GOVERNMENT AND NOT THE WILL OF THE WHOLE COMMUNITY—AND TO LEAVE THE OTHERS UNPROTECTED, A PREY TO ITS AMBITION AND CUPIDITY—just as would be the case between rulers and ruled, if the right to govern was vested exclusively in the hands of the former. They would both be, in reality, absolute and despotic governments: the one as much so as the other.

They would both become mere instruments of cupidity and ambition in the hands of those who wielded them. No one doubts that such would be the case were the government placed under the control of irresponsible rulers, but, unfortunately for the cause of liberty, it is not seen with equal clearness that it must as necessarily be so when controlled by an absolute majority; and yet, the former is not more certain than the latter. To this we may attribute the mistake so often and so fatally repeated, that TO EXPEL A DESPOT IS TO ESTABLISH LIBERTY—a mistake to which we may trace the failure of many noble and generous efforts in favor of liberty. The error consists in considering communities as formed of interests strictly identical throughout, instead of being composed, as they in reality are, of as many distinct interests as there are individuals. The interests of no two persons are the same, regarded in reference to each other, though they may be, viewed in relation to the rest of the community. It is this diversity which the several portions of the community bear to each other, in reference to the whole, that renders the principle of the concurring majority necessary to preserve liberty. Place the power in the hands of the absolute majority, and the strongest of these would certainly pervert the government from the object for which it was instituted—the equal protection of the rights of all—into an instrument of advancing itself at the expense of the rest of the community. Against this abuse of power no remedy can be devised but that of the concurring majority. Neither the right of suffrage nor public opinion can possibly check it. They, in fact, but tend to aggravate the disease. . . .

In stating what I have, I have but repeated the experience of ages, comprehending all free governments preceding ours, and ours as far as it has progressed. The PRACTICAL operation of ours has been substantially on the principle of *the absolute* majority. We have acted, with some exceptions, as if the General Government had the right to interpret its own powers, without limitation or check; and though many circumstances have favored us, and greatly impeded the natural progress of events, under such an operation of the system, yet we already see, in whatever direction we turn our eyes, the growing symptoms of disorder and decay—the growth of faction, cupidity, and corruption; and the decay of patriotism, integrity, and disinterestedness. In the midst of youth, we see the flushed cheek, and the short and feverish breath, that mark the approach of the fatal hour; and come it will, unless there be a speedy and radical change—a return to the great conservative principles which brought the Republican party into authority, but which, with the possession of power and prosperity, it has long ceased to remember.

I have now finished the task which your request imposed. If I have been so fortunate as to add to your fund a single new illustration of this great conservative principle of our Government, or to furnish an additional argument calculated to sustain the State in her noble and patriotic struggle to revive and maintain it, and in which you have acted a part long to be remembered by the friends of freedom, I shall feel amply compensated for the time occupied in so long a communication. I believe the cause to be the cause of truth and justice, of union, liberty, and the Constitution, before which the ordinary party struggles of the day sink into perfect insignificance; and that it will be so regarded by the most distant posterity, I have not the slightest doubt.

With great and sincere regard,

I am yours, &c., &c.,

JOHN C. CALHOUN

Discussion Starters

1. On what did Calhoun rest his belief that the General Government must be the agent of the State government? In what respects does this differ from earlier explanations by the founding fathers of the relationship between the states and the central government?

2. What was Calhoun's interpretation of the principle of sovereignty in the American system of government? Was this fact or theory to him?

3. Why did Calhoun make a distinction between nullification and secession?

4. How does Calhoun's concept of the "concurring majority" differ from what today is termed "minority rule"?

5. Which arguments used by Calhoun to justify nullification carry the greatest weight in giving validity to his position?

Related Documents

I. The Nullification Convention: A Speech and the Ordinance

The passage of the Tariff of 1832, without the redress of Southern grievances, resulted in the election of a special convention in South Carolina to consider the tariff system of the United States. The convention met in Columbia, South Carolina, on November 19, 1832, and on November 24 passed an ordinance nullifying the federal tariff laws. How does the following speech given by Governor James Hamilton, Jr., to the convention reflect Calhoun's arguments for nullification in his letter? To what extent do Calhoun's reasons for nullification appear in the ordinance passed by the convention?

Gentlemen: On looking round this convention, and seeing of whom it is composed, no impulse of self-love could lead me to attribute the distinction which has just been given me to anything else than the high and responsible station I already fill. When I see in this assembly so many individuals whose experience is more mature, and whose claims are paramount to my own, I can attribute it to no other cause. I feel deeply penetrated with a sense of your kindness, as well as the great responsibility which is thus cast on me. A crisis of no ordinary character has brought us together, and we have solemn duties, involving high considerations, to discharge. Results the most important and lasting are to flow from a faithful and inflexible discharge of those duties.

It is scarcely a solecism to say, that here are the PEOPLE. This is the concentration of their sovereignty. An intermediate class of the people's agents have determined that a convention of South Carolina should be called. This act was passed in wisdom and discretion. We are convened under the solemn injunction from the people to consider the acts of the congress of the United States, imposing duties on goods, wares, and merchandise imported into the United States, for the protection of American manufactures, which are, in the opinion of the people of South Carolina, infringements of their rights, and violations of the constitution, and to devise the mode and measure of redress. These are our duties, and it becomes us to discharge them in a spirit of enlightened moderation, and of inflexible firmness. If there is, and belongs to political bodies a reasonable forecast, and a high moral courage, let us, in the language of the immortal martyr of constitutional liberty, "put on athletic habits for the contest," and nerve our souls to the struggle.

I shall be often compelled to throw myself on your indulgence, as this is the first occasion that I have been called upon to preside over a deliberative assembly.—All I can do is to pledge my best endeavors to preserve decorum, and to admit of all the latitude of debate compatible with the usual parliamentary rules, and in a spirit of kindness to those who are politically opposed to me.

Permit me to say, that ours is no ordinary position.—We have the incontestible power of a sovereign state. Ours is the first convention which has been held for reviewing the terms and conditions of the federal compact—not the revision of our state constitution, but the consideration of high and ulterior questions of sovereignty. Our present circumstances are a commentary on the safety and beauty of our constitution. In other countries we should render ourselves obnoxious to the charge of an attempt to disturb and change the very elements of government. Here, all goes on with tranquillity, and with the harmony of the spheres themselves.

In conclusion, permit me to say, that, in taking the matters under consideration submitted to us, my anxious prayer is, that our deliberations, in their results, may tend to establish *our own* liberties—to maintain the rights and privileges of *our own* people, and with those to give stability to the union, to restore harmony to our altars and our firesides—that harmony and affection out of which the union sprung, and which are its best refuge and defence.

With these remarks, I proceed to discharge the duties of the chair. . . .

AN ORDINANCE,

To provide for arresting the operation of certain acts of the congress of the United States, purporting to be laws laying duties and imposts on the importation of foreign commodities.

1. *Whereas* the congress of the United States, by various acts, purporting to be acts laying duties and imposts on foreign imports, but in reality intended for the protection of domestic manufactures, and the giving of bounties to classes and individuals engaged in particular employments, at the expense, and to the injury and oppression of other classes and individuals, and by wholly exempting from taxation certain foreign commodities, such as are not produced or manufactured in the United States, to afford a pretext for imposing higher and excessive duties on articles similar to those intended to be protected, hath exceeded its just powers under the constitution, which confers on it no authority to afford such protection, and hath violated the true meaning and intent of the constitution, which provides for equality in imposing the burdens of taxation upon the several states and portions of the confederacy; And, whereas, the said congress, exceeding its just power to impose taxes and collect revenue for the purpose of effecting and accomplishing the specific objects and purposes which the constitution of the United States authorises it to effect and accomplish, hath raised and collected unnecessary revenue, for objects unauthorised by the constitution:

2. We, therefore, the people of the state of South Carolina, in convention assembled, do declare and ordain, and it is hereby declared and ordained, that the several acts and parts of acts of the congress of the United States, purporting to be laws for the imposing of duties and imposts on the importation of foreign commodities, and now having actual operation and effect within the

United States, and more especially an act entitled "an act in alteration of the several acts imposing duties on imports," approved on the nineteenth day of May, one thousand eight hundred and twenty-eight, and also an act entitled "an act to alter and amend the several acts imposing duties on imports," approved on the fourteenth day of July, one thousand eight hundred and thirty-two, are unauthorised by the constitution of the United States, and violate the true meaning and intent thereof, and are null, void, and no law, nor binding upon this state, it officers or citizens; and all promises, contracts and obligations, made or entered into, or to be made or entered into, with purpose to secure the duties imposed by the said acts, and all judicial proceedings which shall be hereafter had in affirmance thereof, are and shall be held utterly null and void.

3. *And it is further, ordained,* That it shall not be lawful for any of the constituted authorities, whether of this state or of the United States, to enforce the payment of duties imposed by the said acts, within the limits of this state; but that it shall be the duty of the legislature to adopt such measures and pass such acts as may be necessary to give full effect to this ordinance, and to prevent the enforcement and arrest the operation of the said acts and parts of acts of the congress of the United States, within the limits of this state, from and after the first day of February next. . . .

4. *And it is further ordained,* That in no case of law or equity, decided in the courts of this state, wherein shall be drawn in question the authority of this ordinance, or the validity of such act or acts of the legislature as may be passed for the purpose of giving effect thereto, or the validity of the foresaid acts of congress, imposing duties, shall any appeal be taken or allowed to the supreme court of the United States. . . .

5. *And it is further ordained,* That all persons now holding any office of honor, profit or trust, civil or military, under this state, shall, within such time, and in such manner as the legislature shall prescribe, take an oath, well and truly to obey, execute and enforce this ordinance, and such act or acts of the legislature as may be passed in pursuance thereof, according to the true intent and meaning of the same, and on the neglect or omission of any such person or persons so to do, his or their office or offices shall be forthwith vacated, and shall be filled up, as if such person or persons were dead or had resigned. . . .

6. And we, the people of South Carolina, to the end that it may be fully understood by the government of the United States, and the people of the co-states, that we are determined to maintain this, our ordinance and declaration, at every hazard, do further declare, that we will not submit to the application of force, on the part of the federal government, to reduce this state to obedience; but that we will consider the passage by congress of any act authorising the employment of a military or naval force against the state of South Carolina, her constituted authorities or citizens; or any act abolishing or closing the ports of this state, or any of them, or otherwise obstructing the free ingress and egress of vessels, to and from the said ports; or any other act, on the part of the federal government, to coerce the state, shut up her ports,

destroy or harrass her commerce, or to enforce the acts hereby declared to be null and void, otherwise than through the civil tribunals of the country, as inconsistent with the longer continuance of South Carolina in the union; and that the people of this state will thenceforth hold themselves absolved from all further obligation to maintain or preserve their political connexion with the people of the other states, and will forthwith proceed to organize a separate government, and do all other acts and things, which sovereign and independent states may of right do.

II. A Proclamation to the People of South Carolina

ANDREW JACKSON

President Jackson answered the Ordinance of the South Carolina Convention on December 10, 1832, with a Proclamation to the People of South Carolina. Jackson had been elected in 1828 by a coalition of Northeastern, Southern, and Western Democrats on a platform designed to benefit the "common man." But once he was elected, each section tried to master the new president and use him for its own purposes. The Northeastern and Western Democrats were somewhat successful in this, especially the faction led by Martin Van Buren of New York, but the Southerners, led by Calhoun, failed to gain any sway over Jackson. The personal conflict between Jackson and Calhoun did not help the Southern cause, for the new president demanded a loyalty and obedience that the proud Calhoun was not inclined to give. Much of this conflict was generated by Jackson's new-found nationalism and Calhoun's insistent demands based on sectional interest.

What arguments did Jackson use to support his view of the relationship between the states and the federal government? How did these arguments answer Calhoun's views on the role of the majority in the governing of the United States?

DECEMBER 10, 1832

Whereas a convention assembled in the State of South Carolina have passed an ordinance by which they declare "that the several acts and parts of acts of the Congress of the United States purporting to be laws for the imposing of duties and imposts on the importation of foreign commodities, and now having actual operation and effect within the United States, and more especially" two acts for the same purposes passed on the 29th of May, 1828, and on the 14th of July, 1832, "are unauthorized by the Constitution of the United States, and

James D. Richardson, ed., *A Compilation of the Messages and Papers of the Presidents, 1789–1897* (Washington, D.C.: Government Printing Office, 1896), II, pp. 640–44, 647–48, 650, 652–53, 655–56.

violate the true meaning and intent thereof, and are null and void and no law," nor binding on the citizens of that State or its officers. . . .

To preserve this bond of our political existence from destruction, to maintain inviolate this state of national honor and prosperity, and to justify the confidence my fellow-citizens have reposed in me, I, Andrew Jackson, President of the United States, have thought proper to issue this my proclamation, stating my views of the Constitution and laws applicable to the measures adopted by the convention of South Carolina. . . .

The ordinance is founded, not on the indefeasible right of resisting acts which are plainly unconstitutional and too oppressive to be endured, but on the strange position that any one State may not only declare an act of Congress void, but prohibit its execution; that they may do this consistently with the Constitution; that the true construction of that instrument permits a State to retain its place in the Union and yet be bound by no other of its laws than those it may choose to consider as constitutional. It is true, they add, that to justify this abrogation of a law it must be palpably contrary to the Constitution; but it is evident that to give the right of resisting laws of that description, coupled with the uncontrolled right to decide what laws deserve that character, is to give the power of resisting all laws; for as by the theory there is no appeal, the reasons alleged by the State, good or bad, must prevail. If it should be said that public opinion is a sufficient check against the abuse of this power, it may be asked why it is not deemed a sufficient guard against the passage of an unconstitutional act by Congress? There is however a restraint in this last case which makes the assumed power of a State more indefensible, and which does not exist in the other. There are two appeals from an unconstitutional act passed by Congress—one to the judiciary, the other to the people and the States. There is no appeal from the State decision in theory, and the practical illustration shows that the courts are closed against an application to review it, both judges and jurors being sworn to decide in its favor. But reasoning on this subject is superfluous when our social compact, in express terms, declares that the laws of the United States, its Constitution, and treaties made under it are the supreme law of the land, and, for greater caution, adds "that the judges in every State shall be bound thereby, anything in the constitution or laws of any State to the contrary notwithstanding." And it may be asserted without fear of refutation that no federative government could exist without a similar provision. . . .

If the doctrine of a State veto upon the laws of the Union carries with it internal evidence of its impracticable absurdity, our constitutional history will also afford abundant proof that it would have been repudiated with indignation had it been proposed to form a feature in our Government.

In our colonial state, although dependent on another power, we very early considered ourselves as connected by common interest with each other. Leagues were formed for common defense, and before the declaration of independence we were known in our aggregate character as *the United Colo-*

nies of America. That decisive and important step was taken jointly.

. . . In the instrument forming that Union is found an article which declares that "every State shall abide by the determinations of Congress on all questions which by that Confederation should be submitted to them."

Under the Confederation, then, no State could legally annul a decision of the Congress or refuse to submit to its execution; but no provision was made to enforce these decisions. Congress made requisitions, but they were not complied with. The Government could not operate on individuals. They had no judiciary, no means of collecting revenue.

But the defects of the Confederation need not be detailed. Under its operation we could scarcely be called a nation. We had neither prosperity at home nor consideration abroad. This state of things could not be endured, and our present happy Constitution was formed, but formed in vain if this fatal doctrine prevails. It was formed for important objects that are announced in the preamble, made in the name and by the authority of the people of the United States, whose delegates framed and whose conventions approved it. The most important among these objects—that which is placed first in rank, on which all the others rest—is *"to form a more perfect union."* Now, is it possible that even if there were no express provision giving supremacy to the Constitution and laws of the United States over those of the States, can it be conceived that an instrument made for the purpose of *"forming a more perfect union"* than that of the Confederation could be so constructed by the assembled wisdom of our country as to substitute for that Confederation a form of government dependent for its existence on the local interest, the party spirit, of a State, or of a prevailing faction in a State? Every man of plain, unsophisticated understanding who hears the question will give such an answer as will preserve the Union. Metaphysical sublety, in pursuit of an impracticable theory, could alone have devised one that is calculated to destroy it.

I consider, then, the power to annul a law of the United States, assumed by one State, *incompatible with the existence of the Union, contradicted expressly by the letter of the Constitution, unauthorized by its spirit, inconsistent with every principle on which it was founded, and destructive of the great object for which it was formed.* . . .

The preamble rests its justification on these grounds: It assumes as a fact that the obnoxious laws, although they purport to be laws for raising revenue, were in reality intended for the protection of manufactures, which purpose it asserts to be unconstitutional; that the operation of these laws is unequal; that the amount raised by them is greater than is required by the wants of the Government; and, finally, that the proceeds are to be applied to objects unauthorized by the Constitution.

. . . The first virtually acknowledges that the law in question was passed under a power expressly given by the Constitution to lay and collect imposts; but its constitutionality is drawn in question from the *motives* of those who passed it. However apparent this purpose may be in the present case, nothing can be more dangerous than to admit the position that an unconstitutional purpose entertained by the members who assent to a law enacted under a constitutional power shall make that law void. For how is that purpose to be ascertained? Who is to make the scrutiny? How often may bad purposes be falsely imputed, in how many cases are they concealed by false professions, in how many is no declaration of motive made? Admit this doctrine, and you give to the States an uncontrolled right to decide, and every law may be annulled under this pretext. . . .

The next objection is that the laws in question operate unequally. This objection may be made with truth to every law that has been or can be passed. The wisdom of man never yet contrived a system of taxation that would operate with perfect equality. If the unequal operation of a law makes it unconstitutional, and if all laws of that description may be abrogated by any State for that cause, then, indeed, is the Federal Constitution unworthy of the slightest effort for its preservation. We have hitherto relied on it as the perpetual bond of our Union; we have received it as the work of the assembled wisdom of the nation; we have trusted to it as to the sheet anchor of our safety in the stormy times of conflict with a foreign or domestic foe; we have looked to it with sacred awe as the palladium of our liberties, and with all the solemnities of religion have pledged to each other our lives and fortunes here and our hopes of happiness hereafter in its defense and support. . . .

On such expositions and reasonings the ordinance grounds not only an assertion of the right to annul the laws of which it complains, but to enforce it by a threat of seceding from the Union if any attempt is made to execute them.

This right to secede is deduced from the nature of the Constitution, which, they say, is a compact between sovereign States who have preserved their whole sovereignty and therefore are subject to no superior; that because they made the compact they can break it when in their opinion it has been departed from by the other States. Fallacious as this course of reasoning is, it enlists State pride and finds advocates in the honest prejudices of those who have not studied the nature of our Government sufficiently to see the radical error on which it rests. . . .

The States severally have not retained their entire sovereignty. It has been shown that in becoming parts of a nation, not members of a league, they surrendered many of their essential parts of sovereignty. The right to make treaties, declare war, levy taxes, exercise exclusive judicial and legislative powers, were all of them functions of sovereign power. The States, then, for all these important purposes were no longer sovereign. The allegiance of their citizens was transferred, in the first instance, to the Government of the United States; they became American citizens and owed obedience to the Constitution of the United States and to laws made in conformity with the powers it vested in Congress. This last position has not been and can not be denied. . . .

Fellow-citizens of my native State, let me not only admonish you, as the First Magistrate of our common country, not to incur the penalty of its laws, but use the influence that a father would over his children whom he saw rushing to certain ruin. In that paternal language, with that paternal feeling, let me tell you, my countrymen, that you are deluded by men who are either deceived themselves or wish to deceive you. . . . They are not champions of liberty, emulating the fame of our Revolutionary fathers, nor are you an oppressed people, contending, as they repeat to you, against worse than colonial vassalage. You are free members of a flourishing and happy Union. There is no settled design to oppress you. You have indeed felt the unequal operation of laws which may have been unwisely, not unconstitutionally, passed; but that inequality must necessarily be removed. . . .

Fellow-citizens of the United States, the threat of unhallowed disunion, the names of those once respected by whom it is uttered, the array of military force to support it, denote the approach of a crisis in our affairs on which the continuance of our unexampled prosperity, our political existence, and perhaps that of all free governments may depend. . . .

Fellow-citizens, the momentous case is before you. On your undivided support of your Government depends the decision of the great question it involves—whether your sacred Union will be preserved and the blessing it secures to us as one people shall perpetuated. . . .

May the Great Ruler of Nations grant that the signal blessings with which He has favored ours may not, by the madness of party or personal ambition, be disregarded and lost; and may His wise providence bring those who have produced this crisis to see the folly before they feel the misery of civil strife, and inspire a returning veneration for that Union which, if we may dare to penetrate His designs, He has chosen as the only means of attaining the high destinies to which we may reasonably aspire.

In testimony whereof I have caused the seal of the United States to be hereunto affixed, having signed the same with my hand. Done at the city of Washington, this 10th day of December, A. D. 1832, and of the Independence of the United States the fifty-seventh.

III. The Architects of Ruin

DANIEL WEBSTER

President Jackson faced a difficult decision in January 1833, for the Ordinance of Nullification was to go into effect on February 1 and the Convention of South Carolina had resolved that they would not permit the tariffs of 1828 and 1832 to operate within the borders of the state. The President had several alternatives: he could back down and let South Carolina go its own way; he could invade South Carolina and force the state to recognize federal statutes; or he could attempt to compel the Congress to bring about a tariff that would satisfy South

Daniel Webster, *The Works of Daniel Webster* (Boston: Little, Brown and Company, 1853), III, pp. 463–66, 503–4.

Carolinian demands. Jackson decided to ask Congress for the authority to use force to collect the customs duties and to present Congress with a compromise tariff proposal. The first was enacted by Congress as the Force Bill and the second as the Compromise Tariff (Verplanck Bill) of 1833.

The Northern reaction to the Force Bill was one of approval, but the Compromise Tariff was condemned as a sellout to the Southern interests. The sharpest attacks on the new tariff came from the Northeastern manufacturers, who saw it as the end of protection for their industries. On February 16, 1833, in an effort to block the passage of the tariff (which had the backing of the West and the South), Daniel Webster rose in the Senate to instruct his colleagues on the nature of the Constitution.

Restate Webster's concept of the Constitution. In what ways does this differ with Calhoun's view of the Constitution?

FEBRUARY 16, 1833

Mr. President, if we are to receive the Constitution as the text, and then to lay down in its margin the contradictory commentaries which have been, and which may be, made by different States, the whole page would be a polyglot indeed. It would speak with as many tongues as the builders of Babel, and in dialects as much confused, and mutually as unintelligible. The very instance now before us presents a practical illustration. The law of the last session is declared unconstitutional in South Carolina, and obedience to it is refused. In other States, it is admitted to be strictly constitutional. You walk over the limit of its authority, therefore, when you pass a State line. On one side it is law, on the other side a nullity; and yet it is passed by a common government, having the same authority in all the States.

Such, Sir, are the inevitable results of this doctrine. Beginning with the original error, that the Constitution of the United States is nothing but a compact between sovereign States; asserting, in the next step, that each State has a right to be its own sole judge of the extent of its own obligations, and consequently of the constitutionality of laws of Congress; and, in the next, that it may oppose whatever it sees fit to declare unconstitutional, and that it decides for itself on the mode and measure of redress,—the argument arrives at once at the conclusion, that what a State dissents from, it may nullify; what it opposes, it may oppose by force; what it decides for itself, it may execute by its own power; and that, in short, it is itself supreme over the legislation of Congress, and supreme over the decisions of the national judicature; supreme over the constitution of the country, supreme over the supreme law of the land. . . .

This, Sir, is practical nullification.

And now, Sir, against all these theories and opinions, I maintain,—

1. That the Constitution of the United States is not a league, confederacy, or compact between the people of the several States in their sovereign capacities; but a government proper, founded on the adoption of the people, and creating direct relations between itself and individuals.

2. That no State authority has power to dissolve these relations; that

nothing can dissolve them but revolution; and that, consequently, there can be no such thing as secession without revolution.

3. That there is a supreme law, consisting of the Constitution of the United States, and acts of Congress passed in pursuance of it, and treaties; and that, in cases not capable of assuming the character of a suit in law or equity, Congress must judge of, and finally interpret, this supreme law so often as it has occasion to pass acts of legislation; and in cases capable of assuming, and actually assuming, the character of a suit, the Supreme Court of the United States is the final interpreter.

4. That an attempt by a State to abrogate, annul, or nullify an act of Congress, or to arrest its operation within her limits, on the ground that, in her opinion, such law is unconstitutional, is a direct usurpation on the just powers of the general government, and on the equal rights of other States; a plain violation of the Constitution, and a proceeding essentially revolutionary in its character and tendency.

Whether the Constitution be a compact between States in their sovereign capacities, is a question which must be mainly argued from what is contained in the instrument itself. . . . What the Constitution says of itself . . . is as conclusive as what it says on any other point. Does it call itself a "compact"? Certainly not. It uses the word *compact* but once, and that is when it declares that the States shall enter into no compact. Does it call itself a "league," a "confederacy," a "subsisting treaty between the States"? Certainly not. There is not a particle of such language in all its pages. But it declares itself a CONSTITUTION. What is a *constitution?* Certainly not a league, compact, or confederacy, but a *fundamental law.* That fundamental regulation which determines the manner in which the public authority is to be executed, is what forms the *constitution* of a State. Those primary rules which concern the body itself, and the very being of the political society, the form of government, and the manner in which power is to be exercised,—all, in a word, which form together the *constitution of a state,*—these are the fundamental laws. This, Sir, is the language of the public writers. But do we need to be informed, in this country, what a *constitution* is? Is it not an idea perfectly familiar, definite, and well settled? We are at no loss to understand what is meant by the constitution of one of the States; and the Constitution of the United States speaks of itself as being an instrument of the same nature. It says, this *Constitution* shall be the law of the land, any thing in any State *constitution* to the contrary notwithstanding. And it speaks of itself, too, in plain contradistinction from a confederation; for it says that all debts contracted, and all engagements entered into, by the United States, shall be as valid under this *Constitution* as under the *Confederation.* It does not say, as valid under this *compact,* or this league, or this confederation, as under the former confederation, but as valid under this *Constitution.* . . .

Mr. President, if the friends of nullification should be able to propagate their opinions, and give them practical effect, they would, in my judgment, prove themselves the most skilful "architects of ruin," the most effectual extinguishers of high-raised expectation, the greatest blasters of human hopes, that any age has produced. . . .

IV. The Glories of South Carolina: An Editorial

On March 1, 1833, the Force Bill and the Compromise Tariff were approved by Congress and signed the next day by President Jackson. The response in South Carolina was one of celebration for the victory of their cause, while in the Northeast Jackson was characterized as the captive of the Southern nullifiers. The West generally agreed with the compromise and Henry Clay of Kentucky helped to guide the bill through Congress. On March 15, 1833, the South Carolina Convention passed a resolution rescinding the Nullification Ordinance of November 24, 1832, and on March 18 passed an ordinance nullifying the Force Bill and then adjourned. The controversy was over, but who had won?

The Columbia Telescope *thought it knew, and ran an editorial on March 12, one day after the convention had convened to consider the situation. How does this editorial demonstrate the failure of the solution to the nullification controversy?*

MARCH 12, 1833

The convention of South Carolina has once more assembled. Expectation will be strongly fixed upon its proceedings. We will endeavor to say what they are like to be.

The convention will accede to the present arrangement of the tariff, by Mr. Clay's bill. The state feels that the present adjustment is less than was due. But she will not, for the degree by no means important, in which this bill falls short of a perfectly fair settlement, disturb the peace of the confederacy.

The adjustment, indeed, is one, at which all men must feel bound to rejoice, while it is impossible to be contented with it. Yet it is much to have been gained, *at a single effort, and against such vast odds.* Never was there a prouder instance of the might of just principles, backed by a high courage. This little state, in the mere panoply of courage and high principles, has foiled the swaggering giant of the union. 30,000 Carolinians have not only awed the wild west into respect,—compelled Pennsylvania stolidity into something like sense —New York corruption into something like decency—Yankee rapacity into a sort of image of honesty; but all this has been loftily and steadily done, in the face of 17,000—what shall we call them? What epithet is of a shame wide, lasting and deep enough, for the betrayers of the liberties of their own country —the instigators of merciless slaughter—the contrivers of irretrievable servitude, against their own struggling state?

Niles' Weekly Register, March 23, 1833.

The tariff, then, is overthrown; the corrupt majorities in congress have yielded. The madness of the government has, at last, found a slight lucid interval. It is an interval only. For, as if in the mere wantonness of folly, they have joined to the concession, *thus wrung from them by mere fear and interest,* ANOTHER ACT, capable in its consequences of utterly defeating the compromise, at which they grasp.

We speak of . . . the "bloody bill;" which they have passed, we believe, in mere bravado—only to cover the shame of their defeat. *They may find it,* however, *in the hands of the chief of this atrocious administration,* not the mere *brutem fulmen* that it was intended to be.

Whether or not he seize at once upon the dangerous powers of this act, and brandish them, to drive this state into a conflict, *it is quite certain that the bloody bill will not be submitted to by this state.* The convention, we make no doubt, will nullify it. Such seems distinctly the public view.

We have as little doubt, too, that the state, taught by the recent events, will adopt an oath of paramount allegiance to her authorities. This whole contest, indeed, has been nothing else than one of allegiance. If we ever consent again to place ourselves in the same difficulty, in any future struggle with the general government, we shall almost deserve that loss of liberty, which had so nearly been the fruit of our past omission of that which no civilized state ever yet omitted, that had been visited, (as all states must sooner or later be), by a domestic contest for liberty.

For Further Reading

To obtain a more detailed account of the background of the nullification controversy and the controversy itself, see two early, but not outdated, books on the period: Chauncy S. Boucher, *The Nullification Controversy in South Carolina* (1916; reprinted in 1968) and David F. Houston, *A Critical Study of Nullification in South Carolina* (1896; reprinted in 1967). A more recent study of the events and how they affected South Carolina is William H. Freehling's *Prelude to Civil War** (1966).

Since the tariff was of prime importance in the controversy one should consult *The Tariff History of the United States** (1931; reprinted in 1967), by F. W. Taussig. Edward Pessen's *Jacksonian America** (1969), the thought-provoking *Age of Jackson** (1945) by Arthur M. Schlesinger, Jr., and Leonard D. White's *The Jacksonians** (1954) are more general accounts of the period.

Biographies of the leading participants include: Marquis James, *The Life of Andrew Jackson* (1938); Robert V. Remini, *Andrew Jackson** (1966); Gerald Capers, *John C. Calhoun: Opportunist* (1960); Richard Current, *John C. Calhoun* (1966); and Charles M. Wiltse, *John C. Calhoun,* 3 vols. (1944–51; reprinted in 1968).

Two collections of essays are Frank Otto Gattell's *Essays on Jacksonian America** (1970) and Margaret L. Coit's *John C. Calhoun** (1970).

---

*Paperbound edition available.

Problems books concerned with the period and the controversy are: James L. Bugg, Jr., ed., *Jacksonian Democracy** (1962); Charles Sellers, ed., *Andrew Jackson, Nullification, and the State-Rights Tradition** (1963); and George Rogers Taylor, ed., *The Great Tariff Debate, 1820–1830** (1953).

*Paperbound edition available.

10. The Cherokee Nation: Toward the Trail of Tears

When the United States emerged as a nation, the new government immediately faced the problem of dealing with the Indian tribes residing within its boundaries. The likelihood of the white population's expansion into Indian territories made this an especially crucial problem. In response to this problem a point of view began to develop in the Confederation period, and during Washington's first administration it became stated policy. This policy, first envisioned by Secretary of War Henry Knox, provided that western lands would be purchased from the Indian tribes by Congress and that the tribes would be removed farther West, outside the reach of white settlements. Through this "removal" policy the westward movement by whites was encouraged.

From the white man's point of view the policy might have been desirable, but the Indians accepted it reluctantly or not at all. Following the War of 1812 the tribes living in the Southeast presented a specific obstacle to its easy implementation on behalf of the cotton growers in that region. These tribes, including the Creeks, Cherokees, Choctaws, and Chickasaws, were opposed, if not openly hostile, to any incursion by whites into their ancestral lands.

From 1816 to 1821 the federal government was able to sign treaties of removal for several tracts of land in Georgia, Alabama, and Tennessee, but this did not satisfy the demands of land-hungry whites. Those demands became more insistent during the administrations of presidents Monroe and Adams, and finally brought about a treaty for the removal of the entire Creek tribe in 1826. Typically, a removal treaty provided for presents to be given to the chiefs and the ceding to the Indians of an amount of land west of the Mississippi River equal to that they were forced to vacate east of the river.

The principal barrier to more effective, widespread implementation of the removal policy was the development of an agricultural way of life among the tribes in the Southeast. This new life style, modeled after the neighboring white settlements, meant that the government would be removing not wandering tribes in a state of barbarism, but settled people living in a "civilized" way. The difficulty was compounded in the case of the Cherokees, who had formulated an alphabet, printed a newspaper, and established schools and churches. In 1827 they proclaimed themselves to be self-governing under a constitution patterned after the United States Constitution. Despite the difficulties, however, the removal of all tribes living on coveted lands was persistently demanded by the various Southeastern states.

The most noteworthy problems appeared in Georgia, where removal demands by whites and by the state government became more shrill when gold was discovered on the lands of the Cherokee Nation in July 1829. To bring the situation to the desired conclusion the Georgia legislature passed a bill in December 1829, annexing a large section of the Cherokee territory. Similar laws were subsequently passed in Alabama and Mississippi. The Georgia law also annulled Cherokee laws, decreeing that Indians were not to be considered competent witnesses in any state court action involving a white person. The Indians were therefore effectively stripped of all legal protection from white aggression.

The Cherokees (and other tribes similarly victimized) had no recourse, short of war, but to appeal to the federal government for protection from the state legislatures. In 1828, however, Andrew Jackson, no friend to the Indians, had been elected president, so the nature of the government's response was almost predictable.

Core Documents

Memorial of the Cherokee Nation: December 1829

When the Cherokees proclaimed themselves a nation in 1827, the state of Georgia became concerned that they would become too settled, too civilized for removal. Such fears were soon dispelled by Jackson in his First Annual Message on December 8, 1829. Although the new president declared, "We are at peace with all mankind, and . . . our great desire is to see our brethren of the human

Niles' Weekly Register, March 13, 1830.

race secured in the blessings enjoyed by ourselves, and advancing in knowledge, in freedom, and in happiness," he also made it clear that this rhetoric of freedom was not to extend to the Indians.

Jackson, a noted Indian fighter, had represented the War Department in signing partial removal treaties in 1817 and 1820. In 1829, as president, he continued to see the Indian question through the eyes of his earlier experiences. For him the situation was simple: The Indians could not set up independent nations within areas under the jurisdiction of the states. Indian presence could not be permitted to prevent the expansion of the United States. Therefore the Indians, if dissatisfied, should consider removal to areas where they could live in peace under their own laws. Nevertheless, his presidential message on December 8 stated, "This emigration should be voluntary, for it would be as cruel as unjust to compel the aborigines to abandon the graves of their fathers and seek a home in a distant land. But they should be distinctly informed that if they remain within the limits of the States they must be subject to their laws."

The Indians had not found a friend in the White House, for their alternatives assured either an undesirable move to the West and an uncertain future or a perilous existence on their ancestral lands as noncitizens of the states.

The president's position on the Indian problem encouraged the introduction of legislation in Congress for the removal of the tribes in the Southeast. This legislation, finally passed as the Indian Removal Bill, found stiff resistance in Congress from many Northern members and acceptance by most from the South. To aid their cause and their supporters in Congress, the Cherokees wrote to the House and Senate in December 1829, pleading their case.

In the first document in this section, the "Memorial of the Cherokee Nation" to the Congress of the United States, give close attention to:

- *the Cherokees' views of the historical relationship between the Indians and the whites.*
- *their praise of the American civilization.*
- *their belief that they had a right to the lands in question.*

To the honorable the senate and house of representatives of the United States of America, in congress assembled:

The undersigned memorialists, humbly make known to your honorable bodies, that they are free citizens of the Cherokee nation. Circumstances of late occurrence have troubled our hearts, and induced us at this time to appeal to you, knowing that you are generous and just. As weak and poor children are accustomed to look to their guardians and patrons for protection, so we would come and make our grievances known. Will you listen to us? Will you have pity on us? You are great and renowned—the nation which you represent, is like a mighty man who stands in his strength. But we are small—our name is not renowned. You are wealthy, and have need of nothing; but we are poor in life, and have not the arm and power of the rich. . . .

Brothers—we address you according to usage adopted by our forefathers. . . . The land on which we stand, we have received as an inheritance from our fathers, who possessed it from time immemorial, as a gift from our common father in heaven. We have already said, that when the white man came to the shores of America, our ancestors were found in peaceable possession of this very land. They bequeathed it to us as their children, and we have sacredly kept it as containing the remains of our beloved men. This right of inheritance we have *never ceded,* nor ever *forfeited.* Permit us to ask, what better right can a people have to a country, than the right of *inheritance* and *immemorial peaceable possession?* We know it is said of late by the state of Georgia, and by the executive of the United States, that we have forfeited this right—but we think this is said gratuitously. At what time have we made the forfeit? What crime have we committed, whereby we must forever be divested of our country and rights? Was it when we were hostile to the United States, and took part with the king of Great Britain during the struggle for independence? If so, why was not this forfeiture declared in the first treaty of peace between the United States and our beloved men? Why was not such an article as the following inserted in the treaty: "The United States give peace to the Cherokees, but, for the part they took in the late war, declare them to be but tenants at will, to be removed when the convenience of the states within whose chartered limits they live shall require it." This was the proper time to assume such a position. But it was not thought of, nor would our forefathers have agreed to any treaty, whose tendency was to deprive them of their rights and their country. All that they have conceded and relinquished are inserted in the treaties open to the investigation of all people. We would repeat, then, the right of inheritance and peaceable possession which we claim, we have never ceded nor forfeited.

In addition to that first of all rights, the right of inheritance and peaceable possession, we have the faith and pledge of the U. States, repeated over and over again in treaties made at various times. By these treaties our rights as a separate people are distinctly acknowledged, and guarantees given that they shall be secured and protected. So we have always understood the treaties. The conduct of the government toward us, from its organization until very lately, the talks given to our beloved men by the presidents of the United States, and the speeches of the agents and commissioners, all concur to show that we are not mistaken in our interpretation. . . .

In view of the strong ground upon which their rights are founded, your memorialists solemnly protest against being considered as tenants at will, or as mere occupants of the soil, without possessing the sovereignty. We have already stated to your honorable bodies, that our forefathers were found in possession of this soil in full sovereignty, by the first European settlers; and as we have never ceded nor forfeited the occupancy of the soil and the sover-eignty over it, we do solemnly protest against being forced to leave it, either direct or by indirect measures. To the land of which we are now in possession we are attached—it is our fathers' gift—it contains their ashes—it is the land of our nativity, and the land of our intellectual birth. We cannot consent to abandon it, for another *far inferior,* and which holds out to us no inducements. We do moreover protest against the arbitrary measures of our neighbor, the state of Georgia, in her attempt to extend her laws over us, in surveying our lands without our consent and in direct opposition to treaties and the intercourse law of the United States, and interfering with our municipal regulations in such a manner as to derange the regular operations of our own laws. To deliver and protect them from all these and every encroachment upon their rights, the undersigned memorialists do most earnestly pray your honorable bodies. Their existence and future happiness are at stake—divest them of their liberty and country, and you sink them in degradation, and put a check, if not a final stop, to their present progress in the arts of civilized life, and in the knowledge of the Christian religion. Your memorialists humbly conceive, that such an act would be in the highest degree oppressive. From the people of these United States, who perhaps, of all men under heaven, are the most religious and free, it cannot be expected.—Your memorialists, therefore, cannot anticipate such a result. You represent a virtuous, intelligent and Christian nation. To you they willingly submit their cause for your righteous decision.

Memorial of the Cherokee Nation: July 17, 1830

When the Removal Bill was passed on May 28, 1830, the Cherokee Nation addressed another memorial, this time to the "People of the United States," reminding them and their government of the existing obligations resulting from the treaties that had been agreed to between the two nations.

In this memorial, the second one in this section, note:

- *what the Cherokees believed to be the role that treaties should play in the controversy.*
- *the Cherokee concept of the relationship between their Nation and the United States Government.*
- *the reasons why the Cherokees did not want to remove west of the Mississippi River.*
- *the Cherokees' appeal to the Christianity of the whites.*

More than a year ago we were officially given to understand by the secretary of war, that the president could not protect us against the laws of Georgia. This information was entirely unexpected; as it went upon the principle, that treaties made between the United States and the Cherokee nation have no power to withstand the legislation of separate states; and of course, that they have no efficacy whatever, but leave our people to the mercy of the neighboring whites, whose supposed interests would be promoted by our expulsion, or extermination. It would be impossible to describe the sorrow, which affected our minds on learning that the chief magistrate of the United States had come to this conclusion, that all his illustrious predecessors had held intercourse with us on principles which could not be sustained; that they had made promises of vital importance to us, which could not be fulfilled—promises made hundreds of times in almost every conceivable manner,—often in the form of solemn treaties, sometimes in letters written by the chief magistrate with his own hand, very often in letters written by the secretary of war under his direction, sometimes orally by the president and the secretary to our chiefs, and frequently and always, both orally and in writing by the agent of the United States residing among us, whose most important business it was, to see the guaranty of the United States faithfully executed.

Soon after the war of the revolution, as we have learned from our fathers, the Cherokees looked upon the promises of the whites with great distrust and suspicion; but the frank and magnanimous conduct of General Washington did much to allay these feelings. The perseverance of successive presidents, and especially of Mr. Jefferson, in the same course of policy, and in the constant assurance that our country should remain inviolate, except so far as we voluntarily ceded it, nearly banished anxiety in regard to encroachments from the whites. To this result the aid which we received from the United States in the attempts of our people to become civilized, and the kind efforts of benevolent societies, have greatly contributed. Of late years, however, much solicitude was occasioned among our people by the claims of Georgia. This solicitude arose from the apprehension, that by extreme importunity, threats, and other undue influence, a treaty would be made, which should cede the territory, and thus compel the inhabitants to remove. But it never occurred to us for a moment, that without any new treaty, without any assent of our rulers and people, without even a pretended compact, and against our vehement and unanimous protestations, we should be delivered over to the discretion of those, who had declared by a legislative act, that they wanted the Cherokee lands and would have them.

Finding that relief could not be obtained from the chief magistrate, and not doubting that our claim to protection was just, we made our application to congress. During four long months our delegation waited, at the doors of the national legislature of the United States, and the people at home, in the most painful suspense, to learn in what manner our application would be answered; and, now that congress has adjourned, on the very day before the date fixed by Georgia for the extension of her oppressive laws over the greater part of our country, the distressing intelligence has been received that we have received no answer at all; and no department of the government has assured us, that we are to receive the desired protection. But just at the close of the session, an act was passed, by which an half a million of dollars was appropriated towards effecting a removal of Indians; and we have great reason to fear that the influence of this act will be brought to bear most injuriously upon us. The passage of this act was certainly understood by the representatives of Georgia as abandoning us to the oppressive and cruel measures of the state, and as sanctioning the opinion that treaties with Indians do not restrain state legislation. We are informed by those, who are competent to judge, that the recent act does not admit of such construction; but that the passage of it, under the actual circumstances of the controversy, will be considered as sanctioning the pretensions of Georgia, there is too much reason to fear.

Thus have we realized, with heavy hearts, that our supplication has not been heard; that the protection heretofore experienced is now to be withheld; that the guaranty, in consequence of which our fathers laid aside their arms and ceded the best portions of their country, means nothing; and that we must either emigrate to an unknown region and leave the pleasant land to which we have the strongest attachment, or submit to the legislation of a state, which has already made our people outlaws, and enacted that any Cherokee, who shall endeavor to prevent the selling of his country, shall be imprisoned in the penitentiary of Georgia not less than four years. To our countrymen this has been melancholy intelligence, and with the most bitter disappointment has it been received.

But in the midst of our sorrows, we do not forget our obligations to our friends and benefactors. It was with sensations of inexpressible joy that we have learned that the voice of thousands, in many parts of the United States, has been raised in our behalf, and numerous memorials offered in our favor, in both houses of congress. To those numerous friends, who have thus sympathized with us in our low estate, we tender our grateful acknowledgements. In pleading our cause, they have pleaded the cause of the poor and defenceless throughout the world. Our special thanks are due, however, to those honorable men, who so ably and eloquently asserted our rights, in both branches of the national legislature. Their efforts will be appreciated wherever the merits of this question shall be known; and we cannot but think, that they have secured for themselves a permanent reputation among the disinterested advocates of humanity, equal rights, justice, and good faith. We even cherish the hope, that these efforts, seconded and followed by others of a similar character, will yet be available, so far as to mitigate our sufferings, if not to effect our entire deliverance.

Before we close this address, permit us to state what we conceive to be our relations with the United States. After the peace of 1783, the Cherokees were an independent people; absolutely so, as much as any people on earth. They had been allies to Great Britain, and as a faithful ally took a part in the colonial war on her side. They had placed themselves under her protection, and had they, without cause, declared hostility against their protector, and had the colonies been subdued, what might not have been their fate? But her power on this continent was broken. She acknowledged the independence of the United States, and made peace. The Cherokees therefore stood alone; and, in these circumstances, continued the war. They were then under no obligations to the United States any more than to Great Britain, France or Spain. The United States never subjugated the Cherokees; on the contrary, our fathers remained in possession of their country, and with arms in their hands.

The people of the United States sought a peace; and, in 1785, the treaty of Hopewell was formed, by which the Cherokees came under the protection of the United States, and submitted to such limitations of sovereignty as are mentioned in that instrument. None of these limitations, however, affected, in the slightest degree, their rights of self-government and inviolate territory. The citizens of the United States had no right of passage through the Cherokee country till the year 1791, and then only in one direction, and by an express treaty stipulation. When the federal constitution was adopted, the treaty of Hopewell was confirmed, with all other treaties, as the supreme law of the land. In 1791, the treaty of Holston was made, by which the sovereignty of the Cherokees was qualified as follows: The Cherokees acknowledged themselves to be under the protection of the United States, and of no other sovereign.— They engaged that they would not hold any treaty with a foreign power, with any separate state of the union, or with individuals. They agreed that the United States should have the exclusive right of regulating their trade; that the citizens of the United States should have a right of way in one direction through the Cherokee country; and that if an Indian should do injury to a citizen of the United States he should be delivered up to be tried and punished. A cession of lands was also made to the United States. On the other hand, the United States paid a sum of money; offered protection; engaged to punish citizens of the United States who should do any injury to the Cherokees; abandoned white settlers on Cherokee lands to the discretion of the Cherokees; stipulated that white men should not hunt on these lands, nor even enter the country without a passport; and gave a solemn guaranty of all Cherokee lands not ceded. This treaty is the basis of all subsequent compacts; and in none of them are the relations of the parties at all changed.

The Cherokees have always fulfilled their engagements. They have never reclaimed those portions of sovereignty which they surrendered by the treaties of Hopewell and Holston. These portions were surrendered for the purpose of obtaining the guaranty which was recommended to them as the great equivalent. Had they refused to comply with their engagements, there is no doubt the United States would have enforced a compliance. Is the duty of fulfilling engagements on the other side less binding than it would be, if the Cherokees had the power of enforcing their just claims?

The people of the United States will have the fairness to reflect, that all the treaties between them and the Cherokees were made, at the solicitation, and for the benefit, of the whites; that valuable considerations were given for every stipulation, on the part of the United States; that it is impossible to reinstate the parties in their former situation, that there are now hundreds of thousands of citizens of the United States residing upon lands ceded by the Cherokees in these very treaties; and that our people have trusted their country to the guaranty of the United States. If this guaranty fails them, in what can they trust, and where can they look for protection?

We are aware, that some persons suppose it will be for our advantage to remove beyond the Mississippi. We think otherwise. Our people universally think otherwise. Thinking that it would be fatal to their interests, they have almost to a man sent their memorial to congress deprecating the necessity of a removal. This question was distinctly before their minds when they signed their memorial. Not an adult person can be found, who has not an opinion on the subject, and if the people were to understand distinctly, that they could be protected against the laws of the neighboring states, there is probably not an adult person in the nation, who would think it best to remove; though possibly a few might emigrate individually. There are doubtless many, who would flee to an unknown country, however beset with dangers, privations and sufferings, rather than be sentenced to spend six years in a Georgia prison for advising one of their neighbors not to betray his country. And there are others who could not think of living as outlaws in their native land, exposed to numberless vexations, and excluded from being parties or witnesses in a court of justice. It is incredible that Georgia should ever have enacted the oppressive laws to which reference is here made, unless she had supposed that something extremely terrific in its character was necessary in order to make the Cherokees willing to remove. We are not willing to remove; and if we could be brought to this extremity, it would be not by argument, not because our judgment was satisfied, not because our condition will be improved; but only because we cannot endure to be deprived of our national and individual rights and subjected to a process of intolerable oppression.

We wish to remain on the land of our fathers. We have a perfect and original right to remain without interruption or molestation. The treaties with us, and laws of the United States made in pursuance of treaties, guaranty our residence and our privileges, and secure us against intruders. Our only request is, that these treaties may be fulfilled, and these laws executed.

But if we are compelled to leave our country, we see nothing but ruin before us. The country west of the Arkansas territory is unknown to us. From what we can learn of it, we have no prepossessions in its favor. All the inviting parts of it, as we believe, are preoccupied by various Indian nations, to which it has been assigned. They would regard us as intruders, and look upon us with an evil eye. The far greater part of that region is, beyond all controversy, badly supplied with wood and water; and no Indian tribe can live as agriculturists without these articles. All our neighbors, in case of our removal, though crowded into our near vicinity; would speak a language totally different from ours, and practice different customs. The original possessors of that region are now wandering savages lurking for prey in the neighborhood. They have always been at war, and would be easily tempted to turn their arms against peaceful emigrants. Were the country to which we are urged much better than it is represented to be, and were it free from the objections which we have made to it, still it is not the land of our birth, nor of our affections. It contains neither the scenes of our childhood, nor the graves of our fathers.

The removal of families to a new country, even under the most favorable auspices, and when the spirits are sustained by pleasing visions of the future, is attended with much depression of mind and sinking of heart. This is the case, when the removal is a matter of decided preference, and when the persons concerned are in early youth or vigorous manhood. Judge, then, what must be the circumstances of a removal, when a whole community, embracing persons of all classes and every description, from the infant to the man of extreme old age, the sick, the blind, the lame, the improvident, the reckless, the desperate, as well as the prudent, the considerate, the industrious, are compelled to remove by odious and intolerable vexations and persecutions, brought upon them in the forms of law, when all will agree only in this, that they have been cruelly robbed of their country, in violation of the most solemn compacts, which it is possible for communities to form with each other; and that, if they should make themselves comfortable in their new residence, they have nothing to expect hereafter but to be the victims of a future legalized robbery!

Such we deem, and are absolutely certain, will be the feelings of the whole Cherokee people, if they are forcibly compelled, by the laws of Georgia, to remove; and with these feelings, how is it possible that we should pursue our present course of improvement, or avoid sinking into utter despondency? We have been called a poor, ignorant, and degraded people. We certainly are not rich; nor have we ever boasted of our knowledge, or our moral or intellectual elevation. But there is not a man within our limits so ignorant as not to know that he has the right to live on the land of his fathers, in the possession of his immemorial privileges, and that this right has been acknowleged and guaranteed by the United States; nor is there a man so degraded as not to feel a keen sense of injury, on being deprived of this right and driven into exile.

It is under a sense of the most pungent feelings that we make this, perhaps our last appeal to the good people of the United States. It cannot be that the community we are addressing, remarkable for its intelligence and religious sensibilities, and pre-eminent for its devotion to the rights of man, will lay aside this appeal, without considering that we stand in need of its sympathy and commiseration. We know that to the Christian and to the philanthropist the voice of our multiplied sorrows and fiery trials will not appear as an idle tale. In our own land, on our own soil, and in our own dwellings, which we reared for our wives and for our little ones, when there was peace on our mountains and in our valleys, we are encountering troubles which cannot but try our very souls. But shall we, on account of these troubles, forsake our beloved country? Shall we be compelled by a civilized and Christian people, with whom we have lived in perfect peace for the last forty years, and for whom we have willingly bled in war, to bid a final adieu to our homes, our farms, our streams and our beautiful forests? No. We are still firm. We intend still to cling, with our wonted affection, to the land which gave us birth, and which, every day of our lives, brings to us new and stronger ties of attachment. We appeal to the judge of all the earth, who will finally award us justice, and to the good sense of the American people, whether we are intruders upon the land of others. Our consciences bear us witness that we are the invaders of no man's rights—we have robbed no man of his territory—we have usurped no man's authority, nor have we deprived any one of his unalienable privileges. How then shall we indirectly confess the right of another people to our land by leaving it forever? On the soil which contains the ashes of our beloved men we wish to live—on this soil we wish to die.

We intreat those to whom the foregoing paragraphs are addressed, to remember the great law of love. "Do to others as ye would that others should do to you"—Let them remember that of all nations on the earth, they are under the greatest obligation to obey this law. We pray them to remember that, for the sake of principle, their forefathers were *compelled* to leave, therefore *driven* from the old world, and that the winds of persecution wafted them over the great waters and landed them on the shores of the new world, when the Indian was the sole lord and proprietor of these extensive domains—Let them remember in what way they were received by the savage of America, when power was in his hand, and his ferocity could not be restrained by any human arm. We urge them to bear in mind, that those who would now ask of them a cup of cold water, and a spot of earth, a portion of their own patrimonial possessions, on which to live and die in peace, are the descendants of those, whose origin, as inhabitants of North America, history and tradition are alike insufficient to reveal. Let them bring to remembrance all these facts, and they *cannot*, and we are sure, they *will* not fail to remember, and sympathize with us in these our trials and sufferings.

Discussion Starters

1. Evaluate the contention of the Cherokee Nation that because they had occupied the land in question for generations it was their land and that they were therefore exempt from the laws of the United States.

2. What basis, if any, did the Cherokees have for asking the federal government for protection from the laws of Georgia?

3. If the treaty obligations listed by the Cherokees in their memorials had been agreed to by the United States Government, how might the Executive branch have justified its ignoring those treaties and supporting Georgia in its attempts to cause the removal of the Indians?

4. How would you have solved the problem of the conflict of cultures and desire for the same land between the whites and the Indians? What programs should the government enact at the present time to help the Indians?

Related Documents

I. A Defense of the Indians

THEODORE FRELINGHUYSEN

Theodore Frelinghuysen, a member of a well-known New Jersey family, was elected to the Senate by the New Jersey legislature in 1829. Although he served

Register of Debates in Congress, First Session, Twenty-First Congress (Washington, D.C.: Gales & Seaton, 1830), VI, p. 311.

only one term, his performance marked the beginning of a long career in which he became nationally influential in not only political affairs, but also in religion and in higher education.

Frelinghuysen's political fame came primarily from a six-hour speech delivered to the Senate on April 7, 8, and 9, 1830, opposing the Indian Removal Bill. He was not able to muster enough votes to defeat the bill, but in fighting the removal he won the respect of many Americans, including William Lloyd Garrison. Garrison became so convinced of the "higher" motives of the senator from New Jersey that he wrote a poem about the "Patriot and Christian" Frelinghuysen. Subsequently, the senator became popularly known as the "Christian Statesman."

In the following excerpt from Senator Frelinghuysen's speech, how did he try to establish the right of the Indians to hold claim to territory desired by the states?

APRIL 7, 1830

I now proceed to the discussion of those principles which, in my humble judgment, fully and clearly sustain the claims of the Indians to all their political and civil rights, as by them asserted. And here, I insist that, by immemorial possession, as the original tenants of the soil, they hold a title beyond and superior to the British Crown and her colonies, and to all adverse pretensions of our confederation and subsequent Union. God, in his providence, planted these tribes on this Western continent, so far as we know, before Great Britain herself had a political existence. I believe, sir, it is not now seriously denied that the Indians are men, endowed with kindred faculties and powers with ourselves; that they have a place in human sympathy, and are justly entitled to a share in the common bounties of a benignant Providence. And, with this conceded, I ask in what code of the law of nations, or by what process of abstract deduction, their rights have been extinguished?

Where is the decree or ordinance that has stripped these early and first lords of the soil. Sir, no record of such measure can be found. And I might triumphantly rest the hopes of these feeble fragments of once great nations upon this impregnable foundation. However mere human policy, or the law of power, or the tyrant's plea of expediency, may have found it convenient at any or in all times to recede from the unchangeable principles of eternal justice, no argument can shake the political maxim, that, where the Indian always has been, he enjoys an absolute right still to be, in the free exercise of his own modes of thought, government, and conduct.

In the light of natural law, can a reason for a distinction exist in the mode of enjoying that which is my own? If I use it for hunting, may another take it because he needs it for agriculture? I am aware that some writers have, by a system of artificial reasoning, endeavored to justify, or rather excuse the encroachments made upon Indian territory; and they denominate these abstractions the law of nations, and, in this ready way, the question is despatched. Sir, as we trace the sources of this law, we find its authority to depend either upon the conventions or common consent of nations. And when, permit me to inquire, were the Indian tribes ever consulted on the establishment of such a law? Whoever represented them or their interests in any Congress of nations, to confer upon the public rules of intercourse, and the proper foundations of dominion and property? The plain matter of fact is, that all these partial doctrines have resulted from the selfish plans and pursuits of more enlightened nations; and it is not matter for any great wonder, that they should so largely partake of a mercenary and exclusive spirit toward the claims of the Indians.

It is, however, admitted, sir, that, when the increase of population and the wants of mankind demand the cultivation of the earth, a duty is thereby devolved upon the proprietors of large and uncultivated regions, of devoting them to such useful purposes. But such appropriations are to be obtained by fair contract, and for reasonable compensation. It is, in such a case, the duty of the proprietor to sell: we may properly address his reason to induce him; but we cannot rightfully compel the cession of his lands, or take them by violence, if his consent be withheld. It is with great satisfaction that I am enabled, upon the best authority, to affirm, that this duty has been largely and generously met and fulfilled on the part of the aboriginal proprietors of this continent. Several years ago, official reports to Congress stated the amount of Indian grants to the United States to exceed two hundred and fourteen millions of acres. Yes, sir, we have acquired, and now own, more land as the fruits of their bounty than we shall dispose of at the present rate to actual settlers in two hundred years. For, very recently, it has been ascertained, on this floor, that our public sales average not more than about one million of acres annually. It greatly aggravates the wrong that is now meditated against these tribes, to survey the rich and ample districts of their territories, that either force or persuasion have incorporated into our public domains. As the tide of our population has rolled on, we have added purchase to purchase. The confiding Indian listened to our professions of friendship: we called him brother, and he believed us. Millions after millions he has yielded to our importunity, until we have acquired more than can be cultivated in centuries—and yet we crave more. We have crowded the tribes upon a few miserable acres on our Southern frontier: it is all that is left to them of their once boundless forests: and still, like the horse-leech, our insatiated cupidity cries, give! give!

II. President Jackson on the Indian Question

Senator Frelinghuysen's Senate speech was the first of a series of protests made by white Americans against the treatment of the Indians. These protests and the numerous petitions sent to Congress requesting federal protection for the Indians ultimately led the Senate to pass a resolution on February 15, 1831, asking President Jackson "to inform the Senate whether the provisions of the act

James D. Richarson, ed., *A Compilation of the Messages and Papers of the Presidents* (Washington, D.C.: Government Printing Office, 1896), II, pp. 536–41.

entitled 'An act to regulate trade and intercourse with the Indian tribes and to preserve peace on the frontiers,' passed the 30th of March, 1802, have been fully complied with on the part of the United States Government, and if they have not that he inform the Senate of the reasons that have induced the government to decline the enforcement of said act."

The president's answer demonstrated once and for all which side of the controversy he would support. How did his interpretation of the role of the federal government in Indian affairs differ from the Cherokees' view as expressed in their memorials? How did Jackson's position on the disposition of Indian lands strengthen the advocates of a states'-rights interpretation of the Constitution?

FEBRUARY 22, 1831

To the Senate of the United States:
    I have received your resolution of the 15th instant . . . and I now reply to the same. . . .

The numerous provisions of that act designed to secure to the Indians the peaceable possession of their lands may be reduced, substantially, to the following: That citizens of the United States are restrained under sufficient penalties from entering upon the lands for the purpose of hunting thereon, or of settling them, or of giving their horses and cattle the benefit of a range upon them, or of traveling through them without a written permission; and that the President of the United States is authorized to employ the military force of the country to secure the observance of these provisions. The authority to the President, however, is not imperative. The language is:

It shall be lawful for the President to take such measures and to employ such military force as he may judge necessary to remove from lands belonging to or secured by treaty to any Indian tribe any citizen who shall make a settlement thereon.

By the nineteenth section of this act it is provided that nothing in it "shall be construed to prevent any trade or intercourse with Indians living on lands surrounded by settlements of citizens of the United States and being within the ordinary jurisdiction of any of the individual States." This provision I have interpreted as being prospective in its operation and as applicable not only to Indian tribes which at the date of its passage were subject to the jurisdiction of any State, but to such also as should thereafter become so. To this construction of its meaning I have endeavored to conform, and have taken no step inconsistent with it. As soon, therefore, as the sovereign power of the State of Georgia was exercised by an extension of her laws throughout her limits, and I had received information of the same, orders were given to withdraw from the State the troops which had been detailed to prevent intrusion upon the Indian lands within it, and these orders were executed. The reasons which dictated them shall be frankly communicated.

The principle recognized in the section last quoted was not for the first time then avowed. It is conformable to the uniform practice of the Government before the adoption of the Constitution, and amounts to a distinct recognition by Congress at that early day of the doctrine that that instrument had not varied the powers of the Federal Government over Indian affairs from what they were under the Articles of Confederation. It is not believed that there is a single instance in the legislation of the country in which the Indians have been regarded as possessing political rights independent of the control and authority of the States within the limits of which they resided. . . .

There is no assertion of the right of Congress under the Articles of Confederation to interfere with the jurisdiction of the States over Indians within their limits, but rather a negation of it. They refused to interfere with the subject, and referred it under a general recommendation back to the State, to be disposed of as her wisdom might decide. . . .

It was not then pretended that the General Government had the power in their relations with the Indians to control or oppose the internal policy of the individual States of this Union, and if such was the case under the Articles of Confederation the only question on the subject since must arise out of some more enlarged power or authority given to the General Government by the present Constitution. Does any such exist?

Amongst the enumerated grants of the Constitution that which relates to this subject is expressed in these words: "Congress shall have power to regulate commerce with the Indian tribes." In the interpretation of this power we ought certainly to be guided by what had been the practice of the Government and the meaning which had been generally attached to the resolves of the old Congress if the words used to convey it do not clearly import a different one, as far as it affects the question of jurisdiction in the individual States. The States ought not to be divested of any part of their antecedent jurisdiction by implication or doubtful construction. Tested by this rule it seems to me to be unquestionable that the jurisdiction of the States is left untouched by this clause of the Constitution, and that it was designed to give to the General Government complete control over the trade and intercourse of those Indians only who were not within the limits of any State. From a view of the acts referred to and the uniform practice of the Government it is manifest that until recently it has never been maintained that the right of jurisdiction by a State over Indians within its territory was subordinate to the power of the Federal Government. That doctrine has not been enforced nor even asserted in any of the States of New England where tribes of Indians have resided, and where a few of them yet remain. These tribes have been left to the undisturbed control of the States in which they were found, in conformity with the view which has been taken of the opinions prevailing up to 1789 and the clear interpretation of the act of 1802. . . . The Southern States present an exception to this policy. As early as 1784 the settlements within the limits of North Carolina were advanced farther to the west than the authority of the State to enforce an obedience of its laws. Others were in a similar condition. The necessities, therefore, and not the acknowledged principles, of the Government must have suggested the policy of treating with the Indians in that quarter as the only practicable mode of conciliating their good will. The United States at that period had just emerged from a protracted war for the achievement of their independence. At the moment of its conclusion many of these tribes as powerful as they were ferocious in their mode of warfare, remained in arms, desolating our frontier settlements. Under these circumstances the first treaties, in 1785 and 1790, with the Cherokees, were concluded by the Government of the United States, and were evidently sanctioned as measures of necessity adapted to the character of the Indians and indispensable to the peace and security of the western frontier. But they can not be understood as changing the political relations of the Indians to the States or to the Federal Government. To effect this would have required the operation of quite a different principle and the intervention of a tribunal higher than that of the treaty-making power.

To infer from the assent of the Government to this deviation from the practice which had before governed its intercourse with the Indians, and the accidental forbearance of the States to assert their right of jurisdiction over them, that they had surrendered this portion of their sovereignty, and that its assumption now is usurpation, is conceding too much to the necessity which dictated those treaties, and doing violence to the principles of the Government and the rights of the States without benefiting in the least degree the Indians. The Indians thus situated can not be regarded in any other light than as members of a foreign government or of that of the State within whose chartered limits they reside. If in the former, the ordinary legislation of Congress in relation to them is not warranted by the Constitution, which was established for the benefit of our own, not of a foreign people. If in the latter, then, like other citizens or people resident within the limits of the States, they are subject to their jurisdiction and control. To maintain a contrary doctrine and to require the Executive to enforce it by the employment of a military force would be to place in his hands a power to make war upon the rights of the States and the liberties of the country—a power which should be placed in the hands of no individual.

The steps taken to prevent intrusion upon Indian lands had their origin with the commencement of our Government, and became the subject of special legislation in 1802, with the reservations which have been mentioned in favor of the jurisdiction of the States. With the exception of South Carolina, who has uniformly regulated the Indians within her limits without the aid of the General Government, they have been felt within all the States of the South without being understood to affect their rights or prevent the exercise of their jurisdiction, whenever they were in a situation to assume and enforce it. Georgia, though materially concerned, has on this principle forborne to spread her legislation farther than the settlements of her own white citizens, until she has recently perceived within her limits a people claiming to be capable to self-government, sitting in legislative council, organizing courts and administering justice. To disarm such an anomalous invasion of her sovereignty she has declared her determination to execute her own laws throughout her limits —a step which seems to have been anticipated by the proclamation of 1783, and which is perfectly consistent with the nineteenth section of the act of 1802.

According to the language and reasoning of that section, the tribes to the South and the Southwest are not only "surrounded by settlements of the citizens of the United States," but are now also "within the ordinary jurisdiction of the individual States." They became so from the moment the laws of the State were extended over them, and the same result follows the similar determination of Alabama and Mississippi. These States have each a right to claim in behalf of their position now on this question the same respect which is conceded to the other States of the Union.

Toward this race of people I entertain the kindest feelings, and am not sensible that the views which I have taken of their true interests are less favorable to them than those which oppose their emigration to the West. Years since I stated to them my belief that if the States chose to extend their laws over them it would not be in the power of the Federal Government to prevent it. My opinion remains the same, and I can see no alternative for them but that of their removal to the West or a quiet submission to the State laws. If they prefer to remove, the United States agree to defray their expenses, to supply them the means of transportation and a year's support after they reach their new homes—a provision too liberal and kind to deserve the stamp of injustice. Either course promises them peace and happiness, whilst an obstinate perseverance in the effort to maintain their possessions independent of the State authority can not fail to render their condition still more helpless and miserable. Such an effort ought, therefore, to be discountenanced by all who sincerely sympathize in the fortunes of this peculiar people, and especially by the political bodies of the Union, as calculated to disturb the harmony of the two Governments and to endanger the safety of the many blessings which they enable us to enjoy.

ANDREW JACKSON

III. "Let Equal Justice Be Done Between the Red and the White Man"

JOHN ROSS

John Ross was the most influential chief in the Cherokee Nation during the period of the removal. The son of a Scottish emigrant and a Cherokee woman, he served as principal chief from 1828–39. Although some Cherokees were tempted to resort to violence to protect their lands, Ross reasoned that such action would be terribly destructive to his people and could not succeed. His reasoning took on greater significance when a faction of Sacs and Foxes in Illinois resisted removal in 1832 and were virtually exterminated by a force of U.S. regulars and Illinois militia in the Black Hawk War. With such an exam-

United States Senate Document, No. 512, Twenty-Third Congress, First Session, "Indian Removal," IV, pp. 97–100.

ple of what could happen, the Cherokees continued to pursue a peaceful and lawful course of action. Consistent with this approach, Ross led numerous delegations to Washington protesting the government's refusal to fulfill the obligations of the treaties between the Cherokees and the United States.

It was during one of those visits that Ross and several other chiefs wrote a letter to the secretary of war, Lewis Cass, asking federal recognition of the rights of the Cherokee Nation. Note Ross' answer to Jackson's assertions that removal would be in the best interest of both Indian and white man.

Brown's Hotel, Washington City, February 14, 1833

Sir: ... We are told that the President looks with great anxiety and solicitation to our situation; that he knows our position is an embarrassing one, and that change is called for by every consideration of present convenience and future security; and that the Government is desirous of entering into a satisfactory arrangement, by which all our difficulties will be terminated, and the prosperity of our people fixed upon a permanent basis. Yet we are assured that you are well convinced that these objects *can only be attained by a cession of our possessory rights* in Georgia, and by *our removal* to the country west of the Mississippi; that you can see no cause of apprehension, as we do, that such removal will be injurious, either in its immediate or remote consequences; a mild climate, a fertile soil, an inviting and extensive country, a government of our own, adequate protection against other tribes and against your own citizens, within a reasonable expectation, are freely offered to us. You cannot, therefore, see that the subject presents itself in the melancholy light in which we view it. You have also referred to the President's message to the Senate, of February 22, 1831, to show his views on the subject of the existing relations between the Indian tribes and the States in which they reside. In reviewing the principles upon which these views are predicated, we have been impelled to look into those upon which the primitive and conventional rights of the Cherokee nation have been recognized and established by the solemn acts of this Government. And it is with deep regret and great diffidence we are constrained to say, that, in this scheme of Indian removal, we can see more of expediency and policy to get rid of them, than to perpetuate their race upon any fundamental principles. Were it possible for you to be placed, or to imagine yourself for a moment to be in the peculiar situation in which we stand, with the existing treaties and laws, and the subsequent acts of the Government, all before your eyes, you cannot but feel and see as we do. It is impossible, then, for us to see, that by a removal to the country west of the Mississippi, all our difficulties would be terminated, and the prosperity of our people fixed upon a permanent basis.

Would not a removal to the country west of the Mississippi, upon lands of the United States, by Indian tribes, under the provisions of the act of Congress, denationalize their character as distinct communities? By what tenure would such tribes occupy the lands to be assigned to them? Is not the fee simple title vested in and will be retained by the United States? What kind of a Government of their own, then, is designed for them to establish, and how is it possible for the United States to afford them more adequate protection against your own citizens there, than where we are? These questions have never as yet been definitively settled down upon any fundamental law of Congress that we know of, and we cannot avoid believing that the present system of policy towards the Indians, is founded upon contingencies growing out of the interests and desires of the States, without regarding the permanent prosperity and happiness of the Indians. We intend no reflection upon the Government, in thus frankly communicating our views, but we deem it essential to a perfect understanding upon the subject. As to the climate, soil, and extent of the country, to which you have alluded, and the future propects of the Cherokees who are living there, our people are currently informed on those points, from personal observations and otherwise. Withal, they have no wish to remove there.

What, then, would be the consequence of a whole nation of people, driven by the force of necessity to leave their native land for a distant one, in a strange and inhospitable region, and there to experience the sad effects of injured disappointments? To what source could they seek indemnity for their injuries, and what tribunal will there redress their wrongs? for in vain have our nation appealed to the protecting arm of the General Government to fulfil treaty obligations; to shield our suffering people against illegal encroachments; and in vain will your supreme judicial tribunal have declared a verdict in favor of our nation, against the exercise of usurped power on the part of State authority.

In the suggestions which we took the liberty to submit for the considera- tion of the President, that some practicable arrangement might be entered into between the United States and Georgia, to relieve our nation of its present embarrassments, we had entertained no doubt that, with a corresponding desire on the part of the General Government, such an arrangement could be effected, and, in that event, that Georgia would not be permitted to subject our people to the obedience of her laws, inasmuch as the Supreme Court of the United States had already pronounced the exercise of her jurisdiction over our territory and people, to be unconstitutional and void; and we are at a loss to see the grounds you have taken in arriving to the opinion that "we would still be subject to the laws of Georgia." We cannot subscribe to the correctness of the idea, which has been so frequently recurred to by the advocates of Indian removal, that the evils which have befallen and swept away the numerous tribes that once inhabited the old States, are to be traced to the *mere circum- stance* of their contiguity to a white population; but we humbly conceive that the true causes of their extinction are to be found in the catalogue of wrongs which have been heaped upon their ignorance and credulity, by the superior policies of the white man, when dictated by avarice and cupidity.

You appeal to our better feelings in regard to the situation of our people, and suggest that, under existing circumstances, some sacrifices may well be encountered in removing from a contact with the white population, in order to escape the fate which has swept away so many Indian tribes. Should the doctrine that Indian tribes cannot exist contiguously to a white population, prevail, and they be compelled to remove west of the States and Territories of this republic, what is to prevent a similar removal of them from there for the same reason? We can only plead, let equal justice be done between the red and the white man, and so long as the faith of contracts is preserved inviolate there will be no just cause for complaints, much less for aggressions on the rights of the one or the other, and that, so far as our (individually) sense of right, justice, and honor, will dictate to us a course to meet the wishes, the interest, and the permanent prosperity and happiness of our nation, that no pecuniary sacrifices or human sufferings ever so great, can or will deter us from encountering them.

Contrary to treaty stipulations and the intercourse act of 1802, there are numerous white families who have intruded upon the lands of our nation within the chartered limits of several of the adjoining States, and the repeated complaints made of the same to the agent, have not been regarded, and the trespassers, instead of being removed, have greatly increased in numbers, and are daily multiplying. We are constrained to bring this grievous subject before the department, that the evil be corrected.

In addition to these, there are others who threaten to overrun and dispossess our nation of its territory, under the sanction of State authority. Under the assumption of the right to exercise jurisdiction, it is known that Georgia has passed legislative acts to survey and draw a lottery for the occupation of our land, and which, in part, have been carried into effect; and without the timely interposition of this Government, will, doubtless, rob us of our lands.

Can this be permitted, or will the President extend the constitutional arm of the Government to save us from this impending calamity? His determination upon this delicate and important question, we most respectfully solicit. . . .

With great respect,
We have the honor to be, sir,
Your obedient servants,
JOHN ROSS,
R. TAYLOR,
JOHN F. BALDRIDGE, his x mark.
JOSEPH VANN

Hon. LEWIS CASS, *Secretary of War*

IV. The Trail of Tears

On March 14, 1835, a small dissident group of Cherokees and the U.S. Commissioner, the Reverend J. F. Schermerhorn, negotiated a removal treaty. The treaty, known as the Schermerhorn Treaty (later revised as the New Echota Treaty), was subsequently approved by three percent of the estimated sixteen

From *Indian Removal: The Emigration of the Five Civilized Tribes of Indians*, pp. 305–7, by Grant Foreman. Copyright 1932, 1953 by the University of Oklahoma Press.

thousand people in the Cherokee Nation and then transmitted to Washington as a binding treaty with all Cherokees. In response to the treaty the antiremoval Cherokees sent a petition to the Senate that contained nearly sixteen thousand names to protest the illegality of the document. But on May 18, 1835, the Senate ratified the treaty by a one-vote margin.

The treaty was a fraud, and meetings held in the Cherokee Nation and in many Northern states denounced the actions of the president and the Senate. But fraudulent or not, the Jackson administration, and later that of Martin Van Buren, was determined to carry out the "voluntary" removal of the Cherokees. In order to give the Indians time to prepare and the government time to organize the emigrations, the removals did not begin in earnest until two years after the ratification of the treaty. On May 10, 1838, Major General Winfield Scott, in charge of the removal, warned the Cherokees not to resist and to accept their fate. This done, he ordered his troops to round up the Indians in a firm but humane fashion so they could be sent westward.

Between fifteen and seventeen thousand Cherokees were collected into camps where they were divided into groups of a thousand, and, under the supervision of soldiers and Indian agents, they began their journey to their new homes. Of the men, women, and children removed about four thousand died on the Cherokees' "Trail of Tears." But to official Washington the event was described by President Van Buren as the successful completion of a beneficial governmental program, and that the Cherokees had "emigrated without any apparent reluctance."

The Cherokees left few accounts of the Trail of Tears, but the following document is a description of that event by a white man from Maine who encountered the Indians while traveling in the West. How does this account demonstrate that the fears of the Cherokees in removing to the West were not unfounded fantasies?

1838–1839

A sympathetic traveler who met them on the road describes the appearance of these unhappy people:

". . . On Tuesday evening we fell in with a detachment of the poor Cherokee Indians . . . about eleven hundred Indians—sixty waggons—six hundred horses, and perhaps forty pairs of oxen. We found them in the forest camped for the night by the road side . . . under a severe fall of rain accompanied by heavy wind. With their canvas for a shield from the inclemency of the weather, and the cold wet ground for a resting place, after the fatigue of the day, they spent the night . . . many of the aged Indians were suffering extremely from the fatigue of the journey, and the ill health consequent upon it . . . several were then quite ill, and one aged man we were informed was then in the last struggles of death.

". . . About ten officers and overseers in each detachment whose business it was to provide supplies for the journey, and attend to the general wants of the company. . . . We met several detachments in the southern part of Kentucky on the 4th, 5th and 6th of December. . . . The last detachment which we passed on the 7th embraced rising two thousand Indians with horses and mules in proportion. The forward part of the train we found just pitching their tents for the night, and notwithstanding some thirty or forty waggons were already stationed, we found the road literally filled with the procession for about three miles in length. The sick and feeble were carried in waggons—about as comfortable for traveling as a New England ox cart with a covering over it—a great many ride on horseback and multitudes go on foot—even aged females, apparently nearly ready to drop into the grave, were traveling with heavy burdens attached to the back—on the sometimes frozen ground, and sometimes muddy streets, with no covering for the feet except what nature had given them. We were some hours making our way through the crowd, which brought us in close contact with the wagons and multitude, so much that we felt fortunate to find ourselves freed from the crowd without leaving any part of our carriage. We learned from the inhabitants on the road where the Indians passed, that they buried fourteen or fifteen at every stopping place, and they make a journey of ten miles per day only on an average. One fact which to my own mind seemed a lesson indeed to the American nation is, that they will not travel on the Sabbath . . . when the Sabbath came, they must stop, and not merely stop—they must worship the Great Spirit too, for they had divine service on the Sabbath—a camp-meeting in truth. One aged Indian who was commander of the friendly Creeks and Seminoles in a very important engagement in the company with General Jackson, was accosted on arriving in a little village in Kentucky by an aged man residing there, and who was one of Jackson's men in the engagement referred to, and asking him if he (the Indian) recollected him? The aged Chieftain looked him in the face and recognized him, and with a down-cast look and heavy sigh, referring to the engagement, he said 'Ah! my life and the lives of my people were then at stake for you and your country. I then thought Jackson my best friend. But ah! Jackson no serve me right. Your country no do me justice now!'

"The Indians as a whole carry in their countenances every thing but the appearance of happiness. Some carry a downcast dejected look bordering upon the appearance of despair; others a wild frantic appearance as if about to burst the chains of nature and pounce like a tiger upon their enemies. . . . Most of them seemed intelligent and refined. Mr. Bushyhead, son of an aged man of the same name, is a very intelligent and interesting Baptist clergyman. Several missionaries were accompanying them to their destination. Some of the Cherokees are wealthy and travel in style. One lady passed on in her hack in company with her husband, apparently with as much refinement and equipage as any of the mothers of New England; and she was a mother too and her youngest child about three years old was sick in her arms, and all she could do was to make it comfortable as circumstances would permit . . . she could only carry her dying child in her arms a few miles farther, and then she must stop in a stranger-land and consign her much loved babe to the cold ground, and that too without pomp or ceremony, and pass on with the multitude. . . .

". . . When I past the last detachment of those suffering exiles and thought that my native countrymen had thus expelled them from their native soil and their much loved homes, and that too in this inclement season of the year in all their suffering, I turned from the sight with feelings which language cannot express and 'wept like childhood then.' I felt that I would not encounter the secret silent prayer of one of these sufferers armed with the energy that faith and hope would give it (if there be a God who avenges the wrongs of the injured) for all the lands of Georgia! . . . When I read in the President's Message that he was happy to inform the Senate that the Cherokees were peaceably and without reluctance removed—and remember that it was on the third day of December when not one of the detachments had reached their destination; and that a large majority had not made even half their journey when he made that declaration, I thought I wished the President could have been there that very day in Kentucky with myself, and have seen the comfort and the willingness with which the Cherokees were making their journey. But I forbear, full well I know that many prayers have gone up to the King of Heaven from Maine in behalf of the poor Cherokees."

For Further Reading

Books dealing specifically with the removal of the Indians are: Grant Foreman, *Indian Removal* (1932; reprinted in 1969); Francis Paul Prucha, *American Indian Policy in the Formative Years** (1962); and Dale Van Every, *Disinherited: The Lost Birthright of the American Indian** (1966). See also Mary E. Young, "Indian Removal and Land Allotment," *American Historical Review,* LXIV (October, 1958).

Background for the period and histories of the Indians include: Robert S. Cotterill, *The Southern Indians* (1954; reprinted in 1966); William T. Hagan, *American Indians** (1961); Henry T. Malone, *Cherokees of the Old South* (1956); and Grace Steele Woodward, *The Cherokees* (1963).

A problems book is *The Removal of the Cherokee Nation** (1962), edited by Louis Filler and Allen Guttmann.

A collection of primary sources can be found in Wilcomb E. Washburn's *The Indian and the White Man** (1964).

*Paperbound edition available.

11. An Idea of Community: Brook Farm

"What a fertility of projects for the salvation of the world!" wrote Ralph Waldo Emerson in 1844. Disposition to scrutiny and dissent, he noted, appeared in all facets of society. The record of the middle decades of the nineteenth century supports Emerson's observation. Reforms in education, in labor practices, and in prisons and hospitals attracted national attention. Crusades for women's rights, for temperance, and for peace thrived; attacks on slavery intensified; and aroused moral concerns everywhere demanded social change.

Social change comes in various forms. Few Americans favored revolution, the most sudden and drastic form of change. Some sought change by focusing on regeneration of individuals, assuming that a regenerated society would follow. Most reformers chose to attack evil elements in the social system and to work within the system for their gradual correction. But here and there were groups of persons who preferred a collectivist yet evolutionary approach to social change.

These groups were concerned with the regeneration of both individuals and society. Toward this end they formed small experimental communities, hoping to exert a force that would produce needed changes in society and at the same time permit rewarding and uplifting experiences for the community's participants. Although disenchanted with the larger society, these communitarians, as they are referred to here, were not sufficiently alienated to discount the possibilities of reform, both personal and social. Their romantic faith in the perfectibility of man and society inspired them to seek in community living the path to a new and brighter day.

In numbers these societies were not impressive. According to John Humphrey Noyes, the founder of the Oneida community, less than one hundred such communities were formed in the United States, including some which preceded the reform thrust of the middle decades. Fewer than ten thousand persons were associated with these communities, and in many cases their association was brief. And few of these communities existed longer than several years.

Despite the unimpressiveness of their numbers, however, the idea represented by these communitarian societies is significant. Their idea, simply stated, was this: The regeneration of individuals and of society can be achieved through association in communities in which participants live and work and grow together.

Core Document

Plan of the West Roxbury Community

ELIZABETH PEABODY

No single community can be properly identified as typical of the communitarian movement. It is possible, though, to point to some as being representative of the idea of community. One such example is the community at Brook Farm. The relative completeness of the Brook Farm account, much of it left by its distinguished members, friends, and visitors, provides an account of an experiment with an idea that merits attention.

The Brook Farm Institute of Agriculture and Education was founded in 1841 on a 160-acre tract of land nine miles from Boston. The inspiration and guidance for the new community was provided by George Ripley, a former Unitarian minister. Always richer in culture than in material wealth, the struggling community gradually moved toward acceptance of the elaborate theory of "association" developed by the French socialist Charles Fourier. This theory emphasized cooperation over competition, and sought to put society on a harmonious basis. Early in 1844, perhaps more from poverty than conviction, Brook Farm reorganized itself into a "phalanx," the term given to the communal unit advocated by Fourier. About two years later a major fire destroyed what was to have been upon completion the community's major building. This disaster was greater than the community could bear. Already in serious financial trouble and beset with divisions over the transition to Fourierism, the rate of decline increased

The Dial, January 1842 (reprinted in New York: Russell and Russell, 1961), pp. 361–72.

rapidly. The property was sold at auction in the spring of 1849, less than eight years after Ripley had acquired it.

Ripley's idea of community was no doubt formulated through his association with transcendentalists in the Boston area. New England transcendentalism, in some ways a descendant of Puritanism and Unitarianism, assumed the existence of realities that could be grasped by intuition, transcending reason and the physical senses. Essentially a moral philosophy, transcendentalism called for respect for man's dignity and extolled his possibilities as a human being. Brook Farm might be properly regarded as a missionary enterprise of those transcendentalists who saw man's possibilities as best developed through community living. Transcendentalists who preferred radical individualism, as did Ralph Waldo Emerson and Henry David Thoreau, shied away from such an organized effort as Brook Farm.

Brook Farm did not really develop into a communitarian society as that term is usually used, not even after it became a phalanx. It was a joint-stock enterprise, privately owned, engaged in production (chiefly education and agricultural products; it faltered when it tried to go further), and was practical almost to a fault. Yet it was also spiritual, for not only did it respect all faiths, it aimed at developing a unique freedom, a freedom for persons to live simply and to become self-sacrificing, gentle, kind, wise, and good. In their rustic clothes, many with long hair and beards (not in style at the time), the Brook Farmers sought communion not only with each other but with nature and life.

Most of the contemporary accounts of Brook Farm were written by sympathetic observers rather than by members and residents. Perhaps the most detailed description of what they were doing came from a Boston literary figure and social reformer, Elizabeth Peabody. A member of the Transcendentalist Club, she was, with Emerson, an editor of The Dial, *the transcendentalist journal in which the following article appeared. In reading this selection, note:*

- *the reasons given for organizing the community.*
- *the spiritual references and overtones.*
- *the concern for agriculture and education.*
- *the writer's concern that the community remain "exclusive."*
- *the writer's hope that the community not be corrupted by material things.*
- *the writer's misgivings about the community.*

In the last number of the Dial were some remarks, under the perhaps ambitious title, of "A Glimpse of Christ's Idea of Society;" in a note to which, it was intimated, that in this number, would be given an account of an attempt to realize in some degree this great Ideal, by a little company in the midst of us, as yet without name or visible existence. The attempt is made on a very small scale. A few individuals, who, unknown to each other, under different disciplines of life, reacting from different social evils, but aiming at the same object,—of being wholly true to their natures as men and women; have been made acquainted with one another, and have determined to become the Faculty of the Embryo University.

In order to live a religious and moral life worthy the name, they feel it is necessary to come out in some degree from the world, and to form themselves into a community of property, so far as to exclude competition and the ordinary rules of trade;—while they reserve sufficient private property, or the means of obtaining it, for all purposes of independence, and isolation at will. They have bought a farm, in order to make agriculture the basis of their life, it being the most direct and simple in relation to nature.

A true life, although it aims beyond the highest star, is redolent of the healthy earth. The perfume of clover lingers about it. The lowing of cattle is the natural bass to the melody of human voices.

On the other hand, what absurdity can be imagined greater than the institution of cities? They originated not in love, but in war. It was war that drove men together in multitudes, and compelled them to stand so close, and build walls around them. This crowded condition produces wants of an unnatural character, which resulted in occupations that regenerated the evil, by creating artificial wants. Even when that thought of grief,

"I know, where'er I go
That there hath passed away a glory from the Earth,"

came to our first parents, as they saw the angel, with the flaming sword of self-consciousness, standing between them and the recovery of spontaneous Life and Joy, we cannot believe they could have anticipated a time would come, when the sensuous apprehension of Creation—the great symbol of God —would be taken away from their unfortunate children,—crowded together in such a manner as to shut out the free breath and the Universal Dome of Heaven, some opening their eyes in the dark cellars of the narrow, crowded streets of walled cities. How could they have believed in such a conspiracy against the soul, as to deprive it of the sun and sky, and glorious apparelled Earth!—The growth of cities, which were the embryo of nations hostile to each other, is a subject worthy the thoughts and pen of the philosophic historian. Perhaps nothing would stimulate courage to seek, and hope to attain social good, so much, as a profound history of the origin, in the mixed nature of man, and the exasperation by society, of the various organized Evils under which humanity groans. Is there anything, which exists in social or political life contrary to the soul's Ideal? That thing is not eternal, but finite, saith the Pure Reason. It has a beginning, and so a history. What man has done, man may *undo*. "By man came death; by man also cometh the resurrection from the dead."

The plan of the Community, as an Economy, is in brief this; for all who have property to take stock, and receive a fixed interest thereon; then to keep house or board in commons, as they shall severally desire, at the cost of provisions purchased at wholesale, or raised on the farm; and for all to labor in community, and be paid at a certain rate an hour, choosing their own number of hours, and their own kind of work. With the results of this labor, and their interest, they are to pay their board, and also purchase whatever else they require at cost, at the warehouses of the Community, which are to be filled by the Community as such. To perfect this economy, in the course of time they must have all trades, and all modes of business carried on among themselves, from the lowest mechanical trade, which contributes to the health and comfort of life, to the finest art which adorns it with food or drapery for the mind.

All labor, whether bodily or intellectual, is to be paid at the same rate of wages; on the principle, that as the labor becomes merely bodily, it is a greater sacrifice to the individual laborer, to give his time to it; because time is desirable for the cultivation of the intellect, in exact proportion to ignorance. Besides intellectual labor involves in itself higher pleasures, and is more its own reward, than bodily labor.

Another reason, for setting the same pecuniary value on every kind of labor, is, to give outward expression to the great truth, that all labor is sacred, when done for a common interest. Saints and philosophers already know this, but the childish world does not; and very decided measures must be taken to equalize labors, in the eyes of the young of the community, who are not beyond the moral influences of the world without them. The community will have nothing done within its precincts, but what is done by its own members, who stand all in social equality;—that the children may not "learn to expect one kind of service from Love and Goodwill, and another from the obligation of others to render it,"—a grievance of the common society stated, by one of the associated mothers, as destructive of the soul's simplicity. Consequently, as the Universal Education will involve all kinds of operation, necessary to the comforts and elegances of life, every associate, even if he be the digger of a ditch as his highest accomplishment, will be an instructer in that to the young members. Nor will this elevation of bodily labor be liable to lower the tone of manners and refinement in the community. The "children of light" are not altogether unwise in their generation. They have an invisible but all-powerful guard of principles. Minds incapable of refinement, will not be attracted into this association. It is an Ideal community, and only to the ideally inclined will it be attractive; but these are to be found in every rank of life, under every shadow of circumstance. Even among the diggers in the ditch are to be found some, who through religious cultivation, can look down, in meek superiority, upon the outwardly refined, and the book-learned.

Besides, after becoming members of this community, none will be engaged merely in bodily labor. The hours of labor for the Association will be limited by a general law, and can be curtailed at the will of the individual still more; and means will be given to all for intellectual improvement and for social intercourse, calculated to refine and expand. The hours redeemed from labor by community, will not be reapplied to the acquisition of wealth, but to the production of intellectual goods. This community aims to be rich, not in the metallic representative of wealth, but in the wealth itself, which money should represent; namely, LEISURE TO LIVE IN ALL THE FACULTIES OF THE SOUL. As a community, it will traffic with the world at large, in the products of Agricultural labor; and it will sell education to as many young persons as can be domesticated in the families, and enter into the common life with their own children. In the end, it hopes to be enabled to provide—not only all the necessaries, but all the elegances desirable for bodily and for spiritual health; books, apparatus, collections for science, works of art, means of beautiful amusement. These things are to be common to all; and thus that object, which alone gilds and refines the passion for individual accumulation, will no longer exist for desire, and whenever the Sordid passion appears, it will be seen in its naked selfishness. In its ultimate success, the community will realize all the ends which selfishness seeks, but involved in spiritual blessings, which only greatness of soul can aspire after.

And the requisitions on the individuals, it is believed, will make this the order forever. The spiritual good will always be the condition of the temporal. Every one must labor for the community in a reasonable degree, or not taste its benefits. The principles of the organization therefore, and not its probable results in future time, will determine its members. These principles are coöperation in social matters, instead of competition or balance of interests; and individual self-unfolding, in the faith that the whole soul of humanity is in each man and woman. The former is the application of the love of man; the latter of the love of God, to life. Whoever is satisfied with society, as it is; whose sense of justice is not wounded by its common action, institutions, spirit of commerce, has no business with this community; neither has any one who is willing to have other men (needing more time for intellectual cultivation than himself) give their best hours and strength to bodily labor, to secure himself immunity therefrom. And whoever does not measure what society owes to its members of cherishing and instruction, by the needs of the individuals that compose it, has no lot in this new society. Whoever is willing to receive from his fellow men that, for which he gives no equivalent, will stay away from its precincts forever.

But whoever shall surrender himself to its principles, shall find that its yoke is easy and its burden light. Everything can be said of it, in a degree, which Christ said of his kingdom, and therefore it is believed that in some measure it does embody his Idea. For its Gate of entrance is strait and narrow. It is literally a pearl *hidden in a field.* Those only who are willing to lose their life for its sake shall find it. Its voice is that which sent the young man sorrowing away. "Go sell all thy goods and give to the poor, and then come and follow me." "Seek first the kingdom of Heaven, and its righteousness, and all other things shall be added to you."

This principle, with regard to labor, lies at the root of moral and religious life; for it is not more true that "money is the root of all evil," than that *labor is the germ of all good.*

All the work is to be offered for the free choice of the members of the community, at stated seasons, and such as is not chosen, will be hired. But it is not anticipated that any work will be set aside to be hired, for which there is actual ability in the community. It is so desirable that the hired labor should be avoided, that it is believed the work will all be done freely, even though at voluntary sacrifice. If there is some exception at first, it is because the material means are inadequate to the reception of all who desire to go. They cannot go, unless they have shelter; and in this climate, they cannot have shelter unless they can build houses; and they cannot build houses unless they have money. It is not here as in Robinson Crusoe's Island, or in the prairies and rocky mountains of the far west, where the land and the wood are not appropriated. A single farm, in the midst of Massachusetts, does not afford range enough for men to create out of the Earth a living, with no other means; as the wild Indians, or the United States Army in Florida may do.

This plan, of letting all persons choose their own departments of action, will immediately place the Genius of Instruction on its throne. Communication is the life of spiritual life. Knowledge pours itself out upon ignorance by a native impulse. All the arts crave response. "WISDOM CRIES." If every man and woman taught only what they loved, and so many hours as they could naturally communicate, instruction would cease to be a drudgery, and we may add, learning would be no longer a task. The known accomplishments of many of the members of this association have already secured it an interest in the public mind, as a school of literary advantages quite superior. Most of the associates have had long practical experience in the details of teaching, and have groaned under the necessity of taking their method and law from custom and caprice, when they would rather have found it in the nature of the thing taught, and the condition of the pupil to be instructed. Each instructer appoints his hours of study or recitation, and the scholars, or the parents of the children, or the educational committee, choose the studies, for the time, and the pupils submit, as long as they pursue their studies with any teacher, to his regulations.

As agriculture is the basis of their external life, scientific agriculture, connected with practice, will be a prominent part of the instruction from the first. This obviously involves the natural sciences, mathematics, and accounts. But to classical learning justice is also to be done. Boys may be fitted for our colleges there, and even be carried through the college course. The particular studies of the individual pupils, whether old or young, male or female, are to be strictly regulated, according to their inward needs. As the children of the community can remain in the community after they become of age, as associates, if they will; there will not be an entire subserviency to the end of preparing the means of earning a material subsistence, as is frequently the case now. Nevertheless, as they will have had an opportunity, in the course of their minority, to earn three or four hundred dollars, they can leave the community at twenty years of age, if they will, with that sufficient capital, which, together with their extensive education, will gain *a subsistence* anywhere, in the best society of the world. It is this feature of the plan, which may preclude from parents any question as to their right to go into this community, and forego forever all hope of great individual accumulation *for their children;* a customary plea for spending life in making money. Their children will be supported at free board, until they are ten years of age; educated gratuitously; taken care of in case of their parents' sickness and death; and they themselves will be supported, after seventy years of age, by the community, unless their accumulated capital supports them.

There are some persons who have entered the community without money.

It is believed that these will be able to support themselves and dependents, by less work, more completely, and with more ease than elsewhere; while their labor will be of advantage to the community. It is in no sense an eleemosynary establishment, but it is hoped that in the end it will be able to receive all who have the spiritual qualifications.

It seems impossible that the little organization can be looked on with any unkindness by the world without it. Those, who have not the faith that the principles of Christ's kingdom are applicable to real life in the world, will smile at it, as a visionary attempt. But even they must acknowledge it can do no harm, in any event. If it realizes the hope of its founders, it will immediately become a manifold blessing. Its moral *aura* must be salutary. As long as it lasts, it will be an example of the beauty of brotherly love. If it succeeds in uniting successful labor with improvement in mind and manners, it will teach a noble lesson to the agricultural population, and do something to check that rush from the country to the city, which is now stimulated by ambition, and by something better, even a desire for learning. Many a young man leaves the farmer's life, because only by so doing can he have intellectual companionship and opportunity; and yet, did he but know it, professional life is ordinarily more unfavorable to the perfection of the mind, than the farmer's life; if the latter is lived with wisdom and moderation, and the labor mingled as it might be with study. This community will be a school for young agriculturalists, who may learn within its precincts, not only the skilful practice, but the scientific reasons of their work, and be enabled afterwards to improve their art continuously. It will also prove the best of normal schools, and as such, may claim the interest of those, who mourn over the inefficiency of our common school system, with its present ill-instructed teachers.

It should be understood also, that after all the working and teaching, which individuals of the community may do, they will still have leisure, and in that leisure can employ themselves in connexion with the world around them. Some will not teach at all; and those especially can write books, pursue the Fine Arts, for private emolument if they will, and exercise various functions of men.—From this community might go forth preachers of the gospel of Christ, who would not have upon them the odium, or the burthen, that now diminishes the power of the clergy. And even if *pastors* were to go from this community, to reside among congregations as now, for a salary given, the fact that they would have something to retreat upon, at any moment, would save them from that virtual dependence on their congregations, which now corrupts the relation. There are doubtless beautiful instances of the old true relation of pastor and people, even of teacher and taught, in the decaying churches around us, but it is in vain to attempt to conceal the ghastly fact, that many a taper is burning dimly in the candlestick, no longer silver or golden, because compassion forbids to put it quite out. But let the spirit again blow "where it listeth," and not circumscribe itself by salary and other commodity,—and the Preached word might reassume the awful Dignity which is its appropriate garment; and though it sit down with publicans and sinners, again speak "with authority and not as the scribes."

We write, as is evident perhaps, not as members, which we are not, but interested spectators of the growth of this little community. It is due to their modesty to apologize for bringing out so openly, what they have done simply and without pretension. We rest on the spirit of the day, which is that of communication. No sooner does the life of man become visible, but it is a part of the great phenomenon of nature, which never seeks display, but suffers all to speculate thereon. When this speculation is made in respect, and in love of truth, it is most to be defended. We shall now proceed to make some observations that may sound like criticism, but this we do without apology, for earnest seekers of a true life are not liable to be petulant.

The very liberality, and truth to nature of the plan, is a legitimate reason for fearing it will not succeed as a special community in any given time. The vineyard does not always yield according to the reasonable expectation of its Lord. When he looks for grapes, behold it brings forth wild grapes. For outward success there must always be compromise, and where it is so much the object to avoid the dangers of compromise, as there very properly is here, there is perhaps danger of not taking advantage of such as nature offers.

One of these is the principle of antagonism. It is fair to take advantage of this in one respect. The members may be stimulated to faithfulness and hope, by the spectacle of society around them, whose unnecessary evils can be clearly seen to be folly, as well as sin, from their retreat. The spirit of liberality must be discriminated from the spirit of accommodation. Love is a stern principle, a severe winnower, when it is one with the pure Reason; as it must be, to be holy, and to be effective. It is a very different thing from indulgence. Some persons have said that in order to a true experiment, and to enact a really generous faith in man, there should be any neighborhood taken without discrimination, with the proportion that may happen to be in it, of the good and bad, the strong and weak. But we differ as to the application in this instance. They are so little fenced about with rules and barriers, that they have no chance but by being strong in the spirit. "Touch not, taste not, handle not," must be their watchword, with respect to the organized falsehoods they have protested against; and with respect to means of successful manifestation, the aphorism of St. Augustine, "God is patient because he is Eternal."

To be a little more explicit. The men and women of the world, as they rise, are not at the present moment wise enough, in the Hebrew sense of the word wisdom, even if they are good-intentioned enough, to enter into a plan of so great mutual confidence. To all the evils arising from constitutional infirmity and perversion they must, especially at first, be exposed. There will always be natures too cold to satisfy the warm-hearted, too narrow for the enjoyment of the wide-visioned, some will be deficient in reason, and some in sensibility, and there will be many who, from defect of personal power, will let run to waste beautiful hearts, and not turn to account great insight of natural wisdom. Love, justice, patience, forbearance, every virtue under heaven, are always necessary in order to do the social duties. There is no knot that magnanimity cannot untie; but the Almighty Wisdom and Goodness will not allow any tower to be builded by the children of men, where they can understand one another *without* this solvent magnanimity. There must ever be sincerity of good design, and organic truth, for the evolution of Beauty.

Now there can be only one way of selecting and winnowing their company. The power to do this must be inherent in their constitution; they must keep sternly true to their principles.

In the first place, they must not compromise their principle of labor, in receiving members. Every one, who has any personal power, whether bodily or mental, must bring the contribution of personal service, no matter how much money he brings besides. This personal service is not to amount to drudgery in any instance, but in every able-bodied or sound-minded person, it should be at least equivalent to the care of their own persons. Exchange, or barter of labor, so as to distribute to each according to his genius, is to be the means of ease, indefinitely, but no absolute dispensation should be given, except for actual infirmity. "My Father worketh hitherto, and I work," is always the word of the divine humanity.

But granting that they keep the gate of entrance narrow, as the gate of life, which is being as liberal as the moral Law, a subtle temptation assails them from the side of their Organization. Wo be unto them if they lean upon it; if they ever forget that it is only what they have made it, and what they sustain it to be. It not only must be ever instinct with spirit, but it must never be thought, even then, to circumscribe the spirit. It can do nothing more, even if it work miracles, than make bread out of stones, and after all, man liveth not by bread alone, but by *every word that proceedeth out of the mouth of God.* Another temptation assails them, clothed as an angel of light. The lover of man finds in his benevolence a persuasive advocate, when the Devil proposes to him to begin by taking possession of the kingdoms of this world, according to his ability. In their ardor for means of success, they may touch the mammon of unrighteousness. They will be exposed to endowment. Many persons, enlightened enough to be unwilling to let the wealth, they have gained by the accident of birth or of personal talent, go to exasperate the evil of present society, will be disposed to give it, or to leave it as a legacy to this community, and it would be asceticism to refuse it absolutely. But they should receive it greatly. "Thou shalt worship the Lord thy God, and Him *only* shalt thou *serve.*" No person who proposes to endow the community as a University, or as the true system of life, understands what he does, unless he surrenders what he gives, unconditionally, in the same spirit of faith, with which the members throw themselves in, with their lives, their property, and sacred honor. At all events it would violate their principle of progress to accept anything with conditions; unless indeed it may be considered a condition, that they remain an association, governed by the majority of members, according to its present general constitution.

It were better even to forego the advantage of good buildings, apparatus, library, than to have these shackles. —Though space cannot now be given to do more than state these points, it might be demonstrated that to keep to them is essential to independence, and can alone justify the conscience of endower and endowed.

Another danger which should be largely treated is the spirit of coterie. The breadth of their platform, which admits all sects; and the generality of their plan, which demands all degrees of intellectual culture to begin with, is some security against this. But the ultimate security must be in numbers. Some may say, "already this taint has come upon them, for they are doubtless *transcendentalists.*" But to mass a few protestants together and call them transcendentalists, is a popular cant. Transcendentalism belongs to no sect of religion, and no social party. It is the common ground to which all sects may rise, and be purified of their narrowness; for it consists in seeking the spiritual ground of all manifestations. As already in the pages of this periodical, Calvinist, and Unitarian, and Episcopalian, and Baptist, and Quaker, and Swedenborgian, have met and spoken in love and freedom, on this common basis; so it would be seen, if the word were understood, that transcendentalism, notwithstanding its name is taken in vain by many moonshiny youths and misses who assume it, would be the best of all guards against the spirit of coterie. Much as we respect our friends of the community, we dare not hope for them quite so much, as to aver that they *transcend,* as yet, all the limitations that separate men from love and mutual trust.

> *Serene will be our days and bright,*
> *And happy will our nature be,*
> *When Love is an unerring light*
> *And Joy its own security.*
> *And blest are they who in the main*
> *This faith, even now, do entertain;*
> *Live in the spirit of this creed;*
> *Yet find the strength of Law* according to their need!

We had intended to subjoin some further remarks, by way of inquiry, into the possibility of other portions of society, not able to emancipate themselves from the thraldom of city life, beginning also to act, in a degree, on the principles of coöperation. Ameliorations of present evils, initiations into truer life, may be made we believe everywhere. Worldly wisdom, for its own purposes, avails itself of what is outward in the community plan; at least of the labor-saving element. Why may not the children of light be equally wise?

There may be some persons, at a distance, who will ask, to what degree has this community gone into operation? We cannot answer this with precision, for we do not write as organs of this association, and have reason to feel, that if we applied to them for information, they would refuse it, out of their dislike to appear in public. We desire this to be distinctly understood. But we can see, and think we have a right to say, that it has purchased the Farm, which some of its members cultivated for a year with success, by way of trying their love and skill for agricultural labor;—that in the only house they are as yet rich enough to own, is collected a large family, including several boarding scholars, and that all work and study together. They seem to be glad to know of all, who desire to join them in the spirit, that at any moment, when they are able to enlarge their habitations, they may call together those that belong to them.

Discussion Starters

1. Identify the economic and social principles on which the community rested and evaluate their soundness.

2. What personal characteristics would be required of those who would wish to live successfully in this sort of community? How would "successful living" be defined? What would be the rewards for each individual?

3. How did Brook Farm attempt to relate to the larger society?

4. What are the chief similiarities and differences between this community and the typical commune created in recent years by disenchanted youth in America? Aside from their availability, why do drugs figure so prominently in contemporary communes?

5. In what sense might it be possible for an individual to gain freedom by committing himself to community living?

Related Documents

I. On Joining Brook Farm: An Inquiry and a Reply

Elizabeth Peabody's article in The Dial *attracted wide attention. Included next is a letter to Ripley from a potential participant, along with his response. What does this exchange show about the appeal of the community and about Ripley's sense of values?*

Dear Friends, if I may so call you. I read in the "New York Tribune" a piece taken from the "Dial," headed the West Roxbury Community. Now what I want to know is, can I and my children be admitted into your society, and be better off than we are here? I have enough of the plainest kind to eat and wear here. I have no home but what we hire from year to year. I have no property but movables, and not a cent to spare when the year comes round. I have three children: two boys and a girl; the oldest fourteen, the youngest nine; now I want to educate them—how to do it where there is no chance but ordinary schools,—to move into the village, I could not bring the year round, and the

Octavius Brooks Frothingham, *George Ripley* (Boston: Houghton Mifflin, 1882), pp. 141–46.

danger they would be exposed to without a father to restrain their wanderings would be undertaking more than I dare attempt. Now, if you should presume to let me come, where can I live? Can our industry and economy clothe and feed us for the year? Can I keep a cow? How can I be supplied with fire in that dear place, how can I pay my school bills, and how can I find all the necessary requisites for my children to advance in learning? If I should wish to leave in two, three, or five years, could I and mine, if I paid my way whilst there? If you should let me come, and I should think best to go, *how shall I get there,* what would be my best and cheapest route, how should I proceed with what I have here—sell all off or bring a part? I have three beds and bedding, one cow, and ordinary things enough to keep house. My children are called tolerable scholars; my daughter is the youngest. The neighbors call her an uninteresting child. I have no pretensions to make; my only object is to enjoy the good of the society, and have my children educated and accomplished.

Am I to send my boys off to work alone, or will they have a kind friend to say, Come, boys; and teach them how in love and good will, and relieve me of this heavy task of bringing up boys with nothing to do it with? If your religion has a name I should like well enough to know it; if not, and the substance is love to God and good will to man, my mind is well enough satisfied. I have reflected upon this subject ever since I read the article alluded to, and now I want you to write me every particular. Then, if you and I think best in the spring, I will come to you. We are none of us what can be called weakly. I am forty-six years old, able to do as much every day as to spin what is called a day's work. Not that I expect you spin much there, only that is the amount of my strength as it now holds out. I should wish to seek intelligence, which, as you must know, I lack greatly; and I cannot endure the thought that my children must lack as greatly, while multitudes are going so far in advance, no better qualified by nature than they. I want you to send me quite a number of names of your leading characters; if it should seem strange to you that I make the demand I will explain it to you when I get there. I want you to answer every item of this letter, and as much more as can have any bearing on my mind either way. Whether you accept this letter kindly or not, I want you to write me an answer without delay. Are there meetings for us to attend? Do you have singing schools? I do thus far feel friendly to your society. Direct my letter to New York—

To the leading members of the Roxbury Community, near Boston.

DEAR SIR,—It gives me the most sincere pleasure to reply to the inquiries proposed in your favor of the 31st instant. I welcome the extended and increasing interest which is manifested in our apparently humble enterprise, as a proof that it is founded in nature and truth, and as a cheering omen of its ultimate success. Like yourself, we are seekers of universal truth. We worship only reality. We are striving to establish a mode of life which shall combine the enchantments of poetry with the facts of daily experience. This we believe can be done by a rigid adherence to justice, by fidelity to human rights, by loving and honoring man as man, by rejecting all arbitrary, factitious distinctions. We are not in the interest of any sect, party, or coterie; we have faith in the soul of man, in the universal soul of things. Trusting to the might of benignant Providence which is over all, we are here sowing in weakness a seed which will be raised in power. But I need not dwell on these general considerations, with which you are doubtless familiar.

In regard to the *connection* of a family with us, our arrangements are liberal and comprehensive. We are not bound by fixed rules which apply to all cases. One general principle we are obliged to adhere to rigidly: not to receive any person who would increase the expenses more than the revenue of the establishment. Within the limits of this principle we can make any arrangement which shall suit particular cases.

A family with resources sufficient for self-support, independent of the exertion of its members, would find a favorable situation with us for the education of its children and for social enjoyment. . . . With the intelligent zeal which you manifest in our enterprise, I need not say that we highly value your sympathy, and should rejoice in any arrangement which might bring us into closer relations. It is only from the faith and love of those whose hearts are filled with the hopes of a better future for humanity that we look for the building up of our "city of God." So far we have been prospered in our highest expectations. We are more and more convinced of the beauty and justice of our mode of life. We love to breathe this pure, healthy atmosphere; we feel that we are living in the bosom of Nature, and all things seem to expand under the freedom and truth which we worship in our hearts.

I should regret to think that this was to be our last communication with each other. May I not hope to hear from you again? And with the sincere wish that your views of the philosophy of life may bring you still nearer to us, I am, with great respect,

Sincerely your friend,
GEO. RIPLEY

II. Letter to George Ripley

RALPH WALDO EMERSON

A fellow transcendentalist invited by Ripley to join the Brook Farm community could not bring himself to do so. Ralph Waldo Emerson, a frequent and welcomed (but not worshiped) visitor, would have given it a stature that might have improved its possibilities for survival, but for the reasons given in this letter, he declined Ripley's invitation. In this letter note Emerson's preference for in-

Ralph L. Rusk, ed., *The Letters of Ralph Waldo Emerson* (New York: Columbia University Press, 1939), II, pp. 368–71. This draft of the letter was corrected but not rewritten by Emerson. Words and phrases he deleted are omitted here. Indications are that he wished to incorporate the fifth paragraph into the fourth, after the words "usage permits."

dividualism. To what extent is the self-reliance of which he wrote so eloquently elsewhere evident in this letter?

DECEMBER 15, 1840

My dear Sir,
    It is quite time I made an answer to your proposition that I should join you in your new enterprise. The design appears to me so noble & humane, proceeding, as I plainly see, from a manly & expanding heart & mind that it makes me & all men its friends & debtors It becomes a matter of conscience to entertain it friendly & to examine what it has for us.
    I have decided not to join it & yet very slowly & I may almost say penitentially. I am greatly relieved by learning that your coadjutors are now so many that you will no longer ascribe that importance to the defection of individuals which you hinted in your letter to me . . . might attach to mine.
    The ground of my decision is almost purely personal to myself. I have some remains of skepticism in regard to the general practicability of the plan, but these have not much weighed with me. That which determines me is the conviction that the Community is not good for me. Whilst I see it may hold out many inducements for others it has little to offer me which with resolution I cannot procure for myself. It seems to me that it would not be worth my while to make the difficult exchange of my property in Concord for a share in the new Household. I am in many respects suitably placed . . . in an agreeable neighborhood, in a town which I have many reasons to love & which has respected my freedom so far that I may presume it will indulge me farther if I need it. Here I have friends & kindred. Here I have builded & planted: & here I have greater facilities to prosecute such practical enterprises as I may cherish, than I could probably find by any removal. I cannot accuse my townsmen or my social position of my domestic grievances:—only my own sloth & conformity. It seems to me a circuitous & operose way of relieving myself of any irksome circumstances, to put on your community the task of my emancipation which I ought to take on myself.
    The principal particulars in which I wish to mend my domestic life are in acquiring habits of regular manual labor, and in ameliorating or abolishing in my house the condition of hired menial service. I should like to come one step nearer to nature than this usage permits. But surely I need not sell my house & remove my family to Newton in order to make the experiment of labor & self help. I am already in the act of trying some domestic & social experiments which my present position favors. And I think that my present position has even greater advantages than yours would offer me for testing my improvements in those small private parties into which men are all set off already throughout the world.
    . . .—But I own I almost shrink from making any statement of my objections to our ways of living because I see how slowly I shall mend them. My own health & habits & those of my wife & my mother are not of that robustness which should give any pledge of enterprize & ability in reform. And

whenever I am engaged in literary composition I find myself not inclined to insist with heat on new methods. Yet I think that all I shall solidly do, I must do alone. I do not think I should gain anything—I who have little skill to converse with people—by a plan of so many parts and which I comprehend so slowly & imperfectly as the proposed Association.

If the community is not good for me neither am I good for it. I do not look on myself as a valuable member to any community which is not either very large or very small & select I fear that yours would not find me as profitable & pleasant an associate as I should wish to be and as so important a project seems imperatively to require in all its constituents Moreover I am so ignorant & uncertain in my improvements that I would fain hide my attempts & failures in solitude where they shall perplex none or very few beside myself The result of our secretest improvements will certainly have as much renown as shall be due to them.

In regard to the plan as far as it respects the formation of a School or College, I have more hesitation, inasmuch as a concentration of scholars in one place seems to me to have certain great advantages. Perhaps as the school emerges to more distinct consideration out of the Farm, I shall yet find it attractive And yet I am very apt to relapse into the same skepticism as to modes & arrangements the same magnifying of the men—the men alone. According to your ability & mine, you & I do now keep school for all comers, & the energy of our thought & will measures our influence. In the community we shall utter not a word more—not a word less.

Whilst I refuse to be an active member of your company I must yet declare that of all the philanthropic projects of which I have heard yours is the most pleasing to me and if it is prosecuted in the same spirit in which it is begun, I shall regard it with lively sympathy & with a sort of gratitude.

Yours affectionately
R W Emerson

III. Charles Lane on Brook Farm

Charles Lane, an eccentric Englishman who espoused communitarianism, regarded Brook Farm with both admiration and criticism. As cofounder of Fruitlands, with Amos Bronson Alcott, Lane might have had the opportunity to implement or experiment with his more radical ideas, but this community had only a brief and disastrous existence.

In this short excerpt from an article about Brook Farm, Lane discusses one of the issues that would have had to be confronted at Fruitlands, had it survived. How valid is his assertion that association and family life are incompatible? What are the implications of this assertion for those who want to form communes or simply to promote a greater sense of community concern in our society today?

The Dial, January 1844 (reprinted in New York: Russell and Russell, 1961), pp. 351–57.

Wherever we recognize the principle of progress, our sympathies and affections are engaged. However small may be the innovation, however limited the effort towards the attainment of pure good, that effort is worthy of our best encouragement and succor. The Institution at Brook Farm, West Roxbury, though sufficiently extensive in respect to number of persons, perhaps is not to be considered an experiment of large intent. Its aims are moderate; too humble indeed to satisfy the extreme demands of the age; yet, for that reason probably, the effort is more valuable, as likely to exhibit a larger share of actual success.

Though familiarly designated a "Community," it is only so in the process of eating in commons; a practice at least, as antiquated, as the collegiate halls of old England, where it still continues without producing, as far as we can learn, any of the Spartan virtues. A residence at Brook Farm does not involve either a community of money, of opinions, or of sympathy. The motives which bring individuals there, may be as various as their numbers. In fact, the present residents are divisible into three distinct classes; and if the majority in numbers were considered, it is possible that a vote in favor of self-sacrifice for the common good would not be very strongly carried. The leading portion of the adult inmates, they whose presence imparts the greatest peculiarity and the fraternal tone to the household, believe that an improved state of existence would be developed in association, and are therefore anxious to promote it. Another class consists of those who join with the view of bettering their condition, by being exempted from some portion of worldly strife. The third portion, comprises those who have their own development or education, for their principal object. . . .

Of about seventy persons now assembled there, about thirty are children sent thither for education; some adult persons also place themselves there chiefly for mental assistance; and in the society there are only four married couples. With such materials it is almost certain that the sensitive and vital points of communication cannot well be tested. A joint-stock company, working with some of its own members and with others as agents, cannot bring to issue the great question, whether the existence of the marital family is compatible with that of the universal family, which the term "Community" signifies. This is now the grand problem. By mothers it has ever been felt to be so. The maternal instinct, as hitherto educated, has declared itself so strongly in favor of the separate fire-side, that association, which appears so beautiful to the young and unattached soul, has yet accomplished little progress in the affections of that important section of the human race—the mothers. With fathers, the feeling in favor of the separate family is certainly less strong; but there is an undefinable tie, a sort of magnetic *rapport,* an invisible, inseverable, umbilical chord between the mother and child, which in most cases circumscribes her desires and ambition to her own immediate family. All the accepted adages and wise saws of society, all the precepts of morality, all the sanctions of theology, have for ages been employed to confirm this feeling. This is the chief corner stone of present society; and to this maternal instinct have, till very lately, our most heartfelt appeals been made for the progress of the human race, by means of a deeper and more vital education. Pestalozzi and his most enlightened disciples are distinguished by this sentiment. And are we all at once to abandon, to deny, to destroy this supposed stronghold of virtue? Is it questioned whether the family arrangement of mankind is to be preserved? Is it discovered that the sanctuary, till now deemed the holiest on earth, is to be invaded by intermeddling skepticism, and its altars sacrilegiously destroyed by the rude hands of innovating progress? Here "social science" must be brought to issue.The question of association and of marriage are one. If, as we have been popularly led to believe, the individual or separate family is in the true order of Providence, then the associative life is a false effort. If the associative life is true, then is the separate family a false arrangement. By the maternal feeling, it appears to be decided that the coexistence of both is incompatible, is impossible. So also say some religious sects. Social science ventures to assert their harmony. This is the grand problem now remaining to be solved, for at least, the enlightening, if not for the vital elevation of humanity. That the affections can be divided or bent with equal ardor on two objects, so opposed as universal and individual love, may at least be rationally doubted. History has not yet exhibited such phenomena in an associate body, and scarcely perhaps in any individual. The monasteries and convents, which have existed in all ages, have been maintained solely by the annihilation of that peculiar affection on which the separate family is based. The Shaker families, in which the two sexes are not entirely dissociated, can yet only maintain their union by forbidding and preventing the growth of personal affection other than that of a spiritual character. And this in fact is not personal in the sense of individual, but ever a manifestation of universal affection. Spite of the speculations of hopeful bachelors and aesthetic spinsters, there is somewhat in the marriage bond which is found to counteract the universal nature of the affections, to a degree tending at least to make the considerate pause, before they assert that, by any social arrangements whatever, the two can be blended into one harmony. The general condition of married persons at this time is some evidence of the existence of such a doubt in their minds. Were they as convinced as the unmarried of the beauty and truth of associate life, the demonstration would be now presented. But might it not be enforced that the two family ideas really neutralize each other? Is it not quite certain that the human heart cannot be set in two places; that man cannot worship at two altars? It is only the determination to do what parents consider the best for themselves and their families, which renders the o'er populous world such a wilderness of selfhood as it is. Destroy this feeling, they say, and you prohibit every motive to exertion. Much truth is there in this affirmation. For to them, no other motive remains, nor indeed to any one else, save that of the universal good, which does not permit the building up of supposed self-good; and therefore, forecloses all possibility of an individual family.

IV. Remembering Brook Farm

JOHN CODMAN

Brook Farm was particularly noted for the stimulating education it offered to children. The effectiveness of classroom instruction was no doubt enhanced by the life style of the community, for learning and life were expected to be in harmony with each other and with nature.

Writing about fifty years after his Brook Farm experiences, John Codman recalled what life there as a child had meant to him. How important are the things about Brook Farm that Codman regarded as good? How might they be developed in learning situations today?

A pun is a part of the sunshine of words. It gives a sparkle and a glow to language. It is a big pendulum that swings from torrid to frigid zone quicker than a telegram goes. If you hold on to it, you will find yourself in both places in a jiffy, and back again to the spot where you start from without being hurt, and the jog to your intellect, if you happen to have any, is only of an agreeable nature.

But it was not alone in puns and conundrums that the social life of Brook Farm was rich. It was rich in cheerful buzz. The bumble-bees had no more melodious hum than the Brook Farmers. They had thrown aside the forms that bind outside humanity. They were sailing on a voyage of discovery, seeking a modern El Dorado, but they did not carry with them the lust for gold. They were seeking something which, had they found the realization of, would have carried peace to troubled hearts, contentment and joy to all conditions and classes. They were builders, not destroyers. They proposed to begin again the social structure with new foundations. They were at war with none personally; as high-toned, large-souled men and women they were ready with their expressions of hatred and contempt for the unchristian social life of our generation, but they were never ranters.

In general little was said on the farm of these matters, except in private discussions; all were too busy with the active work. We felt that we had put our ears down to the earth and heard nature's whisperings of harmony; that we had gone back from the uncertain and flimsy foundations of present society, and placed our corner stone on the eternal rock of science and justice; that the social laws God ordained from the beginning had been discovered; there could be no possibility of a mistake, and therefore, we felt that our feet were on eternal foundations, and our souls growing more and more in harmony with man and God.

Imagine, different reader of my story, the state of mind you would be in if you could feel that you were placed in a position of positive harmony with all your race; that you carried with you a balm that could heal every earthly

John T. Codman, *Brook Farm: Historic and Personal Memoirs* (Boston: Arena, 1894), pp. 176–79.

wound; an earthly gospel, even as the church thinks it has a heavenly gospel
—a remedy for poverty, crime, outrage and over-taxed hand, heart and brain.
And every night as you laid your head on your pillow, you could say: "I have
this day wronged no man. I have this day worked for my race, I have let all
my little plans go and have worked on the grand plan that the Eternal Father
has intended shall sometime be completed. I feel that I am in harmony with
Him. Now I know He *is* truly our Father. With an unending list of crimes and
social wrongs staring me in the face I doubted and my heart was cast down.
Now the light is given me by which I see the way through the labyrinth! It
is our Father's beautiful garden in which we are. I have learned that all is
intended for order and beauty, but as children we cannot yet walk so as not
to stumble. Natural science has explained a thousand mysteries. Social science
—understand the word; not schemes, plans or guessing, but genuine science,
as far from guess or scheme as astronomy or chemistry is—will reveal to us
as many truths and beauties as ever any other science has done. I now see
clearly! Blessed be God for the light!"

And after sound sleep, waking in the rosy morning, with the fresh air from
balmy fields blowing into your window, penetrated still with the afflatus of last
night's thoughts and reveries, wouldn't you be cheerful? Wouldn't the unity
of all things come to you, and wouldn't you chirrup like a bird, and buzz like
a bee, and turn imaginary somersaults and dance and sing, and feel like cutting
up "didoes," and talk a little high strung, and be chipper with the lowliest and
level with the highest? Wouldn't your heart flow over with ever so much love
and gratitude? Wouldn't it infuse so much spirit into your poor, weak life that
your words would sparkle with cheeriness, frolic and wit? I believe so! I know
so!

Such was to me the secret of the fun, wit and frolic of the Brook Farmers.
The jokes were, it is true, largely superficial, but they were inseparable from
the position. The bottom fact was, *the associates there were leading a just life,*
and could go to their labor, hard beds and simple fare—down to plain bread
and sometimes mythical butter—with cheerfulness just in proportion as they
were penetrated by these great ideas. They could make merry with their friends
over a cup of coffee, and sought not the stimulants that college days and college
habits might have allowed.

It was with one of our little social groups of friends, that Mr. Dwight gave
the toast, "Here's to the coffee-pot! If it is not *spiritual,* it's not *material!*"

For Further Reading

Two recent books on Brook Farm are: Henry W. Sams, ed., *Autobiography of
Brook Farm** (1958), which contains excerpts from key documents; and Edith
R. Curtis, *A Season in Utopia: The Story of Brook Farm* (1961). A third has
been reprinted: Lindsay Swift, *Brook Farm, Its Members, Scholars, and Visitors*
(1908, 1961).

*Paperbound edition available.

The Story of Utopias (1922, 1962), by Lewis Mumford, is a classic study of utopian ideas and practices. Alice Felt Tyler's *Freedom's Ferment** (1944) and C. S. Griffin's *The Ferment of Reform** (1969) tell of the restlessness that led to the reform movement of which Brook Farm was a part. *The Era of Reform** (1960), edited by Henry S. Commager, is a short book of documents. *Ante-Bellum Reform** (1967), edited by David Brion Davis, is a collection of essays on the movement. Arthur Bestor's *Backwoods Utopias* (1950) deals with communitarian societies between 1663 and 1829. *Heaven's on Earth** (1966), by Mark Holloway, contains interesting descriptions of a number of communities. John Humphrey Noyes, founder of the Oneida community, provides descriptions of numerous communities in *History of American Socialisms** (1870; reprinted in 1966). Additional firsthand accounts are given by Charles Nordhoff in *The Communistic Societies of the United States** (1875; reprinted in 1966).

Socialism and American Life, 2 vol. (1952), edited by Donald Egbert and Stow Persons, is valuable both for its narrative and its extensive bibliography. An appropriate biography is Charles Crowe's *George Ripley: Transcendentalist and Utopian Socialist* (1967).

The Alternative: Communal Life in America (1970), by William Hedgepeth and Dennis Stock, is a description of modern communal life by actual participants in it.

---

*Paperbound edition available.

12. Beyond Abolitionism: The Black Quest for Social Equality

The inconsistency of slavery with American ideals and values was recognized by many people long before the emergence of the abolitionist movement in the 1830s. Early abolitionist societies, founded between 1775 and 1800, were strongly religious in orientation, gradualistic in philosophy, and conciliatory in approach. While counseling blacks to bear and forbear, they made special efforts to gain the support of the South. The principal achievements of these early, low-keyed societies were the rescuing of blacks held illegally in bondage, the promotion of free education for blacks and the temporary popularization of the idea of colonization. They did not succeed, however, in arousing widespread opposition to slavery.

A new abolitionist movement that appeared in the 1830s was significantly different in character and goals. The fervor it exhibited was moral rather than religious. It quickly adopted the principle of immediacy rather than gradualism, and its demands for uncompensated emancipation of slaves were hardly intended to be conciliatory. By the mid-1840s the movement had become highly political in its methods and purposes, but the earlier moralism continued to play an important role.

The persistence and effectiveness of the abolitionist movement reflect its gifted and dedicated leaders, of whom the best known was William Lloyd Garrison. His oratorical and literary abilities, along with those of other men and women, provided the backbone of the movement. One wonders what success the movement would have reached if these abolitionists had matched their oratory and writings with comparable efforts and skill in political organizing.

The expressed goal of the abolitionists was the emancipation of slaves. It might be assumed, therefore, that freed slaves and other blacks played a major part in the movement. As the history of the movement has been recorded, however, they played a parallel rather than an integral part.

How can the relations between blacks and whites in the abolition movement be explained? In part, the explanation lies in the nature of the Southern response to abolitionism. The character of any movement as it unfolds and as it is recounted by historians is determined in part by the enmity it arouses. For the South to have focused attention on the black abolitionists would have contradicted its assertion that slaves were not only inherently inferior, but also that they were contented in their condition. The South had to avoid doing anything to make the abolitionist cause believable.

A further, more important explanation lies in the differences between the concerns and goals of white abolitionists and their black counterparts. White abolitionists directed their attention almost exclusively to slavery, and often to slavery in an abstract sense. Blacks were little more than symbols of their struggle and the recipients of their good works. White abolitionists were thus able to continue to hold their beliefs in black inferiority and to accept and practice rigid social separation, even to the extent of creating black auxiliaries to white antislavery societies.[1]

Black abolitionists, on the other hand, wished to push for more comprehensive goals. They were concerned with such matters as voting, improving their economic status, erasing ideas of racial inferiority, and establishing equal educational, social, and civic privileges.

In the early stages of the movement it was natural for the black abolitionists to give their support to the white leaders and their movement. They respected their courage and appreciated their sincerity. But it was just as natural that a general parting of the ways should develop as the movement achieved maturity and as blacks gained leadership experience. In the white movement the blacks were, for the most part, bit players or extras. On their own, given the restricted sphere in which they could operate, their achievements were quite substantial.

---

[1] *Editors' note:* They were called "antislavery" societies as a way of setting themselves apart from the abolitionist societies of earlier years.

Core Document

A National Convention of the Free People of Color of the United States

Conventions played a remarkably prominent part in the activities of the various state and national antislavery societies. Their purpose was to disseminate information, rally support, and nourish faith in the cause. With a few significant exceptions, blacks played only minor roles in these conventions, and only rarely did they hold offices in the societies sponsoring them.

Given their commitment to the cause of abolishing slavery, their different circumstances, and the greater breadth of their concerns, it is not surprising that blacks early decided to hold their own meetings. They held national conventions annually from 1830 to 1837 and occasionally thereafter. The 1843 convention attracted considerable attention because of a speech by Henry Highland Garnet (included later in this chapter).

The most significant National Negro Convention was held at Rochester, New York, July 6–8, 1853. More than one hundred delegates and officers from eight states were in attendance. They displayed an ideology of self-help and racial solidarity as the convention aimed at racial uplift and economic improvement of blacks. Harriet Beecher Stowe and William Lloyd Garrison spoke and were given respectful tributes, but the delegates proceeded to think and act for themselves, recognizing that real improvement in their condition depended on their own efforts.

Three documents of the convention are included here. In studying these documents, pay particular attention to:

- *the reasons for calling the convention.*
- *the grievances of both slaves and free blacks.*
- *indications of militant feelings and racial pride among the convention's callers and participants.*
- *appeals to American political ideals as a basis for improving the condition of black Americans.*
- *the nature of the convention's requests.*
- *the means proposed to assure the granting of its requests.*
- *the necessity of establishing the validity of citizenship for blacks.*
- *the analysis of the reasons for the continuation of racial discrimination.*
- *the pertinence of the plan for a national council to pursue the grievances and goals expressed in the convention's address.*

Herbert Aptheker, ed., *A Documentary History of the Negro People in the United States* (New York: Citadel Press, 1951), I, pp. 342–52.

JULY 1853

Call for the Convention

Fellow Citizens:—In the exercise of a liberty which we hope, you will not deem unwarrantable, and which is given us, in virtue of our connection and identity with you, the undersigned do hereby, most earnestly and affectionately, invite you, by your appropriate and chosen representatives, to assemble at ROCHES-TER, N.Y., on the 6th of July, 1853 under the form and title of a National Convention of the free people of color of the United States.

After due thought and reflection upon the subject, in which has entered a profound desire to serve a common cause, we have arrived at the conclusion, that the time has now fully come when the free colored people from all parts of the United States, should meet together, to confer and deliberate upon their present condition, and upon principles and measures important to their welfare, progress and general improvement.

The aspects of our cause, whether viewed as being hostile or friendly, are alike full of argument in favor of such a Convention. Both reason and feeling have assigned us to a place in the conflict now going on in our land between liberty and equality on the one hand, and slavery and caste on the other—a place which we cannot fail to occupy without branding ourselves as unworthy of our natural post, and recreant to the cause we profess to love. Under the whole heavens, there is not to be found a people which can show better cause for assembling in such a Convention than we.

Our fellow-countrymen now in chains, to whom we are united in a common destiny demand it; and a wise solicitude for our own honor, and that of our children, impels us to this course of action. We have gross and flagrant wrongs against which, if we are men of spirit we are bound to protest. We have high and holy rights, which every instinct of human nature and every sentiment of manly virtue bid us to preserve and protect to the full extent of our ability. We have opportunities to improve—difficulties peculiar to our condition to meet—mistakes and errors of our own to correct—and therefore we need the accumulated knowledge, the united character, and the combined wisdom of our people to make us (under God) sufficient for these things.

The Fugitive Slave Act, the most cruel, unconstitutional and scandalous outrage of modern times—the proscriptive legislation of several States with a view to drive our people from their borders—the exclusion of our children from schools supported by our money—the prohibition of the exercise of the franchise—the exclusion of colored citizens from the jury box—the social barriers erected against our learning trades—the wily and vigorous efforts of the American Colonization Society to employ the arm of government to expel us from our native land—and withal the propitious awakening to the fact of our condition at home and abroad, which has followed the publication of "Uncle Tom's Cabin"—call trumpet-tongued for our union, co-operation and action in the premises.

Convinced that the number amongst us must be small, who so far miscalculate and undervalue the importance of united and intelligent moral action, as to regard it as useless, the undersigned do not feel called upon here for an argument in its favor. Our warfare is not one where force can be employed; we battle against false and hurtful customs, and against the great errors [of] opinion which support such customs. Nations are more and more guided by the enlightened and energetically expressed judgment of mankind. On the subject of our condition and welfare, we may safely and properly appeal to that judgment. Let us meet, then, near the anniversary of this nation's independence, and enforce anew the great principles and self-evident truths which were proclaimed at the beginning of the Republic.

Among the matters which will engage the attention of our Convention will be a proposition to establish a NATIONAL COUNCIL of our people with a view to permanent existence. This subject is one of vast importance, and should only be disposed of in the light of a wise deliberation. There will come before the Convention matters touching the disposition of such funds as our friends abroad, through Mrs. Harriet Beecher Stowe, may appropriate to the cause of our progress and improvement. In a word, the whole field of our interests will be opened to enquiry, investigation and determination.

That this be done successfully, it is desirable that each delegate to the Convention should bring with him an accurate statement as to the number of colored inhabitants in his town or neighborhood—the amount of property owned by them—their business or occupation—the state of education—the extent of their school privileges and the number of children in attendance, and any other information which may serve the great purposes of the Convention.

It is recommended that all colored churches, literary and other societies, banded together for laudable purposes, proceed at once to the appointment of at least one, and not more than three, delegates to attend the National Convention. Such persons as come from towns, villages or counties, where no regular delgate may have been chosen; shall be received and enrolled as honorary members of the Convention.

Address, of the Colored National Convention to the People of the United States

Fellow Citizens: Met in convention as delegates, representing the Free Colored people of the United States; charged with the responsibility of inquiring into the general condition of our people, and of devising measures which may, with the blessing of God, tend to our mutual improvement and elevation; conscious of entertaining no motives, ideas, or aspirations, but such as are in accordance with truth and justice, are compatible with the highest good of our country and the world, with a cause as vital and worthy as that for which (nearly eighty years ago) your fathers and our fathers bravely contended, and in which they gloriously triumphed—we deem it proper, on this occasion, as one method of promoting the honorable ends for which we have met, and of discharging our duty to those in whose name we speak, to present the claims of our common cause to your candid, earnest, and favorable consideration.

As an apology for addressing you, fellow-citizens! we cannot announce the discovery of any new principle adapted to ameliorate the condition of mankind. The great truths of moral and political science, upon which we rely and which we press upon your consideration, have been evolved and enunciated by you. We point to your principles, your wisdom, and to your great example for the full justification of our cause this day. That "ALL MEN ARE CREATED EQUAL": that "LIFE, LIBERTY, AND THE PURSUIT OF HAPPINESS" ARE THE RIGHT OF ALL; that "TAXATION AND REPRESENTATION" SHOULD GO TOGETHER; that GOVERNMENTS ARE TO PROTECT, NOT TO DESTROY, THE RIGHTS OF MANKIND; that THE CONSTITUTION OF THE UNITED STATES WAS FORMED TO ESTABLISH JUSTICE, PROMOTE THE GENERAL WELFARE, AND SECURE THE BLESSING OF LIBERTY TO ALL THE PEOPLE OF THIS COUNTRY; THAT RESISTANCE TO TYRANTS IS OBEDIENCE TO GOD—are American principles and maxims, and together they form and constitute the constructive elements of the American government. From this elevated platform, provided by the Republic for us, and for all the children of men, we address you. In doing so, we would have our spirit properly discerned. On this point we would gladly free ourselves and our cause from all misconception. We shall affect no especial timidity, nor can we pretend to any great boldness. We know our poverty and weakness, and your wealth and greatness. Yet we will not attempt to repress the spirit of liberty within us, or to conceal, in any wise, our sense of justice and the dignity of our cause.

We are Americans, and as Americans, we would speak to Americans. We address you not as aliens nor as exiles, humbly asking to be permitted to dwell among you in peace; but we address you as American citizens asserting their rights on their own native soil. Neither do we address you as enemies, (although the recipients of innumerable wrongs;) but in the spirit of patriotic good will. In assembling together as we have done, our object is not to excite pity for ourselves, but to command respect for our cause, and to obtain justice for our people. We are not malefactors imploring mercy; but we trust we are honest men, honestly appealing for righteous judgment, and ready to stand or fall by that judgment. We do not solicit unusual favor, but will be content with rough-handed "fair play." We are neither lame nor blind, that we should seek to throw off the responsibility of our own existence, or to cast ourselves upon public charity for support. We would not lay our burdens upon other men's shoulders; but we do ask, in the name of all that is just and magnanimous among men, to be freed from all the unnatural burdens and impediments with which American customs and American legislation have hindered our progress and improvement. We ask to be disencumbered of the load of popular reproach heaped upon us—for no better cause than that we wear the complexion given us by our God and our Creator.

We ask that in our native land, we shall not be treated as strangers, and worse than strangers.

We ask that, being friends of America, we should not be treated as enemies of America.

We ask that, speaking the same language, and being of the same religion, worshipping the same God, owing our redemption to the same Savior, and learning our duties from the same Bible, we shall not be treated as barbarians.

We ask that, having the same physical, moral, mental, and spiritual wants, common to other members of the human family, we shall also have the same means which are granted and secured to others to supply those wants.

We ask that the doors of the school-houses, the work-shop, the church, the college, shall be thrown open as freely to our children as to the children of other members of the community.

We ask that the American government shall be so administered as that beneath the broad shield of the Constitution, the colored American seaman, shall be secure in his life, liberty and property, in every State in the Union.

We ask that as justice knows no rich, no poor, no black, no white, but, like the government of God, renders alike to every man reward or punishment, according as his works shall be—the white and black may stand upon an equal footing before the laws of the lands.

We ask that (since the right of trial by jury is a safeguard of liberty, against the encroachments of power, only as it is a trial by impartial men, drawn indiscriminately from the country) colored men shall not, in every instance, be tried by white persons; and that colored men shall not be either by custom or enactment excluded from the jury-box.

We ask that (inasmuch as we are, in common with other American citizens, supporters of the State, subject to its laws, interested in its welfare, liable to be called upon to defend it in time of war, contributors to its wealth in time of peace) the complete and unrestricted right of suffrage, which is essential to the dignity even of the white man, be extended to the Free Colored man also.

Whereas, the colored people of the United States have too long been retarded and impeded in the development and improvement of their natural faculties and powers, ever to become dangerous rivals to white men, in the honorable pursuits of life, liberty and happiness; and whereas, the proud Anglo-Saxon can need no arbitrary protection from open and equal competition with any variety of the human family; and whereas, laws have been enacted limiting the aspirations of colored men, as against white men—we respectfully submit that such laws are flagrantly unjust to the man of color, and plainly discreditable to white men; and for these and other reasons, such laws ought to be repealed.

We especially urge that all laws and usages which preclude the enrollment of colored men in the militia, and prohibit their bearing arms in the navy, disallow their rising, agreeable to their merits and attainments—are unconstitutional—the constitution knowing no color—are anti-Democratic, since Democracy respects men as equals—are unmagnanimous, since such laws are made by the many, against the few, and by the strong against the weak.

We ask that all those cruel and oppressive laws, whether enacted at the South or the North, which aim at the expatriation of the free people of color, shall be stamped with national reprobation, denounced as contrary to the humanity of the American people, and as an outrage upon the Christianity and civilization of the nineteenth century.

We ask that the right of pre-emption, enjoyed by all white settlers upon the public lands, shall be enjoyed by colored settlers; and that the word *"white"* be struck from the pre-emption act. We ask that no appropriations whatever, state or national, shall be granted to the colonization scheme; and we would have our right to leave or to remain in the United States placed above legislative interference.

We ask that the Fugitive Slave Law of 1850, that legislative monster of modern times, by whose atrocious provisions the writ "of habeas corpus," the "right of trial by jury," have been virtually abolished, shall be repealed.

We ask, that the law of 1793 be so construed as to apply only to apprentices, and others really owing service or labor; and not to slaves, who can *owe* nothing. Finally, we ask that slavery in the United States shall be immediately, unconditionally, and forever abolished.

To accomplish these just and reasonable ends, we solemnly pledge ourselves to God, to each other, to our country, and to the world, to use all and every means consistent with the just rights of our fellow men, and with the precepts of Christianity.

We shall speak, write and publish, organize and combine to accomplish them.

We shall invoke the aid of the pulpit and the press to gain them.

We shall appeal to the church and to the government to gain them.

We shall vote, and expend our money to gain them.

We shall send eloquent men of our own condition to plead our cause before the people.

We shall invite the co-operation of good men in this country and throughout the world—and above all, we shall look to God, the Father and Creator of all men, for wisdom to direct us and strength to support us in the holy cause to which we this day solemnly pledge ourselves.

Such, fellow-citizens are our aims, ends, aspirations and determinations. We place them before you, with the earnest hope that upon further investigation, they will meet your cordial and active approval.

And yet, again, we would free ourselves from the charge of unreasonableness and self-sufficiency.

In numbers we are few and feeble; but in the goodness of our cause, in the rectitude of our motives, and in the abundance of argument on our side, we are many and strong.

We count our friends in the heavens above, in the earth beneath, among good men and holy angels. The subtle and mysterious cords of human sympathy have connected us with philanthropic hearts throughout the civilized world. The number in our own land who already recognize the injustice of our cause, and are laboring to promote it, is great and increasing.

It is also a source of encouragement, that the genuine American, brave and independent himself, will respect bravery and independence in others. He spurns servility and meanness, whether they be manifested by nations or by individuals. We submit, therefore, that there is neither necessity for, nor disposition on our part to assume a tone of excessive humility. While we would be respectful, we must address you as men, as citizens, as brothers, as dwellers in a common country, equally interested with you for its welfare, its honor and for its prosperity.

To be still more explicit: we would, first of all, be understood to range ourselves no lower among our fellow-countrymen than is implied in the high appellation of *"citizen."*

Notwithstanding the impositions and deprivations which have fettered us —notwithstanding the disabilities and liabilities, pending and impending— notwithstanding the cunning, cruel and scandalous efforts to blot out that right, we declare that we are, and of right we ought to be *American citizens.* We claim this right, and we claim all the rights and privileges, and duties which, properly, attach to it.

It may, and it will, probably, be disputed that we are citizens. We may, and probably shall be denounced for this declaration, as making an inconsiderate, impertinent and absurd claim to citizenship; but a very little reflection will vindicate the position we have assumed, from so unfavorable a judgement. Justice is never inconsiderate; truth is never impertinent; right is never absurd. If the claim we set up be just, true and right, it will not be deemed improper or ridiculous in us to declare it. Nor is it disrespectful to our fellow-citizens, who repudiate the aristocratic notions of the old world that we range ourselves with them in respect to all the rights and prerogatives belonging to American citizens. Indeed, we believe, when you have duly considered this subject, you will commend us for the mildness and modesty with which we have taken our ground.

By birth, we are American citizens; by the principles of the Declaration of Independence, we are American citizens; within the meaning of the United States Constitution, we are American Citizens; by the facts of history, and the admissions of American statesmen, we are American citizens; by the hardships and trials endured; by the courage and fidelity displayed by our ancestors in defending the liberties and in achieving the independence of our land, we are American citizens. In proof of the justice of this primary claim, we might cite numerous authorities, facts and testimonies,—a few only must suffice. . . . We hope you will now permit us to address you in the plainness of speech becoming the dignity of American citizens.

Fellow-citizens, we have had, and still have, great wrongs of which to complain. A heavy and cruel hand has been laid on us.

As a people, we feel ourselves to be not only deeply injured, but grossly misunderstood. Our white fellow-countrymen do not know us. They are strangers to our character, ignorant of our capacity, oblivious of our history and progress, and are misinformed as to the principles and ideas that control and guide us as a people. The great mass of American citizens estimate us as being a characterless and purposeless people; and hence we hold up our heads, if at all, against the withering influence of a nation's scorn and contempt.

It will not be surprising that we are so misunderstood and misused when the motives for misrepresenting us and for degrading us are duly considered. Indeed, it will seem strange, upon such consideration, (and in view of the ten thousand channels through which malign feelings find utterance and influence) that we have not even fallen lower in public estimation than we have done. For, with the single exception of the Jews, under the whole heavens, there is not to be found a people pursued with a more relentless prejudice and persecution, than are the Free Colored people of the United States.

Without pretending to have exerted ourselves as we ought, in view of an intelligent understanding of our interest, to avert from us the unfavorable opinions and unfriendly action of the American people, we feel that the imputations cast upon us, for our want of intelligence, morality and exalted character, may be mainly accounted for by the injustice we have received at your hands. What stone has been left unturned to degrade us? What hand has refused to fan the flame of popular prejudice against us? What American artist has not caricatured us? What wit has not laughed at us in our wretchedness? What songster has not made merry over our depressed spirits? What press has not ridiculed and contemned us? What pulpit has withheld from our devoted heads its angry lightning or its sanctimonious hate? Few, few, very few; and that we have borne up with it all—that we have tried to be wise, though denounced by all to be fools—that we have tried to be upright, when all around us have esteemed us as knaves—that we have striven to be gentlemen, although all around us have been teaching us its impossibility—that we have remained here, when all our neighbors have advised us to leave, proves that we possess qualities of head and heart such as cannot but be commended by impartial men. It is believed that no other nation on the globe could have made more progress in the midst of such an universal and stringent disparagement. It would humble the proudest, crush the energies of the strongest, and retard the progress of the swiftest. In view of our circumstances, we can, without boasting, thank God, and take courage, having placed ourselves where we may fairly challenge comparison with more highly favored men.

Among the colored people we can point, with pride and hope, to men of education and refinement, who have become such, despite of the most unfavorable influences, we can point to mechanics, farmers, merchants, teachers, ministers, doctors, lawyers, editors, and authors against whose progress the concentrated energies of American prejudice have proved quite unavailing. Now, what is the motive for ignoring and discouraging our improvement in this country? The answer is ready. The intelligent and upright free man of color is an unanswerable argument in favor of liberty, and a killing condemnation of American slavery. It is easily seen that, in proportion to the progress of the free man of color in knowledge, temperance, industry, and righteousness, in just that proportion will he endanger the stability of slavery; hence, all the powers of slavery are exerted to prevent the elevation of the free people of color.

The force of fifteen hundred million dollars is arrayed against us; hence, the press, the pulpit, and the platform, against all the natural promptings of uncontaminated manhood, point their deadly missiles of ridicule, scorn and contempt at us; and bid us on pain of being pierced through and through, to remain in our degradation.

Let the same amount of money be employed against the interest of any other class of persons, however favored by nature they may be, the result could scarcely be different from that seen in our own case. Such a people would be regarded with aversion; the money-ruled multitude would heap contumely upon them, and money-ruled institutions would proscribe them. Besides this money consideration, fellow-citizens, an explanation of the erroneous opinions prevalent concerning us is furnished in the fact, less creditable to human nature, that men are apt to hate most those whom they injure most. Having despised us, it is not strange that Americans should seek to render us despicable; having enslaved us, it is natural that they should strive to prove us unfit for freedom; having denounced us as indolent, it is not strange that they should cripple our enterprise; having assumed our inferiority, it would be extraordinary if they sought to surround us with circumstances which would serve to make us direct contradictions to their assumption.

In conclusion, fellow-citizens, while conscious of the immense disadvantages which beset our pathway, and fully appreciating our own weakness, we are encouraged to persevere in efforts adapted to our improvement, by a firm reliance upon God, and a settled conviction, as immovable as the everlasting hills, that all the truths in the whole universe of God are allied to our cause.

Plan for National Council

For the purpose of improving the character, developing the intelligence, maintaining the rights, and organizing a Union of the Colored People of the Free States, the National Convention does hereby ordain and institute the "NATIONAL COUNCIL OF THE COLORED PEOPLE."

Article 1. The Council shall consist of two members from each State, represented in this Convention, to be elected by this Convention, and two other members from each State to be elected as follows: On the 15th day of November next, and biennially thereafter, there shall be held in each State, a Poll, at which each colored inhabitant[1] may vote who pays ten cents as a poll-tax; and each State shall elect, at such election, delegates to State Councils, twenty in number from each State, at large. The election to be held in such places and under such conditions as the public meetings in such localities may determine. The members of the National Council in each State shall receive, canvass and declare the result of such vote. The State Council thus elected, shall meet to select a location in the State designated by the National Council, to erect buildings, appoint or dismiss instructors in the literary or mechanical branches. There shall be a farm attached to the School. . . .

Article 4. The Committee on Protective Union, shall institute a Protective Union for the purchase and sale of articles of domestic consumption, and shall unite and aid in the formation of branches auxiliary to their own.

Article 5. The Committee on Business Relations, shall establish an office, in which they shall keep a registry of colored mechanics, artizans and business men throughout the Union. They shall keep a registry of all persons willing to employ colored men in business, to teach colored boys mechanical

---

[1]Note that this does not say "male."

trades, liberal and scientific professions, and farming; and, also, a registry of colored men and youth seeking employment or instruction. They also shall report upon any avenues of business or trade which they deem inviting to colored capital, skill or labor. Their reports and advertisements to be in papers of the widest circulation. They shall receive for sale or exhibition, products of the skill and labor of colored people.

Article 6. The Committee on Publication shall collect all facts, statistics and statements, all laws and historical records and biographies of the Colored People, and all books by colored authors. They shall have for the safe keeping of these documents, a Library, with a Reading Room and Museum. The Committee shall also publish replies to any assaults, worthy of note, made upon the character or condition of the Colored People.

Article 7. Each Committee shall have absolute control over its special department; shall make its own by-laws, and in case of any vacancy occurring, shall fill up the same forthwith, subject to the confirmation of the Council. Each Committee shall meet at least once a month or as often as possible; shall keep a minute of its proceedings, executive and financial, and shall submit a full statement of the same, with the accounts audited, at every regular meeting of the National Council.

Article 8. The National Council shall meet at least once in six months, to receive the reports of the Committees, and to consider any new plan for the general good, for which it shall have power, at its option, to appoint a new Committee, and shall be empowered to receive and appropriate donations for the carrying out of the objects of the same. At all such meetings, eleven members shall constitute a quorum. In case any Committee neglect or refuse to send in its report, according to article 8th, then the Council shall have power to enter the bureau, examine the books and papers of such Committee; and in case the Committee shall persist in its refusal or neglect, then the Council shall declare their offices vacant, and appoint others in their stead.

Article 9. In all cases of the meetings of the National Council, or the Committees, the travelling expenses (if any) of the members shall be paid out of their respective funds.

Article 10. The Council shall immediately establish a bureau in the place of its meeting; and the same rooms shall, as far as possible, be used by the several Committees for their various purposes. The Council shall have a clerk, at a moderate salary, who shall keep a record of their transactions, and prepare a condensed report of the Committees for publication; and also a registry of the friends of the cause.

Article 11. The expenses of the Council shall be defrayed by the fees of membership of sub-societies or Councils, to be organized throughout the States. The membership fee shall be one cent per week.

Article 12. A member of the Council shall be a member of only one of the Committees thereof.

Article 13. All officers holding funds, shall give security in double the amount likely to be in their hands. This security to be given to the three first officers of the Council.

Article 14.   The Council shall have power to make such By-Laws as are necessary for their proper government.

Discussion Starters

1. Evaluate the convention's analysis of the black peoples' plight and the reasonableness of its requests.

2. As the convention saw it, how would improving the lot of free blacks constitute an attack upon slavery? Why would white abolitionists prefer a more direct assault on slavery?

3. What are the similarities and differences between the requests of this convention and the demands of blacks in recent years? How did the resistance to the movement then differ from the resistance blacks are meeting today?

4. The convention placed considerable emphasis on establishing citizenship of blacks as a basis for pressing their requests. The Dred Scott decision in 1857, which decreed that persons of African descent could not be citizens, was therefore a deadly blow to their aspirations. Why, on the other hand, did the establishment of citizenship in 1868 by the Fourteenth Amendment not provide full rights of citizenship for blacks, as might have been expected? What have been the long-term implications of the reluctance or refusal to permit blacks full rights of citizenship?

5. Immediately following the convention, Frederick Douglass, one of the principal writers of the convention's Address, wrote to a friend, "I hope you will like my address to the people of the United States. It is somewhat tame, but perhaps it will reach some minds which a more spirited document would not." Evaluate this strategy.

Related Documents

I. An Address to the Slaves of the United States of America

HENRY HIGHLAND GARNET

Considering the circumstances under which black Americans lived, the 1853 National Negro Convention reveals that they possessed noteworthy restraint and

Herbert Aptheker, ed., *A Documentary History of the Negro People in the United States* (New York: Citadel Press, 1951), I, pp. 228–31, 232–33.

common sense. Appeals to violence or even forcible resistance were not offered. This does not mean, however, that blacks lacked courage or that they favored only nonviolent methods. As early as 1823 a militant, inflammatory pamphlet, Walker's Appeal, *by David Walker, received wide circulation (and condemnation).*

Another passionate appeal for black freedom came in the call to rebellion raised by the Reverend Henry Highland Garnet at the 1843 National Negro Convention. Garnet, according to tradition a grandson of an African chieftain, escaped from slavery with his family through the Underground Railroad when he was only 10 years old. Despite obstacles he received a good education and became a Presbyterian clergyman. Only 27 when he delivered his famous address, Garnet was just beginning an outstanding career of service to the abolitionist cause.

A resolution calling for the adoption of Garnet's speech as the sentiment of the convention failed by one vote. The speech was later published and circulated by John Brown, and the ideas presented eventually became acceptable to many who had earlier opposed them, including the leading black abolitionist, Frederick Douglass.

Recognizing that Garnet's speech was directed toward slaves, while the address of the 1853 convention was intended for a white audience, what similarities of grievances can be noted? Had a similar call to resistance been given to free blacks, what purposeful resistance tactics might have been advocated?

SLAVERY! How much misery is comprehended in that single word. What mind is there that does not shrink from its direful effects? Unless the image of God be obliterated from the soul, all men cherish the love of liberty. The nice discerning political economist does not regard the sacred right more than the untutored African who roams in the wilds of Congo. Nor has the one more right to the full enjoyment of his freedom than the other. In every man's mind the good seeds of liberty are planted, and he who brings his fellow down so low, as to make him contented with a condition of slavery, commits the highest crime against God and man. Brethren, your oppressors aim to do this. They endeavor to make you as much like brutes as possible. When they have blinded the eyes of your mind—when they have embittered the sweet waters of life— when they have shut out the light which shines from the word of God—then, and not till then, has American slavery done its perfect work.

TO SUCH DEGRADATION IT IS SINFUL IN THE EXTREME FOR YOU TO MAKE VOLUNTARY SUBMISSION. The divine commandments you are in duty bound to reverence and obey. If you do not obey them, you will surely meet with the displeasure of the Almighty. He requires you to love Him supremely, and your neighbor as yourself—to keep the Sabbath day holy—to search the Scriptures—and bring up your children with respect for His laws, and to worship no other God but Him. But slavery sets all these at nought, and hurls defiance in the face of Jehovah. The forlorn condition in which you are placed does not destroy your obligation to God. You are not certain of heaven, because you allow yourselves to remain in a state of slavery, where you cannot obey the commandments of the Sovereign of the universe. If the ignorance of slavery is a passport to heaven, then it is a blessing, and no curse, and you should rather desire its perpetuity than its abolition. God will not receive slavery, nor ignorance, nor any other state of mind, for love and obedience to Him. Your condition does not absolve you from your moral obligation. The diabolical injustice by which your liberties are cloven down, NEITHER GOD NOR ANGELS, OR JUST MEN, COMMAND YOU TO SUFFER FOR A SINGLE MOMENT. THEREFORE IT IS YOUR SOLEMN AND IMPERATIVE DUTY TO USE EVERY MEANS, BOTH MORAL, INTELLECTUAL, AND PHYSICAL, THAT PROMISES SUCCESS. If a band of heathen men should attempt to enslave a race of Christians, and to place their children under the influence of some false religion, surely Heaven would frown upon the men who would not resist such aggression, even to death. If, on the other hand, a band of Christians should attempt to enslave a race of heathen men and to entail slavery upon them, and to keep them in heathenism in the midst of Christianity, the God of heaven would smile upon every effort which the injured might make to disenthral themselves.

Brethren, it is as wrong for your lordly oppressors to keep you in slavery as it was for the man thief to steal our ancestors from the coast of Africa. You should therefore now use the same manner of resistance as would have been just in our ancestors when the bloody foot-prints of the first remorseless soul-thief was placed upon the shores of our fatherland. The humblest peasant is as free in the sight of God as the proudest monarch that ever swayed a sceptre. Liberty is a spirit sent out from God, and like its great Author, is no respecter of persons.

Brethren, the time has come when you must act for yourselves. It is an old and true saying that, "if hereditary bondmen would be free, they must themselves strike the blow." You can plead your own cause, and do the work of emancipation better than any others. The nations of the Old World are moving in the great cause of universal freedom, and some of them at least will, ere long, do you justice. The combined powers of Europe have placed their broad seal of disapprobation upon the African slave-trade. But in the slave-holding parts of the United States the trade is as brisk as ever. They buy and sell you as though you were brute beasts. The North has done much—her opinion of slavery in the abstract is known. But in regard to the South, we adopt the opinion of the *New York Evangelist*—"We have advanced so far, that the cause apparently waits for a more effectual door to be thrown open than has been yet." We are about to point you to that more effectual door. Look around you, and behold the bosoms of your loving wives heaving with untold agonies! Here the cries of your poor children! Remember the stripes your fathers bore. Think of the torture and disgrace of your noble mothers. Think of your wretched sisters, loving virtue and purity, as they are driven into concubinage and are exposed to the unbridled lusts of incarnate devils. Think of the undying glory that hangs around the ancient name of Africa—and forget not that you are native-born American citizens, and as such you are justly entitled to all the rights that are granted to the freest. Think how many tears you have poured out upon the soil which you have cultivated with unrequited toil and enriched with your blood; and then go to your lordly enslavers and tell them plainly, that you *are determined to be free.* Appeal to their sense of justice, and tell them that they have no more right to oppress you than you have to enslave them. Entreat them to remove the grievous burdens which they have imposed upon you, and to remunerate you for your labor. Promise them renewed diligence in the cultivation of the soil, if they will render to you an equivalent for your services. Point them to the increase of happiness and prosperity in the British West Indies since the Act of Emancipation. Tell them in language which they cannot misunderstand of the exceeding sinfulness of slavery, and of a future judgment, and of the righteous retributions of an indignant God. Inform them that all you desire is FREEDOM, and that nothing else will suffice. Do this, and forever after cease to toil for the heartless tyrants, who give you no other reward but stripes and abuse. If they then commence work of death, they, and not you, will be responsible for the consequences. You had far better all die—*die immediately,* than live slaves, and entail your wretchedness upon your posterity. If you would be free in this generation, here is your only hope. However much you and all of us may desire it, there is not much hope of redemption without the shedding of blood. If you must bleed, let it all come at once—rather *die freemen than live to be the slaves. . . .*

You will not be compelled to spend much time in order to become inured to hardships. From the first movement that you breathed the air of heaven, you have been accustomed to nothing else but hardships. The heroes of the American Revolution were never put upon harder fare than a peck of corn and few herrings per week. You have not become enervated by the luxuries of life. Your sternest energies have been beaten out upon the anvil of severe trial. Slavery has done this to make you subservient to its own purposes; but it has done more than this, it has prepared you for any emergency. If you receive good treatment, it is what you can hardly expect; if you meet with pain, sorrow, and even death, these are the common lot of the slaves.

Fellowmen! patient sufferers! behold your dearest rights crushed to the earth! See your sons murdered, and your wives, mothers and sisters doomed to prostitution. In the name of the merciful God, and by all that life is worth, let it no longer be a debatable question, whether it is better to choose *liberty* or *death. . . .*

Brethren, arise, arise! Strike for your lives and liberties. Now is the day and the hour. Let every slave throughout the land do this, and the days of slavery are numbered. You cannot be more oppressed than you have been—you cannot suffer greater cruelties than you have already. *Rather die freemen than live to be slaves.* Remember that you are FOUR MILLIONS!

It is in your power so to torment the God-cursed slaveholders that they will be glad to let you go free. If the scale was turned, and black men were the masters and white men the slaves, every destructive agent and element would be employed to lay the oppressor low. Danger and death would hang over their heads day and night. Yes, the tyrants would meet with plagues more terrible than those of Pharaoh. But you are a patient people. You act as though you were made for the special use of these devils. You act as though your daughters were born to pamper the lusts of your masters and overseers. And worse than all, you tamely submit while your lords tear your wives from your embraces and defile them before your eyes. In the name of God, we ask, are you men? Where is the blood of your fathers? Has it all run out of your veins? Awake, awake; millions of voices are calling you! Your dead fathers speak to you from their graves. Heaven, as with a voice of thunder, calls on you to arise from the dust.

Let your motto be resistance! *resistance!* RESISTANCE! No oppressed people have ever secured their liberty without resistance. What kind of resistance you had better make you must decide by the circumstances that surround you, and according to the suggestion of expediency. Brethren, adieu! Trust in the living God. Labor for the peace of the human race, and remember that you are FOUR MILLIONS!

II. "What to Slaves is the Fourth of July?"

FREDERICK DOUGLASS

Although the citizenship of free blacks was stressed by the 1853 convention, black abolitionists were well aware of their second-class status. When called upon to speak at the 1852 Fourth of July Observance in Rochester, New York, Frederick Douglass delivered a caustic indictment of American practices.

In the portions included here, identify Douglass' most potent accusation. How "reasonable" are his charges? How does knowledge of the attitude reflected here alter one's interpretation of the documents of the 1853 convention, in which Douglass played a major role?

JULY 5, 1852

Fellow-citizens, pardon me, allow me to ask, why am I called upon to speak here to-day? What have I, or those I represent, to do with your national independence? Are the great principles of political freedom and of natural justice, embodied in that Declaration of Independence, extended to us? and am I, therefore, called upon to bring our humble offering to the national altar, and to confess the benefits and express devout gratitude for the blessings resulting from your independence to us?

Would to God, both for your sakes and ours, that an affirmative answer could be truthfully returned to these questions! Then would my task be light, and my burden easy and delightful. For *who* is there so cold, that a nation's

Philip S. Foner, ed. *The Life and Writings of Frederick Douglass,* II, pp. 188–89, 191–92. Reprinted by permission of International Publishers Co., Inc. Copyright © 1950.

sympathy could not warm him? Who so obdurate and dead to the claims of gratitude, that would not thankfully acknowledge such priceless benefits? Who so stolid and selfish, that would not give his voice to swell the hallelujahs of a nation's jubilee, when the chains of servitude had been torn from his limbs? I am not that man. In a case like that, the dumb might eloquently speak, and the "lame man leap as an hart."

But such is not the state of the case. I say it with a sad sense of the disparity between us. I am not included within the pale of this glorious anniversary! Your high independence only reveals the immeasurable distance between us. The blessings in which you, this day, rejoice, are not enjoyed in common. —The rich inheritance of justice, liberty, prosperity and independence, bequeathed by your fathers, is shared by you, not by me. The sunlight that brought light and healing to you, has brought stripes and death to me. This Fourth July is *yours*, not *mine*. *You* may rejoice, I must mourn. To drag a man in fetters into the grand illuminated temple of liberty, and call upon him to join you in joyous anthems, were inhuman mockery and sacrilegious irony. Do you mean, citizens, to mock me, by asking me to speak to-day? If so, there is a parallel to your conduct. And let me warn you that it is dangerous to copy the example of a nation whose crimes, towering up to heaven, were thrown down by the breath of the Almighty, burying that nation in irrevocable ruin! I can to-day take up the plaintive lament of a peeled and woe-smitten people!

"By the rivers of Babylon, there we sat down. Yea! we wept when we remembered Zion. We hanged our harps upon the willows in the midst thereof. For there, they that carried us away captive, required of us a song; and they who wasted us required of us mirth, saying, Sing us one of the songs of Zion. How can we sing the Lord's song in a strange land? If I forget thee, O Jerusalem, let my right hand forget her cunning. If I do not remember thee, let my tongue cleave to the roof of my mouth." . . .

Would you have me argue that man is entitled to liberty? that he is the rightful owner of his own body? You have already declared it. Must I argue the wrongfulness of slavery? Is that a question for Republicans? Is it to be settled by the rules of logic and argumentation, as a matter beset with great difficulty, involving a doubtful application of the principle of justice, hard to be understood? How should I look to-day, in the presence of Americans, dividing, and subdividing a discourse, to show that men have a natural right to freedom? speaking of it relatively and positively, negatively and affirmatively. To do so, would be to make myself ridiculous, and to offer an insult to your understanding.—There is not a man beneath the canopy of heaven that does not know that slavery is wrong *for him*.

What, am I to argue that it is wrong to make men brutes, to rob them of their liberty, to work them without wages, to keep them ignorant of their relations to their fellow men, to beat them with sticks, to flay their flesh with the lash, to load their limbs with irons, to hunt them with dogs, to sell them at auction, to sunder their families, to knock out their teeth, to burn their flesh, to starve them into obedience and submission to their masters? Must I argue that a system thus marked with blood, and stained with pollution, is *wrong*?

No! I will not. I have better employment for my time and strength than such arguments would imply.

What, then, remains to be argued? Is it that slavery is not divine; that God did not establish it; that our doctors of divinity are mistaken? There is blasphemy in the thought. That which is inhuman, cannot be divine! *Who* can reason on such a proposition? They that can, may; I cannot. The time for such argument is passed.

At a time like this, scorching irony, not convincing argument, is needed. O! had I the ability, and could I reach the nation's ear, I would, to-day, pour out a fiery stream of biting ridicule, blasting reproach, withering sarcasm, and stern rebuke. For it is not light that is needed, but fire; it is not the gentle shower, but thunder. We need the storm, the whirlwind, and the earthquake. The feeling of the nation must be quickened; the conscience of the nation must be roused; the propriety of the nation must be startled; the hypocrisy of the nation must be exposed; and its crimes against God and man must be proclaimed and denounced.

What, to the American slave, is your 4th of July? I answer; a day that reveals to him, more than all other days in the year, the gross injustice and cruelty to which he is the constant victim. To him, your celebration is a sham; your boasted liberty, an unholy license; your national greatness, swelling vanity; your sounds of rejoicing are empty and heartless; your denunciation of tyrants, brass fronted impudence; your shouts of liberty and equality, hollow mockery; your prayers and hymns, your sermons and thanksgivings, with all your religious parade and solemnity, are, to Him, mere bombast, fraud, deception, impiety, and hypocrisy—a thin veil to cover up crimes which would disgrace a nation of savages. There is not a nation on the earth guilty of practices more shocking and bloody than are the people of the United States, at this very hour.

Go where you may, search where you will, roam through all the monarchies and despotisms of the Old World, travel through South America, search out every abuse, and when you have found the last, lay your facts by the side of the everyday practices of this nation, and you will say with me, that, for revolting barbarity and shameless hypocrisy, America reigns without a rival.

III. The Possible Amelioration of Slavery: A Review of Uncle Tom's Cabin

From the perspective of the twentieth century it may be difficult to comprehend the magnitude of the obstacles faced by black Americans in the 1850s. A sympathetic review of Uncle Tom's Cabin, *by Harriet Beecher Stowe, in the literary journal* North American Review *reveals how blacks were regarded by even those who opposed slavery.*

The review called not for abolition of slavery, but for amelioration of the slave's plight. What could black abolitionists in the 1853 convention have done

Unsigned review, *North American Review,* October 1853 (Boston: Little, Brown), pp. 475–79.

to counter these ideas? Considering the attitudes expressed here, what would be the likely response of the reviewer to the militancy of blacks today?

OCTOBER 1853

The wealth and greatness of the South are the result of the labor of about 4,000,000 of negroes, directed by the superior intelligence of the whites. These negroes are, as a race, inferior in mental and moral force to the white race with whom they live. This inferiority is proved by their condition here and everywhere. Being the result of organization, it is a permanent inferiority. The negro is improvable to a certain point by contact with the civilized white, but only to a certain point. When that contact ceases, he relapses speedily into barbarism.

It is a law of nature, that the intellectually strong shall govern the weak; in other words, that the weak shall serve and obey the strong. As the white race is the permanently strong, and the negro race the permanently weak, it follows that so long as the two races live together, the negro must be the servant of the white.

But the negro, though inferior to the white, is still a man. He has intelligence, passions, moral sentiments, affections. He is capable of happiness and misery, of other pains and pleasures than those of the body. The laws of nature are all beneficent. If superior strength implies government, government implies duty and responsibility. The duty of the governing party is care, guidance, and protection, and it is responsible for the well-being of the party governed. From this duty and responsibility there is no escape. Whoever has charge of another incurs thereby an obligation of the highest character, which cannot be neglected, either by an individual or a nation, without incurring a heavy penalty. This obligation is a consequence of the great moral law of nature, which commands us to do good when in our power, to love our neighbor, to love even our enemies, to do unto others as we would that others should do unto us, and which binds together all men in one brotherhood, whatever the differences and distinctions of rank or race or nation.

If these principles be correct, it follows, that the negroes in the South are naturally and permanently the servants of the white race; that it is the duty of Southern legislatures to provide for their proper treatment, and to protect them from violence and outrage. The masters must be required to perform the duty of masters; so far as the law can compel, they must be compelled to exercise justice and humanity, kindness and care. It follows, also, that these same legislatures are responsible for the happiness of these 4,000,000 of toiling human beings; that in withdrawing from them the protection of law, in declaring that they do not and will not regard their welfare, but simply the profit of their owners, and thus delivering them up helpless victims to occasional brutality and vice, they have failed to perform a solemn duty.

These 4,000,000 of negroes, with their humble capacities for enjoyment and improvement, are worthy and meritorious objects for the attention and care of a wise and humane government. They are here. To send them away is impossible; to emancipate them, equally so. It would destroy great interests, it would endanger the peace of society, it would be disastrous to themselves. Ignorant, improvident, without self-sustaining energy of character, and of limited intellectual faculties, they are incapable of providing for their own support or caring for their own interests. Freedom to them would be like freedom to children, or to the domestic animals. It would be helplessness, abandonment, the absence of guidance and protection. Thus deserted, indolence, vice, and poverty would speedily degrade them below even their present condition, and they would gradually dwindle away and disappear, as they are disappearing in the North, where they are left to themselves to struggle with difficulties too great for their strength, difficulties arising from climate and social circumstances which do not exist in the original seat of their race, and which therefore they are not fitted, by nature, to encounter.

The negro is naturally the servant of the white man, because all mental inferiority is naturally the servant of mental superiority, the degree of servitude varying with the degree of inferiority. It is his happiest position. His docility, his good temper, his bodily vigor, his intellectual weakness, all fit him for it. As a servant, under just treatment, he thrives and rejoices, and is tormented by no ambition for a higher sphere. He is a servant in the North. The menial labors, the drudgery of society, to obey always and never to command, to be forever one of a degraded caste, are his portion there. He has the privilege of choosing his master and his employment; but on the other hand, he must take care of himself and his family, a task often too great for his feeble powers, amid the energetic stir and competition of a stronger race. But he has one advantage. Servant though he be; inferior by nature though he be; though he may neither sit in the legislature, nor on the bench, nor vote, nor enter the jury-box,—the law cares for him and protects him. He has civil rights, the right of self-defence, the right to wife and child, the right to hold property. Acts criminal and punished by law if committed against a white man, are equally criminal and punishable if committed against him. These rights are accorded to him in the North by the governing race,—some of them because it is just under all and any circumstances to give them; others, because the condition of society makes it safe to give them.

The negro is a servant in the North, but he is a slave in the South. Slavery is another and stricter form of servitude. The slave cannot choose his master, or his employment, or his place of residence, or acquire property. He may be compelled to labor, and his master has control over him, and may punish his vices, his idleness, his disobedience, or insubordination. This condition is imposed on the negro in the South, because the circumstances and interests of society there require it. It is rightfully imposed; for the white race are the natural rulers, and may justly regard their own safety and welfare as objects of paramount consideration. For these they must provide at all hazards; but, in doing so, they must not violate humanity and justice. They have among them this vast multitude of helpless and dependent beings, from whose labor they derive their wealth and importance. Slavery with them is a necessity, whatever may be its evils. The peace, security, and prosperity of society, the interests of commerce and the arts require it; the well being and safety of the negro himself require it. But the laborer is worthy of his hire; and thou shalt not muzzle the ox that treadeth out the corn. The free negro of the North makes his contract for his labor, and the law enforces it; he can defend himself and his family from aggression and outrage, and the law sustains him. The slave is deprived of the right to make a contract, of the right to defend himself and those dear to him, and the law should itself be to him all that it has taken away. The very helplessness, dependence, mental inferiority, and hard fate of this humble race call loudly, with the commanding voice of duty, on government to interpose, with special care, its protecting arm, to shield the slave from wrong by all the force and terrors of the law; to secure for him all the happiness of which his condition is capable.

The enormities of the law of the South, as it exists in the statutes and judicial decisions of the several States, arise from one great principle upon which the whole system is founded—that a slave is property.

This is an error. A slave is not, and cannot be, property. Such an idea is equally inconsistent with the nature of property and the nature of slavery; and it is because the institution has been thus founded on an untruth, that so much evil has flowed from it; for error is the source of all evil, and evil continually.

A slave is not property, because he is a man. A man cannot be the subject of property, though his labor may. He is not a thing. Even in the lowest forms of humanity, he has intellect, passions, sentiments, conscience, which establish his brotherhood with all men, which establish the theoretic equality of man as man, and separate him from the lower animals and material things. To man, to the race of men, the earth was given as an inheritance. Whatever he can make, or modify, or add value to, is property. But man was not given to man to possess. He is not a product of industry, but himself a producer.

A proposition so plain, it is difficult to make plainer by argument. Its truth is self-evident. No man can imagine himself to be property. Every instinct and impulse of his nature revolt at the idea. But the idea of subjection to a superior nature, of obedience and service in return for protection and care, of looking up to another for guidance and direction, is natural, arises at once from inequality of intellectual force, and pervades, in a greater or less degree, all the relations of life.

IV. The Liberator on Frederick Douglass

Frederick Douglass came to a parting of the ways with William Lloyd Garrison in 1851 when Douglass decided that the Constitution need not be regarded as a proslavery document. Contrary to Garrison, Douglass chose to believe that the Constitution could be interpreted in the light of its preamble, and that political means should be used to achieve political ends.

Journal of Negro History, July 1925, X, 380–84.

An unfortunate hostility developed between the two men, culminating in a diatribe by Garrison in The Liberator *in December 1853. To what extent does the breach, as revealed in this article, reflect honest differences of opinion on methods and approaches? How important a part did racial matters play in aggravating the differences? Might it be that Douglass' black militancy was at the root of Garrison's resentment?*

SEPTEMBER 16, 1853

> '*Either he must*
> *Confess himself wondrous malicious,*
> *Or be accused of folly.*'—CORIOLANUS.

In his paper of the 9th instant, FREDERICK DOUGLASS occupies twelve columns in reply to sundry brief articles in the *Pennsylvania Freeman, Anti-Slavery Standard, Bugle,* and *Liberator,* respecting his feelings and attitude towards his old friends and associates in the cause of emancipation. Such portions of it as relate to the other journals referred to, we leave them to dispose of as they may think proper. We quote all that is personal to us, in addition to a considerable portion of Mr. D's exordium; and from this sample, our readers can easily infer what the remainder must be.

The history of the Anti-Slavery struggle has been marked by instances of defection, alienation, apostasy, on the part of some of its most efficient supporters for a given time; but by none more signal, venomous, or extraordinary, than the present. Mr. DOUGLASS now stands self-unmasked, his features flushed with passion, his air scornful and defiant, his language bitter as wormwood, his pen dipped in poison; as thoroughly changed in his spirit as was ever 'arch-angel ruined,' and as artful and unscrupulous a schismatic as has yet appeared in the abolition ranks.

Having long endeavored, by extreme forbearance, to avoid any collision with him; having omitted in many cases to make even a passing reference to what we deemed unworthy of his position; having criticised, with brevity and moderation, some very objectionable articles from his pen, only because we could not be true to our convictions of duty, if we suppressed the expression of our surprise and sorrow; and having no feelings of personal animosity to gratify; we have no intention to make a protracted rejoinder in the present case, but shall submit the whole matter, in a very few words, to the impartial judgment of all who take any interest in the controversy.

It is difficult to believe that the author of the article of 'enormous' length and character, now under consideration, is the FREDERICK DOUGLASS once so manly, generous, and faithful. The transformation—or, rather, the revelation—is the most astounding and severely painful event in our experience; and 'the end is not yet.' He now assumes an attitude which is eliciting the warmest encomiums from the most malignant enemies of the Anti-Slavery movement, and which is undisguisedly hostile to his old companion in arms. No marvel, therefore, that he can speak of the 'Garrisonians' with as much flippancy as any of our pro-slavery contemners; or that he can aver, '*Word*-wise, these Garrisonians are my best friends—*deed*-wise, I have no more vigilant enemies'; or that he is able to say of the 'REFUGE OF OPPRESSION,' that, 'of late, it has become about the best part of Mr. Garrison's paper, and about which nobody cares a single straw;' or that he can utter the monstrous untruth, that 'a fierce and bitter warfare' is waged against him, 'under the generalship of William Lloyd Garrison,' with a view to destroy *his anti-slavery usefulness!!*

The untruthfulness of Mr. D. is matched only by his adroitness in striving to excite popular sympathy, as though he were a poor innocent lamb, about to be torn in pieces by a pack of famished wolves! Though he is the aggressor, he affects to have made no effort even in self-defence, and whiningly says— 'I shall be silent no longer (!) The impunity allowed to my adversaries, by my silence, like all other submission to wrong, has failed to soften the heart of the wrong-doers (!) They have waxed more arrogant as I have waxed humble' (!) 'Gerrit Smith is an independent nation. Alas! I am but a rebel. While those against whom I have rebelled would treat with Mr. Smith, they would hang me.' Again—'I had reason to know that prejudice against color—yes, prejudice against my race, would be invoked, as it has been invoked, on the side of my adversaries (!)—and in all the likelihoods of the case, the question between me and my old friends would be decided in this case as between white and black—in favor of the former, and against the latter—the white man to rise, as an injured benefactor, and the black man to fall, as a miserable ingrate' (!) Again—'The spectacle of a rich (!) and powerful (!) organization, largely provided with the appliances of moral warfare, is not seen marshalling its forces, its presses, and its speakers, for the moral extermination of one humble, solitary individual (!!!)—for the purpose of silencing, and putting to open shame, *a fugitive slave,* (!) simply because that fugitive slave has dared to differ from that Society, or from the leading individuals in it, as to the manner in which he shall exercise his powers for the promotion of the anti-slavery cause, and the elevation of the free people of color in the United States (!!) Again— 'The hatchet of fratricidal war is uplifted; nay, it is now flung at the head of its appointed victim, with the combined force of three strong arms, and with the deadly aim of three good marksmen' (!!!) And this is his estimate of the American Anti-Slavery Society, its presses, and its speakers! Now, as a specimen of low cunning and malignant defamation, we have never seen this surpassed. It is too palpable to need a single word in reply, and we should be lost to all self-respect to treat it as worthy of serious consideration.

Mr. Douglass sneers at the regret expressed by us, and others, at the necessity of noticing his hostile assaults, and scoffingly says—'They have had to overcome mountains of reluctance in getting at me; and it is amazing, considering the ruggedness of these mountains, that they ever succeeded in crossing their Alpine heights!' If this does not indicate either that we have never, in his opinion, been his true friends, or that, ever selfish and untrue himself, he is incapable of experiencing the pang of misplaced confidence and disappointed friendship, we know not how to interpret language. In either case, it places him in a most unenviable position.

Jaundiced in vision, and inflamed with passion, he affects to regard us as the 'disparager' (!) of the colored race, and artfully endeavors to excite their jealousy and opposition by utterly perverting the meaning of our language. We said, that 'the Anti-Slavery cause, both religiously and politically, has transcended the ability of the sufferers from American slavery and prejudice, *as a class,* to keep pace with it, or to perceive what are its demands, or to understand the philosophy of its operations'—meaning by this, that the cause requires religious and political sacrifices, which, 'as a class,' they do not yet see, or, seeing, are not yet prepared to make, even though they are the victims to be delivered—and also meaning that what was at first supposed to be local, is now seen to have a world-wide bearing, and must be advocated upon world-wide principles, irrespective of complexional differences. There is nothing really or intentionally invidious in a statement like this: and yet, how does Mr. Douglass treat it? 'The colored man,' he says, 'ought to feel profoundly grateful for this magnificent compliment to their high moral worth and breadth of comprehension, so generously bestowed by William Lloyd Garrison! Who will doubt, hereafter, the *natural* inferiority of the negro, when the great champion of the negroes rights *thus broadly concedes all that is claimed respecting the negro's inferiority by the bitterest despisers of the negro race'!!!* Now, if this were blundering stupidity, it might readily be pardoned; but it is unmitigated baseness, and therefore inexcusable.

Again we said—'It does not follow, that, because a man is or has been a slave, or because he is identified with a class meted out and trodden under foot, therefore he will be the truest to the cause of human freedom'—a truism which nothing can make plainer. Yet Mr. Douglass presumes upon the color of his skin to vindicate his superior fidelity to that cause, and to screen himself from criticism and rebuke! This trick cannot succeed. Of the colored people he says—'What is theory to others, is practice to them. Every day and hour is crowded with lessons to them on the subject, to which the whites, as a class, are strangers.' Very true—but what then? Does it indicate the same regard for universal justice, for those who are oppressed to desire to gain their freedom, as it does for others, not of their complexion, and not involved in their suffering, to encounter deadly perils and make liberal sacrifices in seeking their liberation? The former may be animated by motives limited to a narrow selfishness; the latter must be actuated by feelings of disinterested benevolence and world-wide philanthropy. Once, Mr. Douglass would have promptly recognized this distinction; now, beneath the blackness of his skin he is attempting to hide the blackness of his treachery.

For Further Reading

The most important book on this subject is *Black Abolitionists** (1969), by Benjamin Quarles. Several related volumes are *American Slavery: The Question of Black Resistance** (1971) and *Blacks in the Abolitionist's Movement** (1971), edited by John H. Bracey, August Meier, and Elliott Rudwick. An out-of-print

*Paperbound edition available.

but still useful work is Herbert Aptheker's *The Negro in the Abolitionist Movement* (1941). See also the Aptheker volumes from which the core document of this chapter was taken.

An account of what slavery meant to blacks who had fled to Canada was provided by Daniel Drew in *The Refugee* (1856; reprinted in 1968). On the subject of free blacks there is Leon F. Litwack's *North of Slavery* (1961).

Recent interpretations of abolitionism, including a highly pertinent one by Litwack, are found in *The Antislavery Vanguard** (1965), edited by Martin Duberman. More general studies of abolitionism are: John L. Thomas, *Slavery Attacked: The Abolitionist Crusade* (1964); Dwight L. Dumond, *Antislavery: The Crusade for Freedom in America** (1961); Carlton Mabee, *Black Freedom: The Nonviolent Abolitionists from 1830 Through the Civil War* (1970); and Sherman W. Savage, *The Controversy over the Distribution of Abolition Literature, 1830–1860* (1938; reprinted in 1968).

Documents on abolitionism are found in *The Abolitionists: A Collection of Their Writings** (1963); and in *And Why Not Every Man: A Documentary Story of the Fight Against Slavery in the United States* (1969), both edited by Herbert Aptheker.

Problems books are: Richard Curry, ed., *The Abolitionists: Reformers or Fanatics?** (1965); Hugh Hawkins, ed., *The Abolitionists: Immediatism and the Question of Means** (1964); and Bernard Weisberger, ed., *Abolitionism: Disrupter of the Democratic System or Agent of Progress?** (1963).

On the leading black abolitionist, see *Life and Times of Frederick Douglass** (1892, 1962), written by himself. Also available is *Frederick Douglass** (1968), edited by Benjamin Quarles.

*Paperbound edition available.

13. Manifest Destiny Challenged

Since the day they first set foot on North American soil, Americans have been moving westward almost as if their destiny was to be found there. By the 1840s the westward movement was linked with expansionism, and the concept of manifest destiny became popular. The term "manifest destiny" was coined by John L. O'Sullivan, editor of the *United States Magazine and National Review*. In July 1845 he proclaimed in his newspaper that it was America's "manifest destiny to overspread the continent allotted by Providence for the free development of our yearly multiplying millions."

A wave of national enthusiasm for expansion had brought James K. Polk and the Democrats to power in the elections of 1844 on a platform calling for the annexation of Texas and Oregon. Lame-duck President John Tyler seized the opportunity to preside over the admission of Texas to the Union by a joint resolution of Congress in the winter of 1845, and the Oregon question was resolved early in 1846. But expansionist sentiment was not yet satisfied. Covetous eyes were still looking toward territory held by Mexico.

In the winter of 1846 expansionist designs upon Mexican territory had hit a roadblock. John Slidell had been sent by Polk to negotiate the purchase of the desired territory, but the Mexican government had refused to meet with him. His lack of success prompted Polk to order General Zachary Taylor to move his American forces into the land between the Nueces and Rio Grande rivers, the territory in question. In response to this movement, regarded by the Mexicans as an invasion, fighting broke out in April. On May 13, 1846, war was declared by the United States against the Republic of Mexico.

The actions of the Polk administration in precipitating the war concerned many groups in the United States, especially the Whig party. The opposition by the Whigs and some antislavery Democrats, such as Congressman David Wilmot of Pennsylvania, was a constant irritation to the Polk administration. This irritation intensified after the Whig and antislavery Democrats increased their strength in Congress in the elections of 1846.

The rising dissent against the war, especially in the North, aroused considerable feeling in Congress against war appropriations. With the prospect of a congressional revolt over administration policies, and with the successful American occupation of Mexico City in September 1847, President Polk sent a peace treaty to the Senate in February 1848. Known as the Treaty of Guadalupe Hidalgo, it had been negotiated by Nicholas Trist, who, because he had been recalled earlier by Polk, was not authorized to negotiate for the United States. But authorized or not, Trist negotiated a treaty, which was later ratified by the Senate, that brought the last third of the present continental United States under the American flag.

Thus ended the Mexican War, a war seen by some as aggression and by others as the fulfillment of destiny. It was a war that brought to a head the issues that were to occupy the minds of Americans for the next ten years and to finally bring civil war in 1861. It was a war in which dissent became a major factor in bringing about peace. The documents in this chapter offer insights into the arguments and attitudes of the principal dissenters of "manifest destiny."

Core Document

Let Us Call Home Our Armies

THOMAS CORWIN

Thomas Corwin, the Whig senator from Ohio during the years of the Mexican War, helped to lead the antiwar protest in the Senate. Corwin was not new to Congress, for he had served for ten years in the House of Representatives during the Democratic administrations of Jackson and Van Buren. In 1840 he was elected on the Whig platform as governor of Ohio. Although the Democrats won the presidency in 1844 with James Knox Polk, in Ohio the Whigs retained a majority in the General Assembly. This majority chose former Governor Corwin in 1844 to represent Ohio in the Senate.

Josiah Morrow, ed., *Life and Speeches of Thomas Corwin* (Cincinnati: W. H. Anderson, 1896), pp. 278–81, 283–84, 288–90, 294–95, 298–302, 305–8, 311–14.

Corwin's stand on the war again placed him in the minority, but he still spoke out against what he believed to be an unjust war. His dissent brought criticism from both Democrats and Whigs, who in their most extreme forms condemned him as a traitor to his country. The protest against Corwin became so great that petitions were sent to the General Assembly of Ohio demanding his removal from office. After considerable pressure and publicity, an investigating committee reported a vote of confidence to the Assembly and Corwin served out his term.

But it was the congressional pressure of Corwin and men like him that helped Polk decide to send the Treaty of Guadalupe Hidalgo to the Senate, thereby ending the war. Corwin later served as secretary of the treasury under President Millard Fillmore, but more important, he was chosen by Abraham Lincoln as ambassador to Mexico during the crucial years of 1861–64.

In reading Senator Corwin's speech note what he believed to be:

- *the relationship between Congress and the president over the declaration of war.*
- *the only defense Congress had against a tyrannical president.*
- *the reasons why the Mexican War was an unjust war.*
- *the answer to the administration's desire to "conquer a peace."*
- *the justice or injustice of fighting for indemnity and more room for Americans.*
- *the answer to the argument that territorial expansion was the destiny of America.*
- *the expected result of the war.*

FEBRUARY 11, 1847

Mr. President:

... The Senator from Michigan [MR. CASS], in contemplating the present aspects and probably future course of our public affairs, declared that he saw nothing to alarm the fears or depress the hopes of the patriot. To his serene, and, as I fear, too apathetic mind, all is calm; the sentinel might sleep securely on his watch-tower. The ship of State seems to him to expand her sails under a clear sky, and move on, with prosperous gales, upon a smooth sea. He admonishes all not to anticipate evil to come, but to fold their hands and close their eyes in quietude, ever mindful of the consolatory text, "sufficient unto the day is the evil thereof." But the Senator from South Carolina [MR. CALHOUN], summoning from the depths of his thoughtful and powerful mind all its energies, and looking abroad on the present condition of the republic, is pained with fearful apprehension, doubt, distrust and dismay. To his vision, made strong by a long life of careful observation, made keen by a comprehensive view of past history, the sky seems overcast with impending storms, and the dark future is shrouded in impenetrable gloom. When two such minds thus differ, those less familiar with great subjects affecting the happiness of nations may well pause, before they rush to a conclusion on this, a subject which, in all its bearings, immediate and remote, affects *certainly* the present prosperity, and *probably* the liberty, of two republics, embracing together nearly thirty millions of people. Mr. President, it is a fearful responsibility we have assumed; engaged in flagrant, desolating war with a neighboring republic, to us thirty millions of God's creatures look up for that moderated wisdom which, if possible, may stay the march of misery, and restore to them, if it may be so, mutual feelings of good-will, with all the best blessings of peace.

I sincerely wish it were in my power to cherish those placid convictions of security which have settled upon the mind of the Senator from Michigan. So far from this, I have been, in common with the Senator from South Carolina, oppressed with melancholy forebodings of evils to come, and not unfrequently by a conviction that each step we take in this unjust war, may be the last in our career; that each chapter we write in Mexican blood, may close the volume of our history as a free people. . . .

. . . Mr. President, it is no purpose of mine to arraign the conduct of the United States upon that occasion; it is no purpose of mine to treat this young and newly-adopted sister—the State of Texas—as an alien or stranger in this family of republics. I allude to this only to show how little reliance is to be placed upon those favorable anticipations in which gentlemen indulge with regard to consequences which may flow from measures to which they are strongly wedded, either by feeling or party attachment.

Is there nothing else in our history of even the past year to justify the Senator from South Carolina in the pregnant declaration, that in the whole period of his public life, comprehending the most eventful in the history of the Republic, there had never been a time when so much danger was threatened to the interests, happiness and liberties of the people. Sir, if any one could sit down, free from the excitements and biases which belong to public affairs— could such a one betake himself to those sequestered solitudes, where thoughtful men extract the philosophy of history from its facts, I am quite sure no song of "all's well" would be heard from his retired cell. . . .

He would find written in that Constitution, *Congress* shall have power to declare war; he would find everywhere, in that old charter, proofs clear and strong, that they who framed it intended that Congress, composed of two Houses, the representatives of the States, and the people, should (if any were pre-eminent) be the controlling power. He would find there a President designated; whose general and almost exclusive duty it is to *execute*, not to *make* the law. Turning from this to the history of the last ten months, he would find that the President alone, without the advice or consent of Congress, had, by a bold usurpation, made war on a neighboring republic; and what is quite as much to be deplored, that Congress, whose high powers were thus set at naught and defied, had, with ready and tame submission, yielded to the usurper the wealth and power of the nation to execute his will, as if to swell his iniquitous triumph over the very Constitution which he and they had alike sworn to support. . . .

Now, Mr. President, I have already stated that I do not intend to occupy the Senate with a discussion of those varieties of topics which naturally enforce themselves upon my attention in considering this subject. It must have occurred to everybody how utterly impotent the Congress of the United States *now* is for any purpose whatever, but that of yielding to the President every demand which he makes for men and money, unless they assume that *only* position which is left—that which, in the history of other countries, in times favorable to human liberty, has been so often resorted to as a check upon arbitrary power—withholding money, refusing to grant the services of men when demanded for purposes which are not deemed to be proper.

When I review the doctrines of the Majority here, and consider their application to the existing war, I confess I am at a loss to determine whether the world is to consider our conduct as a ridiculous farce, or be lost in amazement at such absurdity in a people calling themselves free. The President, without asking the consent of Congress, involves us in war, and the majority here, without reference to the justice or necessity of the war, call upon us to grant men and money at the pleasure of the President, who they say, is charged with the duty of carrying on the war and responsible for its result. If we grant the means thus demanded, the President can carry forward this war for any end, or from any motive, without limit of time or place. . . .

Mr. President, I trust we shall abandon the idea, the heathen, barbarian notion, that our true national glory is to be won, or retained, by military prowess or skill in the art of destroying life. And, while I cannot but lament, for the permanent and lasting renown of my country, that she should command the sevice of her children in what I must consider wanton, unprovoked, *unnecessary*, and, therefore, unjust war, I can yield to the brave soldier, whose trade is war, and whose duty is obedience, the highest meed of praise for his courage, his enterprise and perpetual endurance of the fatigues and horrors of war. I know the gallant men who are engaged in fighting your battles possess personal bravery equal to any troops, in any land, anywhere engaged in the business of war. I do not believe we are less capable in the art of destruction than others, or less willing, on the slightest pretext, to unsheath the sword, and consider "revenge a virtue." I could wish, also, that your brave soldiers, while they bleed and die on the battle-field, might have (what in this war is impossible) the consolation to feel and know that their blood flowed in defense of a great right—that their lives were a meet sacrifice to an exalted principle.

But, sir, I return to our relations with Mexico. Texas, I have shown, having won her independence, and torn from Mexico about one-fourth part of her territory, comes to the United States, sinks her national character into the less elevated, but more secure, position of *one* of the United States of America. The revolt of Texas, her successful war with Mexico, and a consequent loss of a valuable province, all inured to the ultimate benefit of our Government and our country. While Mexico was weakened and humbled, we, in the same proportion, were strengthened and elevated. All this was done against the wish, the interest and the earnest remonstrance of Mexico. . . .

I do not say that Mexico had a right to make war upon us because our citizens chose to seek their fortunes in the fields of Texas. I do not say she had a right to treat you as a belligerent power because you permitted your citizens to march in battalions and regiments from your shores, for the avowed purpose of insurrectionary war in Texas—but I was not alone at the time in expressing my astonishment that all this did not work an open rupture between the two Republics at that time. We all remember your proclamations of neutrality— we know that in defiance of these, your citizens armed themselves and engaged in the Texan revolt; and it is true that without such aid Texas would this day have been, as she then was, an integral portion of the Mexican republic. Sir, Mexicans knew this then, they knew it when, seven years after, you coolly took this province under your protection and made it your own. Do you wonder, therefore, after all this, that when Texas did thus forcibly pass away from them and come to us, that prejudice amounting to hate, resentment implacable as revenge toward us, should seize and possess and madden the entire population of a country thus weakened, humbled, contemned? . . .

It is therefore a mere question of fact; and how will it be pretended that that country, lying between the Nueces and the Del Norte, to which your army was ordered, and of which it took possession, was subject to Texan law and not Mexican law? What did your general find there? What did he write home? Do you hear of any trial by jury on the east bank of the Rio Grande—of Anglo Saxons making cotton there with their negroes? No! You hear of Mexicans residing peacefully there, but fleeing from their cotton-fields at the approach of your army—no slaves, for it had been a decree of the Mexican government, years ago, that no slaves should exist there. If there were a Texan population on the east bank of the Rio Grande, why did not General Taylor hear something of those Texans hailing the advent of the American army, coming to protect them from the ravages of the Mexicans, and the more murderous onslaughts of the neighboring savages?

Do you hear anything of that? No! On the contrary, the population fled at the approach of your army. In God's name, I wish to know if it has come to this, that when an American army goes to protect American citizens on American territory, they flee from it as if from the most barbarous enemy? Yet such is the ridiculous assumption of those who pretend that, on the east bank of the Rio Grande, where your arms took possession, there were Texan population, Texan power, Texan laws, and American United States power and law! No, Mr. President, when I see that stated in an Executive document, written by the finger of a President of the United States, and when you read in those documents, with which your tables groan, the veracious account of that noble old General Taylor, of his reception in that country, and of those men—to use the language of one of his officers—fleeing before the invaders; when you compare these two documents together, is it not a biting sarcasm upon the *sincerity* of public men—a bitter satire upon the *gravity* of all public affairs?

Can it be, Mr. President, that the honest, generous, Christian people of the United States will give contenance to this egregious, palpable misrepresentation of fact—this bold falsification of history? Shall it be written down in your public annals, when the world looking on and you yourselves know, that

Mexico, and not Texas, possessed this territory to which your armies marched? As Mexico had never been dispossessed by Texan power, neither Texas nor your Government had any more claim to it than you now have to California, that other possession of Mexico over which your all-grasping avarice has already extended its remorseless dominion. . . .

While the American President can command the army, thank Heaven I can command the purse. While the President, under the penalty of death, can command your officers to proceed, I can tell them to come back, or the President can supply them as he may. He shall have no funds from me in the prosecution of a war which I cannot approve. That I conceive to be the duty of a Senator. I am not mistaken in that. If it be my duty to grant whatever the President demands, for what am I here? Have I no will upon the subject? Is it not placed at my discretion, understanding, judgment? Have an American Senate and House of Representatives nothing to do but obey the bidding of the President, as the army he commands is compelled to obey under penalty of death? No! The representatives of the sovereign people and sovereign States were never elected for such purposes as that.

Have Senators reflected on the great power which the command of armies in war confers upon any one, but especially on him who is at once the civil and military chief of the government? . . .

. . . [I]n England, since 1688, it has not been in the power of a British sovereign to do that, which in your boasted Republic, an American president, under the auspices of what you call Democracy, has done—make war, without consent of the legislative power. In England, supplies are at once refused, if Parliament does not approve the objects of the war. *Here*, as we are told, we must not look to the objects of the war, being *in the war*—made by the President—we must help him to fight it out, should it even please him to carry it to the utter extermination of the Mexican race. Sir, I believe it must proceed to this shocking extreme, if you are, by war, to "conquer a peace." Here, then, is your condition. The President involves you in war without your consent. Being *in* such a war, it is demanded as a duty, that we grant men and money to carry it on. The President tells us he shall prosecute this war, till Mexico pays us, or agrees to pay us, all its expenses. I am not willing to scourge Mexico thus; and the only means left me is to say to the commander-in-chief, "Call home your army, I will feed and clothe it no longer; you have whipped Mexico into three pitched battles, this is revenge enough; this is punishment enough."

The President has said he does not expect to hold Mexican territory by conquest. Why then conquer it? Why waste thousands of lives and millions of money fortifying towns and creating governments, if, at the end of the war, you retire from the graves of your soldiers and the desolated country of your foes, only to get money from Mexico for the expense of all your toil and sacrifice? Who ever heard, since Christianity was propagated among men, of a nation taxing its people, enlisting its young men and marching off two thousand miles to fight a people merely to be paid for it in money? . . . Sir, I have no patience with this flagitious notion of fighting for indemnity, and this under the equally absurd and hypocritical pretense of securing an honorable peace. An honorable peace! If you have accomplished the objects of the war (if indeed you had an object which you dare to avow), cease to fight, and you will have peace. Conquer your insane love of false glory, and you will "conquer a peace." Sir, if your commander-in-chief will not do this, I will endeavor to compel him, and as I find no other means, I shall refuse supplies—without the money of the people, he cannot go further. He asks me for that money; I wish him to bring your armies home, to cease shedding blood *for* money; if he refuses, I will refuse supplies, and then I know he *must*, he will cease his further sale of the lives of my countrymen. May we not, *ought* we not now to do this? I can hear no reason why we should not, except this: It is said that we are *in* war, wrongfully it may be, but, being in, the President is responsible, and we must give *him* the means *he* requires! He responsible! Sir, we, we are responsible, if having the power to stay this plague, we refuse to do so. When it shall be so—when the American Senate and the American House of Representatives can stoop from their high position, and yield a dumb compliance with the behests of a president who is, for the time being, commander of your army; when they will open the treasury with one hand, and the veins of all the soldiers in the land with the other, *merely because* the President commands, then, sir, it matters little how soon some Cromwell shall come into this Hall and say, "the Lord hath no further need of you here." When we fail to do the work, "whereunto we were sent," we shall be, we ought to be, removed, and give place to others who will. The fate of the barren fig-tree will be ours— Christ cursed it and it withered.

. . . [Y]ou have overrun half of Mexico, you have exasperated and irritated her people, you claim indemnity for all expenses incurred in doing this mischief, and boldly ask her to give up New Mexico and California; and, as a bribe to her patriotism, seizing on her property, you offer three millions to pay the soldiers she has called out to repel your invasion, on condition that she will give up to you at least one-third of her whole territory. . . .

What is the territory, Mr. President, which you propose to wrest from Mexico? It is consecrated to the heart of the Mexican by many a well-fought battle, with his old Castilian master. His Bunker Hills, and Saratogas, and Yorktowns are there. The Mexican can say, "There I bled for Liberty! and shall I surrender that consecrated home of my affections to the Anglo-Saxon invaders? What do they want with it? They have Texas already. They have possessed themselves of the territory between the Nueces and the Rio Grande. What else do they want? To what shall I point my children as memorials of that independence which I bequeath to them, when those battle-fields shall have passed from my possession?"

Sir, had one come and demanded Bunker Hill of the people of Massachusetts, had England's lion ever showed himself there, is there a man over thirteen, and under ninety who would not have been ready to meet him—is there a river on this continent that would not have run red with blood—is there a field but would have been piled high with the unburied bones of slaughtered Americans before these consecrated battle-fields of liberty should have been wrested from us? But this same American goes into a sister republic, and says to poor, weak Mexico, "Give up your territory—you are unworthy to possess it—I have got one-half already—all I ask of you is to give up the other!" England might as well, in the circumstances I have described, have come and demanded of us, "Give up the Atlantic slope—give up this trifling territory from the Alleghany mountains to the sea; it is only from Maine to St. Mary's —only about one-third of your Republic, and the least interesting portion of it." What would be the response? They would say, we must give this up to John Bull. Why? "He wants room." The Senator from Michigan says he must have this. Why, my worthy Christian brother, on what principle of justice? "I want room!"

Sir, look at this pretense of want of room. With twenty millions of people, you have about one thousand millions of acres of land, inviting settlement by every conceivable argument—bringing them down to a quarter of a dollar an acre, and allowing every man to squat where he pleases. But the Senator from Michigan says we will be two hundred millions in a few years, and we want room. If I were a Mexican I would tell you, "Have you not room in your own country to bury your dead men? If you come into mine we will greet you with bloody hands, and welcome you to hospitable graves."

Why, says the Chairman of this Committee of Foreign Relations, it is the most reasonable thing in the world! We ought to have the Bay of San Francisco. Why? Because it is the best harbor on the Pacific! It has been my fortune, Mr. President, to have practiced a good deal in criminal courts in the course of my life, but I never yet heard of a thief, arraigned for stealing a horse, plead that it was the best horse that he could find in the country! We want California. What for? Why, says the Senator from Michigan, we will have it; and the Senator from South Carolina, with a very mistaken view, I think, of policy, says, you can't keep our people from going there. I don't desire to prevent them. Let them go and seek their happiness in whatever country or clime it pleases them.

All I ask of them is, not to require this Government to protect them with that banner consecrated to war waged for principles—eternal, enduring truth. Sir, it is not meet that our old flag should throw its protecting folds over expeditions for lucre or for land. But you still say, you want room for your people. This has been the plea of every robber-chief from Nimrod to the present hour. I dare say, when Tamerlane descended from his throne built of seventy thousand human skulls, and marched his ferocious battalions to further slaughter, I dare say he said, "I want room." . . .

Why is it, sir, that we of the United States, a people of yesterday compared with the older nations of the world, should be waging war for territory—for "room?" Look at your country, extending from the Alleghany Mountains to the Pacific Ocean, capable itself of sustaining, in comfort, a larger population than will be in the whole Union for one hundred years to come. Over this vast expanse of territory your population is now so sparse that I believe we provided, at the last session, a regiment of mounted men to guard the mail, from the frontier of Missouri to the mouth of the Columbia: and yet you persist in the ridiculous assertion, "I want room." One would imag ʌe, from the frequent reiteration of the complaint, that you had a bursting, teeming population, whose energy was paralyzed, whose enterprise was crushed, for want of space. Why should we be so weak or wicked as to offer this idle apology for ravaging a neighboring republic? It will impose on no one at home or abroad.

Mr. President, this uneasy desire to augment our territory has depraved the moral sense and blunted the otherwise keen sagacity of our people. What has been the fate of all nations who have acted upon the idea that they must advance! Our young orators cherish this notion with a fervid, but fatally mistaken zeal. They call it by the mysterious name of "destiny." "Our destiny," they say is "onward," and hence they argue, with ready sophistry, the propriety of seizing upon any territory and any people that may lie in the way of our "fated" advance. . . .

Mr. President, if the history of our race has established any truth, it is but a confirmation of what is written, "the way of the transgressor is hard." Inordinate ambition, wantoning in power and spurning the humble maxims of justice has—ever has—and ever shall end in ruin. Strength cannot always trample upon weakness—the humble shall be exalted, the bowed down will at length be lifted up. It is by faith in the law of strict justice, and the practice of its precepts, that nations alone can be saved. All the annals of the human race, sacred and profane, are written over with this great truth, in characters of living light. It is my fear, my fixed belief, that in this invasion, this war with Mexico, we have forgotten this vital truth. Why is it, that we have been drawn into this whirlpool of war? How clear and strong was the light that shone upon the path of duty a year ago! The last disturbing question with England was settled—our power extended its peaceful sway from the Atlantic to the Pacific; from the Alleghanies we looked out upon Europe, and from the tops of the Stony Mountains we could descry the shores of Asia; a rich commerce with all the nations of Europe poured wealth and abundance into our lap on the Atlantic side, while an unoccupied commerce of three hundred millions of Asiatics waited on the Pacific for our enterprise to come and possess it. One hundred millions of dollars will be wasted in this fruitless war. Had this money of the people been expended in making a railroad from your northern lakes to the Pacific, as one of your citizens has begged of you in vain, you would have made a highway for the world between Asia and Europe. Your Capital then would be within thirty or forty days' travel of any and every point on the map of the civilized world. Through this great artery of trade, you would have carried through the heart of your own country, the teas of China and the spices of India to the markets of England and France. Why, why, Mr. President, did we abandon the enterprises of peace, and betake ourselves to the barbarous achievements of war? Why did we "forsake *this* fair and fertile field to batten on that moor."

But, Mr. President, if further acquisition of territory is to be the result either of conquest or treaty, then I scarcely know which should be preferred, eternal war with Mexico, or the hazards of internal commotion at home, which last, I fear, *may* come if another province is to be added to our territory. There is one topic connected with this subject which I tremble when I approach, and yet I cannot forbear to notice it. It meets you in every step you take. It threatens you which way soever you go in the prosecution of this war. I allude to the question of Slavery. Opposition to its further extension, it must be obvious to every one, is a deeply-rooted determination with men of all parties in what we call the non-slaveholding States. New York, Pennsylvania and Ohio, three of the most powerful, have already sent their legislative instructions here—so it will be, I doubt not, in all the rest. It is vain now to speculate about the reasons for this. Gentlemen of the South may call it prejudice, passion, hypocrisy, fanaticism. I shall not dispute with them now on that point. The great fact that it is so, and not otherwise, is what it concerns us to know. You nor I cannot alter or change this opinion if we would. These people only say, we will not, cannot consent that you shall carry slavery where it does not already exist. They do not seek to disturb you in that institution, as it exists in your States. Enjoy it if you will, and as you will. This is their language, this their determination. How is it in the South? Can it be expected that they should expend in common, their blood and their treasure, in the acquisition of immense territory, and then willingly forgo the right to carry thither their slaves, and inhabit the conquered country if they please to do so? Sir, I know the feelings and opinions of the South too well to calculate on this. Nay, I believe they would even contend to any extremity for the mere *right*, had they no wish to exert it. I believe (and I confess I tremble when the conviction presses upon me) that there is equal obstinacy on both sides of this fearful question. If then, we persist in war, which if it terminate in anything short of a more wanton waste of blood as well as money, must end (as this bill proposes) in the acquisition of territory, to which at once this controversy must attach—this bill would seem to be nothing less than a bill to produce internal commotion. Should we prosecute this war another moment or expend one dollar in the purchase or conquest of a single acre of Mexican land, the North and the South are brought into collison on a point where neither will yield. Who can foresee or foretell the result? Who so bold or reckless as to look such a conflict in the face unmoved? I do not envy the heart of him who can realize the possibility of such a conflict without emotions too painful to be endured. Why then shall we, the representatives of the sovereign States of this Union—the chosen guardians of this confederated Republic, why should we precipitate this fearful struggle, by continuing a war, the results of which must be to force us at once upon it? Sir, rightly considered, *this* is treason, treason to the Union, treason to the dearest interests, the loftiest aspirations, the most cherished hopes of our constituents. It is a crime to risk the possibility of such a contest. It is a crime of such infernal hue, that every other in the catalogue of iniquity, when compared with it, whitens into virtue. Oh, Mr. President, it does seem to me, if hell itself could yawn and vomit up the fiends that inhabit its penal abodes, commissioned to disturb the harmony of this world, and dash the fairest prospect of happiness that ever allured the hopes of men, the first step in the consummation of this diabolical purpose would be, to light up the fires of internal war, and plunge the sister States of this Union into the bottomless gulf of civil strife. We stand this day on the crumbling brink of that gulf—we see its bloody eddies wheeling and boiling before us—shall we not pause before it be too late? How plain again is here the path, I may add the only way of duty, of prudence, of true patriotism. Let us abandon all idea of acquiring further territory, and by consequence cease at once to prosecute this war. Let us call home our armies, and bring them at once within our own acknowledged limits. Show Mexico that you are sincere when you say you desire nothing by conquest. She has learned that she cannot encounter you in war, and if she had not, she is too weak to disturb you here. Tender her peace, and my life on it, she will then accept it. But whether she shall or not, you will have peace without her consent. It is your invasion that has made war, your retreat will restore peace. Let us then close forever the approaches of internal feud, and so return to the ancient concord and the old way of national prosperity and permanent glory. Let us here, in this temple consecrated to the Union, perform a solemn lustration; let us wash Mexican blood from our hands, and on these altars, in the presence of that image of the Father of his country that looks down upon us, swear to preserve honorable peace with all the world, and eternal brotherhood with each other.

Discussion Starters

1. On what did Senator Corwin base his belief that the war was a danger to the fundamental relationship between the presidency and the Congress? Cite similar difficulties between these two branches of government that have existed before or since?

2. How valid was Corwin's suggestion that as a representative of the minority in Congress he should do everything legally possible to block the conduct of the war even though the majority of Congress was for the war? How would his position have been affected if such things as public opinion polls had shown that a majority of the American people, as well as a majority of Congress, supported the war?

3. What standards would one use in evaluating Corwin's responses to the concept of manifest destiny, or his convictions that America should restrain its territorial ambitions?

4. How does one measure whether a dissenting position such as Corwin's is patriotic or unpatriotic?

Related Documents

I. Inaugural Address

JAMES KNOX POLK

Polk, the Democratic candidate, was elected to the presidency in 1844. He had run on a platform espousing manifest destiny and he took his election as a mandate to fulfill American "rights" in Oregon and Mexico. The Oregon question was settled, after sword-rattling by both England and the United States, with a compromise that divided the territory at the 49th parallel. The Mexican situation was not so easily decided.

In his inaugural address, Polk mapped out the program for his administration based upon a policy of expansion. How does Polk's justification for extending American authority over Oregon, Texas, and other areas differ from Corwin's objections to such expansionism? Why did Polk see the annexation of Texas as a reunion of territory of the United States?

MARCH 4, 1845

I regard the question of annexation as belonging exclusively to the United States and Texas. They are independent powers competent to contract, and foreign nations have no right to interfere with them or to take exceptions to their reunion. Foreign powers do not seem to appreciate the true character of our Government. Our Union is a confederation of independent States, whose policy is peace with each other and all the world. To enlarge its limits is to extend the dominions of peace over additional territories and increasing millions. They world has nothing to fear from military ambition in our Government. While the Chief Magistrate and the popular branch of Congress are elected for short terms by the suffrages of those millions who must in their own persons bear all the burdens and miseries of war, our Government can not be otherwise than pacific. Foreign powers should therefore look on the annexation of Texas to the United States not as the conquest of a nation seeking to extend her dominions by arms and violence, but as the peaceful acquisition of a territory once her own, by adding another member to our confederation, with the consent of that member, thereby diminishing the chances of war and opening to them new and ever-increasing markets for their products.

To Texas the reunion is important, because the strong protecting arm of our Government would be extended over her, and the vast resources of her fertile soil and genial climate would be speedily developed, while the safety of New Orleans and of our whole southwestern frontier against hostile aggres-

James D. Richardson, ed., *A Compilation of the Messages and Papers of the Presidents* (Washington, D.C.: Government Printing Office, 1897), IV, pp. 379–81.

sion, as well as the interests of the whole Union, would be promoted by it.

In the earlier stages of our national existence the opinion prevailed with some that our system of confederated States could not operate successfully over an extended territory, and serious objections have at different times been made to the enlargement of our boundaries. These objections were earnestly urged when we acquired Louisiana. Experience has shown that they were not well founded. The title of numerous Indian tribes to vast tracts of country has been extinguished; new States have been admitted into the Union; new Territories have been created and our jurisdiction and laws extended over them. As our population has expanded, the Union has been cemented and strengthened. As our boundaries have been enlarged and our agricultural population has been spread over a large surface, our federative system has acquired additional strength and security. It may well be doubted whether it would not be a greater danger of overthrow if our present population were confined to the comparatively narrow limits of the original thirteen States than it is now that they are sparsely settled over a more expanded territory. It is confidently believed that our system may be safely extended to the utmost bounds of our territorial limits, and that as it shall be extended the bonds of our Union, so far from being weakened, will become stronger. . . .

. . . I shall on the broad principle which formed the basis and produced the adoption of our Constitution, and not in any narrow spirit of sectional policy, endeavor by all constitutional, honorable, and appropriate means to consummate the expressed will of the people and Government of the United States by the reannexation of Texas to our Union at the earliest practicable period. . . .

Nor will it become in a less degree my duty to assert and maintain by all constitutional means the right of the United States to that portion of our territory which lies beyond the Rocky Mountains. Our title to the country of the Oregon is "clear and unquestionable," and already are our people preparing to perfect that title by occupying it with their wives and children. But eighty years ago our population was confined on the west by the ridge of the Alleghanies. Within that period—within the lifetime, I might say, of some of my hearers—our people, increasing to many millions, have filled the eastern valley of the Mississippi, adventurously ascended the Missouri to its headsprings, and are already engaged in establishing the blessings of self-government in valleys of which the rivers flow to the Pacific. The world beholds the peaceful triumphs of the industry of our emigrants. To us belongs the duty of protecting them adequately wherever they may be upon our soil. The jurisdiction of our laws and the benefits of our republican institutions should be extended over them in the distant regions which they have selected for their homes. . . .

II. Hosea Biglow and the Mexican War

JAMES RUSSELL LOWELL

James Russell Lowell was one of the outstanding men of letters in America during the nineteenth century. In 1848, at the age of 29, he published the first of a series of poems of political satire entitled the Biglow Papers. *The poems, which protested the American involvement in the Mexican War, were written in the New England dialect of a ficticious Hosea Biglow and reflected the growing unrest in the Northeast toward the war.*

Identify the parallels between the thoughts of the following poem and the arguments used by Corwin to indict the war.

THRASH away, you'll *hev* to rattle
　On them kittle drums o' yourn,—
'Taint a knowin' kind o' cattle
　Thet is ketched with mouldy corn;
Put in stiff, you fifer feller,
　Let folks see how spry you be,—
Guess you'll toot till you are yeller
　'Fore you git ahold o' me!

● ● ●

Ez fer war, I call it murder,—
　There you hev it plain an' flat;
I don't want to go no furder
　Than my Testament fer that;
God hez sed so plump an' fairly,
　It 's ez long ez it is broad,
An' you 've gut to git up airly
　Ef you want to take in God.

'Taint your eppyletts an' feathers
　Make the thing a grain more right;
'Taint afollerin' your bell-wethers
　Will excuse ye in His sight;
Ef you take a sword an' dror it,
　An' go stick a feller thru,
Guv'ment aint to answer for it,
　God'll send the bill to you.

Wut 's the use o' meetin-goin'
　Every Sabbath, wet or dry,

James Russell Lowell, *The Biglow Papers* (Boston: Ticknor, Reed, and Fields, 1854), pp. 3–11.

Ef it 's right to go amowin'
   Feller-men like oats an' rye?
I dunno but wut it 's pooty
   Trainin' round in bobtail coats,—
But it 's curus Christian dooty
   This ere cuttin' folks's throats.

They may talk o' Freedom's airy
   Tell they 're pupple in the face,—
It 's a grand gret cemetary
   Fer the barthrights of our race;
They jest want this Californy
   So 's to lug new slave-states in
To abuse ye, an' to scorn ye,
   An' to plunder ye like sin.

        • • •

Tell ye jest the eend I 've come to
   Arter cipherin' plaguy smart,
An' it makes a handy sum, tu,
   Any gump could larn by heart;
Laborin' man an' laborin' woman
   Hev one glory an' one shame,
Ev'y thin' thet 's done inhuman
   Injers all on 'em the same.

'Taint by turnin' out to hack folks
   You 're agoin' to git your right,
Nor by lookin' down on black folks
   Coz you 're put upon by wite;
Slavery aint o' nary color,
   'Taint the hide thet makes it wus,
All it keers fer in a feller
   'S jest to make him fill its pus.

Want to tackle *me* in, du ye?
   I expect you 'll hev to wait;
Wen cold lead puts daylight thru ye
   You 'll begin to kal'late;
'Spose the crows wun't fall to pickin'
   All the carkiss from your bones,
Coz you helped to give a lickin'
   To them poor half-Spanish drones?

Jest go home an' ask our Nancy
   Wether I 'd be sech a goose

Ez to jine ye,—guess you'd fancy
    The etarnal bung wuz loose!
She wants me fer home consumption,
    Let alone the hay 's to mow,—
Ef you 're arter folks o' gumption,
    You 've a darned long row to hoe.

Take them editors thet 's crowin'
    Like a cockerel three months old,—
Don't ketch any on 'em goin',
    Though they *be* so blasted bold;
Aint they a prime set o' fellers?
    'Fore they think on 't they will sprout,
(Like a peach thet's got the yellers,)
    With the meanness bustin' out.

Wal, go 'long to help 'em stealin'
    Bigger pens to cram with slaves,
Help the men thet 's ollers dealin'
    Insults on your fathers' graves;
Help the strong to grind the feeble,
    Help the many agin the few,
Help the men thet call your people
    Witewashed slaves an' peddlin' crew!

Massachusetts, God forgive her,
    She 's akneelin' with the rest,
She, thet ough' to ha' clung fer ever
    In her grand old eagle-nest;
She thet ough' to stand so fearless
    Wile the wracks are round her hurled,
Holdin' up a beacon peerless
    To the oppressed of all the world!

Haint they sold your colored seamen?
    Haint they made your env'ys wiz?
Wut 'll make ye act like freemen?
    Wut 'll git your dander riz?
Come, I 'll tell ye wut I 'm thinkin'
    Is our dooty in this fix,
They 'd ha' done 't ez quick ez winkin'
    In the days o' seventy-six.

Clang the bells in every steeple,
    Call all true men to disown
The tradoocers of our people,

The enslavers o' their own;
Let our dear old Bay State proudly
Put the trumpet to her mouth,
Let her ring this messidge loudly
In the ears of all the South:—

"I'll return ye good fer evil
Much ez we frail mortils can,
But I wun't go help the Devil
Makin' man the cus o' man;
Call me coward, call me traiter,
Jest ez suits your mean idees,—
Here I stand a tyrant-hater,
An' the friend o' God an' Peace!"

Ef I 'd *my* way I hed ruther
We should go to work an' part,—
They take one way, we take t'other,—
Guess it would n't break my heart;
Man hed ough' to put asunder
Them thet God has noways jined;
An' I should n't gretly wonder
Ef there 's thousands o' my mind.

III. A Southern Senator Speaks Out Against the War

JOHN C. CALHOUN

John C. Calhoun saw the Mexican War in different terms than Polk. As senator from South Carolina, he advocated peaceful negotiation of boundary questions between the United States and Mexico. The declaration of war against Mexico in May 1846 brought Calhoun to the forefront of those opposing the war.

In the following speech to Congress why would Calhoun, the chief exponent of Southern rights, be against the acquisition of territory? How are Calhoun's arguments similar to those of Corwin?

JANUARY 4, 1848

We make a great mistake in supposing all people are capable of self-govern-ment. Acting under that impression, many are anxious to force free govern-

Richard K. Cralle, ed., *Speeches of John C. Calhoun* (New York: D. Appelton, 1854), IV, pp. 416–18.

ments on all the people of this continent, and over the world, if they had the power. It has been lately urged in a very respectable quarter, that it is the mission of this country to spread civil and religious liberty over all the globe, and especially over this continent—even by force, if necessary. It is a sad delusion. None but a people advanced to a high state of moral and intellectual excellence are capable in a civilized condition, of forming and maintaining free governments; and among those who are so far advanced, very few indeed have had the good fortune to form constitutions capable of endurance. It is a remarkable fact in the political history of man, that there is scarcely an instance of a free constitutional government, which has been the work exclusively of foresight and wisdom. They have all been the result of a fortunate combination of circumstances. It is a very difficult task to make a constitution worthy of being called so. This admirable federal constitution of ours, is the result of such a combination. It is superior to the wisdom of any or all of the men by whose agency it was made. The force of circumstances, and not foresight or wisdom, induced them to adopt many of its wisest provisions.

But of the few nations who have been so fortunate as to adopt a wise constitution, still fewer have had the wisdom long to preserve one. It is harder to preserve than to obtain liberty. After years of prosperity, the tenure by which it is held is but too often forgotten; and I fear, Senators, that such is the case with us. There is no solicitude now about liberty. It was not so in the early days of the republic. Then it was the first object of our solicitude. The maxim then was, that "Power is always stealing from the many to the few;" "The price of liberty is perpetual vigilance." Then no question of any magnitude came up, in which the first inquiry was not, "Is it constitutional?"—"Is it consistent with our free, popular institutions?"—"How is it to affect our liberty?" It is not so now. Questions of the greatest magnitude are now discussed without reference or allusion to these vital considerations. I have been often struck with the fact, that in the discussions of the great questions in which we are now engaged, relating to the origin and the conduct of this war, their effect on the free institutions and the liberty of the people have scarcely been alluded to, although their bearing in that respect is so direct and disastrous. They would, in former days, have been the great and leading topics of discussion; and would, above all others, have had the most powerful effect in arousing the attention of the country. But now, other topics occupy the attention of Congress and of the country—military glory, extension of the empire, and the aggrandizement of the country. To what is this great change to be attributed? Is it because there has been a decay of the spirit of liberty among the people? I think not. I believe that it was never more ardent. The true cause is, that we have ceased to remember the tenure by which liberty alone can be preserved. We have had so many years of prosperity—passed through so many difficulties and dangers without the loss of liberty—that we begin to think that we hold it by right divine from heaven itself. Under this impression, without thinking or reflecting, we plunge into war, contract heavy debts, increase vastly the patronage of the Executive, and indulge in every species of extravagance, without thinking that we expose our liberty to hazard. It is a great and fatal mistake. The day of retribution will come; and when it does, awful will be the reckoning, and heavy the responsibility somewhere.

IV. Civil Disobedience

HENRY DAVID THOREAU

Henry David Thoreau, a New England transcendentalist, took a different course of action in resisting the Mexican War than did the politicians in Congress. He was best known during his own time for his book Walden, *published in 1854. In* Walden *he presented his experiences living alone in nature and trying to understand life.*

Before this, however, during the Mexican War, Thoreau became convinced, as did many abolitionists, that the war was a conspiracy to extend slavery. Hence Thoreau refused to pay his poll taxes, for he was convinced that the money would be used to buy weapons to kill the hapless Mexicans. For this he was jailed by the authorities. The experience of his confinement, one day and a night, led him to write a pamphlet entitled, Resistance to Civil Government *(1849), later popularly known as* Civil Disobedience. *His essay, although ignored during his own time, became the basis for such twentieth-century theories of nonviolent resistance as practiced by Mahatma Gandhi in India and Martin Luther King, Jr., in the United States.*

According to Thoreau, what should be a citizen's response to an unjust war? In what respects was his resistance to the war compatible with Corwin's stand?

I heartily accept the motto, "That government is best which governs least;" and I should like to see it acted up to more rapidly and systematically. Carried out, it finally amounts to this, which also I believe,—"That government is best which governs not at all;" and when men are prepared for it that will be the kind of government which they will have. Government is at best but an expedient; but most governments are usually, and all governments are sometimes, inexpedient. The objections which have been brought against a standing army, and they are many and weighty, and deserve to prevail, may also at last be brought against a standing government. The government itself, which is only the mode which the people have chosen to execute their will, is equally liable to be abused and perverted before the people can act through it. Witness the present Mexican war, the work of comparatively a few individuals using the standing government as their tool; for, in the outset, the people would not have consented to this measure.

This American government,—what is it but a tradition, though a recent one, endeavoring to transmit itself unimpaired to posterity, but each instant losing some of its integrity? It has not the vitality and force of a single living

Owen Thomas, ed., *Walden and Civil Disobedience* (New York: W. W. Norton, Norton Critical Edition, 1966), pp. 224–27, 229–31, 233, 236, 243.

man; for a single man can bend it to his will. It is a sort of wooden gun to the people themselves. But it is not the less necessary for this; for the people must have some complicated machinery or other, and hear its din, to satisfy that idea of government which they have. Governments show thus how successfully men can be imposed on, even impose on themselves, for their own advantage. It is excellent, we must all allow. Yet this government never of itself furthered any enterprise, but by the alacrity with which it got out of its way. . . .

After all, the practical reason why, when the power is once in the hands of the people, a majority are permitted, and for a long period continue, to rule is not because they are most likely to be in the right, nor because this seems fairest to the minority, but because they are physically the strongest. But a government in which the majority rule in all cases cannot be based on justice, even as far as men understand it. Can there not be a government in which majorities do not virtually decide right and wrong, but conscience?—in which majorities decide only those questions to which the rule of expediency is applicable? Must the citizen ever for a moment, or in the least degree, resign his conscience to the legislator? Why has every man a conscience, then? I think that we should be men first, and subjects afterward. It is not desirable to cultivate a respect for the law, so much as for the right. The only obligation which I have a right to assume is to do at any time what I think right. It is truly enough said that a corporation has no conscience; but a corporation of conscientious men is a corporation *with* a conscience. Law never made men a whit more just; and, by means of their respect for it, even the well-disposed are daily made the agents of injustice. . . .

The mass of men serve the state thus, not as men mainly, but as machines, with their bodies. They are the standing army, and the militia, jailers, constables, *posse comitatus,* etc. In most cases there is no free exercise whatever of the judgment or of the moral sense; but they put themselves on a level with wood and earth and stones; and wooden men can perhaps be manufactured that will serve the purpose as well. . . .

How does it become a man to behave toward this American government to-day? I answer, that he cannot without disgrace be associated with it. I cannot for an instant recognize that political organization as *my* government which is the *slave's* government also. . . .

It is not a man's duty, as a matter of course, to devote himself to the eradication of any, even the most enormous, wrong; he may still properly have other concerns to engage him; but it is his duty, at least, to wash his hands of it, and, if he gives it no thought longer, not to give it practically his support. If I devote myself to other pursuits and contemplations, I must first see, at least, that I do not pursue them sitting upon another man's shoulders. I must get off him first, that he may pursue his contemplations too. See what gross inconsistency is tolerated. I have heard some of my townsmen say, "I should like to have them order me out to help put down an insurrection of the slaves, or to march to Mexico;—see if I would go;" and yet these very men have each,

directly by their allegiance, and so indirectly, at least, by their money, furnished a substitute. . . .

Unjust laws exist: shall we be content to obey them, or shall we endeavor
to amend them, and obey them until we have succeeded, or shall we transgress
them at once? Men generally, under such a government as this, think that they
ought to wait until they have persuaded the majority to alter them. They think
that, if they should resist, the remedy would be worse than the evil. But it is
the fault of the government itself that the remedy *is* worse than the evil. *It*
makes it worse. Why is it not more apt to anticipate and provide for reform?
Why does it not cherish its wise minority? Why does it cry and resist before
it is hurt? Why does it not encourage its citizens to be on the alert to point
out its faults, and *do* better than it would have them? Why does it always
crucify Christ, and excommunicate Copernicus and Luther, and pronounce
Washington and Franklin rebels? . . .

Under a government which imprisons any unjustly, the true place for a
just man is also a prison. The proper place to-day, the only place which
Massachusetts has provided for her freer and less desponding spirits, is in her
prisons, to be put out and locked out of the State by her own act, as they have
already put themselves out by their principles. It is there that the fugitive slave,
and the Mexican prisoner on parole, and the Indian come to plead the wrongs
of his race should find them; on that separate, but more free and honorable,
ground, where the State places those who are not *with* her, but *against* her,
—the only house in a slave State in which a free man can abide with honor.
. . . A minority is powerless while it conforms to the majority then; but it is
irresistible when it clogs by its whole weight. If the alternative is to keep all
just men in prison, or give up war and slavery, the State will not hesitate which
to choose. If a thousand men were not to pay their tax-bills this year, that
would not be a violent and bloody measure, as it would be to pay them, and
enable the State to commit violence and shed innocent blood. This is, in fact,
the definition of a peaceable revolution, if any such is possible. . . .

I have paid no poll-tax for six years. I was put into a jail once on this
account, for one night; and, as I stood considering the walls of solid stone, two
or three feet thick, the door of wood and iron, a foot thick, and the iron grating
which strained the light, I could not help being struck with the foolishness of
that institution which treated me as if I were mere flesh and blood and bones,
to be locked up. I wondered that it should have concluded at length that this
was the best use it could put me to, and had never thought to avail itself of
my services in some way. I saw that, if there was a wall of stone between me
and my townsmen, there was a still more difficult one to climb or break
through before they could get to be as free as I was. I did not for a moment
feel confined, and the walls seemed a great waste of stone and mortar.
. . . I could not but smile to see how industriously they locked the door on my
meditations, which followed them out again without let or hindrance, and *they*

were really all that was dangerous. As they could not reach me, they had resolved to punish my body; just as boys, if they cannot come at some person against whom they have a spite, will abuse his dog. I saw that the State was half-witted, that it was timid as a lone woman with her silver spoons, and that it did not know its friends from its foes, and I lost all my remaining respect for it, and pitied it.

Thus the State never intentionally confronts a man's sense, intellectual or moral, but only his body, his senses. It is not armed with superior wit or honesty, but with superior physical strength. . . .

. . . Is a democracy, such as we know it, the last improvement possible in government? Is it not possible to take a step further towards recognizing and organizing the rights of man? There will never be a really free and enlightened State until the State comes to recognize the individual as a higher and independent power, from which all its own power and authority are derived, and treats him accordingly. I please myself with imagining a State at last which can afford to be just to all men, and to treat the individual with respect as a neighbor; which even would not think it inconsistent with its own repose if a few were to live aloof from it, not meddling with it, nor embraced by it, who fulfilled all the duties of neighbors and fellow-men. A State which bore this kind of fruit, and suffered it to drop off as fast as it ripened, would prepare the way for a still more perfect and glorious State, which also I have imagined, but not yet anywhere seen.

V. Peace!

FREDERICK DOUGLASS

Douglass was born into slavery in Maryland around 1817. In 1838 he escaped and fled to the North, settling in New Bedford, Massachusetts. There Douglass became acquainted with the Massachusetts Anti-Slavery Society, which soon led to his involvement; in 1841 he became an activist in the society. Douglass had been taught to read and write by his former slave mistress and was determined to tell his story to the widest possible audience. This led him to publish his Narrative of the Life of Frederick Douglass, an American Slave *in 1845. The book brought in enough money to enable him to buy his freedom from his former master (he had been subject to extradition under the fugitive slave law), and to start a newspaper. In 1847 the newspaper began publication in Rochester, New York, under the banner of the* North Star.

In reading the following editorial, evaluate Douglass' condemnation of the war and the peace. How does his stand agree with the position taken by Senator Corwin?

The Annals of America: 1841–1849 (Chicago: Encyclopedia Britannica, 1968), VII, p. 422.

MARCH 17, 1848

The shout is on every lip, and emblazoned on every paper. The joyful news is told in every quarter with enthusiastic delight. We are such an exception to the great mass of our fellow countrymen in respect to everything else, and have been so accustomed to hear them rejoice over the most barbarous outrages committed upon an unoffending people, that we find it difficult to unite with them in their general exultation at this time; and, for this reason, we believe that by *peace* they mean *plunder.*

In our judgment, those who have all along been loudly in favor of a vigorous prosecution of the war, and heralding its bloody triumphs with apparent rapture, and glorifying the atrocious deeds of barbarous heroism on the part of wicked men engaged in it, have no sincere love of peace, and are not now rejoicing over *peace* but *plunder.* They have succeeded in robbing Mexico of her territory, and are rejoicing over their success under the hypocritical pretense of a regard for peace. Had they not succeeded in robbing Mexico of the most important and most valuable part of her territory, many of those now loudest in their professions of favor for peace would be loudest and wildest for War—war to the knife.

Our soul is sick of such hypocrisy. We presume the churches of Rochester will return thanks to God for peace they did nothing to bring about, and boast it as a triumph of Christianity! That an end is put to the wholesale murder in Mexico is truly just cause for rejoicing; but we are not the people to rejoice; we ought rather blush and hang our heads for shame, and, in the spirit of profound humility, crave pardon for our crimes at the hands of a God whose mercy endureth forever.

For Further Reading

The concept of manifest destiny is examined in two recent books on the subject: Frederick Merk, *Manifest Destiny and Mission in American History** (1963), and Albert K. Weinberg, *Manifest Destiny** (1963).

An account of the part played by dissent in the conduct of the war is found in the chapter on the Mexican War in Samuel Eliot Morison, Frederick Merk, and Frank Freidel, *Dissent in Three American Wars* (1970).

The relationship, on and off the battlefield, between the United States and Mexico is the concern of Jose F. Ramirez, *Mexico during the War with the United States** (1950); George L. Rives, *The United States and Mexico, 1821– 1848* (1913; reprinted in 1969); and *The Mexican War** (1960) by Otis Singletary.

Biographies of the period include Wilfred H. Callcott, *Santa Anna* (1964); Eugene I. MacCormac, *James K. Polk* (1922; reprinted in 1965); and Charles Sellers, *James K. Polk, Continentalist* (1966).

Collections of contemporary accounts are: Norman Graebner, ed., *Mani-*

*Paperbound edition available.

fest Destiny* (1971), and Grady McWhiney and Sue McWhiney, eds., *To Mexico with Taylor and Scott, 1845–1847** (1969).

Problems books on the war have been edited by Archie P. McDonald, *The Mexican War* (1969); Armin Rappaport, *The War With Mexico* (1964); and Ramon Eduardo Ruiz, *The Mexican War* (1963).

*Paperbound edition available.

14. Confrontation in Kansas

Gold in California! The news spread quickly, and many people in America left their homes and families to travel westward as "49ers." Just as these gold seekers had to adjust to a new life, the nation had to adjust to its new-found wealth and the rush of its citizens to the West. This adjustment was made, but not without difficulty.

California had become a part of the United States in the Treaty of Guadalupe Hildago of 1848, and with the gold rush it had been settled sufficiently to justify its request for statehood in 1850. But the prohibition of slavery by the California constitution added another dimension to the North-South conflict over the slavery question. The debates in Congress and the threats by both sides over granting or denying statehood to California culminated in a series of compromises proposed by Henry Clay of Kentucky.

Clay's proposals, known collectively as the Compromise of 1850, provided for the admission of California as a free state, the enforcement of a more stringent fugitive slave law, restricted boundaries for Texas (with compensation), the prohibition of the slave trade in the national capital, and the opening of the New Southwest by leaving the question of slavery up to the people that settled there. Because of Clay's age these proposals were directed through Congress by the vigorous young senator from Illinois, Stephen A. Douglas.

The promise of the Compromise of 1850 as a solution to the problems of the North and South did not last long. It became increasingly apparent as the decade progressed that the compromise was actually a postponement of the clash over the issues between the two sections. The Fugitive Slave Act, intended as a major concession to the South, did not function as it was intended; the Southern slaveholder found himself blocked from recovering his property by the Northern states, who were prone to ignore or even violate the federal law by protecting the runaways within their borders. Such actions caused the Southern extremists to demand greater enforcement; failing this, they threatened to seek other means to protect their property.

The question of disposition of territory in the struggle between the North and the South did not figure in the initial disenchantment with the compromise. It became an issue in 1852, however, when Secretary of War Jefferson Davis announced that the government planned to help build a railroad from Memphis, Tennessee, to the West Coast. Northern congressmen responded immediately against any plan that would take a southern route. Consequently, in order to provide for a more acceptable route, Senator Douglas suggested that the new railroad take a central route, beginning in Chicago. For this to be feasible the prairie would have to be settled and organized, so to accomplish this, Douglas proposed legislation that became known as the Kansas-Nebraska Act of 1854.

Core Document

Popular Sovereignty

STEPHEN A. DOUGLAS

The rush of emigrants to California in 1849 became a flood by the early 1850s. These new pioneers started from such jumping-off places as Independence, Westport, and St. Joseph on the western frontier of Missouri, with such points as Santa Fe and Fort Bridger serving as halfway places. But what about the land between Missouri and the mountains? What about the great American "desert" that stretched for hundreds of miles between civilization and the new Edens of the West? What about the land known as Kansas?

For the people moving westward in the early 1850s Kansas was a barrier that had to be crossed, just as the mountains had to be surmounted before one reached California. But with the Douglas plan to build a railroad across the plains, the federal government would be extending its civil jurisdiction over the areas the railway was to go through, thus providing for settlement and thereby helping to defray the expenses of the operation. But settlement meant territories

Congressional Globe, 33rd Congress, 1st Session (Washington, D.C.: John C. Rives, 1854), XXVIII—Part I, pp. 275–80.

and eventually statehood, and that could mean raising again the question of slavery in the new states.

The Committee on Territories, chaired by Douglas, reported out a bill to the full Senate organizing the plains into two territories: Kansas and Nebraska. The key issue in the bill was whether slavery would be sanctioned or prohibited in these areas, and how this would affect North-South relations. The bill answered these questions by first declaring the Missouri Compromise of 1820 as "inoperative and void," and then asserting that Congress would not legislate slavery into nor exclude it from any territory or state, but would "leave the people thereof perfectly free to form and regulate their domestic institutions in their own way, subject only to the Constitution of the United States." The new territories of Kansas and Nebraska were therefore to determine their own domestic institutions by what Douglas termed "popular sovereignty."

In reading Douglas' speech in support of the bill, note why he believed that:
- *the bill conformed to the Compromise of 1850.*
- *the Indians in the areas in question had been treated fairly.*
- *the history of the United States supported the concept of popular sovereignty.*
- *the Missouri Compromise was not an issue in the bill.*
- *the abolitionists were misrepresenting the bill.*
- *his character and integrity had been impugned.*

JANUARY 30, 1854

Mr. President, when I proposed on Tuesday last, that the Senate should proceed to the consideration of the bill to organize the Territories of Nebraska and Kansas, it was my purpose only to occupy ten or fifteen minutes in explanation of its provisions. I desired to refer to two points: first, as to those provisions relating to the Indians; and second, to those which might be supposed to bear upon the question of slavery.

The committee, in drafting this bill, had in view the great anxiety which had been expressed by some members of the Senate to protect the rights of the Indians, and prevent infringements upon them. By the provisions of the bill, I think we have so clearly succeeded in that respect as to obviate all possible objection upon that score. The bill itself provides that it shall not operate upon any of the rights of the lands of the Indians; nor shall they be included within the limits of those Territories, until they shall, by treaty with the United States, expressly consent to come under the operations of the act, and be incorporated within the limits of the Territories. This provision certainly is broad enough, clear enough, explicit enough, to protect all the rights of the Indians as to their persons and their property.

Upon the other point—that pertaining to the question of slavery in the Territories—it was the intention of the committee to be equally explicit. We took the principles established by the compromise act of 1850 as our guide, and intended to make each and every provision of the bill accord with those principles. Those measures established and rest upon the great principle of self-government—that the people should be allowed to decide the questions of their domestic institutions for themselves, subject only to such limitations and restrictions as are imposed by the Constitution of the United States, instead of having them determined by an arbitrary or geographical line.

. . . As the object of the committee was to conform to the principles established by the compromise measures of 1850, and to carry those principles into effect in the Territories, we thought it was better to recite in the bill precisely what we understood to have been accomplished by those measures, viz.: That the Missouri compromise having been superseded by the legislation of 1850, has become inoperative, and hence we propose to leave the question to the people of the States and the Territories, subject only to the limitations and provisions of the Constitution.

Sir, this is all that I intended to say, if the question had been taken up for consideration on Tuesday last; but since that time occurrences have transpired which compel me to go more fully into the discussion. It will be borne in the mind that the Senator from Ohio (Mr. Chase) then objected to the consideration of the bill, and asked for its postponement until this day, on the ground that there had not been time to understand and consider its provisions; and the Senator from Massachusetts (Mr. Sumner) suggested that the postponement should be for one week, for that purpose. These suggestions seeming to be reasonable to Senators around me, I yielded to their request, and consented to the postponement of the bill until this day.

Sir, little did I suppose at the time that I granted that act of courtesy to those two Senators, that they had drafted and published to the world a document, over their own signatures, in which they arraigned me as having been guilty of a criminal betrayal of my trust, as having been guilty of an act of bad faith, and been engaged in an atrocious plot against the cause of free government. Little did I suppose that those two Senators had been guilty of such conduct when they called upon me to grant that courtesy, to give them an opportunity of investigating the substitute reported from the committee. I have since discovered that on that very morning the National Era, the Abolition organ in this city, contained an address, signed by certain Abolition confederates, to the people, in which the bill is grossly misrepresented, in which the action of the members of the committee is grossly falsified, in which our motives are arraigned, and our characters calumniated. And, sir, what is more, I find that there was a postscript added to the address, published that very morning, in which the principal amendment reported by the committee was set out, and then coarse epithets applied to me by name. . . .

The argument of this manifesto is predicated upon the assumption that the policy of the fathers of the Republic was to prohibit slavery in all the territory ceded by the old States to the Union and made United States territory, for the purpose of being organized into new States. I take issue upon that statement. Such was not the practice in the early history of the Government. It is true that in the territory northwest of the Ohio river slavery was prohibited by the ordinance of 1787; but it is also true that in the territory south of the Ohio river, to wit, the Territory of Tennessee, slavery was permitted and protected; and it is also true, that in the organization of the Territory of Mississippi, in 1798, the provisions of the ordinance of 1787 were applied to it, with the exception of the sixth article, which prohibited slavery. Then, sir, you find upon the statute-books under Washington and the early Presidents, provisions of law showing that in the southwestern territories the right to hold slaves was clearly implied or recognized, while in the northwest territories it was prohibited. The only conclusion that can be fairly and honestly drawn from that legislation is, that it was the policy of the fathers of the Republic to prescribe a line of demarkation between territories and slaveholding territories by a natural or a geographical line, being sure to make that line correspond, as near as might be, to the laws of climate, of production, and probably of all those other causes that would control the institution and make it either desirable or undesirable to the people inhabiting the respective territories.

Sir, I wish you to bear in mind, too, that this geographical line established by the founders of the Republic, between free Territories and slave Territories, extended as far westward as our territory then reached, the object being to avoid all agitation upon the slavery question by settling that question forever, so far as our territory extended, which was then to the Mississippi river.

When, in 1803, we acquired from France the Territory known as Louisiana, it became necessary to legislate for the protection of the inhabitants residing therein. It will be seen by looking into the bill establishing the territorial government in 1805 for the Territory of New Orleans, embracing the same country now known as the State of Louisiana, that the ordinance of 1787 was expressly extended to that Territory, excepting the sixth section, which prohibited slavery. Then that act implied that the Territory of New Orleans was to be a slave-holding Territory by making that exception in the law. But, sir, when they came to form what was then called the Territory of Louisiana, subsequently known as the Territory of Missouri, north of the thirty-third parallel, they used different language. They did not extend the ordinance of 1787 to it at all. They first provided that it should be governed by laws made by the governor and the judges; and when, in 1812, Congress gave to that Territory, under the name of the Territory of Missouri, a territorial government, the people were allowed to do as they pleased upon the subject of slavery, subject only to the limitations of the Constitution of the United States. Now, what is the inference from that legislation? That slavery was, by implication, recognized south of the thirty-third parallel, and north of that the people were left to exercise their own judgment and do as they pleased upon the subject, without any implication for or against the existence of the institution.

This continued to be the condition of the country in the Missouri Territory up to 1820, when the celebrated act which is now called the Missouri compromise act was passed. Slavery did not exist in, nor was it excluded from, the country now known as Nebraska. There was no code of laws upon the subject of slavery either way: First, for the reason that slavery had never been introduced into Louisiana, and established by positive enactment. It had grown up there by a sort of common law, and been supported and protected. When a common law grows up, when an institution becomes established under a usage, it carries it so far as that usage actually goes, and no further. If it had been established by direct enactment, it might have carried it so far as the political jurisdiction extended; but, be that as it may, by the act of 1812, creating the Territory of Missouri, that Territory was allowed to legislate upon the subject of slavery as it saw proper, subject only to the limitations which I have stated; and the country not inhabited or thrown open to settlement was set apart as Indian country, and rendered subject to Indian laws. Hence the local legislation of the State of Missouri did not reach into that Indian country, but was excluded from it by the Indian code and Indian laws. The municipal regulations of Missouri could not go there until the Indian title had been extinguished, and the country thrown open to settlement. Such being the case, the only legislation in existence in Nebraska Territory at the time that the Missouri act passed, namely, the 6th of March, 1820, was a provision in effect, that the people should be allowed to do as they pleased upon the subject of slavery.

The Territory of Missouri having been left in that legal condition, positive opposition was made to the bill to organize a State government, with a view to its admission into the Union; and a Senator from my State, Mr. Jesse B. Thomas, introduced an amendment, known as the eighth section of the bill, in which it was provided that slavery should be prohibited north of 36° 30′ north latitude, in all that country which we had acquired from France. What was the object of the enactment of that eighth section? Was it not to go back to the original policy of prescribing boundaries to the limitation of free institutions, and of slave institutions, by a geographical line, in order to avoid all controversy in Congress upon the subject? Hence they extended that geographical line through all the territory purchased from France, which was as far as our possessions then reached. It was not simply to settle the question on that piece of country, but it was to carry out a great principle, by extending that dividing line as far west as our territory went, and running it onward on each new acquisition of territory. True, the express enactment of the eighth section of the Missouri act, now called the Missouri compromise act, only covered the territory acquired from France; but the principles of the act, the objects of its adoption, the reasons in its support, required that it should be extended indefinitely westward, so far as our territory might go, whenever new purchases should be made.

Thus stood the question up to 1845, when the joint resolution for the annexation of Texas passed. There was inserted in that a provision, suggested in the first instance and brought before the House of Representatives by myself, extending the Missouri compromise line indefinitely westward through the territory of Texas. Why did I bring forward that proposition? Why did the Congress of the United States adopt it? Not because it was of the least practical importance, so far as the question of slavery within the limits of Texas was concerned, for no man ever dreamed that it had any practical effect there. Then why was it brought forward? It was for the purpose of preserving the principle, in order that it might be extended still further westward, even to the Pacific Ocean, whenever we should acquire the country that far. . . .

Then, sir, in 1848 we acquired from Mexico the country between the Rio Del Norte and the Pacific ocean. Immediately after that acquisition, the Senate, on my own motion, voted into a bill a provision to extend the Missouri compromise indefinitely westward to the Pacific ocean, in the same sense, and with the same understanding with which it was originally adopted. That provision passed this body by a decided majority—I think by ten at least—and went to the House of Representatives, and was there defeated by northern votes.

Now, sir, let us pause and consider for a moment. The first time that the principles of the Missouri compromise were ever abandoned, the first time they were ever rejected by Congress, was by the defeat of that provision in the House of Representatives in 1848. By whom was that defeat effected? By northern votes, with Free-Soil proclivities. It was the defeat of that Missouri compromise that reopened the slavery agitation with all its fury. It was the defeat of that Missouri compromise that created the tremendous struggle of 1850. It was the defeat of that Missouri compromise that created the necessity for making a new compromise in 1850. Had we been faithful to the principles of the Missouri compromise in 1848, this question would not have arisen. Who was it that was faithless? I undertake to say it was the very men who now insist that the Missouri compromise was a solemn compact, and should never be violated or departed from. Every man who is now assailing the principle of the bill under consideration, so far as I am advised, was opposed to the Missouri compromise in 1848. The very men who now arraign me for a departure from the Missouri compromise, are the men who successfully violated it, repudiated it, and caused it to be superseded by the compromise measures of 1850. Sir, it is with rather bad grace that the men who proved false themselves, should charge upon me and others, who were ever faithful, the responsibilities and consequences of their own treachery.

Then, sir, as I before remarked, the defeat of the Missouri compromise in 1848 having created the necessity for the establishment of a new one in 1850, let us see what that compromise was.

The leading feature of the compromise of 1850 was congressional non-intervention as to slavery in the Territories; that the people of the Territories, and of all the States, were to be allowed to do as they pleased upon the subject of slavery, subject only to the provisions of the Constitution of the United States.

That, sir, was the leading feature of the compromise measures of 1850. Those measures therefore, abandoned the idea of a geographical line as the boundary between free States and slave States; abandoned it because compelled to do it from an inability to maintain it; and in lieu of that, substituted a great principle of self-government, which would allow the people to do as they thought proper. Now, the question is, when that new compromise, resting upon that great fundamental principle of freedom, was established, was it not an abandonment of the old one—the geographical line? Was it not a supersedure of the old one within the very language of the substitute for the bill which is now under consideration? I say it did supersede it, because it applied its provisions as well to the north as to the south of 36° 30'. . . .

I say, therefore, that a close examination of this act clearly establishes the fact that it was the intent as well as the legal effect of the compromise measures of 1850 to supersede the Missouri compromise, and all geographical and territorial lines. . . .

Mr. President, I repeat, that so far as the question of slavery is concerned, there is nothing in the bill under consideration which does not carry out the principle of the compromise measures of 1850, by leaving the people to do as they please, subject only to the provisions of the Constitution of the United States. If that principle is wrong, the bill is wrong. If that principle is right, the bill is right. It is unnecessary to quibble about phraseology or words; it is not the mere words, the mere phraseology, that our constituents wish to judge by. They wish to know the legal effect of our legislation.

The legal effect of this bill, if it be passed as reported by the Committee on Territories, is neither to legislate slavery into these Territories nor out of them, but to leave the people do as they please, under the provisions and subject to the limitations of the Constitution of the United States. Why should not this principle prevail? Why should any man, North or South, object to it? I will especially address the argument to my own section of country, and ask why should any northern man object to this principle? If you will review the history of the slavery question in the United States, you will see that all the great results in behalf of free institutions which have been worked out, have been accomplished by the operation of this principle, and by it alone. . . .

Let me ask you where have you succeeded in excluding slavery by an act of Congress from one inch of the American soil? You may tell me that you did it in the northwest territory by the ordinance of 1787. I will show you by the history of the country that you did not accomplish any such thing. You prohibited slavery there by law, but you did not exclude it in fact. Illinois was a part of the northwest territory. With the exception of a few French and white settlements, it was a vast wilderness, filled with hostile savages, when the ordinance of 1787 was adopted. Yet, sir, when Illinois was organized into a territorial government it established and protected slavery, and maintained it in spite of your ordinance, and in defiance of its express prohibition. It is a curious fact, that so long as Congress said the territory of Illinois should not have slavery, she actually had it; and on the very day when you withdrew your congressional prohibition, the people of Illinois of their own free will and accord, provided for a system of emancipation.

Thus you did not succeed in Illinois Territory with your ordinance or your Wilmot Proviso, because the people there regarded it as an invasion of their rights. They regarded it as a usurpation on the part of the Federal Government. They regarded it as violative of the great principles of self-government, and they determined that they would never submit even to have freedom so long as you forced it upon them.

Nor must it be said that slavery was abolished in the constitution of Illinois in order to be admitted into the Union as a State, in compliance with the ordinance of 1787, for they did no such thing. In the constitution with which the people of Illinois were admitted into the Union, they absolutely violated, disregarded, and repudiated your ordinance. The ordinance said that slavery should be forever prohibited in that country. The constitution with which you received them into the Union as a State said that all slaves then in the State should remain slaves for life, and that all persons born of slave parents after a certain day should be free at a certain age, and that all persons born in the State after a certain other day should be free from the time of their birth. Thus their State constitution, as well as their territorial legislation, repudiated your ordinance. Illinois, therefore, is a case in point to prove that whenever you have attempted to dictate institutions to any part of the United States, you have failed. The same is true, though not to the same extent, with reference to the Territory of Indiana, where there were many slaves during the time of its territorial existence; and I believe also there were a few in the Territory of Ohio.

But, sir, these Abolition confederates in their manifesto, have also referred to the wonderful results of their policy in the State of Iowa and the Territory of Minnesota. Here again they happen to be in fault as to the laws of the land. The act to organize the Territory of Iowa did not prohibit slavery, but the people of Iowa were allowed to do as they pleased under the territorial government; for the sixth section of that act provided that the legislative authority should extend to all rightful subjects of legislation, except as to the disposition of the public lands, and taxes in certain cases, but not excepting slavery. It may, however, be said by some that slavery was prohibited in Iowa by virtue of that clause in the Iowa act which declared the laws of Wisconsin to be in force therein, inasmuch as the ordinance of 1787 was one of the laws of Wisconsin. If, however, they say this, they defeat their object, because the very clause which transfers the laws of Wisconsin to Iowa, and makes them of force therein, also provides that those laws are subject to be altered, modified or repealed by the Territorial Legislature of Iowa. Iowa, therefore, was left to do as she pleased. Iowa, when she came to form a constitution and State government, preparatory to admission into the Union, considered the subject of free and slave institutions calmly, dispassionately, without any restraint or dictation, and determined that it would be to the interest of her people in their climate, and with their productions, to prohibit slavery, and hence Iowa became a free State by virtue of this great principle of allowing the people to do as they please, and not in obedience to any federal command.

The Abolitionists are also in the habit of referring to Oregon as another instance of the triumph of their abolition policy. There again they have overlooked or misrepresented the history of the country. Sir, it is well known, or if it is not, it ought to be, that for about twelve years you failed to give Oregon any government or any protection; and during that period the inhabitants of that country established a government of their own, and by virtue of their own laws, passed by their own representatives before you extended your jurisdiction over them, prohibited slavery by a unanimous vote. Slavery was prohibited there by the action of the people themselves, and not by virtue of any legislation of Congress.

It is true that in the midst of the tornado which swept over the country in 1848, 1849, and 1850, a provision was forced into the Oregon bill prohibiting slavery in that Territory; but that only goes to show that the object of those who pressed it was not so much to establish free institutions as to gain a political advantage by giving an ascendancy to their peculiar doctrines, in the laws of the land; for slavery having been already prohibited there, and no man proposing to establish it, what was the necessity for insulting the people of Oregon by saying in your law that they should not do that which they had unanimously said they did not wish to do? That was the only effect of your legislation, so far as the Territory of Oregon was concerned.

How was it in regard to California? Every one of these abolition confederates who have thus arraigned me and the Committee on Territories before the country, who have misrepresented our position, and misquoted the law and the fact, predicted that unless Congress interposed by law, and prohibited slavery in California, it would inevitably become a slave-holding State. Congress did not interfere; Congress did not prohibit slavery. There was no enactment upon the subject; but the people formed a State constitution, and then prohibited slavery.

MR. WELLER. The vote was unanimous in the convention of California for prohibition.

MR. DOUGLAS. So it was in regard to Utah and New Mexico. In 1850, we who resisted any attempt to force institutions upon the people of those Territories, inconsistent with their wishes and their right to decide for themselves, were denounced as slavery propagandists. Every one of us who was in favor of the Compromise measures of 1850 was arraigned for having advocated a principle proposing to introduce slavery into those Territories. . . .

I know of but one Territory of the United States where slavery does exist, and that one is where you have prohibited it by law, and it is this very Nebraska Territory. In defiance of the eighth section of the act of 1820, in defiance of Congressional dictation, there have been, not many, but a few slaves introduced. I heard a minister of the Gospel the other day conversing with a member of the Committee on Territories upon this subject. This preacher was from that country; and a member put this question to him: "Have you any negroes out there?" He said there were a few held by the Indians. I asked him if there were not some held by white men? He said there were a few, under peculiar circumstances, and he gave an instance: An abolition missionary, a very good man, had gone there from Boston, and he took his wife with him. He got out into the country, but could not get any help; hence he, being a kind-hearted man, went down to Missouri, and gave $1,000 for a negro, and took him up there as "help." [Laughter.] So, under peculiar circumstances, when these Free-Soil and Abolition preachers and missionaries go into the country, they can buy a negro for their own use, but they do not like to allow any one else to do the same thing. [Renewed laughter.] I suppose the fact of the matter is simply this: there the people can get no servants—no "help," as they are called in the section of country where I was born—and, from the necessity of the case, they must do the best they can, and for this reason, a few slaves have been taken there. I have no doubt that whether you organize the Territory of Nebraska or not this will continue for sometime to come. It certainly does exist, and it will increase as long as the Missouri compromise applies to the Territory; and I suppose it will continue for a little while during their territorial condition, whether a prohibition is imposed or not. But when settlers rush in—when labor becomes plenty, and therefore cheap, in that climate, with its productions, it is worse than folly to think of its being a slave-holding country. I do not believe there is a man in Congress who thinks it could be permanently a slave-holding country. I have no idea that it could. All I have to say on that subject is, that when you create them into a Territory, you thereby acknowledge that they ought to be considered a distinct political organization. And when you give them in addition a Legislature, you thereby confess that they are competent to exercise the powers of legislation. If they wish slavery they have a right to it. If they do not want it they will not have it, and you should not force it upon them.

I do not like, I never did like, the system of legislation on our part, by which a geographical line, in violation of the laws of nature, and climate, and soil, and of the laws of God, should be run to establish institutions for a people; yet, out of a regard for the peace and quiet of the country, out of respect for past pledges, and out of a desire to adhere faithfully to all compromises, I sustained the Missouri compromise so long as it was in force, and advocated its extension to the Pacific. Now, when that has been abandoned, when it has been superseded, when a great principle of self-government has been substituted for it, I choose to cling to that principle, and abide in good faith, not only by the letter, but by the spirit of the last compromise.

Sir, I do not recognize the right of the Abolitionists of this country to arraign me for being false to sacred pledges, as they have done in their proclamation. Let them show when and where I have ever proposed to violate a compact. I have proved that I stood by the compact of 1820 and 1845, and proposed its continuance and observance in 1848. I have proved that the Free-Soilers and Abolitionists were the guilty parties who violated that compromise then. I should like to compare notes with these Abolition confederates about adherence to compromises. When did they stand by or approve of any one that was ever made?

Did not every Abolitionist and Free-Soiler in America denounce the Missouri compromise in 1820? Did they not for years hunt down ravenously for his blood every man who assisted in making that compromise? Did they not in 1845, when Texas was annexed, denounce all of us who went for the annexation of Texas, and for the continuation of the Missouri compromise line through it? Did they not in 1848 denounce me as a slavery propagandist for standing by the principles of the Missouri compromise, and proposing to continue the Missouri compromise line to the Pacific ocean? Did they not themselves violate and repudiate it then? Is not the charge of bad faith true as to every Abolitionist in America, instead of being true as to me and the committee, and those who advocate this bill?

They talk about the bill being a violation of the compromise measures of 1850. Who can show me a man in either House of Congress who was in favor of the compromise measures of 1850, and who is not now in favor of leaving the people of Nebraska and Kansas to do as they please upon the subject of slavery according to the provisions of my bill? Is there one? If so, I have not heard of him. This tornado has been raised by Abolitionists, and Abolitionists alone. They have made an impression upon the public mind in the way in which I have mentioned, by a falsification of the law and the facts. . . .

Now, I ask the friends and the opponents of this measure to look at it as it is. Is not the question involved the simple one, whether the people of the Territories shall be allowed to do as they please upon the question of slavery, subject only to the limitations of the Constitution? That is all the bill provides; and it does so in clear, explicit, and unequivocal terms. I know there are some men, Whigs and Democrats, who, not willing to repudiate the Baltimore platform of their own party, would be willing to vote for this principle, provided they could do so in such equivocal terms that they could deny that it means what it was intended to mean in certain localities. I do not wish to deal in any equivocal language. If the principle is right, let it be avowed and maintained. If it is wrong, let it be repudiated. Let all this quibbling about the Missouri compromise, about the territory acquired from France, about the act of 1820, be cast behind you; for the simple question is, will you allow the people to legislate for themselves upon the subject of slavery? Why should you not?

When you propose to give them a territorial government do you not acknowledge that they ought to be erected into a political organization; and when you give them a Legislature do you not acknowledge that they are capable of self-government? Having made the acknowledgement, why should you not allow them to exercise the rights of legislation? Oh, these Abolitionists say they are entirely willing to concede all this, with one exception. They say they are willing to trust the Territorial Legislature, under the limitations of the Constitution, to legislate upon the rights of inheritance, to legislate in regard to religion, education, and morals, to legislate in regard to the relations of husband and wife, of parent and child, of guardian and ward, upon everything pertaining to the dearest rights and interests of white men, but they are not willing to trust them to legislate in regard to a few miserable negroes. That is their single exception. They acknowledge that the people of the Territories are capable of deciding for themselves concerning white men, but not in relation to negroes. The real gist of the matter is this: Does it require any higher degree of civilization, and intelligence, and learning, and sagacity, to legislate for negroes than for white men? If it does, we ought to adopt the abolition doctrine, and go with them against this bill. If it does not—if we are willing to trust the people with the great, sacred, fundamental right of prescribing their own institutions, consistent with the Constitution of the country, we must vote for this bill as reported by the Committee on Territories. That is the only question involved in the bill. I hope I have been able to strip it of all the misrepresentation, to wipe away all of that mist and obscurity with which it has been surrounded by this Abolition address.

Discussion Starters

1. How does Douglas' explanation of the historical process by which the question of slavery had been managed in the United States compare with most textbook accounts of the same period? Why was the Missouri Compromise of basic importance to his arguments?

2. Who were the "people" that Douglas kept referring to? In what ways could their identity make a difference in the implementation of this bill once Congress had passed it?

3. Evaluate Douglas' contention that nature, climate, and soil were more important in determining the introduction and perpetuation of slavery in the territories than were acts of Congress. Identify other critical questions confronting the federal government to which expanded versions of this argument might apply. What might justify letting the "people" rather than the federal government decide such critical questions?

4. In his speech Douglas tried to answer the political problems faced by the extension of slavery into the territories. His conclusion called for letting the people do as they pleased about the question, subject only to the limitations of the Constitution. How would his position have been affected if moral limitations—raised by questions pertaining to the extension of a system that permitted one human being to own another—had been applied to the slavery question? Speculate on why Douglas ignored the moral issues in the controversy and concentrated only on its political aspects.

Related Documents

I. The Kansas Emigrants

JOHN GREENLEAF WHITTIER

The popular sovereignty proposed by Douglas may have appeared to be a logical solution to a majority in Congress, but in Kansas it was a different matter. The settlers in western Missouri (a slaveholding state) were determined to make the new territory a slave state, regardless of its geographic suitability for it, and had staked out absentee claims in eastern Kansas. But the antislave forces were also

John Greenleaf Whittier, *Complete Poetical Works* (Boston: Houghton Mifflin, c. 1894), p. 317.

at work, for in 1854 Eli Thayer organized the Emigrant Aid Society in Massachusetts to send free-soil families to settle Kansas. Thayer's concern became the cause of the abolitionists, as they sent families and "Beecher's Bibles" (Sharpe's rifles) to Kansas to keep it free from slavery. The cause was celebrated in the North by songs and poems about Kansas and the virtues of the new crusaders for freedom.

One of the most popular of these works was the following poem by the abolitionist poet John Greenleaf Whittier. How does his poem attempt to discredit Douglas' claim that popular sovereignty would solve the problem of slavery on the frontier?

We cross the prairie as of old
   The Pilgrims crossed the sea,
To make the West, as they the East,
   The homestead of the free!

We go to rear a wall of men
   On freedom's southern line,
And plant beside the cotton tree
   The rugged Northern pine!

We're flowing from our native hills
   As our free rivers flow;
The blessing of our motherland
   Is on us as we go.

We go to plant her common schools
   On distant prairie swells,
And give the Sabbaths of the wild
   The music of her bells.

Up bearing, like the Ark of old,
   The Bible in our van,
We go to test the truth of God
   Against the fraud of man.

No pause, nor rest, save where the streams
   That feed the Kansas run,
Save where our Pilgrim gonfalon
   Shall flout the setting sun!

We'll tread the prairie as of old
   Our fathers sailed the sea,
And make the West, as they the East,
   The homestead of the free!

II. Code of the Border Ruffians

The influx of antislave settlers into Kansas through the programs of the Emigrant Aid Company and other abolitionist organizations caused the proslavery advocates in Missouri to fear a free-soil takeover of their claims and the destruction of slavery in the new territory. As a result, the election of a territorial delegate to Congress proved to be the first test of popular sovereignty in Kansas. Hundreds of armed men streamed from Missouri across the border and elected a proslave candidate. A similar situation occurred on March 30, 1855, when a territorial legislature was elected. This legislature, dubbed the "bogus legislature" by the abolitionists because it was dominated by proslavery forces, established itself at the Shawnee Indian Mission near the Missouri border and began to pass legislation to protect and perpetuate the institution of slavery in the territory of Kansas.

How do these laws attempt to legislate morality and ignore the Constitution?

Be it enacted by the Governor and Legislative Assembly of the Territory of Kansas, as follows:

Section 1.   That every person, bond or free, who shall be convicted of actually raising a rebellion or insurrection of slaves, free negroes, or mulattoes, in this Territory, shall suffer death.

Sec. 2.   Every free person who shall aid or assist in any rebellion or insurrection of slaves free negroes, or mulattoes, or shall furnish arms, or do any overt act in furtherance of such rebellion or insurrection, shall suffer death.

Sec. 3.   If any free person shall, by speaking, writing, or printing, advise, persuade, or induce any slaves to rebel, conspire against, or murder any citizen of this Territory, or shall bring into, print, write, publish or circulate, or cause to be brought into, printed, written, published or circulated, or shall knowingly aid or assist in the bringing into, printing, writing, publishing, or circulating in this Territory, any book, paper, magazine, pamphlet, or circular, for the purpose of exciting insurrection, rebellion, revolt, or conspiracy on the part of the slaves, free negroes, or mulattoes, against the citizens of the Territory or any part of them, such person shall be guilty of felony, and shall suffer death.

Sec. 4.   If any person shall entice, decoy, or carry away out of this Territory, any slave belonging to another, with intent to deprive the owner thereof of the services of such slave, or with intent to effect to procure the freedom of such slave, he shall be adjudged guilty of grand larceny and, on conviction thereof, shall suffer death, or be imprisoned at hard labor for not less than ten years.

Sec. 5.   If any person shall aid or assist in enticing, decoying, or persuading, or carrying away or sending into this Territory any slave belonging to another, with intent to procure or effect the freedom of such slave, or with

The Border Ruffian Code in Kansas (New York, 1856).

intent to deprive the owner thereof of the services of such slave, he shall be adjudged guilty of grand larceny, and, on conviction thereof, shall suffer death, or be imprisoned at hard labor for not less than ten years.

Sec. 6. If any person shall entice, decoy, or carry away out of any State or other Territory of the United States any slave belonging to another, with intent to procure or effect the freedom of such slave, or to deprive the owner thereof of the services of such slave, and, shall bring such slave into this Territory, he shall be adjudged guilty of grand larceny, in the same manner as if such slave had been enticed, decoyed, or carried away out of this Territory, and in such case the larceny may be charged to have been committed in any county of this Territory, into or through which such slave shall have been brought by such person, and on conviction thereof, the person offending shall suffer death, or be imprisoned at hard labor for not less than ten years.

Sec. 7. If any person shall entice, persuade, or induce any slave to escape from the service of his master or owner, in this Territory, or shall aid or assist any slave in escaping from the service of his master or owner, or shall aid, assist, harbor, or conceal any slave who may have escaped from the service of his master or owner, he shall be deemed guilty of felony, and punished by imprisonment at hard labor for a term of not less than five years.

Sec. 8. If any person in this Territory shall aid or assist, harbor or conceal any slave who has escaped from the service of his master or owner, in another State or Territory, such person shall be punished in like manner as if such slave had escaped from the service of his master or owner in this Territory.

Sec. 9. If any person shall resist any officer while attempting to arrest any slave that may have escaped from the service of his master or owner, or shall rescue such slave when in the custody of any officer or other person, or shall entice, persuade, aid or assist such slave to escape from the custody of any officer or other person who may have such slave in custody, whether such slave have escaped from the service of his master or owner in this Territory or in any other State or Territory, the person so offending shall be guilty of felony and punished by imprisonment at hard labor for a term of not less than two years.

Sec. 10. If any marshal, sheriff, or constable, or the deputy of any such officer, shall, when required by any person, refuse to aid or assist in the arrest and capture of any slave that may have escaped from the service of his master or owner, whether such slave shall have escaped from his master or owner in this Territory, or any State or other Territory, such officer shall be fined in a sum of not less than one hundred nor more than five hundred dollars.

Sec. 11. If any person print, write, introduce into, publish or circulate, or cause to be brought into printed, written, published, or circulated, or shall knowingly aid or assist in bringing into, printing, publishing, or circulating within this Territory, any book, paper, pamphlet, magazine, handbill or circular, containing any statements, arguments, opinions, sentiment, doctrine, advice, or innuendo, calculated to produce a disorderly, dangerous, or rebellious disaffection among the slaves in this Territory, or to induce such slaves to escape from the service of their masters, or to resist their authority, he shall be guilty of felony, and be punished by imprisonment and hard labor for a term of not less than five years.

Sec. 12.   If any free person, by speaking or by writing, assert or maintain that persons have not the right to hold slaves in this Territory or shall introduce into this Territory, print, publish, write, circulate, or cause to be introduced into this Territory, written, printed, published, or circulated in this Territory, any book, paper, magazine, pamphlet, or circular, containing any denial of the right of persons to hold slaves in this Territory, such person shall be deemed guilty of felony, and punished by imprisonment at hard labor for a term of not less than two years.

Sec. 13.   No person who is conscientiously opposed to holding slaves, or who does not admit the right to hold slaves in this Territory, shall sit as a juror on the trial of any prosecution for any violation of any of the sections of this act.

III. Appeal to the South

The proslavery men in western Missouri became increasingly concerned over the number of free-soil emigrants to Kansas from the North, especially from New England. As the numbers of free-soil men increased, the proslavery forces saw their hold upon the territorial legislature and their military superiority weaken. In order to counteract this trend, a call went out to the Southern states to send proslavery emigrants to Kansas. This appeal achieved mild success with the organization and emigration of about four hundred men under the direction of Jefferson Buford in the spring of 1856. But four hundred men were not enough to secure Kansas for the South, so new appeals went out.

How does the following article try to use the control of Kansas as the key to the future of the Union?

To the People of the South:
On the undersigned, managers of the "Lafayette Emigration Society," has devolved the important duty of calling the attention of the people of the slaveholding states to the absolute necessity of immediate action on their part in relation to the settlement of Kansas Territory. The crisis is at hand. Prompt and decisive measures must be adopted, or farewell to Southern rights and independence.

The Western counties of Missouri have, for the last two years, been heavily taxed, both in money and time, in fighting the battles of the South. Lafayette County alone has expended more than $100,000 in money, and as much, or more, in time. Up to this time, the border counties of Missouri have upheld and maintained the rights and interests of the South in this struggle, unassisted and unsuccessfully. But the Abolitionists, staking their all upon the Kansas issue, and hesitating at no means, fair or foul, are moving heaven and

De Bow's Review, May 1856, cited in *The Annals of America* (Chicago: Encyclopedia Britannica, 1968), VIII, pp. 365–66.

earth to render that beautiful territory not only a free state, so-called, but a den of Negro thieves and "higher law" incendiaries.

Missouri, we feel confident, has done her duty and will still be found ready and willing to do all she can, fairly and honorably, for the maintenance of the integrity of the South. But the time has come when she can no longer stand up, single-handed, the lone champion of the South, against the myrmidons of the entire North. It requires no great foresight to perceive that if the "higher law" men succeed in this crusade, it will be but the commencement of a war upon the institutions of the South, which will continue until slavery shall cease to exist in any of the states or the Union is dissolved.

How, then, shall these impending evils be avoided? The answer is obvious. *Settle the Territory with emigrants from the South.* The population of the territory at this time is about equal—as many pro-slavery settlers as Abolitionists; but the fanatics have emissaries in all the free states—in almost every village—and by misrepresentation and falsehood are engaged in collecting money and enlisting men to tyrannize over the South. Is it in the nature of Southern men to submit without resistance, to look to the North for their laws and institutions? We do not believe it! . . .

. . . We repeat it, the crisis has arrived. The time has come for action— *bold, determined action;* words will no longer do any good; we must have men in Kansas, and that too by tens of thousands. A few will not answer. If we should need 10,000, and lack one of that number, all will count nothing. Let all, then, who can come, do so at once. Those who cannot come must give their money to help others to come. There are hundreds of thousands of broad acres of rich land, worth from $5 to $20 per acre, open to settlement and preemption, at $1.25 per acre.

Let, then, the farmer come and bring his slaves with him. There are now 1,000 slaves in Kansas whose presence there strengthens our cause. Shall we allow these rich lands and this beautiful country to be overrun by our Abolition enemies? We know of a surety that they have emissaries and spies in almost every town, village, and city in the South, watching our movements and tampering with our slaves. Let us, then, be vigilant and active in the cause; we must maintain our ground. The loss of Kansas to the South will be the death knell of our dear Union.

IV. The Sack of Lawrence

WILLIAM PHILLIPS

The community of Lawrence was the center of the free-soil movement in the Kansas territory. It had been settled by Eli Thayer's Emigrant Aid Society in

William Phillips, *The Conquest of Kansas by Missouri and Her Allies* (Boston: Phillips, Sampson, 1856), pp. 296–301.

July 1854, and had been named after the chief financial contributor to the society, Amos A. Lawrence, a New England manufacturer. This town became the symbol of freedom to the abolitionists, but of rebellion to the South. Lawrence offended the proslavery forces in its newspaper articles, in drumming up free-soil support in the elections, in its military preparations, but most of all because the town existed. The people of Lawrence had been behind the establishment of a free-soil government at Topeka with a constitutuon that declared, "slavery shall not exist in the state," and Charles Robinson of Lawrence had been elected the first free-state governor of Kansas. The proslavery men regarded the town as a haven of "fanatics" who had to be cleaned out by the "law and order" forces of the true territorial legislature. On May 21, 1856, a force of between five hundred and eight hundred proslavery men invaded the town. There was no resistance to the raiders since they were accompanied by the "legal" authorities of the proslavery legislature, but lack of resistance meant cowardice to the Southerners, who were determined to destroy the town.

The following article is an account of the destruction of Lawrence written by William Phillips, a correspondent for Horace Greeley's New York Tribune. Although the basic facts are true, what is there about this account which would make it suspect as objective news reporting?

MAY 21, 1856

The army of invasion formed into line and marched into Lawrence. A motley-looking crew they were; many of them had red flannel shirts, with curious border ruffian devices on them, so that they could be recognized by their friends in travelling. This scarlet uniform gave them some little the appearance of the "red coats;" and certainly never did such "tories" march to desecrate American soil, or trample under foot the rights of American freemen. . . .

The first place attacked was the printing office of the *"Free State."* It was in the second story of a concrete building. There was a store below. One of the ruffian officers entered the store and demanded of the proprietor if there was a mine under the building to blow it up. The merchant assured him there was not, when the interrogator told him that they were going up into the printing office, and that if anything happened he would hold him responsible. The "posse" or ruffians, either or both, entered the office of the *Free State,* and the work of demolition commenced. The press and other articles were first broken, so as to be rendered perfectly useless, and then thrown into the Kansas river. As this was some distance to carry the articles, they got tired of it, and began throwing the remainder in the street. Books and papers were thrown in the street. . . .

The office of the other paper in Lawrence, the *Herald of Freedom,* was entered by the Carolinians, shortly after their compatriots had commenced the work of demolition in the *Free State* office. . . . In the *Herald of Freedom* office the same reckless work of destruction went on. The presses were broken in a thorough and *enlightened* manner, which showed the hand or the direction of a practical printer, the fragments being perfectly useless. Books and papers were thrown out in the street, or stolen. Several members of the posse were marching about the streets with books stuck on the points of their bayonets. Others were tearing books to shreds, but the more prudent carried them off.

The next step in the process was the destruction of the hotel. The enemy planted their artillery in front of the hotel, one hundred and fifty feet distant from it, across Massachusetts-street. The hotel was a very large building, three full stories high besides the basement; it seemed almost impossible that they could miss it. The proprietor of the establishment, Mr. Eldridge, was notified by Jones to remove his furniture in a certain time. This Mr. Eldridge said he could not do. Some of the posse went to work and began to carry articles of furniture out into the street; but they very soon got weary of this, and found a task more congenial. They discovered the wines and liquors, a good stock of which was on hand, and, helping themselves freely to these and to eatables and cigars, the heroes of this gallant campaign were soon in an interesting condition.

. . . Some fifty rounds were fired, when, finding it slow business, the hotel looking, externally, little the worse for it, they undertook to blow it up. Four kegs of gunpowder were placed in it, but only two of them exploded, and they made little report, and still less impression on the walls; but fire was communicated to the building in several places, and it was soon a magnificent sea of flame. . . .

And now commenced a scene of wild and reckless pillage. When the citizens of Lawrence had left their homes, those who could locked them; but locks and bolts were small security; when the marauders could not enter by the doors, they got in by the windows. All the money and jewelry that could be found was taken, and also clothing. In fact, they took everything they wanted, or could carry away. Much of what they could not take, they destroyed. . . .

The closing act was the burning of Governor Robinson's dwelling, which stood upon the brow of Mount Oread. This had been plundered through the day, and at night it was set on fire; and the pyramid of flame from the mount lighted up the pathway of the retreating army.

Besides the plundering in town, these men both before and after the 21st, went about the country, and plundered many houses. It is supposed that not less than two hundred horses were taken, in and around Lawrence. There were also frightful stories of outrages, and of women being ravished. Such cases there may have been, but rare. There were villains in that posse who were certainly none too good for it.

V. An Appeal to the American People

SARA ROBINSON

The news of the sack of Lawrence reached Congress a week after Senator Charles Sumner of Massachusetts had declared in the Senate that "Popular sovereignty, which, when truly understood is a fountain of just power, has ended in popular slavery; not merely in the subjection of the unhappy African race but of this proud Caucasian blood which you boast. The profession with which you began, of All by the People, has been lost in the wretched reality of Nothing for the People." Sumner also bitterly attacked the character of Senator Andrew Butler of South Carolina in his speech. This attack inspired Congressman Preston Brooks to assault Sumner with a cane on the Senate floor. The beating of Sumner, followed by the news from Lawrence, caused a wave of anti-Southern feeling in the North that was only partially mollified by the news that John Brown and his sons had hacked to death five proslavery men near Pottowatomie Creek in Kansas in retaliation for the raid on Lawrence. With the level of violence increasing in Kansas, both sides made new appeals to their constituents for support.

The following selection is from a book on Kansas by the wife of the free-soil governor of the territory, Charles Robinson. Robinson had been arrested for treason by the proslavery legislature and was imprisoned in Kansas awaiting trial while Mrs. Robinson carried his cause to the East. How does Douglas' concept of popular sovereignty stand up in the light of the ideas in this article? How does this article compare with "Appeal to the South"?

Two years have passed since the territory of Kansas was thrown open to settlement. Under the Squatter Sovereignty bill, expecting to be protected, settlers came from the far East and North, as well as from the more Southern and Western States. They had a right to look for such protection to the President of these United States in the very provisions of that bill. How have they been protected? . . .

Lawrence was destroyed. Osawattomie was sacked. Guerilla bands block-aded the highways, and murdered peaceable citizens. Did the President do anything? When by a word he could have given Kansas the long-sought-for peace, he said it not. The White House rose between him and the suffering dwellers in Kansas. He had been struck with official blindness, and saw not how, when he had been their willing agent, their pliant tool, the southern party would cast him off as a worthless thing. . . .

We have fallen upon the evil times, in our country's history, when it is treason to think, to speak a word against the evil of slavery, or in favor of free labor. In Kansas, prisons or instant death by barbarians are the reward; and

Sara T. L. Robinson, *Kansas: Its Interior and Exterior Life* (Boston: Crosby, Nichols, 1856), pp. 343–48.

in the Senate, wielders of bludgeons are honored by the state which has sent ruffians to desolate Kansas. But in this reign of misrule the President and his advisers have failed to note the true effect of such oppression. The fires of liberty have been rekindled in the hearts of our people, and burn in yet brighter flame under midnight skies illumined by their own burning dwellings. The sight of lawless, ruthless invaders, acting under the United States government, has filled them with that "deep, dark, sullen, teeth-clenched silence, bespeaking their hatred of tyranny, which armed a William Tell and Charlotte Corday." The best, the boldest utterance of man's spirit for freedom will not be withheld. The administration, with the most insane malignity, has prepared the way for a civil war, and the extermination of freemen in Kansas. With untiring malice, it has endeavored to effect this by the aid of a corrupt judiciary, packed juries, and reckless officials. In violation of the Constitution of the United States, no regard was paid to the sacred rights of freemen in their persons and property. Against the known sentiment and conviction of half the nation these deeds of infamy have been plotted, and have been diligently carried on. That a people are down-trodden is not evidence that they are subdued. The crushed energies are gathering strength; and, like a strong man resting from the heats and toils of the day, the people of Kansas will arise to do battle for liberty; and, when their mighty shouts for freedom shall ascend over her hills and prairies, slavery will shrink back abashed. Life, without liberty, is valueless, and these are times which demand the noble sacrifice of life. The people of Kansas are in the midst of such times; and amid discomfiture and defeat men will be found who for the right will stand with sterner purpose and bolder front. Kansas will never be surrendered to the slave power. God has willed it! Lawrence, the city where the plundered feasted at the hospitable table, and, Judas-like, went out to betray it, will come forth from its early burial clothed with yet more exceeding beauty. Out of its charred and blood-stained ruins, where the flag of rapine floated, will spring the high walls and strong parapets of freedom. The sad tragedies in Kansas will be avenged, when freedom of speech, of the press, and of the person, are made sure by the downfall of those now in power, and when the song of the reaper is heard again over our prairies, and, instead of the clashing of arms, we see the gleam of the ploughshare in her peaceful valleys. Men of the North, shall the brave hearts in Kansas struggle alone?

VI. The Republican Platform of 1856

Kansas became "Bleeding Kansas" in the summer of 1856. The Democratic party, with President Franklin Pierce at its head, could not—or in the opinion of the free-soil men would not—stop the destruction of freedom in Kansas. This led to the establishment of an opposition party in the Old Northwest. Calling

Republican Platform (New York: 1856).

themselves Republicans, they became strong enough to hold a national convention in Philadelphia to nominate a candidate for the presidential election of 1856. They chose John C. Fremont, the famed soldier-explorer, as their standard-bearer. The Republicans made a good showing; had Fremont carried Illinois and Pennsylvania he would have defeated James Buchanan, the Democratic candidate.

How did the Republican platform of 1856 answer the problems posed by the events in Kansas? What elements of Senator Douglas' popular sovereignty remain in the Republican view of the crisis?

JUNE 18, 1856

This Convention of Delegates, assembled in pursuance of a call addressed to the people of the United States, without regard to past political differences or divisions, who are opposed to the repeal of the Missouri Compromise: to the policy of the present Administration; to the extension of Slavery into Free Territory; in favor of admitting Kansas as a free State; of restoring the action of the Federal Government to the principles of WASHINGTON and JEFFERSON, and who purpose to unite in presenting candidates for the offices of President and Vice President, do resolve as follows:

Resolved, That the maintenance of the principles promulgated in the Declaration of Independence and embodied in the Federal Constitution, are essential to the preservation of our republican institutions, and that the Federal Constitution, the rights of the States, and the union of the States shall be preserved.

Resolved, That with our republican fathers we hold it to be a self-evident truth, that all men are endowed with the inalienable rights to life, liberty, and the pursuit of happiness, and that the primary object and ulterior designs of our federal government were, to secure these rights to all persons within its exclusive jurisdiction; that as our republican fathers, when they had abolished slavery in all our national territory, ordained that no person should be deprived of life, liberty, or property, without due process of law, it becomes our duty to maintain this provision of the Constitution against all attempts to violate it for the purpose of establishing slavery in any territory of the United States, by positive legislation, prohibiting its existence or extension therein. That we deny the authority of Congress, of a territorial legislature, of any individual or association of individuals, to give legal existence to slavery in any territory of the United States, while the present Constitution shall be maintained.

Resolved, That the Constitution confers upon Congress sovereign power over the territories of the United States for their government and that in the exercise of this power it is both the right and the duty of Congress to prohibit in the territories those twin relics of barbarism—polygamy and slavery.

Resolved, That while the Constitution of the United States was ordained and established by the people in order to form a more perfect Union, establish justice, insure domestic tranquillity, provide for the common defence, and secure the blessings of liberty, and contains ample provisions for the protection of the life, liberty, and property of every citizen, the dearest Constitutional rights of the people of Kansas, have been fraudulently and violently taken from them—their territory has been invaded by an armed force—spurious and pretended legislative, judicial, and executive officers have been set over them, by whose usurped authority, sustained by the military power of the government, tyrannical and unconstitutional laws have been enacted and enforced— the rights of the people to keep and bear arms have been infringed—test oaths of an extraordinary and entangling nature have been imposed, as a condition of exercising the right of suffrage and holding office—the right of an accused person to a speedy and public trial by an impartial jury has been denied—the right of the people to be secure in their persons, houses, papers, and effects against unreasonable searches and seizures has been violated—they have been deprived of life, liberty, and property, without due process of law—that the freedom of speech and of the press has been abridged—the right to choose their representatives has been made of no effect—murders, robberies, and arsons have been instigated and encouraged, and the offenders have been allowed to go unpunished—that all these things have been done with the knowledge, sanction and procurement of the present administration, and that for this high crime against the Constitution, the Union, and humanity, we arraign the administration, the President, his advisers, agents, supporters, apologists and accessories, either before or after the facts, before the country and before the world, and that it is our fixed purpose to bring the actual perpetrators of these atrocious outrages and their accomplices to a sure and condign punishment hereafter.

Resolved, That Kansas should be immediately admitted as a State of the Union, with her present free constitution, as at once the most effectual way of securing to her citizens the enjoyments of the rights and privileges to which they are entitled, and of ending the civil strife now raging in her territory. . . .

Resolved, That we invite the affiliation and co-operation of the men of all parties, however different from us in other respects, in support of the principles herein declared; and believing that the spirit of our institutions, as well as the Constitution of our country, guarantees liberty of conscience and equality of rights among citizens, we oppose all legislation impairing their security.

For Further Reading

Books on the conflict in Kansas in the 1850s are: Paul W. Gates, *Fifty Million Acres: Conflicts over Kansas Land Policy** (1954); Samuel A. Johnson, *The Battle Cry of Freedom: The New England Emigrant Aid Company in the Kansas Crusade* (1954); James C. Malin, *The Nebraska Question, 1852–1854* (1953); and James A. Rawley, *Race & Politics** (1969).

A general history of the state is William Frank Zornow's *Kansas: A History of the Jayhawk State* (1957).

*Paperbound edition available.

The developments that led to the conflict in Kansas, and eventually to the break-up of the Union, are analyzed in Thomas B. Alexander, *Sectional Stress and Party Strength* (1967); Avery Craven, *Growth of Southern Nationalism* (1953); *The Causes of the Civil War** (1965), edited by Kenneth M. Stampp; and Roy F. Nichols, *The Disruption of the American Democracy** (1948).

The impact of "Bleeding Kansas" on the formation of the new Republican party is covered in *The Republican Party, 1854–1964** (1964) by George H. Mayer.

Biographies of some of the leading participants in the crisis in Kansas are: David Donald, *Charles Sumner and the Coming of the Civil War* (1960); Allen Johnson, *Stephen A. Douglas* (1908; reprinted in 1970); Philip S. Klein, *President James Buchanan* (1962); James C. Malin, *John Brown and the Legend of Fifty-six* (1942; reprinted in 1970); William E. Parrish, *David Rice Atchinson of Missouri* (1961); Robert Rayback, *Millard Fillmore* (1959); and Oswald G. Villard, *John Brown* (1943).

The plight of the black American during the territorial crisis and after is examined in Eugene H. Berwanger, *The Frontier Against Slavery: Western Anti-Negro Prejudice & the Slavery Extension Controversy* (1967); Leon Litwack, *North of Slavery** (1965); Vincent C. Hopkins, *Dred Scott's Case** (1951); and Stanley I. Kutler, *The Dred Scott Decision** (1967).

Two notable contemporary accounts of the period are *The Impending Crisis in the South** (1857; reprinted in 1968) by Hinton R. Helper, and Harriet Beecher Stowe's *Uncle Tom's Cabin** (1852; reprinted in 1962).

*Paperbound edition available.

15. The Civil War: Why They Fought

Why do men fight wars?

Most Americans would answer: To protect their homes, their families, and their nation from destruction by the forces of evil. In 1860 the forces of evil in America were characterized by the opposing sides as "damn Yankees" or as "Southern traitors."

When Abraham Lincoln was elected president in 1860, the South Carolina legislature took steps to "protect" its Southern way of life by seceding from the Union. By early spring 1861, seven states had left the Union, confiscated federal arms, and occupied federal property within their borders. Such actions could not go unnoticed by the president, and in April he ordered supplies sent to Fort Sumter in Charleston Harbor and weapons to Fort Pickens in Florida to "protect" the property of the people of the United States.

The news that relief ships would be sent to Fort Sumter prompted the government of the new Confederate States of America to interpret Lincoln's action as a declaration of war against the South. But before the relief ships could arrive, Major Robert Anderson, commander of Fort Sumter, was asked to surrender, and he agreed. Anderson's acceptance did not reach the appropriate Confederate officials within the prescribed time and on April 12 the Confederate batteries around the harbor began to shell the fort. On April 13, Major Anderson's message was acknowledged and he surrendered the fort to the forces of General P. G. T. Beauregard, C.S.A. Two days later Lincoln, confronted with active rebellion and the prospect of the destruction of the

Union, called for the loyal state militias to assemble and for Congress to convene on July 4, 1861.

The men who participated in the American Civil War did so for a number of reasons. Some sought the excitement and supposed glory of battle, others responsibility and power over their fellow men, and still others saw the war as a crusade against tyranny. But whatever the personal reasons, the general framework of the war was fought by both sides within the context of protecting a way of life and preserving a nation, and 618,000 Americans lost their lives in protecting their homes, their families, and their country from destruction by what they considered the forces of evil.

Core Document

Our Cause Is Just and Holy

JEFFERSON DAVIS

Jefferson Davis was inaugurated as provisional president of the Confederate States of America at Montgomery, Alabama, on February 18, 1861. He brought to the office a wealth of political and military experience gained over many years of public service. Davis graduated from West Point in 1828 and served for seven years on the frontier. After resigning from the army, he settled in Mississippi as a cotton planter. He was elected to Congress in 1845, but resigned the next year to assume command of a unit of the Mississippi militia known as the Mississippi Rifles in the Mexican War. He became a war hero as a result of the Battle of Buena Vista, when his forces held a sagging American line together and turned defeat into victory. In 1847 the grateful Mississippi legislature rewarded his valor by appointing him to the United States Senate. Four years later he ran unsuccessfully for the governorship of the state, but in 1853 his friend President Pierce appointed him Secretary of War. After serving a successful term he was again sent to the Senate by Mississippi in 1857.

During Davis' second term in the Senate he became the chief congressional spokesman for Southern rights. As such, he opposed the concept of popular sovereignty advocated chiefly by Douglas and the assertion that Congress had the right to judge, by the existence of slavery, whether a territory could be admitted to the Union. Davis defended the institution of slavery, and when Douglas was nominated by the Democrats, he and many other Southerners withdrew from the party. With the split in the Democratic ranks, Lincoln won a plurality to become president.

James D. Richardson, ed., *A Compilation of the Messages and Papers of the Confederacy* (Nashville: United States Publishing, 1905), I, pp. 63–75, 81–82.

To Davis the Republicans were abolitionists out to destroy the South. Therefore, in order to protect his section, he advised secession from the Union and the
establishment of a new Southern government. On January 21, 1861, he removed
himself from the Senate and went home to Mississippi to serve the Southern
cause.

Davis made the following address to the Confederate Congress on April 29,
1861, in answer to Lincoln's call for a special session of the United States
Congress and for volunteers to protect the Union.

In reading Davis' speech pay close attention to his:

- interpretation of the constitutional establishment of the United States.
- arguments that a Northern conspiracy existed with the aim of subverting
  the freedom of the Southern states.
- interpretation of the role of slavery in the conflict between the North and
  the South.
- concept of states' rights.
- evaluation of the Southern attempt to negotiate a peaceful settlement.
- account of the events surrounding the bombardment of Fort Sumter.
- appraisal of Southern spirit and unity.

APRIL 29, 1861

Gentlemen of the Congress:

It is my pleasing duty to announce to you that the Constitution framed
for the establishment of a permanent Government for the Confederate States
has been ratified by conventions in each of those States to which it was referred.
To inaugurate the Government in its full proportions and upon its own substantial basis of the popular will, it only remains that elections should be held
for the designation of the officers to administer it. There is every reason to
believe that at no distant day other States, identified in political principles and
community of interests with those which you represent, will join this Confederacy, giving to its typical constellation increased splendor, to its Government
of free, equal, and sovereign States a wider sphere of usefulness, and to the
friends of constitutional liberty a greater security for its harmonious and
perpetual existence. It was not, however, for the purpose of making this
announcement that I have deemed it my duty to convoke you at an earlier day
than that fixed by yourselves for your meeting. The declaration of war made
against this Confederacy by Abraham Lincoln, the President of the United
States, in his proclamation issued on the 15th day of the present month,
rendered it necessary, in my judgment, that you should convene at the earliest
practicable moment to devise the measures necessary for the defense of the
country. The occasion is indeed an extraordinary one. It justifies me in a brief
review of the relations heretofore existing between us and the States which now
unite in warfare against us and in a succinct statement of the events which have
resulted in this warfare, to the end that mankind may pass intelligent and
impartial judgment on its motives and objects. During the war waged against
Great Britain by her colonies on this continent a common danger impelled

them to a close alliance and to the formation of a Confederation, by the terms of which the colonies, styling themselves States, entered *"severally* into a firm league of friendship with each other for their common defense, the security of their liberties, and their mutual and general welfare, binding themselves to assist each other against all force offered to or attacks made upon them, or any of them, on account of religion, sovereignty, trade, or any other pretense whatever." In order to guard against any misconstruction of their compact, the several States made explicit declaration in a distinct article—that *"each* State *retains its* sovereignty, freedom, and independence, and every power, jurisdiction, and right which is not by this Confederation *expressly delegated* to the United States in Congress assembled."

Under this contract of alliance, the war of the Revolution was successfully waged, and resulted in the treaty of peace with Great Britain in 1783, by the terms of which the several States were *each by name* recognized to be independent. The Articles of Confederation contained a clause whereby all alterations were prohibited unless confirmed by the Legislatures of *every State* after being agreed to by the Congress; and in obedience to this provision, under the resolution of Congress of the 21st of February, 1787, the several States appointed delegates who attended a convention "for the *sole and express purpose* of revising the Articles of Confederation and reporting to Congress and the several Legislatures such alterations and provisions therein as shall, when agreed to in Congress *and confirmed by the States,* render the Federal Constitution adequate to the exigencies of Government and the preservation of the Union." It was by the delegates chosen by the *several States* under the resolution just quoted that the Constitution of the United States was framed in 1787 and submitted to the *several States* for ratification, as shown by the seventh article, which is in these words: "The ratification of the *conventions of nine States* shall be sufficient for the establishment of this Constitution *between the States* so ratifying the same." I have italicized certain words in the quotations just made for the purpose of attracting attention to the singular and marked caution with which the States endeavored in every possible form to exclude the idea that the separate and independent sovereignty of each State was merged into one common government and nation, and the earnest desire they evinced to impress on the Constitution its true character—that of a *compact between* independent States. The Constitution of 1787, having, however, omitted the clause already recited from the Articles of Confederation, which provided in explicit terms that each State *retained* its sovereignty and independence, some alarm was felt in the States, when invited to ratify the Constitution, lest this omission should be construed into an abandonment of their cherished principle, and they refused to be satisfied until amendments were added to the Constitution placing beyond any pretense of doubt the reservation by the States of all their sovereign rights and powers not expressly delegated to the United States by the Constitution.

Strange, indeed, must it appear to the impartial observer, but it is none the less true that all these carefully worded clauses proved unavailing to prevent the rise and growth in the Northern States of a political school which has persistently claimed that the government thus formed was not a compact *between* States, but was in effect a national government, set up *above* and *over* the States. An organization created by the States to secure the blessings of liberty and independence against *foreign* aggression, has been gradually perverted into a machine for their control in their *domestic* affairs. The *creature* has been exalted above its *creators;* the *principals* have been made subordinate to the *agent* appointed by themselves. The people of the Southern States, whose almost exclusive occupation was agriculture, early perceived a tendency in the Northern States to render the common government subservient to their own purposes by imposing burdens on commerce as a protection to their manufacturing and shipping interests. Long and angry controversies grew out of these attempts, often successful, to benefit one section of the country at the expense of the other. And the danger of disruption arising from this cause was enhanced by the fact that the Northern population was increasing, by immigration and other causes, in a greater ratio than the population of the South. By degrees, as the Northern States gained preponderance in the National Congress, self-interest taught their people to yield ready assent to any plausible advocacy of their right as a majority to govern the minority without control. They learned to listen with impatience to the suggestion of any constitutional impediment to the exercise of their will, and so utterly have the principles of the Constitution been corrupted in the Northern mind that, in the inaugural address delivered by President Lincoln in March last, he asserts as an axiom, which he plainly deems to be undeniable, that the theory of the Constitution requires that in all cases the majority shall govern; and in another memorable instance the same Chief Magistrate did not hesitate to liken the relations between a State and the United States to those which exist between a county and the State in which it is situated and by which it was created. This is the lamentable and fundamental error on which rests the policy that has culminated in his declaration of war against these Confederate States. In addition to the long-continued and deep-seated resentment felt by the Southern States at the persistent abuse of the powers they had delegated to the Congress, for the purpose of enriching the manufacturing and shipping classes of the North at the expense of the South, there has existed for nearly half a century another subject of discord, involving interests of such transcendent magnitude as at all times to create the apprehension in the minds of many devoted lovers of the Union that its permanence was impossible. When the several States delegated certain powers to the United States Congress, a large portion of the laboring population consisted of African slaves imported into the colonies by the mother country. In twelve out of the thirteen States negro slavery existed, and the right of property in slaves was protected by law. This property was recognized in the Constitution, and provision was made against its loss by the escape of the slave. The increase in the number of slaves by further importation from Africa was also secured by a clause forbidding Congress to prohibit the slave trade anterior to a certain date, and in no clause can there be found any delegation of power to the Congress authorizing it in any manner to legislate to the prejudice, detriment, or discouragement of the owners of that species of property, or excluding it from the protection of the Government.

The climate and soil of the Northern States soon proved unpropitious to the continuance of slave labor, whilst the converse was the case in the South. Under the unrestricted free intercourse between the two sections, the Northern States consulted their own interests by selling their slaves to the South and prohibiting slavery within their limits. The South were willing purchasers of a property suitable to their wants, and paid the price of the acquisition without harboring a suspicion that their quiet possession was to be disturbed by those who were inhibited not only by want of constitutional authority, but by good faith as vendors, from disquieting a title emanating from themselves. As soon, however, as the Northern States that prohibited African slavery within their limits had reached a number sufficient to give their representation a controlling voice in the Congress, a persistent and organized system of hostile measures against the rights of the owners of slaves in the Southern States was inaugurated and gradually extended. A continuous series of measures was devised and prosecuted for the purpose of rendering insecure the tenure of property in slaves. Fanatical organizations, supplied with money by voluntary subscriptions, were assiduously engaged in exciting amongst the slaves a spirit of discontent and revolt; means were furnished for their escape from their owners, and agents secretly employed to entice them to abscond; the constitutional provision for their rendition to their owners was first evaded, then openly denounced as a violation of conscientious obligation and religious duty; men were taught that it was a merit to elude, disobey, and violently oppose the execution of the laws enacted to secure the performance of the promise contained in the constitutional compact; owners of slaves were mobbed and even murdered in open day solely for applying to a magistrate for the arrest of a fugitive slave; the dogmas of these voluntary organizations soon obtained control of the Legislatures of many of the Northern States, and laws were passed providing for the punishment, by ruinous fines and long-continued imprisonment in jails and penitentiaries, of citizens of the Southern States who should dare to ask aid of the officers of the law for the recovery of their property. Emboldened by success, the theater of agitation and aggression against the clearly expressed constitutional rights of the Southern States was transferred to the Congress; Senators and Representatives were sent to the common councils of the nation, whose chief title to this distinction consisted in the display of a spirit of ultra fanaticism, and whose business was not "to promote the general welfare or insure domestic tranquillity," but to awaken the bitterest hatred against the citizens of sister States by violent denunciation of their institutions; the transaction of public affairs was impeded by repeated efforts to usurp powers not delegated by the Constitution, for the purpose of impairing the security of property in slaves, and reducing those States which held slaves to a condition of inferiority. Finally a great party was organized for the purpose of obtaining the administration of the Government, with the avowed object of using its power for the total exclusion of the slave States from all participation in the benefits of the public domain acquired by all the States in common, whether by conquest or purchase; of surrounding them entirely by States in which slavery should be prohibited; of thus rendering the property in slaves so insecure as to be comparatively worthless, and thereby annihilating in effect property worth thousands of millions of dollars. This party, thus organized, succeeded in the month of November last in the election of its candidate for the Presidency of the United States.

In the meantime, under the mild and genial climate of the Southern States and the increasing care and attention for the well-being and comfort of the laboring class, dictated alike by interest and humanity, the African slaves had augmented in number from about 600,000, at the date of the adoption of the constitutional compact, to upward of 4,000,000. In moral and social condition they had been elevated from brutal savages into docile, intelligent, and civilized agricultural laborers, and supplied not only with bodily comforts but with careful religious instruction. Under the supervision of a superior race their labor had been so directed as not only to allow a gradual and marked amelioration of their own condition, but to convert hundreds of thousands of square miles of the wilderness into cultivated lands covered with a prosperous people; towns and cities had sprung into existence, and had rapidly increased in wealth and population under the social system of the South; the white population of the Southern slave-holding States had augmented from about 1,250,000 at the date of the adoption of the Constitution to more than 8,500,000 in 1860; and the productions of the South in cotton, rice, sugar, and tobacco, for the full development and continuance of which the labor of African slaves was and is indispensable, had swollen to an amount which formed nearly three-forths of the exports of the whole United States and had become absolutely necessary to the wants of civilized man. With interests of such overwhelming magnitude imperiled, the people of the Southern States were driven by the conduct of the North to the adoption of some course of action to avert the danger with which they were openly menaced. With this view the Legislatures of the several States invited the people to select delegates to conventions to be held for the purpose of determining for themselves what measures were best adapted to meet so alarming a crisis in their history. Here it may be proper to observe that from a period as early as 1798 there had existed in *all* of the States of the Union a party almost uninterruptedly in the majority based upon the creed that each State was, in the last resort, the sole judge as well of its wrongs as of the mode and measure of redress. Indeed, it is obvious that under the law of nations this principle is an axiom as applied to the relations of independent sovereign States, such as those which had united themselves under the constitutional compact. The Democratic party of the United States repeated, in its successful canvass in 1856, the declaration made in numerous previous political contests, that it would "faithfully abide by and uphold the principles laid down in the Kentucky and Virginia resolutions of 1798, and in the report of Mr. Madison to the Virginia Legislature in 1799; and that it adopts those principles as constituting one of the main foundations of its political creed." The principles thus emphatically announced embrace that to which I have already adverted —the right of each State to judge of and redress the wrongs of which it complains. These principles were maintained by overwhelming majorities of the people of all the States of the Union at different elections, especially in the elections of Mr. Jefferson in 1805, Mr. Madison in 1809, and Mr. Pierce in 1852. In the exercise of a right so ancient, so well-established, and so necessary for self-preservation, the people of the Confederate States, in their conventions, determined that the wrongs which they had suffered and the evils with which they were menaced required that they should revoke the delegation of powers to the Federal Government which they had ratified in their several conventions. They consequently passed ordinances resuming all their rights as sovereign and independent States and dissolved their connection with the other States of the Union.

Having done this, they proceeded to form a new compact amongst themselves by new articles of confederation, which have been also ratified by the conventions of the several States with an approach to unanimity far exceeding that of the conventions which adopted the Constitution of 1787. They have organized their new Government in all its departments; the functions of the executive, legislative, and judicial magistrates are performed in accordance with the will of the people, as displayed not merely in a cheerful acquiescence, but in the enthusiastic support of the Government thus established by themselves; and but for the interference of the Government of the United States in this legitimate exercise of the right of a people to self-government, peace, happiness, and prosperity would now smile on our land. That peace is ardently desired by this Government and people has been manifested in every possible form. Scarce had you assembled in February last when, prior even to the inauguration of the Chief Magistrate you had elected, you passed a resolution expressive of your desire for the appointment of commissioners to be sent to the Government of the United States "for the purpose of negotiating friendly relations between that Government and the Confederate States of America, and for the settlement of all questions of disagreement between the two Governments upon principles of right, justice, equity, and good faith." It was my pleasure as well as my duty to coöperate with you in this work of peace. Indeed, in my address to you on taking the oath of office, and before receiving from you the communication of this resolution, I had said "as a necessity, not a choice, we have resorted to the remedy of separation, and henceforth our energies must be directed to the conduct of our own affairs and the perpetuity of the Confederacy which we have formed. If a just perception of mutual interests shall permit us peaceably to pursue our separate political career, my most earnest desire will have been fulfilled." It was in furtherance of these accordant views of the Congress and the Executive that I made choice of three discreet, able, and distinguished citizens, who repaired to Washington. Aided by their cordial coöperation and that of the Secretary of State, every effort compatible with self-respect and the dignity of the Confederacy was exhausted before I allowed myself to yield to the conviction that the Government of the United States was determined to attempt the conquest of this people and that our cherished hopes of peace were unattainable.

On the arrival of our commissioners in Washington on the 5th of March they postponed, at the suggestion of a friendly intermediary, doing more than giving informal notice of their arrival. This was done with a view to afford time to the President, who had just been inaugurated, for the discharge of other pressing official duties in the organization of his Administration before engaging his attention in the object of their mission. It was not until the 12th of the month that they officially addressed the Secretary of State, informing him of the purpose of their arrival, and stating, in the language of their instructions, their wish "to make to the Government of the United States overtures for the opening of negotiations, assuring the Government of the United States that the President, Congress, and people of the Confederate States earnestly desire a peaceful solution of these great questions; that it is neither their interest nor their wish to make any demand which is not founded on strictest justice, nor do any act to injure their late confederates."

To this communication no formal reply was received until the 8th of April. During the interval the commissioners had consented to waive all questions of form. With the firm resolve to avoid war if possible, they went so far even as to hold during that long period unofficial intercourse through an intermediary, whose high position and character inspired the hope of success, and through whom constant assurances were received from the Government of the United States of peaceful intentions; of the determination to evacuate Fort Sumter; and further, that no measure changing the existing status prejudicially to the Confederate States, especially at Fort Pickens, was in contemplation, but that in the event of any change of intention on the subject, notice would be given to the commissioners. The crooked paths of diplomacy can scarcely furnish an example so wanting in courtesy, in candor, and directness as was the course of the United States Government toward our commissioners in Washington. . . .

Early in April the attention of the whole country, as well as that of our commissioners, was attracted to extraordinary preparations for an extensive military and naval expedition in New York and other Northern ports. These preparations commenced in secrecy, for an expedition whose destination was concealed, only became known when nearly completed, and on the 5th, 6th, and 7th of April transports and vessels of war with troops, munitions, and military supplies sailed from Northern ports bound southward. Alarmed by so extraordinary a demonstration, the commissioners requested the delivery of an answer to their official communication of the 12th of March, and thereupon received on the 8th of April a reply, dated on the 15th of the previous month, from which it appears that during the whole interval, whilst the commissioners were receiving assurances calculated to inspire hope of the success of their mission, the Secretary of State and the President of the United States had already determined to hold no intercourse with them whatever; to refuse even to listen to any proposals they had to make, and had profited by the delay created by their own assurances in order to prepare secretly the means for effective hostile operations. That these assurances were given has been virtually confessed by the Government of the United States by its sending a messenger to Charleston to give notice of its purpose to use force if opposed in its intention of supplying Fort Sumter. No more striking proof of the absence of good faith in the conduct of the Government of the United States toward this Confederacy can be required than is contained in the circumstances which accompanied this notice. According to the usual course of navigation the vessels composing the expedition designed for the relief of Fort Sumter might be expected to reach Charleston Harbor on the 9th of April. Yet, with our commissioners actually in Washington, detained under assurances that notice should be given of any military movement, the notice was not addressed to *them,* but a messenger was sent to Charleston to give the notice to the Governor of South Carolina, and the notice was so given at a late hour on the 8th of April, the eve of the very day on which the fleet might be expected to arrive.

That this maneuver failed in its purpose was not the fault of those who contrived it. A heavy tempest delayed the arrival of the expedition and gave time to the commander of our forces at Charleston to ask and receive the instructions of this Government. Even then, under all the provocation incident to the contemptuous refusal to listen to our commissioners, and the tortuous course of the Government of the United States, I was sincerely anxious to avoid the effusion of blood, and directed a proposal to be made to the commander of Fort Sumter, who had avowed himself to be nearly out of provisions, that we would abstain from directing our fire on Fort Sumter if he would promise not to open fire on our forces unless first attacked. This proposal was refused and the conclusion was reached that the design of the United States was to place the besieging force at Charleston between the simultaneous fire of the fleet and the fort. There remained, therefore, no alternative but to direct that the fort should at once be reduced. This order was executed by General Beauregard with the skill and success which were naturally to be expected from the well-known character of that gallant officer; and although the bombardment lasted but thirty-three hours our flag did not wave over its battered walls until after the appearance of the hostile fleet off Charleston. Fortunately, not a life was lost on our side, and we were gratified in being spared the necessity of a useless effusion of blood, by the prudent caution of the officers who commanded the fleet in abstaining from the evidently futile effort to enter the harbor for the relief of Major Anderson.

I refer to the report of the Secretary of War, and the papers which accompany it, for further details of this brilliant affair. In this connection I cannot refrain from a well-deserved tribute to the noble State, the eminent soldierly qualities of whose people were so conspicuously displayed in the port of Charleston. For months they had been irritated by the spectacle of a fortress held within their principal harbor as a standing menace against their peace and independence. Built in part with their own money, its custody confided with their own consent to an agent who held no power over them other than such as they had themselves delegated for their own benefit, intended to be used by that agent for their own protection against foreign attack, they saw it held with persistent tenacity as a means of offense against them by the very Government which they had established for their protection. They had beleaguered it for months, felt entire confidence in their power to capture it, yet yielded to the requirements of discipline, curbed their impatience, submitted without complaint to the unaccustomed hardships, labors, and privations of a protracted siege; and when at length their patience was rewarded by the signal for attack, and success had crowned their steady and gallant conduct, even in the very moment of triumph they evinced a chivalrous regard for the feelings of the brave but unfortunate officer who had been compelled to lower his flag. All manifestations of exultation were checked in his presence. Their commanding general, with their cordial approval and the consent of his Government, refrained from imposing any terms that could wound the sensibilities of the commander of the fort. He was permitted to retire with the honors of war, to salute his flag, to depart freely with all his command, and was escorted to the vessel in which he embarked with the highest marks of respect from those against whom his guns had been so recently directed.

Not only does every event connected with the siege reflect the highest honor on South Carolina, but the forbearance of her people and of this Government from making any harsh use of a victory obtained under circumstances of such peculiar provocation attest to the fullest extent the absence of any purpose beyond securing their own tranquillity and the sincere desire to avoid the calamities of war. Scarcely had the President of the United States received intelligence of the failure of the scheme which he had devised for the reënforcement of Fort Sumter, when he issued the declaration of war against this Confederacy which has prompted me to convoke you. In this extraordinary production that high functionary affects total ignorance of the existence of an independent Government, which, possessing the entire and enthusiastic devotion of its people, is exercising its functions without question over seven sovereign States, over more than 5,000,000 of people, and over a territory whose area exceeds half a million of square miles. He terms sovereign States "combinations too powerful to be suppressed by the ordinary course of judicial proceedings or by the powers vested in the marshals by law." He calls for an army of 75,000 men to act as a *posse comitatus* in aid of the process of the courts of justice in States where no courts exist whose mandates and decrees are not cheerfully obeyed and respected by a willing people. He avows that "the *first* service to be assigned to the forces called out" will be not to execute the process of courts, but to capture forts and strongholds situated within the admitted limits of this Confederacy and garrisoned by its troops; and declares that "this effort" is intended "to maintain the perpetuity of popular government." He concludes by commanding "the persons composing the combinations aforesaid"—to wit, the 5,000,000 of inhabitants of these States—"to retire peaceably to their respective abodes within twenty days." Apparently contradictory as are the terms of this singular document, one point is unmistakably evident. The President of the United States called for an army of 75,000 men, whose *first* service was to be to capture our forts. It was a plain declaration of war which I was not at liberty to disregard because of my knowledge that under the Constitution of the United States the President was usurping a power granted exclusively to the Congress. . . .

In conclusion, I congratulate you on the fact that in every portion of our country there has been exhibited the most patriotic devotion to our common cause. Transportation companies have freely tendered the use of their lines for troops and supplies. The presidents of the railroads of the Confederacy, in company with others who control lines of communication with States that we hope soon to greet as sisters, assembled in convention in this city, and not only reduced largely the rates heretofore demanded for mail service and conveyance of troops and munitions, but voluntarily proffered to receive their compensation, at these reduced rates, in the bonds of the Confederacy, for the purpose of leaving all the resources of the Government at its disposal for the common defense. Requisitions for troops have been met with such alacrity that the numbers tendering their services have in every instance greatly exceeded the demand. Men of the highest official and social position are serving as volunteers in the ranks. The gravity of age and the zeal of youth rival each other in the desire to be foremost for the public defense; and though at no other point than the one heretofore noticed have they been stimulated by the excitement incident to actual engagement and the hope of distinction for individual achievement, they have borne what for new troops is the most severe ordeal —patient toil and constant vigil, and all the exposure and discomfort of active service, with a resolution and fortitude such as to command approbation and justify the highest expectation of their conduct when active valor shall be required in place of steady endurance. A people thus united and resolved cannot shrink from any sacrifice which they may be called on to make, nor can there be a reasonable doubt of their final success, however long and severe may be the test of their determination to maintain their birthright of freedom and equality as a trust which it is their first duty to transmit undiminished to their posterity. A bounteous Providence cheers us with the promise of abundant crops. The field of grain which will within a few weeks be ready for the sickle give assurance of the amplest supply of food for man; whilst the corn, cotton, and other staple productions of our soil afford abundant proof that up to this period the season has been propitious. We feel that our cause is just and holy; we protest solemnly in the face of mankind that we desire peace at any sacrifice save that of honor and independence; we seek no conquest, no aggrandizement, no concession of any kind from the States with which we were lately confederated; all we ask is to be let alone; that those who never held power over us shall not now attempt our subjugation by arms. This we will, this we must, resist to the direst extremity. The moment that this pretension is abandoned the sword will drop from our grasp, and we shall be ready to enter into treaties of amity and commerce that cannot but be mutually beneficial. So long as this pretension is maintained, with a firm reliance on that Divine Power which covers with its protection the just cause, we will continue to struggle for our inherent right to freedom, independence, and self-government.

JEFFERSON DAVIS

Discussion Starters

1. To what events and legislation was Jefferson Davis probably referring in his arguments that the North, as a section, had repeatedly tried to use the federal government to benefit itself at the expense of the South? In what ways could the same argument be used as an indictment of the South?

2. Evaluate Davis' charge that Lincoln relied on a corrupted interpretation of the Constituion when he asserted that the majority should govern the United States. How would Davis have defined "majority"?

3. Summarize Davis' interpretation of the development of antislavery elements in the North. How does his description of slavery in the South attempt to counter the Northern arguments against slavery? How effective is his description?

4. What effect does the fact that the state of Mississippi was created by the United States have on Davis' argument against Lincoln's state-county, federal-state analogy?

5. With the secession of seven states and the seizure of federal property an accomplished fact, was Davis being realistic in expecting the federal government to negotiate a peace with the Confederate ambassadors to Washington? What evidence, if any, is there in his speech to lead one to believe that Davis knew the peace initiative would be a failure, but that it was a ploy to gain time for the South?

Related Documents

I. "I Would Save the Union"

ABRAHAM LINCOLN

Abraham Lincoln may have appeared as a "Black Republican" to the Southern radicals, but to many Northern radicals he seemed unsure of his duty and pro-Southern in some of his policies. This point of view was forcefully illustrated in an editorial by Horace Greeley in the New York Tribune. *Greeley lectured the President on his responsibility to carry out the abolition of slavery, and questioned whether he ever intended to follow such a policy. Lincoln's reply was a calm reiteration of his policy to preserve the Union. What Greeley did not know was that Lincoln had decided in July 1862 to follow an emancipation policy as*

Abraham Lincoln, *Complete Works,* ed. John G. Nicolay and John Hay (New York: Lamb Publishing, 1905), VIII, pp. 15–16.

soon as the North appeared to be winning on the battlefield.

How do Lincoln's statements about preserving the Union compare to Jefferson Davis' determination to protect the Southern way of life?

Executive Mansion, Washington, August 22, 1862

Hon. Horace Greeley.

Dear Sir: I have just read yours of the 19th, addressed to myself through the New York *Tribune.* If there be in it any statements or assumptions of fact which I may know to be erroneous, I do not, now and here, controvert them. If there be in it any inferences which I may believe to be falsely drawn, I do not, now and here, argue against them. If there be perceptible in it an impatient and dictatorial tone, I waive it in deference to an old friend whose heart I have always supposed to be right.

As to the policy I "seem to be pursuing," as you say, I have not meant to leave any one in doubt.

I would save the Union. I would save it the shortest way under the Constitution. The sooner the national authority can be restored, the nearer the Union will be "the Union as it was." If there be those who would not save the Union unless they could at the same time save slavery, I do not agree with them. If there be those who would not save the Union unless they could at the same time destroy slavery, I do not agree with them. My paramount object in this struggle is to save the Union, and is not either to save or to destroy slavery. If I could save the Union without freeing any slave, I would do it; and if I could save it by freeing all the slaves, I would do it; and if I could save it by freeing some and leaving others alone, I would also do that. What I do about slavery and the coloured race, I do because I believe it helps to save the Union; and what I forbear, I forbear because I do not believe it would help to save the Union. I shall do less whenever I shall believe what I am doing hurts the cause, and I shall do more whenever I shall believe doing more will help the cause. I shall try to correct errors when shown to be errors, and I shall adopt new views so fast as they shall appear to be true views.

I have here stated my purpose according to my view of official duty; and I intend no modification of my oft-expressed personal wish that all men everywhere could be free.

Yours,

A. LINCOLN

II. The American Flag

HENRY WARD BEECHER

Henry Ward Beecher was one of the most famous clergymen in the United States during the mid-nineteenth century. He was especially known for his talents as a speaker, and people came from all over the country to hear his sermons at the Plymouth Church in Brooklyn, New York. During the 1850s Beecher believed that the extension of slavery into the territories was morally wrong, but that the Constitution protected it in the states where it had become an institution. With the advent of the Civil War, he became convinced that emancipation should be the primary policy of the Lincoln Administration, and he spoke out (as did Horace Greeley) against Lincoln's seeming reluctance to follow such a policy.

The following address was made to two companies of the "Brooklyn Fourteenth" Regiment who were preparing to leave for the front. How does Beecher's interpretation of the conflict between the North and South differ from Jefferson Davis' defense of the Southern cause?

MAY, 1861

A thoughtful mind, when it sees a nation's flag, sees not the flag, but the nation itself. And whatever may be its symbols, its insignia, he reads chiefly in the flag the government, the principles, the truths, the history, that belong to the nation that sets it forth. . . .

This nation has a banner, too; and until recently wherever it streamed abroad men saw day-break bursting on their eyes. For until lately the American flag has been a symbol of Liberty, and men rejoiced in it. Not another flag on the globe had such an errand, or went forth upon the sea carrying everywhere, the world around, such hope to the captive, and such glorious tidings. The stars upon it were to the pining nations like the bright morning stars of God, and the stripes upon it were beams of morning light. As at early dawn the stars shine forth even while it grows light, and then as the sun advances that light breaks into banks and streaming lines of color, the glowing red and intense white striving together, and ribbing the horizon with bars effulgent, so, on the American flag, stars and beams of many-colored light shine out together. And wherever this flag comes, and men behold it, they see in its sacred emblazonry no ramping lion, and no fierce eagle; no embattled castles, or insignia of imperial authority; they see the symbols of light. It is the banner of Dawn. It means *Liberty;* and the galley-slave, the poor, oppressed conscript, the trodden-down creature of foreign despotism, sees in the American flag that very promise and prediction of God,—"The people which sat in darkness saw a great light; and to them which sat in the region and shadow of death light is sprung up." . . .

Henry Ward Beecher, *Patriotic Addresses* (New York: Fords, Howard & Hulbert, 1887), pp. 289–303.

If one, then, asks me the meaning of our flag, I say to him, It means just what Concord and Lexington meant, what Bunker Hill meant; it means the whole glorious Revolutionary War, which was, in short, the rising up of a valiant young people against an old tyranny, to establish the most momentous doctrine that the world had ever known, or has since known,—the right of men to their own selves and to their liberties. . . .

How glorious, then, has been its origin! How glorious has been its history? How divine is its meaning! In all the world is there another banner that carries such hope, such grandeur of spirit, such soul-inspiring truth, as our dear old American flag? made by liberty, made for liberty, nourished in its spirit, carried in its service, and never, not once in all the earth, made to stoop to despotism! Never,—did I say? Alas! Only to that worst despotism, Southern slavery, has it bowed. Remember, every one of you, that the slaveholders of the South, alone of all the world, have put their feet upon the American flag!

And now this banner has been put on trial! It has been condemned. For what? Has it failed of duty? Has liberty lost color by it? Have moths of oppression eaten its folds? Has it refused to shine on freemen and given its light to despots? No. It has been true, brave, loyal. It has become too much a banner of liberty for men who mean and plot despotism. Remember, citizen! remember, Christian soldier! the American flag has been fired upon by Americans, and trodden down because it stood in the way of slavery! . . .

Accept it, then, in all its fullness of meaning. It is not a painted rag. It is a whole national history. It is the Constitution. It is the government. It is the free people that stand in the government on the Constitution. Forget not what it means; and for the sake of its ideas, rather than its mere emblazonry, be true to your country's flag. By your hands lift it; but let your lifting it be no holiday display. It must be advanced *"because of the truth."*. . .

If any man asks me whether I will consent to a compromise, I reply, Yes. I love compromises; they are dear to me—if I may make them. Give me a compromise that shall bring peace. Let me say, "Hang the ringleading traitors; suppress their armies; give peace to their fields; lift up the banner, and make a highway in which every true American citizen, minding his own business, can walk unmolested; free the Territories, and keep them free,"—that is our compromise. Give to us the doctrine of the fathers, renew the Declaration of Independence, refill the Constitution with the original blood of liberty, destroy traitors and treason, make the doctrine of secession a byword and a hissing; make laws equal; let that justice for which they were ordained be the same in Maine or Carolina, to the rich and to the poor, the bond and the free,—and thus we will *compromise*. . . .

You live in a civilized age. You go on a sacred mission. The prayers and sympathies of Christendom are with you. You go to open again the shut-up fountains of liberty, and to restore this disgraced banner to its honor. You go to serve your country in the cause of liberty; and if God brings you into conflict ere long with those misguided men of the South, when you see their miserable, new-vamped banner, remember what that flag means,—Treason, Slavery, Despotism; then look up and see the bright stars and the glorious stripes over your own head, and read in them Liberty, *Liberty,* LIBERTY!

And if you fall in that struggle, may some kind hand wrap around about you the flag of your country, and may you die with its sacred touch upon you. It shall be sweet to go to rest lying in the folds of your country's banner, meaning, as it shall mean, "Liberty *and* Union, now and forever."

We will not forget you. You go forth from us not to be easily and lightly passed over. The waves shall not close over the places which you have held; but when you return,—not as you go, many of you inexperienced, and many of you unknown,—you shall return from the conquests of liberty with a reputation and a character established forever to your children and your children's children. It shall be an honor, it shall be a legend, it shall be a historic truth; and your posterity shall say: "Our fathers stood up in the day of peril, and laid again the foundations of liberty that were shaken; and in their hands the banner of our country streamed forth like the morning star upon the night."

God bless you!

III. All Eager for the Fray: Resolutions by the Colored Citizens of Boston

The response of the black population to the outbreak of hostilities between the North and the South was immediate support for President Lincoln's call for volunteers to protect the nation. But this support was not accepted by the federal government because of the administration's policy to stay clear of the "colored problem" and concern itself only with the preservation of the Union. To enlist free blacks or runaway slaves would play into the hands of the abolitionists, who were trying to make the war a crusade, and run counter to the official explanation of the war as a political question.

There were also the prejudices of the Northern whites against the arming of the blacks, some because they believed the blacks could not become competent soldiers, others because they envisioned a social revolution stemming from such an action. But by the summer of 1862 the official attitude had changed, mainly because of the increasing demands of the war, and Congress authorized the enlistment of blacks into the Union service. By the end of the war over 180,000 black Americans had volunteered for service with the North. Black troops—or as they were referred to at the time, "United States Colored Troops"—fought well and in several actions drew praise from General Grant and other top government officials.

How do the following resolutions, while pledging support for the Union

The Liberator, May 31, 1861.

cause, demonstrate that the Boston "colored" saw the war as more than just a political conflict?

The following Resolutions were adopted at a recent meeting of the colored citizens of Boston:—

Whereas, the traitors of the South have assailed the United States Government, with the intention of overthrowing it for the purpose of perpetuating slavery; and,

Whereas, in such a contest between the North and South—believing, as we do, that it is a contest between liberty and despotism—it is as important for each class of citizens to declare, as it is for the rulers of the Government to know, their sentiments and position; therefore,

Resolved, That our feelings urge us to say to our countrymen that we are ready to stand by and defend the Goverment as the equals of its white defenders—to do so with "our lives, our fortunes, and our sacred honor," for the sake of freedom and as good citizens; and we ask you to modify your laws, that we may enlist—that full scope may be given to the patriotic feelings burning in the colored man's breast—and we pledge ourselves to raise an army in the country of fifty thousand colored men.

Resolved, That more than half of the army which we could raise, being natives of the South, knowing its geography, and being acquainted with the character of the enemy, would be of incalculable service to the Government.

Resolved, That the colored women would go as nurses, seamstresses, and warriors, if need be, to crush rebellion and uphold the Government.

Resolved, That the colored people, almost without an exception, "have their souls in arms, and all eager for the fray," and are ready to go at a moment's warning, if they are allowed to go as soldiers.

Resolved, That we do immediately organize ourselves into drilling companies, to the end of becoming better skilled in the use of fire-arms; so that when we shall be called upon by the country, we shall be better prepared to make a ready and fitting response.

IV. Tennessee Is Disenthralled at Last: An Editorial

The Tennessee legislature voted down a proposal on February 9, 1861, to call a secession convention to remove their state from the Union. But in May, after the bombardment of Fort Sumter and Lincoln's call for volunteers, Tennessee decided to enter into a military alliance with the seceded states. In June the question was submitted to a vote of the people; secession was approved by a large majority. Tennessee's Governor I.G. Harris then declared the state seceded on

Memphis Avalanche, May 6, 1861, cited in Frank Moore, ed., *The Rebellion Record* (New York: G. P. Putnam, 1861), I, pp. 204–5.

June 24. This secession was not endorsed by all of the people in the state, for eastern Tennessee was strongly Unionist. This disagreement was pointedly illustrated when Senator Andrew Johnson of Tennessee refused to resign his seat in Congress to support the Confederacy. After some very bitter fighting within the borders of the state, including the battles of Shiloh and Chickamauga, Tennessee was occupied by Union troops in 1862. Senator Johnson was then appointed military governor, a post he held until he was elected vice president in 1864.

How does the editorial from the Memphis Avalanche, *written one day before the military agreement with the Confederacy, parallel Jefferson Davis' arguments for the removal of the Southern states from the Union?*

Tennessee is disenthralled at last. Freedom has again crowned her with a fresh and fadeless wreath. She has broken through the meshes of tyranny. She has shaken off the shackles which tyrants and usurpers were fastening upon her that they might reduce her to helpless and hopeless bondage. She has left a Union in which she was no longer an equal. She has dissolved her connection with States bent on her subjugation and destruction. She has thrown off the yoke of a Government prostituted to the vile purposes of injustice and oppression. Nobly has she asserted her independence and vindicated her sovereignty. . . .

This important change in the political relations of Tennessee creates new and weighty duties and responsbilities, while it awakens new hopes and aspirations. At this moment they urge her to instant and strenuous action. The advent of the new republic has involked the red thunderbolts of war upon its devoted head. It is no sooner born than it is called upon to defend its right to exist. It seems destined to pass through the fiery ordeal of the fiercest and bloodiest strife which, perhaps, history has yet recorded.

The faithless, meddling, and overbearing North, foiled in her long-cherished scheme of sectional domination, usurpation, and tyranny, by the unexpected revolt of the South, gnashes her teeth, and threatens the extermination of her victim. Her people are frenzied with rage; the hell-born passions of avarice, hate, and revenge, sway her infuriated mobs, thirsting for the blood of a people from whom they have received only benefits and favors. A spirit of wild and bloody atrocity, akin to that which raged in the French Revolution, has seized the entire Northern people, extinguishing at once all the sentiments of Christianity, and the feelings of humanity. . . .

Such are the black and threatening clouds of danger, charged with the lightnings of destruction, which now darken the horizon of the Southern Republic. Tennessee, in this tremendous crisis, will do her entire duty. Great sacrifices are demanded of her, and they will be cheerfully made. Her blood and treasure are offered without stint at the shrine of Southern freedom. She counts not the cost at which independence must be bought. The gallant volunteer State of the South, her brave sons now rushing to the standard of the Southern Confederacy, will sustain by their unflinching valor and deathless devotion, her ancient renown achieved on so many battle fields. In fact our entire people—men, women, and children—have engaged in this fight, and are animated by the single, heroic, and indomitable resolve to perish rather than submit to the despicable invader now threatening us with subjugation. They will ratify the ordinance of secession, amid the smoke and carnage of battle; they will write out their endorsement of it with the blood of their foe—they will enforce it at the point of the bayonet and the sword.

Welcome, thrice welcome, glorious Tennessee, to the thriving family of Southern Confederate States!

V. Reverend Hosmer Goes to War

Many men volunteered for military service during the Civil War. Why did they volunteer? There is no simple answer, but there appears to be a surprising similarity between the reasons given by Northerners and those given by Southerners. In the North and South alike men volunteered out of love for country, for God, and for adventure. Each volunteer may have interpreted these general reasons in light of his own personality and with different priorities, but all three concepts played a part in his enlistment.

In the following letter the Reverend James K. Hosmer explained why he enlisted. Although Hosmer fought for the North his reasons could be applied to Southerners of his own generation. How do Hosmer's reasons for volunteering for the military coincide or conflict with the reasons given by most young men today for enlisting in the military?

Camp Miller, Greenfield, Mass., Nov. 13, 1862

Dear P——, ——

To-night there are in the tent at least fifteen men. There are three sets playing cards. I sit at one end of our table, close under the shelving edge of the tent, with head bent over to get rid of the slant of canvas. My seat is a heap of straw, covered with a blanket. A kerosene lamp gives light to me on one side, and to a set at whist on the other. It is cold out of doors; but the tent is in a sweat, with its stove, and a crowd of men. Slap go the cards on the table. Every moment comes up some point for debate. Throughout the tent there is loud and constant talking, sometimes swearing; generally good-natured, sometimes ill-natured.

You want to know why I have left my pulpit and parish, and enlisted. I had several reasons; all plain, simple, and sensible enough. I have believed in the war from the first. The cause of the North, briefly, is, to me, the cause of civilization and liberty. To help this, I have preached, made speeches, and talked in private. Ought I not to practice what I preach? Ought I to shrink from encountering perils and hardships which I have urged others to encounter?

James K. Hosmer, *The Color-Guard* (Boston: Walker, Wise, and Co., 1864), pp. 9–11.

Then, again, having no family, I can go better than many others in our village,—men liable to be drafted, whose means are straitened, and who have wives and children to support. These are my main reasons; but, besides these, I confess to a love for adventure. Moreover, I hope to gain new robustness from the exposure. I own, also, to something of a military spirit. In every honorable war since the settlement of the country, I believe, some member of the stock from which I am descended has taken part. Generally, these ancestors of mine have been in very humble positions; although my great-grandfather held an important command among the militia at Concord Bridge, and did much toward keeping the "embattled farmers" firm on that day before the British volleys. In our family traditions he is an illustrious character, together with his brother, "Uncle Ben," a sturdy husbandman, who fought faithfully that day throughout the long pursuit, and afterward carried a heavy old blunderbuss in many a hard campaign. I own, it is a sort of fame I covet,—to have my name go down in our modest family annals as the parson, who, in his generation, went with rifle on shoulder to Texas or Louisiana or the Carolinas; doing his duty in honorable fields, as did great-grandfather and "Uncle Ben" of old.

I trust that the motives I have put first were the ones that influenced me for the most part; but these last, too, have had their weight. Ed., my young brother, you know, has been made first sergeant of the company. He goes around, therefore, with a broad stripe down each leg, and a blue diamond, with triple underscoring, upon each arm,—insignia upon which we poor privates and corporals look with reverence. I am now one of the eight corporals whose duty it is to guard the colors. I have a narrow stripe running down each pantaloon, and a double bar, or chevron, on each arm. Ed. and I button up to the chin in our blue and brass; and are a brilliant pair, I assure you.

There seems to be no doubt now about our going with Gen. Banks. We hope it will be soon; for, although we are decently comfortable here, we should prefer some sweet-potato patch for a camp-ground, to this pumpkin field.

Yours very truly,

The "CORPORAL"

For Further Reading

The causes of the Civil War have been examined by many historians in the century since the war. These studies include: Bruce Catton, *The Coming Fury** (1961); E. D. Fite, *The Presidential Campaign of 1860* (1911); Louis M. Hacker, *The Triumph of American Capitalism* (1940); Allan Nevins, *The Ordeal of the Union*, 2 vols. (1947) and *The War for the Union*, Volume I (1959); David M. Potter, *Lincoln and His Party in the Secession Crisis** (1942); and Kenneth Stampp, *And the War Came** (1950).

The history of the Confederacy is covered in E. Merton Coulter, *The Confederate States of America* (1950); Clement Eaton, *History of the Southern Confederacy** (1954) and his more general *History of the Old South* (1949;

*Paperbound edition available.

reprinted in 1966); and Charles P. Roland, *The Confederacy** (1960).

Biographies of the period include: James G. Randall, *Lincoln the President** (1945); Benjamin P. Thomas, *Abraham Lincoln* (1952); Burton J. Hendrick, *Statesmen of the Lost Cause: Jefferson Davis and His Cabinet* (1939); and Hudson Strode, *Jefferson Davis,* 4 vols. (1955–64).

Two collections of interpretations of the period are: E. M. Coulter, ed., *The Course of the South to Secession* (1939), and Thomas J. Pressly, ed., *Americans Interpret Their Civil War** (1954).

The role of the black American in the Civil War is found in *The Negro's Civil War** (1965) edited by J. M. McPherson, and Benjamin Quarles' *The Negro in the Civil War** (1953; reprinted in 1968).

Contemporary accounts of the war include Mary Boykin Chestnut, *A Diary From Dixie** (1905); Robert G. H. Kean, *Inside the Confederate Government* (1957); and Bell I. Wiley, *The Life of Billy Yank** (1952) and *The Life of Johnny Reb** (1943).

Problems books are: Norton Garfinkle, ed., *Lincoln and the Coming of the Civil War** (1959); P. J. Staudenraus, ed., *The Secession Crisis** (1963); and Edwin C. Rozwenc, ed., *The Causes of the Civil War** (1961).

The part played by the newspapers in the coming of the war are amply illustrated in two studies: Dwight L. Dumond, *Southern Editorials on Secession* (1931), and Howard Cecil Perkins, *Northern Editorials on Secession,* 2 vols. (1942).

*Paperbound edition available.

16. Civil War and Civil Liberties

Leaders of a democratic nation fighting a war face three difficult problems simultaneously. First, they must mobilize and maintain their physical resources and manpower for war. Second, they must generate and sustain the support of the citizenry. And third, they must contend with the dissent of those opposed to the war effort.

Because the Constitution of the United States specifically names certain liberties pertaining to dissent, the third problem is particularly vexing to American war leaders. To crush dissent in the name of the war effort requires ignoring or suppressing constitutionally protected liberties. Yet war cannot be waged effectively if dissent is rampant.

No war in the history of the United States has received the unanimous support of the American people. The Civil War is no exception. War dissenters caused President Lincoln great distress, a fact that is minimized in most accounts only because, in the end, Lincoln succeeded and the dissenters failed. The conflict between Lincoln and his dissenters merits attention, however, for it reveals the difficulty of maintaining civil liberties in wartime and thus exposes another dimension of the threat war poses to national welfare.

Core Document

Lincoln and the Democrats of New York: An Exchange of Letters

To prosecute the Civil War successfully the President felt it necessary to suppress dissent in some situations by taking such drastic steps as authorizing the arrest of persons without warrants and without showing in the civil courts the causes of the detentions. This, his opponents claimed, was in direct violation of the constitutional provision that "the privilege of habeas corpus *shall not be suspended, unless when in cases of rebellion or invasion the public safety may require it."* Habeas corpus *provides that upon presentation of a writ, a person in detention must be permitted to appear before a judge to hear the charges filed against him. In the absence of charges he must be released.*

Lincoln responded to these objections pragmatically. In his message to Congress on July 4, 1861, he asserted: "As the provision was plainly made for a dangerous emergency, it cannot be believed the framers of the instrument intended that in every case the danger should run its course until Congress could be called together, the very assembling of which might be prevented . . . by the rebellion."

This position represented a giant leap over the hard questions raised by the habeas corpus provision of the Constitution: What is meant by invasion and rebellion and who determines when they exist? Who determines when, where, and for how long public safety is endangered? Who has the authority to suspend habeas corpus? Not waiting to debate these questions, Lincoln pursued his responsibilities as he interpreted them. As early in the war as April 27, 1861, he issued an order to General Winfield Scott suspending the writ of habeas corpus under specific circumstances. Gradually such orders were widened, arrests and detentions increased, and, in some cases where charges were pressed, the trials were held before military rather than civil courts. On September 24, 1862, Lincoln issued a proclamation that amounted to a general suspension of habeas corpus.

Congress, although reluctant to tolerate executive assumption of a power they regarded as theirs, finally accepted the necessity of suspension. On March 3, 1863, they authorized the President to suspend the privilege of the writ of habeas corpus throughout the United States or in any part of it. Under this authorization Lincoln finally suspended it for the duration of the war on September 15, 1863.

This infringement on essential civil liberties was not accepted without resistance, however, and debate on its implications continued even after the suspension had been lifted. Immediately following the war, the Supreme Court issued

Reprinted by permission of the publishers from Frank Freidel, ed., *Union Pamphlets of the Civil War*, Vol. II, pp. 740–51. Cambridge, Mass.: The Belknap Press of Harvard University Press. Copyright 1967 by the President and Fellows of Harvard College.

a ruling that indirectly assailed Lincoln's policies, saying in part: "The Constitution of the United States is a law for rulers and people, equally in war and in peace, and covers with the shield of its protection all classes of men, at all times, and under all circumstances. No doctrine involving more pernicious consequences was ever invented by the wit of man than that any of its provisions can be suspended during any of the great exigencies of government" (ex parte Milligan).

Yet it is a fact that certain constitutional provisions had been suspended, that civil liberties had been suppressed, and that the president had found a rationale for his actions. The following document contains Lincoln's response to a group of Democrats in New York who challenged his policies. It is perhaps his clearest statement on what he felt were his duties and prerogatives as president. In reading the document, note:

- the attempt of the Democrats to establish their loyalty to the Union and its traditions.
- the specific charges the group directs against Lincoln's policies.
- Lincoln's turning of the question from the treason clause to the habeas corpus provision.
- the reasons Lincoln gives for lack of faith in the ordinary courts during wartime.
- Lincoln's interpretation of the reasons for Mr. Vallandigham's arrest.
- Lincoln's conviction that the suppression of civil liberties was only a temporary necessity and his desire to return to normal times.
- Lincoln's effort to turn partisanship to his advantage.

LETTER OF THE COMMITTEE

Albany, May 19, 1863

To His Excellency the President of the United States:—

The undersigned, officers of a public meeting held at the city of Albany on the 16th day of May, instant, herewith transmit to your Excellency a copy of the resolutions adopted at the said meeting, and respectfully request your earnest consideration of them. They deem it proper on their personal responsibility to state that the meeting was one of the most respectable as to numbers and character, and one of the most earnest in the support of the Union ever held in this city.

Yours with great regard,
ERASTUS CORNING, *President.*

RESOLUTIONS

Adopted at the Meeting Held in Albany, N.Y., on the 16th of May, 1863

Resolved, That the Democrats of New York point to their uniform course of action during the two years of civil war through which we have passed, to the alacrity which they have evinced in filling the ranks of the army, to their contributions and sacrifices, as to the evidence of their patriotism and devotion to the cause of our imperiled country. Never in the history of civil war has a government been sustained with such ample resources of means and men as the people have voluntarily placed in the hands of the Administration.

Resolved, That as Democrats we are determined to maintain this patriotic attitude, and, despite of adverse and disheartening circumstances, to devote all our energies to sustain the cause of the Union, to secure peace through victory, and to bring back the restoration of all the States under the safeguards of the Constitution.

Resolved, That while we will not consent to be misapprehended upon these points, we are determined not to be misunderstood in regard to others not less essential. We demand that the Administration shall be true to the Constitution; shall recognize and maintain the rights of the States and the liberties of the citizen; shall everywhere, outside of the lines of necessary military occupation and the scenes of insurrection, exert all its powers to maintain the supremacy of the civil over military law.

Resolved, That in view of these principles we denounce the recent assumption of a military commander to seize and try a citizen of Ohio, Clement L. Vallandigham, for no other reason than words addressed to a public meeting, in criticism of the course of the Administration, and in condemnation of the military orders of that general.[1]

Resolved, That this assumption of power by a military tribunal, if successfully asserted, not only abrogates the right of the people to assemble and discuss the affairs of government, the liberty of speech and of the press, the right of trial by jury, the law of evidence, and the privilege of habeas corpus, but it strikes a fatal blow at the supremacy of law, and the authority of the State and Federal constitutions.

Resolved, That the Constitution of the United States—the supreme law of the land—has defined the crime of treason against the United States to consist "only in levying war against them, or adhering to their enemies, giving them aid and comfort;" and has provided that "no person shall be convicted of treason, unless on the testimony of two witnesses to the same overt act, or on confession in open court." And it further provides, that "no person shall be held to answer for a capital or otherwise infamous crime, unless on a

---

[1]Vallandigham, who had lost his seat in Congress as a result of Republican gerrymandering, was arrested in Dayton in May 1863 for his vitriolic attack on General Ambrose E. Burnside's "General Orders, No. 38." These orders provided that those who committed acts "for the benefit of our enemies" would be tried as spies or traitors, that the habit of declaring sympathy for the enemy would not be tolerated, and that persons arrested would be subject to military procedure. Civil disorder in Dayton followed Vallandigham's arrest, and his arbitrary conviction before a military commission made him the most distinguished martyr among Lincoln's critics. Following his sentence to close confinement in a federal prison, an application for habeas corpus was denied, but Lincoln changed his sentence to banishment to the Confederacy. After being taken behind Confederate lines, where he insisted he be regarded as a prisoner of war, Vallandigham quickly made his way to Canada. About a year later he returned to Ohio, but Lincoln did nothing to prevent his political activities there. The suspicion of treason Vallandigham bore worked to the Democrats' disadvantage and was thus helpful to Lincoln.

presentment or indictment of a grand jury, except in cases arising in the land and naval forces, or in the militia, when in actual service in time of war or public danger;" and further, that "in all criminal prosecutions, the accused shall enjoy the right of a speedy and public trial by an impartial jury of the State and district wherein the crime was committed."

Resolved, That these safeguards of the rights of the citizen against the pretensions of arbitrary power were intended more especially for his protection in times of civil commotion. They were secured substantially to the English people, after years of protracted civil war, and were adopted into our Constitution at the close of the Revolution. They have stood the test of seventy-six years of trial under our republican system, under circumstances which show that, while they constitute the foundation of all free government, they are the elements of the enduring stability of the Republic.

Resolved, That in adopting the language of Daniel Webster, we declare "it is the ancient and undoubted prerogative of this people to canvass public measures and the merits of public men." It is a "home-bred right," a fireside privilege. It has been enjoyed in every house, cottage, and cabin in the nation. It is as undoubted as the right of breathing the air or walking on the earth. Belonging to private life as a right, it belongs to public life as a duty, and it is the last duty which those whose representatives we are shall find us to abandon. Aiming at all times to be courteous and temperate in its use, except when the right itself is questioned, we shall place ourselves on the extreme boundary of our own right, and bid defiance to any arm that would move us from our ground. "This high constitutional privilege we shall defend and exercise in all places—in time of peace, in time of war, and at all times. Living, we shall assert it; and should we leave no other inheritance to our children, by the blessing of God we will leave them the inheritance of free principles, and the example of a manly, independent, and constitutional defence of them."

Resolved, That in the election of Governor Seymour the people of this State by an emphatic majority, declared their condemnation of the system of arbitrary arrests, and their determination to stand by the Constitution. That the revival of this lawless system can have but one result: to divide and distract the North, and to destroy its confidence in the purposes of the Administration. That we deprecate it as an element of confusion at home, of weakness to our armies in the field, and as calculated to lower the estimate of American character and magnify the apparent peril of our cause abroad. And that, regarding the blow struck at a citizen of Ohio as aimed at the rights of every citizen of the North, we denounce it as against the spirit of our laws and Constitution, and most earnestly call upon the President of the United States to reverse the action of the military tribunal which has passed a "cruel and unusual punishment" upon the party arrested, prohibited in terms by the Constitution, and to restore him to the liberty of which he has been deprived.

Resolved, That the president, vice-presidents, and secretary of this meeting, be requested to transmit a copy of these resolutions to his Excellency the President of the United States, with the assurance of this meeting of their hearty and earnest desire to support the Government in every constitutional and lawful measure to suppress the existing rebellion.

MR. LINCOLN'S REPLY

Executive Mansion, Washington, June 12, 1863

Hon. Erastus Corning, and others:

GENTLEMEN:—Your letter of May 19, inclosing the resolutions of a public meeting held at Albany, N.Y., on the 16th of the same month, was received several days ago.

The resolutions, as I understand them, are resolvable into two propositions, first, the expression of a purpose to sustain the cause of the Union, to secure peace through victory, and to support the Administration in every constitutional and lawful measure to suppress the rebellion; and secondly, a declaration of censure upon the Administration for supposed unconstitutional action, such as the making of military arrests. And, from the two propositions, a third is deduced, which is, that the gentlemen composing the meeting are resolved on doing their part to maintain our common government and country, despite the folly or wickedness, as they may conceive, of any Administration. This position is eminently patriotic, and as such I thank the meeting and congratulate the nation for it. My own purpose is the same; so that the meeting and myself have a common object, and can have no difference except in the choice of means or measures for effecting that object.

And here I ought to close this paper, and would close it, if there were no apprehension that more injurious consequences than any merely personal to myself might follow the censures systematically cast upon me for doing what, in my view of duty, I could not forbear. The resolutions promise to support me in every constitutional and lawful measure to suppress the rebellion; and I have not knowingly employed, nor shall knowingly employ, any other. But the meeting, by their resolutions, assert and argue that certain military arrests, and proceedings following them, for which I am ultimately responsible, are unconstitutional. I think they are not. The resolutions quote from the Constitution the definition of treason, and also the limiting safeguards and guarantees therein provided for the citizen on trial for treason, and on his being held to answer for capital or otherwise infamous crimes, and, in criminal prosecutions, his rights to a speedy and public trial by an impartial jury. They proceed to resolve, "that these safeguards of the rights of the citizen against the pretensions of arbitrary power were intended more especially for his protection in times of civil commotion." And, apparently to demonstrate the proposition, the resolutions proceed: "They were secured substantially to the English people *after* years of protracted civil war, and were adopted into our Constitution at the *close* of the Revolution." Would not the demonstration have been better if it could have been truly said that these safeguards had been adopted and applied *during* the civil wars and *during* our Revolution, instead of *after* the one and at the *close* of the other? I, too, am devotedly for them *after* civil war, and *before* civil war, and at all times, "except when, in cases of rebellion or invasion, the public safety may require" their suspension. The resolutions proceed to tell us that these safeguards "have stood the test of seventy-six years of trial, under our republican system, under circumstances which show that, while they constitute the foundation of all free government, they are the elements of the enduring stability of the Republic." No one denies that they have so stood the test up to the beginning of the present rebellion, if we except a certain occurrence at New Orleans; nor does any one question that they will stand the same test much longer after the rebellion closes. But these provisions of the Constitution have no application to the case we have in hand, because the arrests complained of were not made for treason—that is not for *the* treason defined in the Constitution, and upon conviction of which the punishment is death— nor yet were they made to hold persons to answer for any capital or otherwise infamous crimes; nor were the proceedings following, in any constitutional or legal sense, "criminal prosecutions." The arrests were made on totally different grounds, and the proceedings following accorded with the grounds of the arrests. Let us consider the real case with which we are dealing, and apply to it the parts of the Constitution plainly made for such cases.

Prior to my installation here, it had been inculcated that any State had a lawful right to secede from the national Union, and that it would be expedient to exercise the right whenever the devotees of the doctrine should fail to elect a President to their own liking. I was elected contrary to their liking; and, accordingly, so far as it was legally possible, they had taken seven States out of the Union, had seized many of the United States forts, and had fired upon the United States flag, all before I was inaugurated, and, of course, before I had done any official act whatever. The rebellion thus began soon ran into the present civil war; and, in certain respects, it began on very unequal terms between the parties. The insurgents had been preparing for it more than thirty years, while the Government had taken no steps to resist them. The former had carefully considered all the means which could be turned to their account. It undoubtedly was a well-pondered reliance with them that, in their own unrestricted efforts to destroy Union, Constitution, and Law, all together, the Government would, in great degree, be restrained by the same Constitution and law from arresting their progress. Their sympathizers pervaded all departments of the Government and nearly all communities of the people. From this material, under cover of "liberty of speech," "liberty of the press," and "habeas corpus," they hoped to keep on foot among us a most efficient corps of spies, informers, suppliers, and aiders and abettors of their cause in a thousand ways. They knew that in times such as they were inaugurating, by the Constitution itself, the "habeas corpus" might be suspended; but they also knew they had friends who would make a question as to *who* was to suspend it; meanwhile, their spies and others might remain at large to help on their cause. Or, if, as has happened, the Executive should suspend the writ, without ruinous waste of time, instances of arresting innocent persons might occur, as are always likely to occur in such cases; and then a clamor could be raised in regard to this, which might be, at least, of some service to the insurgent cause. It needed no very keen perception to discover this part of the enemy's programme, so soon as, by open hostilities, their machinery was fairly put in motion. Yet, thoroughly imbued with a reverence for the guaranteed rights of individuals, I was slow to adopt the strong measures which by degrees I have been forced to regard as being within the exceptions of the Constitution, and as indispensable to the public safety. Nothing is better known to history than that courts of justice are utterly incompetent to such cases. Civil courts are organized chiefly for trials of individuals, or, at most, a few individuals acting in concert; and this in quiet times, and on charges of crimes well defined in the law. Even in times of peace, bands of horse-thieves and robbers frequently grow too numerous and powerful for the ordinary courts of justice. But what comparison, in numbers, have such bands ever borne to the insurgent sympathizers even in many of the loyal States? Again: a jury too frequently has at least one member more ready to hang the panel than to hang the traitor. And yet, again, he who dissuades one man from volunteering, or induces one soldier to desert, weakens the Union cause as much as he who kills a Union soldier in battle. Yet this dissuasion or inducement may be so conducted as to be no defined crime of which any civil court would take cognizance.

Ours is a case of rebellion—so called by the resolutions before me—in fact, a clear, flagrant, and gigantic case of rebellion; and the provision of the Constitution that "the privilege of the writ of habeas corpus shall not be suspended, unless when, in cases of rebellion or invasion, the public safety may require it," is *the* provision which specially applies to our present case. This provision plainly attests the understanding of those who made the Constitution, that ordinary courts of justice are inadequate to "cases of rebellion"— attests their purpose that, in such cases, men may be held in custody whom the courts, acting on ordinary rules, would discharge. Habeas corpus does not discharge men who are proved to be guilty of defined crime; and its suspension is allowed by the Constitution on purpose that men may be arrested and held who cannot be proved to be guilty of defined crime, "when, in cases of rebellion or invasion, the public safety may require it." This is precisely our present case —a case of rebellion, wherein the public safety *does* require the suspension. Indeed, arrests by process of courts, and arrests in cases of rebellion, do not proceed altogether upon the same basis. The former is directed at the small per-centage of ordinary and continuous perpetration of crime; while the latter is directed at sudden and extensive uprisings against the Government, which, at most, will succeed or fail in no great length of time. In the latter case, arrests are made, not so much for what has been done, as for what probably would be done. The latter is more for the preventive and less for the vindictive than the former. In such cases, the purposes of men are much more easily understood than in cases of ordinary crime. The man who stands by and says nothing when the peril of his Government is discussed, cannot be misunderstood. If not hindered, he is sure to help the enemy; much more, if he talks ambiguously —talks for his country with "buts" and "ifs" and "ands." Of how little value the constitutional provisions I have quoted will be rendered, if arrest shall never be made until defined crimes shall have been committed, may be illustrated by a few notable examples. Gen. John C. Breckinridge, Gen. Robert E. Lee, Gen. Joseph E. Johnson, Gen. John B. Magruder, Gen. William B. Preston, Gen. Simon B. Buckner, and Commodore Franklin Buchanan, now occupying the very highest places in the Rebel war service, were all within the power of the Government since the Rebellion began, and were nearly as well known to be traitors then as now. Unquestionably if we had seized and held them, the insurgent cause would be much weaker. But no one of them had then committed any crime defined in the law. Every one of them, if arrested, would have been discharged on habeas corpus were the writ allowed to operate. In view of these and similar cases, I think the time not unlikely to come when I shall be blamed for having made too few arrests rather than too many.

By the third resolution, the meeting indicate their opinion that military arrests may be constitutional in localities where rebellion actually exists, but that such arrests are unconstitutional in localities where rebellion or insurrection does *not* actually exist. They insist that such arrests shall not be made "outside of the lines of necessary military occupation, and the scenes of insurrection." Inasmuch, however, as the Constitution itself makes no such distinction, I am unable to believe that there *is* any such constitutional distinction. I concede that the class of arrests complained of can be constitutional only when, in cases of rebellion or invasion, the public safety may require them; and I insist that in such cases they are constitutional *wherever* the public safety may require them; as well in places to which they may prevent the rebellion extending as in those where it may be already prevailing; as well where they may restrain mischievous interference with the raising and supplying of armies to suppress the rebellion, as where the rebellion may actually be; as well where they may restrain the enticing men out of the army, as where they would prevent mutiny in the army; equally constitutional at all places where they will conduce to the public safety, as against the dangers of rebellion or invasion. Take the particular case mentioned by the meeting. It is asserted, in substance, that Mr. Vallandigham was, by a military commander, seized and tried "for no other reason than words addressed to a public meeting, in criticism of the course of the Administration, and in condemnation of the military orders of the General." Now, if there be no mistake about this; if this assertion is the truth and the whole truth; if there was no other reason for the arrest, then I concede that the arrest was wrong. But the arrest, as I understand, was made for a very different reason. Mr. Vallandigham avows his hostility to the war on the part of the Union; and his arrest was made because he was laboring, with some effect, to prevent the raising of troops; to encourage desertions from the army; and to leave the rebellion without an adequate military force to suppress it. He was not arrested because he was damaging the political prospects of the Administration, or the personal interests of the commanding general, but because he was damaging the army, upon the existence and vigor of which the life of the nation depends. He was warring upon the military, and this gave the military constitutional jurisdiction to lay hands upon him. If Mr. Vallandigham was not damaging the military power of the country, then his arrest was made on mistake of fact, which I would be glad to correct on reasonably satisfactory evidence.

I understand the meeting, whose resolutions I am considering, to be in favor of suppressing the rebellion by military force—by armies. Long experience has shown that armies cannot be maintained unless desertions shall be punished by the severe penalty of death. The case requires, and the law and the Constitution sanction, this punishment. Must I shoot a simple-minded soldier-boy who deserts, while I must not touch a hair of a wily agitator who induces him to desert? This is none the less injurious when effected by getting a father, or brother, or friend, into a public meeting, and there working upon his feelings till he is persuaded to write the soldier-boy that he is fighting in a bad cause, for a wicked Administration of a contemptible Government, too weak to arrest and punish him if he shall desert. I think that in such a case to silence the agitator and save the boy is not only constitutional, but withal a great mercy.

If I be wrong on this question of constitutional power, my error lies in believing that certain proceedings are constitutional when, in cases of rebellion or invasion, the public safety requires them, which would not be constitutional when, in the absence of rebellion or invasion, the public safety does *not* require them; in other words, that the Constitution is not, in its application, in all respects the same, in cases of rebellion or invasion involving the public safety, as it is in time of profound peace and public security. The Constitution itself makes the distinction; and I can no more be persuaded that the Government can constitutionally take no strong measures in time of rebellion, because it can be shown that the same could not be lawfully taken in time of peace, than I can be persuaded that a particular drug is not good medicine for a sick man, because it can be shown not to be good food for a well one. Nor am I able to appreciate the danger apprehended by the meeting, that the American people will, by means of military arrests during the rebellion, lose the right of public discussion, the liberty of speech and the press, the law of evidence, trial by jury, and habeas corpus, throughout the indefinite peaceful future which I trust lies before them, any more than I am able to believe that a man could contract so strong an appetite for emetics during temporary illness as to persist in feeding upon them during the remainder of his healthful life.

In giving the resolutions that earnest consideration which you request of me, I cannot overlook the fact that the meeting speak as "Democrats." Nor can I, with full respect for their known intelligence, and the fairly presumed deliberation with which they prepared their resolutions, be permitted to suppose that this occurred by accident, or in any way other than that they preferred to designate themselves as "Democrats" rather than "American citizens." In this time of national peril, I would have preferred to meet you upon a level one step higher than any party platform; because I am sure that, from such more elevated position, we could do better battle for the country we all love than we possibly can from those lower ones where, from the force of habit, the prejudices of the past, and selfish hopes of the future, we are sure to expend much of our ingenuity and strength in finding fault with, and aiming blows at each other. But, since you have denied me this, I will yet be thankful, for the country's sake, that not all Democrats have done so. He on whose discretionary judgment Mr. Vallandigham was arrested and tried is a Democrat, having no old party affinity with me; and the judge who rejected the constitutional view expressed in these resolutions, by refusing to discharge Mr. Vallandigham on habeas corpus, is a Democrat of better days than these, having received his judicial mantle at the hands of President Jackson. And still more, of all those Democrats who are nobly exposing their lives and shedding their blood on the battle-field, I have learned that many approve the course taken with Mr. Vallandigham, while I have not heard of a single one condemning it. I cannot assert that there are none such. And the name of President Jackson recalls an instance of pertinent history: After the battle of New Orleans, and while the fact that the treaty of peace had been concluded was well known in the city, but before official knowledge of it had arrived, Gen. Jackson still maintained martial or military law. Now that it could be said the war was over, the clamor against martial law, which had existed from the first, grew more furious. Among other things, a Mr. Louiallier published a denunciatory newspaper article. Gen. Jackson arrested him. A lawyer by the name of Morel procured the United States Judge Hall to issue a writ of habeas corpus to relieve Mr. Louiallier. Gen. Jackson arrested both the lawyer and the judge. A Mr. Hollander ventured to say of some part of the matter that "it was a dirty trick." Gen. Jackson arrested him. When the officer undertook to serve the writ of habeas corpus, Gen. Jackson took it from him, and sent him away with a copy. Holding the judge in custody a few days, the General sent him beyond the limits of his encampment, and set him at liberty, with an order to remain till the ratification of peace should be regularly announced, or until the British should have left the Southern coast. A day or two more elapsed, the ratification of a treaty of peace was regularly announced, and the judge and others were fully liberated. A few days more, and the judge called Gen. Jackson into court and fined him $1,000 for having arrested him and the others named. The General paid the fine and there the matter rested for nearly thirty years, when Congress refunded principal and interest. The late Senator Douglas, then in the House of Representatives, took a leading part in the debates in which the constitutional question was much discussed. I am not prepared to say whom the journals would show to have voted for the measure.

It may be remarked: First that we had the same Constitution then as now; secondly, that we then had a case of invasion, and now we have a case of rebellion; and thirdly, that the permanent right of the people to public discussion, the liberty of speech and of the press, the trial by jury, the law of evidence, and the habeas corpus, suffered no detriment whatever by that conduct of Gen. Jackson, or its subsequent approval by the American Congress.

And yet, let me say that, in my own discretion, I do not know whether I would have ordered the arrest of Mr. Vallandigham. While I cannot shift the responsibility from myself, I hold that, as a general rule, the commander in the field is the better judge of the necessity in any particular case. Of course I must practice a general directory and revisory power in the matter.

One of the resolutions expresses the opinion of the meeting that arbitrary arrests will have the effect to divide and distract those who should be united in suppressing the rebellion, and I am specifically called on to discharge Mr. Vallandigham. I regard this as at least a fair appeal to me on the expediency of exercising a constitutional power which I think exists. In response to such appeal, I have to say it gave me pain when I learned that Mr. Vallandigham had been arrested; that is, I was pained that there should have seemed to be a necessity for arresting him, and that it will afford me great pleasure to discharge him so soon as I can, by any means, believe the public safety will not suffer by it. I further say that, as the war progresses, it appears to me, opinion and action, which were in great confusion at first, take shape, and fall into more regular channels, so that the necessity for strong dealing with them gradually decreases. I have every reason to desire that it should cease altogether; and far from the least is my regard for the opinions and wishes of those who, like the meeting at Albany, declare their purpose to sustain the Government in every constitutional and lawful measure to suppress the rebellion. Still, I must continue to do so much as may seem to be required by the public safety.

ABRAHAM LINCOLN

Discussion Starters

1. Identify the most convincing arguments in Lincoln's letter and speculate on how the New York Democrats might have responded to them. Identify also the soft spots in Lincoln's case and attack them as the Democrats might have done. By what standards does one decide what is or is not convincing?

2. Lincoln's critics, including some not represented by the viewpoints of the New York Democrats, have been variously described as having been motivated by partisanship, obstructionism, defeatism, or ideological commitment to abstract ideals. To what extent are any of these apparent in the resolutions of the New York Democrats? In a democratic nation, under what conditions may actions based on these motives properly be suppressed?

3. James G. Randall has written that if the government under Lincoln erred it did so under great provocation and with the best of motives, and its policy may not be justly criticized without a full understanding of the alarming situation then facing the nation. What standards would one use, then or in more recent times, for measuring provocation and motives?

4. The size of the federal bureaucracy today and the efficient techniques of suppression made possible by technology suggest that the suspension of civil liberties must be regarded with greater apprehension now than in Lincoln's day. Formulate some guidelines for defining when the public safety is endangered and suspension of civil liberties is justified.

Related Documents

I. Executive Order No. 1, Relating to Political Prisoners

President Lincoln's deep concern over loyalty to the war effort is substantiated by the following executive order issued by Secretary of War Edwin M. Stanton. Assuming the description of the extent of disloyalty in the first eight paragraphs to be accurate, what options were open to Lincoln besides the one he followed (as outlined in the remainder of the order)? Today, how could one verify or refute the accuracy of Stanton's description of the prevailing circumstances?

FEBRUARY 14, 1862

The breaking out of a formidable insurrection based on a conflict of political ideas, being an event without precedent in the United States, was necessarily attended by great confusion and perplexity of the public mind. Disloyalty before unsuspected suddenly became bold, and treason astonished the world by bringing at once into the field military forces superior in number to the standing Army of the United States.

Every department of the Government was paralyzed by treason. Defection appeared in the Senate, in the House of Representatives, in the Cabinet, in the Federal courts; ministers and consuls returned from foreign countries to enter the insurrectionary councils or land or naval forces; commanding and other officers of the Army and in the Navy betrayed our councils or deserted their posts for commands in the insurgent forces. Treason was flagrant in the revenue and in the post-office service, as well as in the Territorial governments and in the Indian reserves.

Not only governors, judges, legislators, and ministerial officers in the States, but even whole States rushed one after another with apparent unanimity into rebellion. The capital was besieged and its connection with all the States cut off.

Even in the portions of the country which were most loyal political combinations and secret societies were formed furthering the work of disunion, while, from motives of disloyalty or cupidity or from excited passions or perverted sympathies, individuals were found furnishing men, money, and materials of war and supplies to the insurgents' military and naval forces. Armies, ships, fortifications, navy-yards, arsenals, military posts, and garrisons one after another were betrayed or abandoned to the insurgents.

Congress had not anticipated, and so had not provided for, the emergency. The municipal authorities were powerless and inactive. The judicial

James D. Richardson, ed., *Messages and Papers of the Presidents* (Washington D.C.: Government Printing Office, 1897), VI, pp. 102–4.

machinery seemed as if it had been designed, not to sustain the Government, but to embarrass and betray it.

Foreign intervention, openly invited and industriously instigated by the abettors of the insurrection, became imminent, and has only been prevented by the practice of strict and imparital justice, with the most perfect moderation, in our intercourse with nations.

The public mind was alarmed and apprehensive, though fortunately not distracted or disheartened. It seemed to be doubtful whether the Federal Government, which one year before had been thought a model worthy of universal acceptance, had indeed the ability to defend and maintain itself.

Some reverses, which, perhaps, were unavoidable, suffered by newly levied and inefficient forces, discouraged the loyal and gave new hopes to the insurgents. Voluntary enlistments seemed about to cease and desertions commenced. Parties speculated upon the question whether conscription had not become necessary to fill up the armies of the United States.

In this emergency the President felt it his duty to employ with energy the extraordinary powers which the Constitution confides to him on cases of insurrection. He called into the field such military and naval forces, unauthorized by the existing laws, as seemed necessary. He directed measures to prevent the use of the post-office for treasonable correspondence. He subjected passengers to and from foreign countries to new passport regulations, and he instituted a blockade, suspended the writ of *habeas corpus* in various places, and caused persons who were represented to him as being or about to engage in disloyal and treasonable practices to be arrested by special civil as well as military agencies and detained in military custody when necessary to prevent them and deter others from such practices. Examinations of such cases were instituted, and some of the persons so arrested have been discharged from time to time under circumstances or upon conditions compatible, as was thought, with the public safety.

Meantime a favorable change of public opinion has occurred. The line between loyalty and disloyalty is plainly defined. The whole structure of the Government is firm and stable. Apprehension of public danger and facilities for treasonable practices have diminished with the passions which prompted heedless persons to adopt them. The insurrection is believed to have culminated and to be declining.

The President, in view of these facts, and anxious to favor a return to the normal course of the Administration as far as regard for the public welfare will allow, directs that all political prisoners or state prisoners now held in military custody be released on their subscribing to a parole engaging them to render no aid or comfort to the enemies in hostility to the United States.

The Secretary of War will, however, in his discretion, except from the effect of this order any persons detained as spies in the service of the insurgents, or others whose release at the present moment may be deemed incompatible with the public safety.

To all persons who shall be so released and who shall keep their parole the President grants an amnesty for any past offenses of treason or disloyalty which they may have committed.

Extraordinary arrests will hereafter be made under the direction of the military authorities alone.

By order of the President:

EDWIN M. STANTON,
Secretary of War

II. Proclamation Suspending the Writ of Habeus Corpus

After a lengthy debate, Congress, in March, 1863, finally granted the President the authority to suspend the privilege of habeas corpus as he saw fit. This proclamation, issued six months later, reveals a bit of the jousting that had taken place between the President and Congress over constitutional prerogatives. What effect might one suppose that this congressional sanction had on such presidential critics as the New York Democrats?

SEPTEMBER 15, 1863

By the President of the United States of America

A Proclamation

Whereas the Constitution of the United States has ordained that the privilege of the Writ of Habeas Corpus shall not be suspended unless when in cases of rebellion or invasion the public safety may require it, And whereas a rebellion was existing on the third day of March, 1863, which rebellion is still existing; and whereas by a statute which was approved on that day, it was enacted by the Senate and House of Representatives of the United States in Congress assembled, that, during the present insurrection, the President of the United States, whenever, in his judgment, the Public safety may require, is authorized to suspend the privilege of the Writ of Habeas Corpus in any case throughout the United States or any part thereof; and whereas in the judgment of the President the public safety does require that the privilege of the said writ shall now be suspended throughout the United States in the cases where, by the authority of the President of the United States, military, naval and civil officers of the United States or any of them hold persons under their command or in their custody either as prisoners of war, spies, or aiders or abettors of the enemy; or officers, soldiers or seamen enrolled or drafted or mustered or enlisted in or belonging to the land or naval forces of the United States or as deserters therefrom or otherwise amenable to military law, or the Rules and

The Collected Works of Abraham Lincoln (New Brunswick, N.J.: Rutgers University Press, 1953), VI, pp. 451–52.

Articles of War or the rules or regulations prescribed for the military or naval services by authority of the President of the United States or for resisting a draft or for any other offence against the military or naval service. Now, therefore, I, Abraham Lincoln, President of the United States, do hereby proclaim and make known to all whom it may concern, that the privilege of the Writ of Habeas Corpus is suspended throughout the United States in the several cases before mentioned, and that this suspension will continue throughout the duration of the said rebellion, or until this proclamation shall, by a subsequent one to be issued by the President of the United States, be modified or revoked. And I do hereby require all magistrates, attorneys and other civil officers within the United States, and all officers and others in the military and naval services of the United States, to take distinct notice of this suspension, and to give it full effect, and all citizens of the United States to conduct and govern themselves accordingly and in conformity with the Constitution of the United States and the laws of Congress in such case made and provided.

In testimony whereof, I have hereunto set my hand, and caused the Seal of the United States to be affixed, this Fifteenth day of September, in the year of our Lord one thousand eight hundred and sixty three and of the Independence of the United States of America the Eighty-eighth.

By the President: ABRAHAM LINCOLN

WILLIAM H. SEWARD, Secretary of State

III. The Liberty of the Citizen

DANIEL W. VOORHEES

The most famous speech opposing congressional authorization of suspension of habeas corpus was delivered by Daniel W. Voorhees. A Democratic congressman from Indiana and a staunch defender of constitutional liberties, Voorhees relied on both history and logic in stating his case. This speech, delivered in the House of Representatives, was later published widely as "The Liberty of the Citizen." Unlike Clement L. Vallandigham, Voorhees continued to serve in the House and later, for more than twenty years, in the Senate without serious harrassment or damage to his reputation.

Several excerpts from Voorhees' lengthy speech are included here. Evaluate his arguments in the light of Lincoln's position as presented to the New York Democrats.

FEBRUARY 18, 1863

Sir, the bill now before the House has no parallel in the history of this or any other free people. It is entitled "An act to indemnify the President and other persons for suspending the privilege of the writ of habeas corpus, and acts done

Speeches of Daniel W. Voorhees (Cincinnati: Robert Clarke, 1875), pp. 63–64, 69–70, 89–90.

in pursuance thereof." But it embraces even more than its startling title would indicate. It gives to the Executive and all his subordinates not merely security for crimes committed against the citizen in times past, but confers a license to continue in the future the same unlimited exercise of arbitrary power which has brought disgrace and danger to the country. I propose, to the best of my ability this day, to show that neither indemnity for the past nor impunity for the future can be bestowed on those who have violated, and who propose further to violate, the great and fundamental principles of constitutional liberty.

Sir, the proper division and lawful exercise of the powers of a government, constitute a question of supreme and paramount importance. It stands pre-eminent over all others. No people in the history of the world ever long maintained security from the foot of the oppressor who lost sight of this fundamental truth. The sentinel who stands guard over the citadel of popular liberty can only protect and defend his sacred trust by keeping his vigilant eye steadily fixed on the movements of power. Every attempt to divert his attention by proclaiming other and more important objects, or by lulling him to sleep at his post, comes from an enemy to free government. Every attempt to convince the public mind that there may be higher duties for the citizen to perform than to preserve inviolate the inalienable rights of person, property, and the pursuit of happiness, is an assault upon the existence of this Republic and a sacrilege against God. . . .

It will not be denied on this floor, or elsewhere, that the suspension of the writ of *habeas corpus* by proclamation, to which I have alluded, closed the civil courts of this country, from one ocean to the other, against the trial of any one arrested by the order of the President or his subordinates. It gave access to the vaults of the prison, but not to the bar of justice. It is a part of the nature of frail man to sin against laws, both human and divine, but God himself secures him a trial before punishment, and tyrants alone repudiate the justice of the Almighty. To deny to an accused person the right to be heard in his defense, is pre-eminently the attribute of the worst ages of brutal despotism. Condemnation without trial, and punishment without limitation, is the exact definition to my mind of the most atrocious tyranny that ever feasted on the groans of the captive, or banqueted on the tears of the widow and the fatherless. And yet on this spectacle of horror and of shame American citizens have been gazing for more than a year! The great bulwark which generations in bloody toil have erected against the wicked exercise of unlawful power, has been torn away with a parricidal hand. Every citizen in this Republic—the farmer at his plow, the mechanic in his shop, the merchant at his counter; every calling and profession in life, from the proud man in his mansion to the good man in his cabin—all stand this day naked and exposed, utterly and entirely at the mercy of one man, and of the fawning minions who crouch before him for pay. I state a fact in the hearing of the country, and wherever my feeble words may penetrate, witnesses will rise up and solemnly attest its truth. . . .

No age, no sex, no condition in life, has been exempt from invasion, unlawful arrest, and imprisonment. I speak simply what every man in the hearing of my voice knows to be true. I have seen the ministers of the gospel of a peaceful Savior on their way to prison, leaving wife, children, and congregation a thousand miles behind, for preaching peace on earth and good will toward men. One, the Rev. Mr. Bundy, as I am informed by my friend from Illinois [Mr. Allen], living in his district, was dragged away from the open grave of his child, over whose remains the burial services had not yet been closed; denied the privilege of returning to his house to take a final leave of another member of his family then dying, and hurried, like an atrocious and dangerous criminal, to the safe-keeping of a cell. I have seen the upright and conscientious lawyer seized by the loathsome instruments of oppression; forbidden to console a sick wife, the mother of his children, with a single word at parting, and conveyed by furtive and rapid movements to a distant and arbitrary military tribunal, because he had dared, as became a freeman, to declare what he conceived the law to be. I have seen men who had been trusted and honored in public life by those who had known them most intimately in every relation, arrested in my own State for no offenses known to any law, and without warrant, without commitment, made to eat "the bread which captives' tears have watered" in every age of despotism. In the month of October last, I met three friends, distinguished citizens of Indiana, who six years ago served as senators together in her legislature. I met them, sir, serving together in the same prison a term of imprisonment which had no other duration or limit, no other beginning or end, no other cause or conclusion, no other condition or circumstance to support it, than the mere arbitrary, unlawful, unenlightened, and audacious will of one man here in Washington City. Sir, as I stood in their guarded room, listened to the story of their wrongs, and looked out upon the sunshine and the air—and the flag of the white man's freedom floating in the distance—strange thoughts possessed my mind, and strange visions arose before me. A new sensation penetrated my heart. I seemed to dwell for awhile beneath the shadow of the Bastile, and hear the cries and groans which finally rent its walls. The dungeons of Austria opened around me, and the prayers of their victims for liberty seemed to fill all space and all time. The damp vaults of Venice and the fearful caverns of the Spanish Inquisition yielded up their horrible secrets. The Tower of London—that melancholy tomb of genius and of beauty—the imperious form of Henry VIII., the headsman's ax, the reeking block, all became distinct to my view; and I looked, as it were, face to face, into the frightful, appalling countenance of tyranny. I studied its ferocious and revolting features in the light of historical associations. But when I came to reflect on all this, and reason from cause to effect, I found that precisely the same terrible principle of oppression which has disgraced the past, and filled other countries with tears and blood, was triumphing in my very presence. I turned away, and took my "appeal from tyranny to God."

IV. The Vallandigham Case Reviewed

The case of Clement L. Vallandigham referred to in Lincoln's exchange with the New York Democrats provoked considerable nationwide controversy. After contrasting the viewpoints on the case as presented in the following selection from the American Annual Cyclopedia *of 1862, evaluate Lincoln's position on civil liberties in general and his actions on this case in particular.*

The arrest, trial, and banishment of Mr. Vallandigham, as has been stated, occasioned much discussion both in public assemblies and in the papers of the day. Without an exception among the Democratic newspapers, the whole transaction was denounced as a violation of the rights of free speech, personal liberty, and trial by the constituted tribunals of the country. The papers in the support of the Administration took different views of the case; some maintained that the necessities of the case justified the measure, while others deprecated the act of Gen. Burnside and the military commission. The "Evening Post," of New York, says:

> Nothing can be clearer or more explicit than this; nothing shows a more tender regard for the rights of the citizen, or a stronger determination on the part of the lawgiver to keep the military power subordinate to the civil power.
>
> Under the provisions of these statutes Vallandigham is a prisoner of State, and the Secretary of War is bound to report him as such to the Circuit Judge of the district in which his supposed offences were committed, to be regularly tried by the civil tribunal. There is no escape from the plain demands of the law, even if there were a desire to do so, which we cannot suppose, and we expect to hear in a few days that the culprit has been handed over to the only legitimate authorities.

The Louisville "Journal" thus treats the case:

> It is a great mistake, it is indeed an inexcusable mistake, to suppose that the all but universal feeling, which the arrest and trial of Vallandigham by the military power has awakened, arises in any degree from sympathy with his peculiar views; on the contrary, it arises in spite of a decided antipathy to those views, as is shown conclusively by the fact that the feeling is shared by such Republican champions as the New York "Tribune," the New York "Evening Post," the New York "Commercial Advertiser," the Albany "Statesman," the Boston "Advertiser," the Boston "Traveller," the Springfield "Republican," and, in short, by the ablest and most influential champions of the Republican party, backed, as the New York "Evening Post" avows, by at least three-fourths of the Republican party itself.
>
> The feeling under notice arises clearly not in consequence of Vallandigham's peculiar views, but in spite of them; it arises in spite of them

and in spite of many other things, from an irrepressible sense of the value and sacredness of the rights which have been violated in his person. In other words, it arises from a rooted and solemn conviction of the truth of the principle which the General Assembly of Kentucky declared a few months ago, as follows: "That the General Assembly of Kentucky declares that the power which has recently been assumed by the President of the United States, whereby under the guise of military necessity, he has proclaimed and extended martial law over the State where war does not exist, and has suspended the writ of *habeas corpus,* is unwarranted by the constitution, and its tendency is to subordinate civil to military authority, and to subvert constitutional and free government." This declaration a few weeks afterward was adopted by the Union State Convention of Kentucky, and has since been adopted in like manner by the Democracy of Pennsylvania and of New York. The principle itself formed a conspicuous part of the platform on which the conservatives of the North won their great triumph at the ballot box last fall. It is a principle dear as life to the whole people. It is one they never will surrender—one they never can surrender without ceasing to be freemen. And the all but universal protest against the arrest and trial of Vallandigham by the military power is simply the expression of his vital devotion.

The peculiar views of Vallandigham have no necessary relation to the question. Such relation as they have but serves to place in yet stronger relief the affecting and inextinguishable devotion of the people to this great principle. "As in the celebrated case of John Wilkes, in the last century," to quote the language of Judge Parker in his letter to the New York meeting, "thousands, many thousands, who differ from the individual, will rally around him in defence of a great principle of constitutional liberty." This natural effect is one of the many witnesses that attest the culpable folly of the proceeding, tending, as the proceeding does, speaking hyperbolically to turn a "a monkey" into a "god," as Dr. Johnson fiercely said of Wilkes. Judge Parker is right. "I earnestly hope," adds this eminent jurist and patriot, "that the national administration will be prompt to repudiate the act, and to forbid all arbitrary arrests hereafter in the Northern States. To fail to do so would go far to discourage the efforts now being made to strengthen the arm of the Government in the suppression of the rebellion." These are words of wisdom and of patriotism. They are the words of one whose loyalty is fervent and unspotted. We entreat the President to heed them. And because they signalize a mighty truth, and are supported by the bulk of the President's own party as well as by the solid body of the conservative opposition, we cannot doubt that he will heed them. It is impossible that the President can deliberately set at defiance the voice of the whole people thus unequivocally and impressively uttered in behalf of what he must own up to be the right. There is not at present on the face of the globe a monarch who would even dream of defying such monitions as President Lincoln is now receiving in this grave matter from the free and loyal people whose Chief Magistrate he is. Let him at once respect these monitions, if he would serve and not freshly imperil his country, to say nothing of his own future renown.

On the other hand, those holding that it was a necessity to proceed in this manner, say:

I think you are wrong about Vallandigham. His offence was essentially a military one, in this aspect, that it demoralized the army, prevented recruiting, encouraged desertion, incited men to resist the arrest of deserters, and tended to make trouble about the increase of the army by conscription, by inciting resistance to the execution of that law. These, mind you, are not problematical results of his course, but actual. Specific cases of all of them, except the last, are continually occurring, invariably among men who call themselves democrats and swear by Vallandigham. The only remedy was by sudden and short stoppage.

This could not possibly be effected by the civil law. His offence is hardly known to civil law, and there would have been no end of trouble in getting him indicited. Then he would have been simply bound to stand his trial at some future day, and would have gone on talking his treason and sedition. And the bad effects before mentioned would have gone on growing in power and influence, and might have got too big to stop.

Moreover, special cases of ill-doing, resulting from and directly in accordance with his teachings, have constantly to be attended to. They cannot be overlooked. Should we punish them and let him go on inciting the commission of just such acts? abusing the courts that try them, and bringing their authority into disrepute.

You have no idea of the amount of open and bold disloyalty—not simply disloyalty by the Republican standard, but by that of any honest man—existing in Ohio, Indiana, and Illinois, among the Vallandigham party. It must be stopped and put down now—not six months hence—and military tribunals are the only ones that can do it. It must be put down if it should take a temporary military despotism out here to do it. It is that, or the loss of the cause. The course of these men prolongs the war and costs lives by thousands, and I tell you either they or the Government must go down, and that speedily.

For Further Reading

Northern dissenters during the Civil War have traditionally been called "Copperheads." Three books dealing with their activities are: Frank L. Klement, *The Copperheads in the Middle West* (1960), which emphasizes their sectionalism, agrarianism, and antiabolitionism; Wood Gray, *The Hidden Civil War: The Story of the Copperheads** (1942, 1964), in which the Copperheads are seen primarily as defeatists; and George Fort Milton, *Abraham Lincoln and*

*Paperbound edition available.

the Fifth Column (1942), a sharp attack on the Copperheads. (The last of these three is now out of print.) Klement has also written *The Limits of Dissent: Clement L. Vallandigham and the Civil War* (1970).

James G. Randall's *Constitutional Problems Under Lincoln** (1926, 1951) offers a good analysis and interpretation of the difficulties Lincoln faced. It contains a good bibliography through 1951. The whole spectrum of problems challenging Lincoln's leadership is discussed in Don Fehrenbacher's *The Leadership of Abraham Lincoln** (1970).

Many of the books suggested at the end of the previous chapter are pertinent here as well.

---

*Paperbound edition available.

17. Jim-Crowism
in the Making

The war aims of the Union during the Civil War progressed through three roughly identifiable stages. In the first stage, lasting more than a year after the firing on Fort Sumter in April 1861, the aim—as stated by President Lincoln —was simply to restore the Union. This implied the continued acceptance of the institution of slavery.

For military and diplomatic reasons, emancipation of slaves became an expressed aim in September 1862 with the announcement of the impending Emancipation Proclamation, and thus a second stage emerged.

As the war neared its conclusion, the radical wing in the Republican Party formulated a third aim: civil equality for the freedmen. In the face of Northern indifference, well-organized Southern intransigence, the illiteracy, inexperience, and poverty of the freedmen themselves, and the frailty of the Republican Party in the South, the Radicals succeeded in making civil equality a national issue for a decade after the war ended.

Early efforts to provide immediate assistance to the freedmen and to establish a long-range program to insure them a viable place in the economy were meager and short-lived. But a remarkable set of laws was enacted to protect the freed slaves from falling back into servitude, either in the old or in some new form. Between 1866 and 1875, eleven acts and three constitutional amendments became law.

The supporters of these laws and amendments believed that civil equality could be promoted through such measures. But as the promise of the black vote diminished, concern for the welfare of the freedmen lessened, and the Radicals lost their grip on national power. The civil rights laws either fell into disuse or were overturned in the courts, and a new set of laws, referred to as "Jim-Crow" laws, developed for the purpose of promoting civil *inequality*.[1]

Successful court challenges to these Jim-Crow laws and enactment of new civil rights laws in the past two decades (a "Second Reconstruction") has awakened interest in the civil rights laws of the First Reconstruction. This chapter is concerned chiefly with the Supreme Court decision in 1883, which marked a turning point in efforts to promote civil equality by law and made Jim-Crowism possible.

Core Document

On the Civil Rights Cases: A Speech by Frederick Douglass at Lincoln Hall

In 1875 Congress passed the last civil rights bill until 1957, when another mild one was enacted. By the time the 1875 bill was passed, the courts had already begun to question the validity of such laws. Between 1871 and 1875 more than 3,000 criminal cases under these laws were handled in federal courts in the South, with only about twenty percent leading to conviction.

It was therefore no surprise when the Supreme Court ruled in 1883 that the key provisions of the 1875 act were unconstitutional. Nevertheless, it was a major blow to the blacks, who had placed their hopes in the federal government working in their behalf. Without knowing the details of either the act or the decision, it is possible to gain an appreciation of their disappointment in the following speech by Frederick Douglass.

Douglass was born a slave around 1817. He escaped from slavery in 1838 and soon became an able orator, journalist, and author in the abolitionist cause. During the war he played a key role in recruiting black troops for the Union army. As a loyal Republican following the war, he served as marshall and recorder of deeds of the District of Columbia and as minister resident and consul general to Haiti. He died in 1895.

In writing about the 1883 Supreme Court decision in his Life and Times, *Douglass noted that the "colored men in the capital of the nation where the deed was done were quick to perceive its disastrous significance." In the helpless horror of the moment, he said, they called upon him and others to express their*

---

[1]The name "Jim Crow" derived from an act by an entertainer who based it on an anonymous song called *Jim Crow.*

Frederick Douglass, *Life and Times of Frederick Douglass* (Boston: DeWolfe and Fisk Co., 1892), pp. 654–69.

grief and indignation. This they did in Lincoln Hall, which was "packed by an audience of all colors." About 2,000 persons were present and about as many more could not get in.

In studying Douglass' speech, pay attention to:
- *the depth of the emotions he expressed.*
- *signs of oratorical restraint.*
- *actions he advocated.*
- *the larger historical context into which he put the decision.*
- *the arguments he raised against the validity of the decision.*
- *his ideas on balance and separation of powers and on the "object and intention" of laws.*
- *the distinction drawn between civil rights and social rights.*

OCTOBER 22, 1883

I have only a few words to say to you this evening. . . . It may be, after all, that the hour calls more loudly for silence than for speech. Later on in this discussion, when we shall have before us the full text of the Supreme Court and the dissenting opinion of Judge Harlan, who must have weighty reasons for separating from his associates and incurring thereby, as he must, an amount of criticism from which even the bravest man might shrink, we may be in a better frame of mind, better supplied with facts, and better prepared to speak calmly, correctly, and wisely than now. The temptation at this time is to speak more from feeling than reason, more from impulse than reflection.

We have been, as a class, grievously wounded, wounded in the house of our friends, and this wound is too deep and too painful for ordinary and measured speech.

> *When a deed is done for freedom,*
> *Through the broad earth's aching breast*
> *Runs a thrill of joy prophetic,*
> *Trembling on from East to West.*

But when a deed is done for slavery, caste, and oppression, and a blow is struck at human progress, whether so intended or not, the heart of humanity sickens in sorrow and writhes in pain. It makes us feel as if some one were stamping upon the graves of our mothers, or desecrating our sacred temples. Only base men and oppressors can rejoice in a triumph of injustice over the weak and defenseless, for weakness ought itself to protect from assaults of pride, prejudice, and power.

The cause which has brought us here tonight is neither common nor trivial. Few events in our national history have surpassed it in magnitude, importance and significance. It has swept over the land like a cyclone, leaving moral desolation in its track. This decision belongs with a class of judicial and legislative wrongs by which we have been oppressed.

We feel it as we felt years ago the furious attempt to force the accursed system of slavery upon the soil of Kansas—as we felt the enactment of the Fugitive Slave Bill, the repeal of the Missouri Compromise, and the Dred Scott decision. I look upon it as one more shocking development of that moral weakness in high places which has attended the conflict between the spirit of liberty and the spirit of slavery, and I venture to predict that it will be so regarded by aftercoming generations. Far down the ages, when men shall wish to inform themselves as to the real state of liberty, law, religion, and civilization in the United States at this juncture of our history, they will overhaul the proceedings of the Supreme Court, and read this strange decision declaring the Civil Rights Bill unconstitutional and void.

From this more than from many volumes they will learn how far we had advanced, in this year of grace, from the barbarism of slavery toward civilization and the rights of man.

Fellow-citizens! Among the great evils which now stalk abroad in our land, the one, I think, which most threatens to undermine and destroy the foundations of our free institutions in this country is the great and apparently increasing want of respect entertained for those to whom are committed the responsibility and the duty of administering our government. On this point I think all good men must agree, and against the evil I trust you feel the deepest repugnance, and that we will, neither here nor elsewhere, give it the least breath of sympathy or encouragement. We should never forget, whatever may be the incidental mistakes or misconduct of rulers, that government is better than anarchy, and that patient reform is better than violent revolution.

But while I would increase this feeling and give it the emphasis of a voice from heaven, it must not be allowed to interfere with free speech, honest expression of opinion, and fair criticism. To give up this would be to give up progress, and to consign the nation to moral stagnation, putrefaction, and death.

In the matter of respect for dignitaries, it should, however, never be forgotten that duties are reciprocal, and that while the people should frown down every manifestation of levity and contempt for those in power, it is the duty of the possessors of power so to use it as to deserve and insure respect and reverence.

To come a little nearer to the case now before us. The Supreme Court of the United States, in the exercise of its high and vast constitutional power, has suddenly and unexpectedly decided that the law intended to secure to colored people the civil rights guaranteed to them by the following provision of the Constitution of the United States, is unconstitutional and void. Here it is:

"No state," says the Fourteenth Amendment, "shall make or enforce any law which shall abridge the privileges or immunities of citizens of the United States; nor shall any state deprive any person of life, liberty, or property, without due process of the law; or deny any person within its jurisdiction the equal protection of the laws."

Now, when a bill has been discussed for weeks and months and even years, in the press and on the platform, in Congress and out of Congress; when it has been calmly debated by the clearest heads and the most skillful and learned lawyers in the land; when every argument against it has been over and over again carefully considered and fairly answered; when its constitutionality has been especially discussed, pro and con; when it has passed the United States House of Representatives and has been solemnly enacted by the United States Senate (perhaps the most imposing legislative body in the world); when such a bill has been submitted to the cabinet of the nation, composed of the ablest men in the land; when it has passed under the scrutinizing eye of the Attorney-General of the United States; when the Executive of the Nation has given to it his name and formal approval; when it has taken its place upon the statute-book and has remained there for nearly a decade, and the country has largely assented to it, you will agree with me that the reasons for declaring such a law unconstitutional and void should be strong, irresistible and absolutely conclusive.

Inasmuch as the law in question is a law in favor of liberty and justice, it ought to have had the benefit of any doubt which could arise as to its strict constitutionality. This, I believe, will be the view taken of it, not only by laymen like myself, but by eminent lawyers as well.

All men who have given any thought to the machinery, structure, and practical operation of our government, must have recognized the importance of absolute harmony between its various departments and their respective powers and duties. They must have seen clearly the mischievous tendency and danger to the body politic of any antagonisms between any of its various branches. . . .

Now let me say here, before I go on a step or two further in this discussion, that if any man has come here tonight with his breast heaving with passion, his heart flooding with acrimony, and wishing and expecting to hear violent denunciation of the Supreme Court on account of this decision, he has mistaken the object of this meeting and the character of the men by whom it is called.

We neither come to bury Caesar nor to praise him. The Supreme Court is the autocratic point in our government. No monarch in Europe has a power more absolute over the laws, lives, and liberties of his people than that court has over our laws, lives, and liberties. Its judges live, and ought to live, an eagle's flight beyond the reach of fear or favor, praise or blame, profit or loss. No vulgar prejudice should touch the members of that court anywhere. Their decisions should come down to us like the calm, clear light of infinite justice. We should be able to think of them and to speak of them with profoundest respect for their wisdom and deepest reverence for their virtue, for what his Holiness the Pope is to the Roman Catholic Church, the Supreme Court is to the American State. Its members are men, to be sure, and may not, like the Pope, claim infallibility, and they are not infallible, but they are the supreme law-giving power of the nation, and their decisions are law until changed by that court.

What will be said here tonight will be spoken, I trust, more in sorrow than in anger—more in a tone of regret than in bitterness and reproach, and more to promote sound views than to find bad motives for unsound views.

We cannot, however, overlook the fact that though not so intended, this decision has inflicted a heavy calamity upon seven millions of the people of this country, and left them naked and defenseless against the action of a malignant, vulgar, and pitiless prejudice from which the Constitution plainly intended to shield them.

It presents the United States before the world as a nation utterly destitute of power to protect the constitutional rights of its own citizens upon its own soil.

It can claim service and allegiance, loyalty and life from them, but it cannot protect them against the most palpable violation of the rights of human nature, rights to secure which governments are established. It can tax their bread and tax their blood, but it has no protecting power for their persons. Its national power extends only to the District of Columbia and the territories— to where the people have no votes, and to where the land has no people. All else is subject to the states. In the name of common sense, I ask what right have we to call ourselves a nation, in view of this decision and of this utter destitution of power? . . .

Today our Republic sits as a queen among the nations of the earth. Peace is within her walls and plenteousness within her palaces, but he is bolder and a far more hopeful man than I am who will affirm that this peace and prosperity will always last. History repeats itself. What has happened once may happen again.

The Negro, in the Revolution, fought for us and with us. In the war of 1812 General Jackson, at New Orleans, found it necessary to call upon the colored people to assist in its defense against England. Abraham Lincoln found it necessary to call upon the Negro to defend the Union against rebellion. In all cases the Negro responded gallantly.

Our legislators, our presidents, and our judges should have a care, lest, by forcing these people outside of law, they destroy that love of country which in the day of trouble is needful to the nation's defense.

I am not here in this presence to discuss the constitutionality or the unconstitutionality of this decision of the Supreme Court. The decision may or may not be constitutional. That is a question for lawyers and not for laymen, and there are lawyers on this platform as learned, able, and eloquent as any who have appeared in this case before the Supreme Court, or as any in the land. To these I leave the exposition of the Constitution, but I claim the right to remark upon a strange and glaring inconsistency of this decision with former decisions, where the rules of law apply. It is a new departure, entirely out of the line of precedents and decisions of the Supreme Court at other times and in other directions where the rights of colored men were concerned. It has utterly ignored and rejected the force and application of the object and intention of the adoption of the Fourteenth Amendment. It has made no account whatever of the intention and purpose of Congress and the President in putting the Civil Rights Bill upon the statute-book of the nation. It has seen fit in this case, affecting a weak and much persecuted people, to be guided by the narrowest and most restricted rules of legal interpretation. It has viewed both the Constitution and the law with a strict regard to their letter, but without any generous recognition and application of their broad and liberal spirit. Upon those narrow principles the decision is logical and legal, of course. But what I complain of, and what every lover of liberty in the United States has a right to complain of, is this sudden and causeless reversal of all the great rules of legal interpretation by which this court was once governed in the construction of the Constitution and of laws respecting colored people.

In the dark days of slavery this court on all occasions gave the greatest importance to intention as a guide to interpretation. The object and intention of the law, it was said, must prevail. Everything in favor of slavery and against the Negro was settled by this object and intention rule. We were over and over again referred to what the framers meant, and plain language itself was sacrificed and perverted from its natural and obvious meaning that the so affirmed intention of these framers might be positively asserted and given the force of law. When we said in behalf of the Negro that the Constitution of the United States was intended to establish justice and to secure the blessings of liberty to ourselves and our posterity, we were told that the words said so, but that that was obviously not its intention—that it was intended to apply only to white people, and that the intention must govern.

When we came to the clause of the Constitution which declares that the immigration or importation of such persons as any of the states may see fit to admit shall not be prohibited, and the friends of liberty declared that this provision of the Constitution did not describe the slave-trade, they were told that while its language applied not to the slaves but to persons, still the object and intention of that clause of the Constitution was plainly to protect the slave-trade, and that that intention was the law and must prevail. When we came to that clause of the Constitution which declares that "No person held to labor or service in one state under the laws thereof, escaping into another, shall in consequence of any law or regulation therein be discharged from such labor or service, but shall be delivered upon claim of the party to whom such labor or service may be due," we insisted that it neither described nor applied to slaves—that it applied only to persons owing service and labor—that slaves did not and could not owe service and labor—that this clause of the Constitution said nothing of slaves or of the masters of slaves—that it was silent as to slave states or free states—that it was simply a provision to enforce a contract and not to force any man into slavery, for the slave could not owe service or make a contract.

We affirmed that it gave no warrant for what was called "The Fugutive Slave Bill," and we contended that the bill was therefore unconstitutional, but our arguments were laughed to scorn by that court and by all the courts of the Country. We were told that the intention of the Constitution was to enable masters to recapture slaves, and that the law of '93 and the Fugitive Slave Law of 1850 were constitutional, binding not only on the state but upon each citizen of the state.

Fellow-citizens! While slavery was the base line of American society, while it ruled the church and state, while it was the interpreter of our law and the exponent of our religion, it admitted no quibbling, no narrow rules of legal or scriptural interpretations of the Bible or of the Constitution. It sternly demanded its pound of flesh, no matter how the scale turned or how much blood was shed in the taking of it. It was enough for it to be able to show the intention to get all it asked in the courts or out of the courts. But now slavery is abolished. Its reign was long, dark, and bloody. Liberty is now the base line of the Republic. Liberty has supplanted slavery, but I fear it has not supplanted the spirit or power of slavery. Where slavery was strong, liberty is now weak.

Oh, for a Supreme Court of the United States which shall be as true to the claims of humanity as the Supreme Court formerly was to the demands of slavery! When that day comes, as come it will, a Civil Rights Bill will not be declared unconstitutional and void, in utter and flagrant disregard of the objects and intentions of the national legislature by which it was enacted and of the rights plainly secured by the Constitution.

This decision of the Supreme Court admits that the Fourteenth Amendment is a prohibition on the states. It admits that a state shall not abridge the privileges or immunities of citizens of the United States, but commits the seeming absurdity of allowing the people of a state to do what it prohibits the state itself from doing.

It used to be thought that the whole was more than a part, that the greater included the less, and that what was unconstitutional for a state to do was equally unconstitutional for an individual member of a state to do. What is a state, in the absence of the people who compose it? Land, air, and water. That is all. Land and water do not discriminate. All are equal before them. This law was made for people. As individuals, the people of the State of South Carolina may stamp out the rights of the Negro wherever they please, so long as they do so as a state, and this absurd conclusion is to be called a law. All the parts can violate the Constitution, but the whole cannot. It is not the act itself, according to this decision, that is unconstitutional. The unconstitutionality of the case depends wholly upon the party committing the act. If the state commits it, the act is wrong; if the citizen of the state commits it, the act is right.

O consistency, thou art indeed a jewel! What does it matter to a colored citizen that a state may not insult and outrage him, if the citizen of the state may? The effect upon him is the same, and it was just this effect that the framers of the Fourteenth Amendment plainly intended by that article to prevent.

It was the act, not the instrument—it was the murder, not the pistol or dagger—which was prohibited. It meant to protect the newly enfranchised citizen from injustice and wrong, not merely from a state, but from the individual members of a state. It meant to give the protection to which his citizenship, his loyalty, his allegiance, and his services entitled him, and this meaning and this purpose and this intention are now declared by the Supreme Court of the United States to be unconstitutional and void.

I say again, fellow-citizens, Oh, for a Supreme Court which shall be as true, as vigilant, as active and exacting in maintaining laws enacted for the protection of human rights, as in other days was that court for the destruction of human rights!

It is said that this decision will make no difference in the treatment of colored people—that the Civil Rights Bill was a dead letter and could not be enforced. There may be some truth in all this, but it is not the whole truth. That bill, like all advance legislation, was a banner on the outer wall of American liberty, a noble moral standard uplifted for the education of the American people. There are tongues in trees, sermons in stones, and books in the running brooks. This law, though dead, did speak. It expressed the sentiment of justice and fair play common to every honest heart. Its voice was against popular prejudice and meanness. It appealed to all the noble and patriotic instincts of the American people. It told the American people that they were all equal before the law—that they belonged to a common country and were equal citizens. The Supreme Court has hauled down this broad and glorious flag of liberty in open day and before all the people, and has thereby given joy to the heart of every man in the land who wishes to deny to others the rights he claims for himself. It is a concession to race pride, selfishness, and meanness, and will be received with joy by every upholder of caste in the land, and for this I deplore and denounce this decision.

It is a frequent and favorite device of an indefensible cause to misstate and pervert the views of those who advocate a good cause, and I have never seen this device more generally resorted to than in the case of the late decision on the Civil Rights Bill. When we dissent from the opinion of the Supreme Court and give the reasons why we think the opinion unsound, we are straightway charged in the papers with denouncing the court itself, and thus put in the attitude of bad citizens. Now, I utterly deny that there has ever been any denunciation of the Supreme Court by the speakers on this platform, and I defy any man to point out one sentence or one syllable of any speech of mine in denunciation of that Court.

Another illustration of this tendency to put opponents in a false position is seen in the persistent effort to stigmatize the Civil Rights Bill as a Social Rights Bill. Now, where under the whole heavens, outside of the United States, could any such perversion of truth have any chance of success? No man in Europe would ever dream that because he has a right to ride on a railway, or stop at a hotel, he therefore has the right to enter into social relations with anybody. No one has a right to speak to another without that other's permission. Social equality and civil equality rest upon an entirely different basis, and well enough the American people know it; yet, in order to inflame a popular prejudice, respectable papers like the *New York Times* and the *Chicago Tribune* persist in describing the Civil Rights Bill as a Social Rights Bill.

When a colored man is in the same room or in the same carriage with white people, as a servant, there is no talk of social equality, but if he is there as a man and a gentleman, he is an offense. What makes the difference? It is not color, for his color is unchanged. The whole essence of the thing is in its purpose to degrade and stamp out the liberties of the race. It is the old spirit of slavery and nothing else. To say that because a man rides in the same car with another he is therefore socially equal is one of the wildest absurdities.

When I was in England, some years ago, I rode upon highways, byways, steamboats, stagecoaches, and omnibuses. I was in the House of Commons, in the House of Lords, in the British Museum, in the Coliseum, in the National Gallery, everywhere—sleeping in rooms where lords and dukes had slept—sitting at tables where lords and dukes [had sat]. I hardly think that some of our Democratic circumstances made me socially the equal of these lords and dukes. I hardly think that some of our Democratic friends would be regarded among those lords as their equals. If riding in the same car makes one equal, I think that the little poodle dog I saw one day sitting in the lap of a lady was made equal by riding in the same car with her. Equality, social equality, is a matter between individuals. It is a reciprocal understanding. I do not think that when I ride with an educated, polished rascal he is thereby made my equal, or that when I ride with a numbskull it makes him my equal. Social equality does not necessarily follow from civil equality, and yet for the purpose of a hell-black and damning prejudice, our papers still insist that the Civil Rights Bill is a bill to establish social equality.

If it is a bill for social equality, so is the Declaration of Independence, which declares that all men have equal rights; so is the Sermon on the Mount; so is the golden rule that commands us to do to others as we would that others should do to us; so is the teaching of the Apostle that of one blood God has made all nations to dwell on the face of the earth; so is the Constitution of the United States, and so are the laws and customs of every civilized country in the world; for nowhere, outside of the United States, is any man denied civil rights on account of his color.

Discussion Starters

1. How important should "object and intention" be in determining constitutionality of laws?

2. How valid was Douglass' claim that "object and intention" had historically been used to the black man's disadvantage?

3. Evaluate the distinction Douglass drew between social equality and civil equality. How important is this distinction today?

4. To what extent was Douglass correct when he asserted that even a dead law on the books has some value? In this light, what damage was done by this decision?

5. What arguments by Douglass might be used in promoting civil equality by law today?

Related Documents

I. "Civil Rights Cases"

The Supreme Court decision discussed by Frederick Douglass was rendered on October 15, 1883. The court had considered five cases on appeal from various circuit courts in which blacks had been denied some accommodation or other privilege because of their color. By an 8 to 1 majority the court held the first two sections of the 1875 Civil Rights Act to be unconstitutional.

In the excerpts from the decision given here, identify the key judgments of the court. Explain why Douglass and other blacks had or did not have reasons to despair over this decision.

Mr. Justice Bradley delivered the opinion of the court. After stating the facts in the above language he continued:

It is obvious that the primary and important question in all the cases is the constitutionality of the law: for if the law is unconstitutional none of the prosecutions can stand.

The sections of the law referred to provide as follows:

"SEC. 1. That all persons within the jurisdiction of the United States shall be entitled to the full and equal enjoyment of the accommodations, advantages, facilities, and privileges of inns, public conveyances on land or water, theatres, and other places of public amusement; subject only to the conditions and limitations established by law, and applicable alike to citizens of every race and color, regardless of any previous condition of servitude.

"SEC. 2. That any person who shall violate the foregoing section by denying to any citizen, except for reasons by law applicable to citizens of every race and color, and regardless of any previous condition of servitude, the full enjoyment of any of the accommodations, advantages, facilities, or privileges in said section enumerated, or by aiding or inciting such denial, shall for every such offence forfeit and pay the sum of five hundred dollars to the person aggrieved therby, to be recovered in an action of debt, with full costs; and shall also, for every such offence, be deemed guilty of a misdemeanor, and, upon conviction thereof, shall be fined not less than five hundred nor more than one thousand dollars, or shall be imprisoned not less than thirty days nor more than one year. . . .

Are these sections constitutional? The first section, which is the principal one, cannot be fairly understood without attending to the last clause, which qualifies the preceding part.

The essence of the law is, not to declare broadly that all persons shall be entitled to the full and equal enjoyment of the accommodations, advantages, facilities, and privileges of inns, public conveyances, and theatres; but that such

109 *U.S. Reports*, pp. 8–11, 13–14, 20, 24–25.

enjoyment shall not be subject to any conditions applicable only to citizens of a particular race or color, or who had been in a previous condition of servitude. . . .

Has Congress constitutional power to make such a law? Of course, no one will contend that the power to pass it was contained in the Constitution before the adoption of the last three amendments. The power is sought, first, in the Fourteenth Amendment, and the views and arguments of distinguished Senators, advanced whilst the law was under consideration, claiming authority to pass it by virtue of that amendment, are the principal arguments adduced in favor of the power. . . .

The first section of the Fourteenth Amendment (which is the one relied on), after declaring who shall be citizens of the United States, and of the several States, is prohibitory in its character, and prohibitory upon the States. It declares that:

"No State shall make or enforce any law which shall abridge the privileges or immunities of citizens of the United States; nor shall any State deprive any person of life, liberty, or property without due process of law; nor deny to any person within its jurisdiction the equal protection of the laws."

It is State action of a particular character that is prohibited. Individual invasion of individual rights is not the subject-matter of the amendment. It has a deeper and broader scope. It nullifies and makes void all State legislation, and State action of every kind, which impairs the privileges and immunities of citizens of the United States, or which injures them in life, liberty or property without due process of law, or which denies to any of them the equal protection of the laws. It not only does this, but, . . . the last section of the amendment invests Congress with power to enforce it by appropriate legislation. To enforce what? To enforce the prohibition. To adopt appropriate legislation for correcting the effects of such prohibited State laws and State acts, and thus to render them effectually null, void, and innocuous. This is the legislative power conferred upon Congress, and this is the whole of it. . . .

And so in the present case, until some State law has been passed, or some State action through its officers or agents has been taken, adverse to the rights of citizens sought to be protected by the Fourteenth Amendment, no legislation of the United States under said amendment, nor any proceeding under such legislation, can be called into activity: for the prohibitions of the amendment are against State laws and acts done under State authority. . . .

An inspection of the law shows that it makes no reference whatever to any supposed or apprehended violation of the Fourteenth Amendment on the part of the States. It is not predicated on any such view. It proceeds *ex directo* to declare that certain acts committed by individuals shall be deemed offences, and shall be prosecuted and punished by proceedings in the courts of the United States. . . .

If this legislation is appropriate for enforcing the prohibitions of the amendment, it is difficult to see where it is to stop. Why may not Congress with equal show of authority enact a code of laws for the enforcement and vindication of all rights of life, liberty, and property? . . .

But the power of Congress to adopt direct and primary, as distinguished from corrective legislation, on the subject in hand, is sought, in the second place from the Thirteenth Amendment, which abolishes slavery. . . .

This amendment, as well as the Fourteenth, is undoubtedly self-executing without any ancillary legislation, so far as its terms are applicable to any existing state of circumstances. By its own unaided force and effect it abolished slavery, and established universal freedom. . . .

It is true, that slavery cannot exist without law, any more than property in lands and goods can exist without law: and, therefore, the Thirteenth Amendment may be regarded as nullifying all State laws which establish or uphold slavery. But it has a reflex character also, establishing and decreeing universal civil and political freedom throughout the United States; and it is assumed, that the power vested in Congress to enforce the article by appropriate legislation, clothes Congress with power to pass all laws necessary and proper for abolishing all badges and incidents of slavery in the United States: and upon this assumption it is claimed, that this is sufficient authority for declaring by law that all persons shall have equal accommodations and privileges in all inns, public conveyances, and places of amusement; the argument being, that the denial of such equal accommodations and privileges is, in itself, a subjection to a species of servitude within the meaning of the amendment. . . .

Now, conceding, for the sake of the argument, that the admission to an inn, a public conveyance, or a place of public amusement, on equal terms with all other citizens, is the right of every man and all classes of men, is it any more than one of those rights which the states by the Fourteenth Amerndment are forbidden to deny to any person? And is the Constitution violated until the denial of the right has some State sanction or authority? Can the act of a mere individual, the owner of the inn, the public conveyance or place of amusement, refusing the accommodation, be justly regarded as imposing any badge of slavery or servitude upon the applicant, or only as inflicting an ordinary civil injury, properly cognizable by the laws of the State, and presumably subject to redress by those laws until the contrary appears?

After giving to these questions all the consideration which their importance demands, we are forced to the conclusion that such an act of refusal has nothing to do with slavery or involuntary servitude, and that if it is violative of any right of the party, his redress is to be sought under the laws of the State; or if those laws are adverse to his rights and do not protect him, his remedy will be found in the corrective legislation which Congress has adopted, or may adopt, for counteracting the effect of State laws, or State action, prohibited by the Fourteenth Amendment. It would be running the slavery argument into the ground to make it apply to every act of discrimination which a person may see fit to make as to the guests he will entertain, or as to the people he will take into his coach or cab or car, or admit to his concert or theatre, or deal with in other matters of intercourse or business. . . .

When a man has emerged from slavery, and by the aid of beneficent legislation has shaken off the inseparable concomitants of that state, there must be some stage in the progress of his elevation when he takes the rank of a mere citizen, and ceases to be the special favorite of the laws, and when his rights as a citizen, or a man, are to be protected in the ordinary modes by which other men's rights are protected. There were thousands of free colored people in this country before the abolition of slavery, enjoying all the essential rights of life, liberty and property the same as white citizens; yet no one, at that time, thought that it was any invasion of his personal status as a freeman because he was not admitted to all the privileges enjoyed by white citizens, or because he was subjected to discriminations in the enjoyment of accommodations in inns, public conveyances and places of amusement. Mere discriminations on account of race or color were not regarded as badges of slavery. If, since that time, the enjoyment of equal rights in all these respects has become established by constitutional enactment, it is not by force of the Thirteenth Amendment (which merely abolishes slavery), but by force of the Thirteenth and Fifteenth Amendments.

On the whole we are of opinion, that no countenance of authority for the passage of the law in question can be found in either the Thirteenth or Fourteenth Amendment of the Constitution; and no other ground of authority for its passage being suggested, it must necessarily be declared void, at least so far as its operation in the several States is concerned.

II. "Civil Rights Cases"—A Dissenting Opinion

In his lengthy dissent, Justice John Marshall Harlan cited numerous precedents to contradict the majority opinion. On the basis of the brief portions included here, try to determine how his views of both law and precedent differed from those of his fellow justices. Where did they agree with Douglass' views?

Mr. Justice Harlan dissenting.

The opinion in these cases proceeds, it seems to me, upon grounds entirely too narrow and artificial. I cannot resist the conclusion that the substance and spirit of the recent amendments of the Constitution have been sacrificed by a subtle and ingenious verbal criticism. "It is not the words of the law but the internal sense of it that makes the law: the letter of the law is the body; the sense and reason of the law is the soul." Constitutional provisions, adopted in the interest of liberty, and for the purpose of securing, through national legislation, if need be, rights inhering in a state of freedom, and belonging to American citizenship, have been so construed as to defeat the ends the people

109 *U.S. Reports*, pp. 26, 61–62.

desired to accomplish, which they attempted to accomplish, and which they supposed they had accomplished by changes in their fundamental law. By this I do not mean that the determination of these cases should have been materially controlled by considerations of mere expediency or policy. I mean only, in this form, to express an earnest conviction that the court has departed from the familiar rule requiring, in the interpretation of constitutional provisions, that full effect be given to the intent with which they were adopted. . . .

My brethren say, that when a man has emerged from slavery, and by the aid of beneficent legislation has shaken off the inseparable concomitants of that state, there must be some stage in the progress of his elevation when he takes the rank of a mere citizen, and ceases to be the special favorite of the laws, and when his rights as a citizen, or a man, are to be protected in the ordinary modes by which other men's rights are protected. It is, I submit, scarcely just to say that the colored race has been the special favorite of the laws. The statute of 1875, now adjudged to be unconstitutional, is for the benefit of citizens of every race and color. What the nation, through Congress, has sought to accomplish in reference to that race, is—what had already been done in every State of the Union for the white race—to secure and protect rights belonging to them as freemen and citizens; nothing more. It was not deemed enough "to help the feeble up, but to support him after." The one underlying purpose of congressional legislation has been to enable the black race to take the rank of mere citizens. The difficulty has been to compel a recognition of the legal right of the black race to take the rank of citizens, and to secure the enjoyment of privileges belonging, under the law, to them as a component part of the people for whose welfare and happiness government is ordained. . . . If the constitutional amendments be enforced, according to the intent with which, as I conceive, they were adopted, there cannot be, in this republic, any class of human beings in practical subjection to another class, with power in the latter to dole out to the former just such privileges as they may choose to grant. The supreme law of the land has decreed that no authority shall be exercised in this country upon the basis of discrimination, in respect of civil rights, against freemen and citizens because of their race, color, or previous condition of servitude. To that decree—for the due enforcement of which, by appropriate legislation, Congress has been invested with express power—every one must bow, whatever may have been, or whatever now are, his individual views as to the wisdom or policy, either of the recent changes in the fundamental law, or of the legislation which has been enacted to give them effect.

For the reasons stated I feel constrained to withhold my assent to the opinion of the court.

III. Editorials

THE NATION

That the constitutionality of the Civil Rights Act was widely challenged is apparent in the general approval given the Supreme Court's decision. One of the magazines that regarded it as unconstitutional was The Nation, *a weekly founded in 1865 with the blessing of William Lloyd Garrison as the successor to* The Liberator. *Although Wendell Phillips Garrison, William's son, was an editor of* The Nation, *its editorial policy after 1870 called for time and education rather than laws as the means of achieving equality.*

Included here is an editorial from The Nation *at the time of the passage of the Civil Rights Act and another at the time of the Supreme Court's voiding of that act. How do you account for the differences between* The Nation's *and Douglass' appraisal of the act and of the effect of the Court's decision?*

MARCH 4, 1875

Congress has at last passed the Civil-Rights Bill, and the President has signed it. The bill, as passed, does not enforce mixed schools, and only secures negroes equal rights in public conveyances, inns, theatres, and other places of amusement. While the bill was on its passage in the Senate, Mr. Tipton of Nebraska moved to insert the word "churches" after the word "theatres," including the former under the head of places of amusement—a suggestion which of course brought down the galleries, though it really is not much more amusing than the bill itself. The negroes of the South, being mainly occupied in tilling the soil, or in labor of some kind, are not as a rule in the habit of travelling much from place to place; and when they do go from time to time to some local court-house or county-seat for a holiday, they are apt to move in crowds on foot, or in wagons not subject to the jurisdiction of Congress. They do not frequent hotels much, for similar reasons, and the number of theatres and opera-houses in the South is not so great as to warrant the expectation of a great advance of the race through the influence of the drama and music. Indeed, it is a harmless bill, and does not seem to have had much effect on public opinion in the South. The chief objection to it is its entire unconstitutionality, which Mr. Carpenter showed, much to the consternation of the Radical Republicans, in an able and convincing speech.

OCTOBER 18, 1883

The calm with which the country receives the news that the leading sections of the celebrated Civil-Rights Act of 1875 have been pronounced unconstitutional by the Supreme Court, shows how completely the extravagant expecta-

The Nation, March 4, 1875, and October 18, 1883.

tions as well as the fierce passions of the war have died out. The Act was forced through Congress as the crowning measure of the plan of reconstructing the South on which the Republican party entered at the close of the war, and under the influence of that feeling of omnipotence with regard to the South which was the natural and unavoidable result of the prolonged exercise of the war power, and which survived the war for fully fifteen years. Some of the ablest lawyers in both houses saw its unconstitutionality clearly enough, and pointed it out; but some voted for it as a useful piece of party work, which might do good and could not possibly do any harm. . . .

The reason why the Fourteenth Amendment had not given Congress power to legislate directly in defence of the social rights of the negroes in the several States was plain enough, too. It was that the Republican party, when the amendment was adopted in 1868, was occupied solely with the defence of the ordinary civil rights of the freedmen against hostile or reactionary State legislation. It was, in short, due to the fear that slavery might be succeeded, for the colored people, by a carefully prepared condition of legal inferiority, and against this the men who abolished slavery determined to guard. An amendment providing for the admission of negroes to hotels and theatres and public conveyances would not have been adopted, because the notion that the social equality of the colored people could be hastened by legislation sprang up later, when they had come more distinctly into view as citizens and property-holders, theatre-goers and travellers; but it never was strong enough to procure either the adoption of a Constitutional amendment or the passage of an act which anybody expected to be enforced. The Civil-Rights Act was really rather an admonition, or statement of moral obligation, than a legal command. Probably nine-tenths of those who voted for it knew very well that whenever it came before the Supreme Court it would be torn to pieces.

Any one who has forgotten, or is not old enough to remember, the arguments which were made to do duty in the service of the bill when it was before Congress, will find an interesting summary of them in the comments of Mr. Greener, the colored lawyer, on the late decision of the Court, in the *Evening Post* of Tuesday. As a reminiscence of ways of thinking about constitutional questions which have almost wholly passed away, they are interesting reading. It will be seen that there is very little flavor even of legality about them. They are almost all based on moral considerations with which courts of law under our system have little or nothing to do. The decision is wrong because it is likely to annoy and inconvenience the colored race. It is wrong because it disregards, in disobedience to the Constitution, certain primeval natural rights brought over here by the first settlers; because it may lead to Catholic bishops or Jewish rabbis being expelled from railroad cars; because it raises inconvenient questions of social equality; and because, coming just after the Ohio election, "it can scarcely be construed as anything else than a covert and insidious blow at the institutions of the Republican party."

What the Court had decided, we need hardly say, is simply that the Fourteenth Amendment does not authorize Congress to protect the civil rights of colored people within the States against anything but hostile State legislation; or, in other words, that the powers of Congress are defined by the Constitution, and not by considerations of humanity, or even general utility, or by the opinions or wishes of prominent politicians. Consequently, nearly all that the arguments originally produced in support of the Act, as well as those of Mr. Greener now against the Court's interpretation of it, really prove is, that the division of powers made by the Constitution between the States and the Union is not a proper one, and that the framers might have made a far better Government than the one they did make, if they had only tried.

IV. News Report

THE NEW YORK TRIBUNE

Among the many newspapers reporting on the Supreme Court's decision was The New York Tribune. *In reading the following article, keep in mind that the sentiments expressed by Justice Donohue and the hotel manager were fairly representative of the public's general reaction: that the Civil Rights Act was unconstitutional. What kind of rebuttal might Frederick Douglass have offered to the statement that, "If a colored person behaves himself, nobody will trouble him or think about him"?*

OCTOBER 17, 1883

Justice Donohue, of the Supreme Court [of New York], was asked by a *Tribune* reporter yesterday what he thought of the decision of the United States Supreme Court declaring the Civil Rights bill unconstitutional. In reply he said: "I think that it shows that we are getting back to our constitutional moorings. . . . The difficulty in this whole matter is due to the fact that there has been too much agitation over the color line. Leave the colored people alone and they will take care of themselves as other people do. The matter will take care of itself on a common-sense basis. . . . If a colored person behaves himself, nobody will trouble him or think about him. Let him alone, just as you would anybody else who attends to his business. . . . I have had darkey clients and got along with them as I did with other clients."

"Do you think that this decision will leave the negro at the mercy of those who dislike him, especially in the South?"

"Not at all. There is not the least danger of it. He will have his rights, as everybody else has. Nobody would turn him out of a theatre or of a street-car any more than before. His status before the law will be essentially unchanged." . . .

Several managers of hotels who were asked for their views regarding the decision thought that it would have little effect on their interests, though it might save them from an occasional suit for damages. Mr. Wetherbee of the Windsor, said that colored people never trouble him and he was never sued by them. "They usually are too sensible to go where they are not wanted," said he, "and they prefer hotels where they are sure to be welcome—usually a cheap class of house."

V. Editorial

THE ST. LOUIS REPUBLICAN

As in the preceding news report, this editorial from The St. Louis Republican *expresses the belief that there had been way too much agitation by colored leaders over supposed prejudice. How valid were such observations? Speculate on how Douglass might have answered these arguments.*

OCTOBER 24, 1883

Probably the most effective answer to the outcry of the colored leaders against the recent civil rights decision is to be found in their own statement of their complaint. Fred Douglass says the decision "has inflicted a heavy calamity upon seven millions of colored people, and left them naked and defenceless against the action of malignant, vulgar and pitiless prejudice." Seven millions is an extravagant estimate of the negro population of the country, and Mr. Douglass evidently imagines that the more negroes there are in the land the greater is the "calamity" which the decision brings upon them. If they were seventy millions the grievance would be augmented ten-fold. But to ordinary eyes a race seven millions strong ought to be able to take care of itself without the aid of special laws, noisy meetings and hulabaloos. If, with such vast numbers—double the population of the colonies in the struggle with Great Britain in the Revolution—is not able to take care of itself without perpetually bringing its complaints before the public, the suspicion is strong that it lacks the fibre by which alone rights can be first conquered, and afterwards maintained. . . .

If the colored people want to enjoy the rights and privileges which the civil rights act never did secure to them, and which the present decision does not deprive them of, they will have to go about the task in some other way than by violent speeches, in which they plead their own helplessness and proclaim their own inferiority.

The St. Louis Republican, October 24, 1883.

VI. *Civil Right Not Social Choice*

GEORGE WASHINGTON CABLE

Many of the opponents of civil rights legislation, in addition to affirming its unconstitutionality, tried to argue that civil equality was identical with social equality and could not be promoted by laws. George Washington Cable, a white native Southerner (who moved to New England in 1884) and a champion of the freedmen's rights, attempted to discuss this matter in practical terms.

Analyze and evaluate his arguments and determine how well they support those of Frederick Douglass.

Let us then make our conception of the right and wrong of this matter unmistakable. Social relations, one will say, are sacred. True, but civil rights are sacred, also. Hence social relations must not impose upon civil rights nor civil rights impose upon social relations. We must have peace. But for peace to be stable we must have justice. Therefore, for peace, we must find that boundary line between social relations and civil rights, from which the one has no warrant ever to push the other; and, for justice, this boundary must remain ever faithfully the same, no matter whose the social relations are on one side or whose the civil rights are on the other.

Suppose a case. Mr. A. takes a lady, not of his own family, to a concert. Neither one is moved by compulsion or any assertion of right on the part of the other. They have chosen each other's company. Their relation is social. It could not exist without mutual agreement. They are strangers in that city, however, and as they sit in the thronged auditorium and look around them, not one other soul in that house, so far as they can discern, has any social relation with them. But see, now, how impregnable the social relation is. That pair, outnumbered a thousand to one, need not yield a pennyweight of social interchange with any third person unless they so choose. Nothing else in human life is so amply sufficient to protect itself as are social relations. Provided one thing—that the law will protect every one impartially in his civil rights, one of the foremost of which is that both men and laws shall let us alone to our personal social preferences. If any person, no matter who or what he is, insists on obtruding himself upon this pair in the concert-hall he can only succeed in getting himself put out. Why? Because he is trying to turn his civil right-to-be-there into a social passport. And even if he make no personal advances, but his behavior or personal condition is so bad as to obtrude itself offensively upon others, the case is the same; the mistake and its consequences are his. But, on the other hand, should Mr. A. and his companion demand the expulsion of this third person when he had made no advances and had encroached no more on their liberty than they had on his, demanding it simply on the ground that he was their social or intellectual inferior or probably had

George Washington Cable, *The Silent South* (New York: Charles Scribner's Sons, 1885), pp. 57–63.

relatives who were, then the error, no matter who or what he is, would be not his, but theirs, and it would be the equally ungenteel error of trying to turn their social choice into a civil right; and it would be simply increasing the error and its offensiveness, for them to suggest that he be given an equally comfortable place elsewhere in the house providing it must indicate his inferiority. There is nothing comfortable in ignominy, nor is it any evidence of high mind for one stranger to put it upon another.

Now, the principles of this case are not disturbed by any multiplication of the number of persons concerned, or by reading for concert-hall either theatre or steamboat or railway station or coach or lecture-hall or street car or public library, or by supposing the social pair to be English, Turk, Jap, Cherokee, Ethiopian, Mexican, or "American." But note the fact that, even so, Mr. A. and his companion's social relations are, under these rulings, as safe from invasion as they were before; nay, even safer, inasmuch as the true distinction is made publicly clearer, between the social and the civil relations. Mr. A. is just as free to decline every sort of unwelcome social advance, much or little, as ever he was; and as to his own house or estate may eject any one from it, not of his own family or a legal tenant, and give no other reason than that it suits him to do so. Do you not see it now, gentlemen of the other side? Is there anything new in it? Is it not as old as truth itself? Honestly, have you not known it all along? Is it not actually the part of good breeding to know it? You cannot say no. Then why have you charged us with proposing "to break down every distinction between the races," and "to insist on their intermingling in all places and in all relations," when in fact we have not proposed to disturb any distinction between the races which nature has made, or molest any private or personal relation in life, whatever? Why have you charged us with "moving to forbid all further assortment of the races," when the utmost we have done is to condemn an *arbitrary* assortment of the races, crude and unreasonable, by the stronger race without the consent of the weaker, and in places and relations where no one, exalted or lowly, has any right to dictate to another because of the class he belongs to? We but turn your own words to our use when we say this battery of charges "is as false as it is infamous." But let that go.

Having made it plain that the question has nothing to do with social relations, we see that it is, and is only, a question of *indiscriminative civil rights.* This is what "The Freedman's Case in Equity" advocates from beginning to end, not as a choice which a *race* may either claim or disclaim, but as every citizen's individual yet impersonal right until he personally waives or forfeits it. The issue, we repeat, is not met at all by the assertion that "Neither race wants it." There is one thing that neither race wants, but even this is not because either of them is one race or another, but simply because they are members of a civilized human community. It is that thing of which our Southern white people have so long had such an absurd fear; neither race, or in other words nobody, wants to see the civil rewards of decency in dress and behavior usurped by the common herd of clowns and ragamuffins. But there is another thing that the colored race certainly does want: the freedom for those of the race who can to earn the indiscriminative and unchallenged *civil* —*not social*—rights of gentility by the simple act of being genteel. This is what we insist the best intelligence of the South is willing—in the interest of right, and therefore of both races—to accord. But the best intelligence is not the majority, and the majority, leaning not upon the equities, but the traditional sentiments of the situation, charge us with "theory" and "sentiment" and give us their word for it that "Neither race wants it." . . .

Would our friends on the other side of the discussion say they mean only, concerning these indiscriminative civil rights, "Neither race wants them *now*"? This would but make bad worse. For two new things have happened to the colored race in these twenty years; first, a natural and spontaneous assortment has taken place within the race itself along scales of virtue and intelligence, knowledge and manners; so that by no small fraction of their number the wrong of treating the whole race alike is more acutely felt than ever it was before; and, second, a long, bitter experience has taught them that "equal accommodations, but separate" means, generally, accommodations of a conspicuously ignominious inferiority. Are these people opposed to an arrangement that would give them instant release from organized and legalized incivility?—For that is what a race distinction in civil relations is when it ignores intelligence and decorum.

For Further Reading

Political questions related to civil rights are given thorough treatment in *Farewell to the Bloody Shirt: Northern Republicans and the Southern Negro, 1877–1893** (1962), by Stanley P. Hirshon, and *Republicans Face the Southern Question: The New Departure Years* (1959), by Vincent P. DeSantis. Legal questions are treated or touched upon in Stanley I. Kutler, *Judicial Power and Reconstruction Politics* (1968); Morroe Berger, *Equality by Statute: The Revolution in Civil Rights* (1967); and in *Discrimination and the Law* (1965), edited by Vern Countryman.

Frederick Douglass' *Life and Times** (1892 reprinted in 1962) is perhaps the best source about him. *Frederick Douglass** (1968), edited by Benjamin Quarles, contains his writings as well as commentaries by his contemporaries and current historians.

General accounts of the Reconstruction years are given in John Hope Franklin's *Reconstruction After the Civil War** (1961), and Kenneth M. Stampp's *The Era of Reconstruction* (1965).

The role of blacks is considered in *The Negro in Reconstruction** (1969), by Robert Cruden; *The Negro in American Life and Thought: The Nadir, 1877–1901* (1954), by Rayford Logan; and *Negro Thought in American, 1880–1915* (1963), by August Meier. Three volumes by C. Vann Woodward are also pertinent: *Origins of the New South, 1877–1913* (1951), *Reunion and Reaction:*

---

*Paperbound edition available.

The Compromise of 1877 and the End of Reconstruction (1956), and *The Strange Career of Jim Crow** (1966). The status of blacks in individual states is dealt with in Frenise Logan, *The Negro in North Carolina, 1876–1894* (1964); George B. Tindall, *South Carolina Negroes, 1877–1900* (1952); Joel Williamson, *After Slavery: The Negro in South Carolina During Reconstruction, 1861–1877** (1965); and Charles E. Wynes, *Race Relations in Virginia, 1870–1902* (1961).

Primary sources are available in the *Documentary History of Reconstruction* (1906–1907; reprinted in 1966), edited by Walter L. Fleming. Problems books include *Reconstruction** (1967), edited by Staughton Lynd, and *Reconstruction: A Tragic Era?** (1968), edited by Seth M. Scheiner.

---

*Paperbound edition available.

71 72 73 74 7 6 5 4 3 2 1